T0213273

Lecture Notes in Computer Science   9929

Commenced Publication in 1973
Founding and Former Series Editors:
Gerhard Goos, Juris Hartmanis, and Jan van Leeuwen

More information about this series at http://www.springer.com/series/7409

Yuhua Luo (Ed.)

Cooperative Design, Visualization, and Engineering

13th International Conference, CDVE 2016
Sydney, NSW, Australia, October 24–27, 2016
Proceedings

 Springer

Editor
Yuhua Luo
University of the Balearic Islands
Palma, Mallorca
Spain

ISSN 0302-9743　　　　　　　　ISSN 1611-3349　(electronic)
Lecture Notes in Computer Science
ISBN 978-3-319-46770-2　　　　ISBN 978-3-319-46771-9　(eBook)
DOI 10.1007/978-3-319-46771-9

Library of Congress Control Number: 2016952870

LNCS Sublibrary: SL3 – Information Systems and Applications, incl. Internet/Web, and HCI

Printed on acid-free paper

This Springer imprint is published by Springer Nature
The registered company is Springer International Publishing AG
The registered company address is: Gewerbestrasse 11, 6330 Cham, Switzerland

Preface

CDVE2016 celebrated in a new continent – Australia, for the first time in the beautiful coast city Sydney. CDVE conferences have become more international and more global after being held in Asia and North America.

Our conferences are very international by having researchers from over 20 countries. This year, we had submissions from some new countries. We welcome the researchers from these countries to join our community.

Among papers this year, we saw a large amount of submissions from the field of cooperative visualization. As we can see, the cooperative visualization research has been very active in recent years. It has been applied to a very broad area of applications. We also find that the cooperative visualization is combined with other techniques such as virtual reality, augmented reality, which provides much more possibilities for better visualization. Applications include for work training, cooperative design using virtual reality, and augmented reality, but via small mobile devices and large-scale display walls. It also finds applications to increase the user experience, visual comprehension such as in disaster preparation, museum, and virtual tourism.

Originated from visualization and using it as a tool, visual analytics has achieved some higher-level analysis of big data and reached some interesting analytic results that have never been achieved before. There are papers analyzing student check-in data and other data such as consumption data to find out student behavior and its relationship with academic performances. There are papers for ranking authors by analyzing their co-authorship from social media and publications. To help to control the network security, visual analytics also finds its own way by visualizing and analyzing the network flow logs to show the communication patterns and network abnormalities. The communication network itself can also be visualized to show its structure.

In the field of cooperative engineering, a couple of papers discuss the new challenges in the networked and cloud manufacturing environment. The key issues discussed in the papers involve: how to model the manufacturing process cooperatively, how to cooperate but keep the enterprise's own information undisclosed, how to tell a network potential partner is trustful, how to choose proper resources from a service cloud etc. The papers present their own solutions and recommendations by analyzing the problems and designing prototypes to evaluate them.

Within the cooperative engineering and a special area of engineering, the construction industry, using BIM (Building Information Modeling), was a central topic for two papers. BIM has been a tool for sharing data through centralized or distributed platforms. Collaboration is not at the center of BIM. There are papers discussing how to make the BIM to be a collaborative platform so as to facilitate the collaboration among stake-holders.

In the field of cooperative design, crowd sourcing has been a concern of a few studies. There are papers comparing the Web-based crowd behavior with the experts.

The basic findings of these papers can be a base for broader use of crowd sourcing and group intelligence in the field of cooperative design.

In the field of cooperative applications, there are many applications such as cooperative learning using mobile devices, using cloud to share resources, using IOT for medical care, traffic congestion monitoring, network security ensuring, etc. Among the techniques used, ontology seems to be a strong tool in many application areas from cooperative manufacturing to patient caring.

The papers published in this volume reflect the progress in our field, which is a result of hard work and ongoing effort for better technological solutions. I would like to express my sincere thanks to all of the authors for submitting their paper to the CDVE 2016 conference and presenting their hard-earned research results.

I would like to thank all of our volunteer reviewers, Program Committee members, Organization Committee members for their continuous support to the conference. My special thanks go to my colleague, the Organization Committee Chair Dr. Tony Huang, and the two co-chairs. I would also like to thank the University of Tasmania for its support of this conference. The success of this year's conference would not have been possible without their generous support.

September 2016   Yuhua Luo

Organization

Conference Chair

Yuhua Luo   University of the Balearic Islands, Spain

International Program Committee

Program Chair

Dieter Roller   University of Stuttgart, Germany

Members

Jose Alfredo Costa	Ursula Kirschner	Mary Lou Maher
Peter Demian	Harald Klein	Manuel Ortega
Carrie Sturts Dossick	Jean-Christophe Lapayre	Niko Salonen
Susan Finger	Francis Lau	Fernando Sanchez
Sebastia Galmes	Pierre Leclercq	Weiming Shen
Halin Gilles	Jang Ho Lee	Ram Sriram
Matti Hannus	Moira C. Norrie	Chengzheng Sun
Shuangxi Huang	Jaime Lloret	Thomas Tamisier
Tony Huang	Jos P. van Leeuwen	Xiangyu Wang
Claudia-Lavinia Ignat	Kwan-Liu Ma	Nobuyoshi Yabuki

Reviewers

Md Morshed Alam	Harald Klein	Romain Pinquié
Jose Alfredo Costa	Xiaodi Huang	Guofeng Qin
Peter Demian	Jean-Christophe Lapayre	Dieter Roler
Selim Erol	Pierre Leclercq	Niko Salonen
Hongfei Fan	Jang Ho Lee	Fernando Sanchez
Susan Finger	Jos P. Leeuwen	Alexandru Senciuc
Sebastia Galmes	Tingting Liu	Weiming Shen
Halin Gilles	Jaime Lloret	Thomas Tamisier
Nam Hyuk Ham	Sungkon Moon	Xiangyu Wang
Patrik Hitzelberger	Manuel Ortega	Nobuyoshi Yabuki
Tony Huang	Roberto Pérez	Li-Nan Zhu

Organization Committee

Chair

Tony Huang   University of Tasmania, Australia

Co-chairs

Quang Vinh Nguyen   Western Sydney University, Australia
Mao Lin Huang   University of Technology Sydney, Australia

Members

Xiaodi Huang
Tomeu Estrany
Alex Garcia
Takayuki Fujimoto
Guofeng Qin

Contents

Facilitating Design Automation in Multi-organization Concurrent Engineering: Insights from Graph-Rewriting Theory

Julian R. Eichhoff[(✉)], Felix Baumann, and Dieter Roller

Institute of Computer-aided Product Development Systems,
University of Stuttgart, Universitätsstr. 38, 70569 Stuttgart, Germany
{julian.eichhoff,felix.baumann,dieter.roller}@informatik.uni-stuttgart.de
http://www.iris.uni-stuttgart.de/en.html

Abstract. The aim of this paper is to introduce emerging technologies for the implementation of graph-rewriting-based design automation applications that can be used in collaborative environments. The paper motivates the use of graph-rewriting for design automation and highlights an important issue: preservation of confidentiality. Approaches to the efficient derivation (using design knowledge) and rule induction (learning design knowledge) are discussed. The crucial feature of these approaches for confidentiality-preserving graph-rewriting is that knowledge-bases of contributing organizations do not have to be disclosed.

Keywords: Design automation · Concurrent engineering · Graph-rewriting · Design grammar · Machine learning

1 Introduction

Engineering projects that face the development of complex, highly specialized systems, like the development of a spacecraft, require the integrated design of all subsystems. The provisioning of multi-disciplinary expertise and associated resources result in high development costs. A common strategy to reduce these costs is rooted in the partnership of contributing organizations.

However, often corporate confidentiality requirements stand against open data and knowledge interchange, which is required for the realization of well integrated subsystems. This does not only apply to the implementation of design processes across partnering organizations. It also sets limits to the use of computational design automation. Multi-disciplinary design optimization methods, for instance, are precluded from application, when necessary design knowledge is withheld from inter-organizational sharing.

In this paper we discuss solutions to this problem in the context of graph-rewriting. Graph-rewriting is an expressive computational model, which produces and modifies graphs. Since graph-based representations are very common to engineering design (particularly systems engineering and concept design), providing methods for what we call confidentiality-preserving graph-rewriting

© Springer International Publishing AG 2016
Y. Luo (Ed.): CDVE 2016, LNCS 9929, pp. 1–8, 2016.
DOI: 10.1007/978-3-319-46771-9_1

systems are a promising approach to the practical implementation of design automation for multi-organization concurrent engineering. Specifically, this paper addresses methods for efficiently deriving graphs (a form of deduction) and for inducing new production rules in such settings.

The remainder of the paper is organized in alignment to the following goals: (1) Motivate the use of graph-rewriting for knowledge-based CAD (Sect. 2). (2) Discuss the principle implementation of graph-rewriting systems as an inter-organizational, distributed system (Sect. 3). (3) Introduce approaches to two central problems in knowledge-based CAD, which specifically target an inter-organizational application of graph-rewriting. (3a) Derivation (Sect. 4): The process of producing graphs using a set of production rules. In a broader knowledge-based systems context this is termed inference or deduction. (3b) Rule Induction (Sect. 5): The process of generating new production rules from existing graphs. This can also be seen as a machine-learning problem. Section 6 provides concluding remarks and highlights research questions for future work.

2   Graph-Rewriting for CAD

Graph-based representations are very common in the field of product development. Many methods in product development use graphs as a visual notation (e.g., to depict functionality, aggregation among components, and modularization). Moreover, many other models in computer-aided product development make use of graphs as their underlying data structure (e.g., geometry, requirements tracing).

Graph-rewriting is an expressive computational model, which operates on graphs as its data structure. Its application is backed by a strong theoretical foundation, called algebraic graph theory. One finding from this field is that general graph-rewriting is touring complete making it possible to implement any conventional computer program as a graph-rewriting system. The connection between graph-rewriting and product design can be defined inductively:

Graphs are used to represent *design states*. *Nodes* reflect design entities, such as components, (sub)assemblies, functions, requirements, etc. *Edges* between nodes represent relations among design entities, e.g., component-to-assembly, function-to-component, requirement-to-function, etc. Nodes and edges can be attributed by means of labels. *Labels* represent parameters (masses, prices, geometric properties, etc.) or classifications (e.g., to refer to component classes or principle solutions). A move from one graph to another graph is understood as a *design decision*. Making an informed choice over a set of possible design alternatives corresponds in graph-rewriting to choosing a new graph from a set of possible graphs based on the information encoded on the current graph. Such a process step is termed *direct derivation*. The term *derivation* is used to denote a chain of subsequent direct derivations.

Two reasons account for a direct derivation: First, the differences between the subsequent graphs do correspond to an existing pattern of allowed graph changes, a so-called *production rule* or rule for short. Only transformations suggested by a rule are considered valid transformations. Second, the accountable rule must have been under consideration for application at that point in derivation. There are various strategies for controlling what rules are considered for application. The usefulness of a strategy depends on the desired behavior of a graph-rewriting system and hence its purpose. In context of graph-rewriting systems for design automation two emerging patterns can be observed:

<u>Pattern of use A</u>: Use graph-rewriting to have a rigorous, formal documentation of the design decisions which lead to a final product design. Therefore, a deterministic program for rule application is defined, e.g., in form of a fixed rule application sequence. Especially design teams benefit from this, as each design decision that was once "programmed" by a designer remains replicable and accountable. Besides this, the transparent and detailed documentation facilitates the creation of variant designs through point-wise adaption of the program.

<u>Pattern of use B</u>: Use graph-rewriting to non-deterministically explore a design space for a given design problem. The design problem itself is stated within an initial source graph. A space of feasible designs is then constructed by considering all possible derivations over a set of rules starting from this source graph. More specifically, we are considering all derivable graphs (the graph-rewriting system's *language*), which results from the positive transitive closure of the rule set. It is most likely that this will cause a "combinatorial explosion" making it impractical or impossible to enumerate all possible designs. Thus, various approaches conceptualize design space exploration as an optimization problem, where only a limited number of (relatively) optimal designs are of interest. With respect to graph-rewriting such an optimization can be implemented as a guided search towards a rule application sequence which is able to derive a graph that is optimal in the sense of some predefined optimization criteria (e.g., minimal weight/price, maximal stability, etc.).

From these points we conclude that graph-rewriting is a powerful and flexible method suited for implementing CAD applications, particularly because of its concise theory on performing modifications to graph-structured data. Figure 1 illustrates some central points of graph-rewriting for CAD.

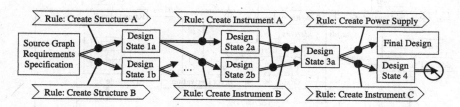

Fig. 1. Very simplified example of using graph-rewriting for spacecraft design. Double-edged arcs depict direct derivations. Varying applications of different rule sequences result in different design graphs. Feasibility of designs is reflected by the applicability/not-applicability of production rules, e.g., adding instrument C to the spacecraft would yield a power consumption that cannot be satisfied by the power subsystem. Moreover, adding instrument A before B or vice versa does not matter, due to the independence of these rules.

3   Confidentiality-Preserving Graph-Rewriting

An application in the sense of pattern A is the work of Schaefer and Rudolph [10]. Here, a graph-rewriting-based CAD environment named "design compiler 43" is employed to create a complete satellite design with several subsystems from an initial graph defining the satellite mission architecture. The program starts with defining the structure subsystem. Then all other subsystems (propulsion, telecommunications, power, etc.) are subsequently added by means of derivation. All design entities and relations including the satellites geometry are formalized in the graphical notation of the Unified Modeling Language (UML).

Though this is an excellent example demonstrating the capabilities of graph-rewriting, in a cooperative project there may be organizational barriers that hinder the implementation of such an approach. Unless all subsystems are designed by one authority, contributing organizations need to provide their domain specific production rules to a common graph-rewriting engine. We assume most organizations will be reluctant to do so, since production rules essentially encode proprietary knowledge on why their products are designed the way they are.

However, research about cooperating/distributed graph-rewriting systems is not new. Csuhaj-Varju et al. [1] coin the term *cooperating/distributed grammar system*. Csuhaj-Varju and Kelemen [2] draw the connection between graph-rewriting systems and *blackboard* architectures. The blackboard software design pattern is a way of implementing a shared-repository system [8], where multiple contributors work on a common (design) model. Figure 2 illustrates how the blackboard pattern has been used to implement a form of confidentially-preserving system for cooperating/distributed graph-rewriting. It contains three main components:

Knowledge sources: These correspond to the production rule sets of each partnering organization. They are contributed to a global graph-rewriting system.

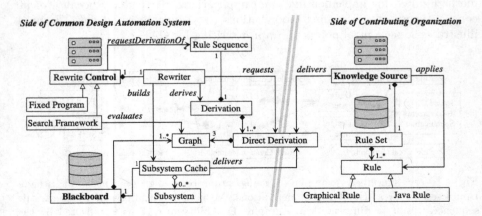

Fig. 2. Confidentiality-preserving architecture for graph-rewriting

<u>The blackboard</u>: A model to store the current progress in design, hence, the graph which has been generated up to the current time in derivation.

<u>The control component</u>: This is the graph-rewriting engine per se being responsible for steering the course of derivation. In case of pattern of use A this is a program and in case of pattern of use B a search framework.

Several research has been done with respect to this notion of graph-rewriting. Kari et al. [7] discuss the creation of "teams" of knowledge sources. Later Csuhaj-Varju et al. [3] discuss the implementation of so-called eco-grammar systems, which are a kind of extension of cooperating/distributed grammar systems that allow for parallel rewriting and the evolution of knowledge sources (here called agents). The goal of this was to create a system with lifelike features.

We address two problems in the context of cooperating/distributed graph-rewriting systems having an substantial impact on the practical use of such systems for design, but which have not been sufficiently investigated so far: The problem of efficient *inference*, i.e., making use of the knowledge-base to deduce results, and the problem of *learning*, i.e. extending the knowledge-base by means of induction. In the context of graph-rewriting, inference refers to the efficient computation of derivations (particularly with respect to pattern B) and learning corresponds to the introduction of new production rules to a graph-rewriting system. Moreover, within a cooperative design setting with confidentially constraints, both problems have to be solved without access to the existing rules' definitions.

4   Derivation

When computing multiple derivations of a set of rules (pattern B), one is easily confronted with the exponentially increasing number of possible derivations. This results from (a) the possible sequences in which rules may be applied, and (b) alternative possibilities for applying a rule to the current host graph. However, there is a property of graph-rewriting systems that is of special interest in design called *confluence*. Confluence states the fact that multiple derivations yield similar resulting graphs (equivalent up to isomorphism). As we are most likely interested in distinct design alternatives, *confluence* can be exploited to avoid unnecessary derivations that would lead to existing results.

Eichhoff and Roller [6] compared two approaches to determining confluence without knowing the definitions of rules. The key to this is to determine which rules can be applied independently from each other, as the derivation over a set of mutually independent rules always yields the same results no matter what application sequence is chosen. In contrast to the common critical-pair analysis, which analyzes rule definitions upfront to derivation for independence, [6] proposed a dynamic approach that does not need access to possibly confidential rule definitions.

The method tests pairs of rules for independence while computing derivations and builds up a cache graph-rewriting subsystems, where each of these subsystems contains only rules that are all independent to each other with respect to the subsystem's source graph. Derivations that still need to be computed can

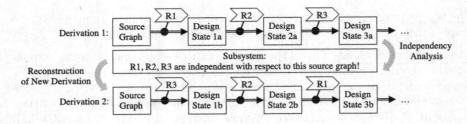

Fig. 3. Derivation approach

then be (partly) re-constructed using this cache. If a derivation can be completely re-constructed it is evident that the derivation will only result in graphs that have already been derived. A simplified example of this principle is shown in Fig. 3. For the mathematical details the reader is referred to [6].

[6] showed that this approach requires significantly less rule applications. This has several effects for our cooperative scenario: First, there is less data traffic among the network of rule contributors, since existing results can be reused from cache. Second, the rule contributors benefit from a decreased computational burden. This is particularly important if the application of a rule involves considerable computation time. And finally, discovered dependencies among rules can be used to initiate a inter-organizational dialogue about considering an even closer cooperation, where some confidentially requirements are dropped for the sake of computational efficiency.

5   Rule Induction

The second problem deals with the extension of an existing rule set. From the view of artificial intelligence, the concept of *learning* can be stated as a search or optimization problem [9]. More specifically, it is a search over a set of possible hypothesis that best explains some given data.

In our application scenario this data is an existing product design graph and we seek an explanation of why it is designed the way it is. The space of possible hypothesis corresponds to the space of possible derivations. While in some cases the target design graph can be derived using an existing rule set, in some cases this set is insufficient for reaching the given example design. In this case, one or more new rules need to be added to the rule set to establish reachability.

Often it is sufficient to learn one additional rule to reach the target graph, due to the so-called *amalgamation* theorem of rules [4]. Amalgamation principally states that multiple rules can be joined to form one composite rule. Vice versa, one rule performing various simultaneous operations can be split up into multiple rules, which are then applied subsequently.

In Eichhoff and Roller [5] a search algorithm is presented that can be used to induce such a missing production rule in context of a set of existing rules. Moreover, it suffices the confidentially requirements as it does not need to inspect the definitions of existing rules. Three aspects are essential to this approach:

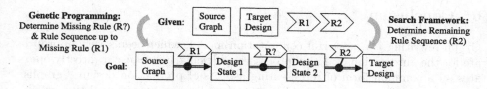

Fig. 4. Rule induction approach

(1) A production rule is formalized as a sequence of elementary graph operations, just like a procedural computer program.

(2) The exploration of possible candidates for the missing rule is performed by a Genetic Programming search heuristic. It tries different sequences of elementary graph operations with different parameters. The sampling of rule candidates incorporates both randomness and goal-directedness: What combinations are to be tried is determined by evolutionary principles: Mutation performs random changes on candidates, recombination randomly mates pairs of promising candidates, and selection directs search towards the survival of the fittest solutions.

(3) The fitness of a rule candidate is determined with respect to the graphs it is capable to derive. More specifically, the rule candidate is tested in derivation together with the existing rules. The produced graphs are then compared with the target graph. The rule's fitness is set proportional to the highest value that can be achieved when comparing each produced graph with the target graph by means of a graph-similarity measure.

Instead of using a fixed rule sequence (pattern A) this approach can directly be extended to consider variable rule sequences (pattern B). Therefore, the rule sequence up to the missing rule is also encoded by rule candidates of Genetic Programming using a simple list of rule indices. This list is then also exposed to the evolutionary optimization driven by mutation, recombination and selection. For the remaining rule sequence, a search framework is employed, to search for a derivation (starting from the missing rule) for a derivation producing a graph similar to the given target graph. Figure 4 provides a sketch of this.

Results from experiments with this combined approach provided a proof of concept. A sufficient rule can be found by the rule induction mechanism and the needed rule sequence can be determined as well. However, the precision of the results remains an issue for future work. In the current version, the rule induction algorithm may "take over" existing rules by adding their operations to the rule candidate as well. A further issue is the frequent computation of derivations for testing rule candidates which may cause long learning times. Depending on the complexity of the rule and the embedding derivation this may take up to several hours on a state-of-the-art PC.

6   Conclusion

Graph-rewriting is a powerful computation model, which seems very appropriate for the automation of design processes, particularly because it directly operates on a common form of representing aspects of production design – graphs. For being used in a cooperative/distributed application scenario existing graph-rewriting methods need to be extended. In this paper we focused on the confidentially of design knowledge and how this can be reflected in derivation (use design knowledge) and rule induction (learn design knowledge). As a common ground for these approaches, a system architecture was presented building on the blackboard design pattern for distributed systems. Future work should be targeted at further improvements to the efficiency of derivation and rule induction.

References

1. Csuhaj-Varjú, E., Dassow, J.: On cooperating/distributed Grammar systems. J. Inf. Process. Cybern. **26**(1–2), 49–63 (1990)
2. Csuhaj-Varjú, E., Kelemen, J.: Cooperating grammar systems: a syntactical framework for the blackboard model of problem solving. In: Proceeding on Artificial Intelligence and Information-Control systems of Robots, pp. 121–127 (1989)
3. Csuhaj-Varjú, E., Kelemen, J., Kelemenová, A., Pun, G.: Eco-grammar systems: a grammatical framework for studying lifelike interactions. Artificial Life **3**(1), 1–28 (1997)
4. Ehrig, H., Golas, U., Habel, A., Lambers, L., Orejas, F.: M-adhesive transformation systems with nested application conditions. part 1: parallelism, concurrency and amalgamation. Math. Struct. Comput. Sci. **24**(04), 1–48 (2014)
5. Eichhoff, J.R., Roller, D.: Genetic Programming for Design Grammar Rule Induction. In: Bassiliades, N., Fodor, P., Giurca, A., Gottlob, G., Kliegr, T., Nalepa, G.J., Palmirani, M., Paschke, A., Proctor, M., Roman, D., Sadri, F., Stojanovic, N. (eds.) Proceeding of the RuleML 2015 Challenge, the Special Track on Rule-based Recommender Systems for the Web of Data, the Special Industry Track and the RuleML 2015 Doctoral Consortium hosted by the 9th International Web Rule Symposium, vol. 1417, pp. 1–8. Aachen (2015). CEUR-WS.org
6. Eichhoff, J.R., Roller, D.: Designing the same, but in different ways: determinism in graph-rewriting systems for function-based design synthesis. J. Comput. Inf. Sci. Eng. **16**(1), 011006 (2016)
7. Kari, L., Mateescu, A., Pun, G., Salomaa, A.: Teams in cooperating grammar systems. J. Exp. Theor. Artif. Intell. **7**(4), 347–359 (1995)
8. Lalanda, P.: Shared repository pattern. In: Proceeding of the 5th Pattern Languages of Programs Conference (PLoP 1998) (1998)
9. Sammut, C.: Learning as Search. In: Sammut, C., Webb, G.I. (eds.) Encyclopedia of Machine Learning, pp. 572–576. Springer, New York (2010)
10. Schaefer, J., Rudolph, S.: Satellite design by design grammars - Satellitenentwurf mit Entwurfsgrammatiken. Aerosp. Sci. Technol. **9**(1), 81–91 (2005)

The Design and Development of Manufacturing Process Knowledge Base System Based on Ontology

Haojie Song[1], Huifen Wang[1(✉)], Tingyu Liu[1(✉)], Qiqi Zhang[1], and Binbin Gao[2]

[1] Nanjing University of Sciences and Technology, Nanjing, 210094, China
15051891899@163.com, {wanghf,tyliu}@njust.edu.cn
[2] North Institute of Science and Technology Information, Beijing, 100089, China

Abstract. The distributed collaboration based on process knowledge has become a main mode for manufacturing. Making good use of the manufacturing process knowledge is becoming more and more critical. In this paper, the manufacturing process knowledge is firstly defined and organized. A knowledge base construction method based on ontology is introduced. A three-tier system architecture of the manufacturing process knowledge base system is then illustrated with detailed main functions. Afterwards, a manufacturing process knowledge base system based on ontology is presented with respect to multi-technology fields. The implementation shows that the effective management and reuse of the knowledge can be realized.

Keywords: Manufacturing process · Knowledge · Ontology · Multi-technology fields · Knowledge base system

1 Introduction

In the information era, the knowledge has been the key issue for the manufacturing development and innovation. The manufacturing industry involves a very wide range of technical fields which include Precision and Ultra-Precision Machining, Non-Traditional Machining, Advanced Welding, Micro-Nano Manufacturing, Composite Forming, Assembly Technique, Digital Design and Manufacturing, Precision Forming, Heat Treatment and Surface Engineering. Therefore, it's important to well integrate, reuse, create and manage knowledge to maximize the benefits for enterprises.

In the past few years, the manufacturing process management focuses on the management of process data, such as Computer Aided Process Planning (CAPP), Electronic Bill of Process, etc. But the process data management only cannot satisfy the fast development of the manufacturing industry. Some domestic enterprises and research institutes have begun the research of the manufacturing process knowledge management.

To deal with process-related problems in Numerical Control Machining (NCM), authors in [1] designed a NCM cloud platform which could coordinate the whole process from drawing to parts and support various Cloud Manufacturing application modes.

To solve the problem that it was difficult to retrieve the process design knowledge due to the complicated production process in iron and steel industry, authors in [2]

© Springer International Publishing AG 2016
Y. Luo (Ed.): CDVE 2016, LNCS 9929, pp. 9–16, 2016.
DOI: 10.1007/978-3-319-46771-9_2

introduced a process knowledge discovery approach which could direct the decision makers' practice based on rough set attribute reduction.

To apply the rubber pad forming knowledge into digital manufacture of sheet metal parts, authors in [3] developed the web-based process knowledge base and its application system and designed the integrated application mode of the process knowledge into components hydraulic forming.

Authors in [4] analyzed the characteristics of manufacturing process management of mold &die. Based on the technology of knowledge reuse, manufacturing process planning finished rapidly and the quality of products is under control.

In order to realize the digital integrated manufacturing of tube bending, authors in [5] built the manufacturing process knowledge management system to analyze a tube's machinability and select manufacturing resources in the process planning. The efficiency of tube process planning was improved.

Authors in [6] developed a knowledge base system for machining process based on ontology to solve the problem of selecting machining parameters in high-speed machining field, which provides a method to select the machining process parameters.

According to the characteristics of automobile body and the establishment of drawing process, authors in [7] developed a knowledge base system based on relation typed database. Efficiency of design for drawing die was improved.

Analyzing the current research and application situation of the manufacturing process knowledge management, several problems are organized as follows:

- Due to the heterogeneity of the process knowledge, there exits lots of isolated information islands and overlap.
- The relevant research is mainly done in a theoretical way and lack of application development in this field.
- There is no knowledge management system oriented multi-technology fields.
- An effective process knowledge model needs to be developed.
- The variety of manufacturing levels, unequal resource allocation and complex production status of a manufacturer hinders the management and reusability of the manufacturing process knowledge.

In this paper, considering those analyses above, the manufacturing process knowledge and its organization are presented. A methodology for constructing knowledge base is proposed. Then the architecture, function and application of the system are described in details. Finally, a Manufacturing Process Knowledge Base System (MPKBS) oriented to multi-technology fields is developed based on the ontology and hybrid recommendation method.

2   The Process Knowledge Base Based on Ontology

2.1   Manufacturing Process Knowledge

In this paper, the manufacturing process knowledge refers to the process and its management knowledge which is generated during the product design and manufacturing process. The manufacturing process knowledge includes both the explicit and tacit knowledge and is mainly composed of four types:

- The statement knowledge describes the process technology, technical specifications, the application scope of technology and its current development situation, and the static properties of products in a quantitative and qualitative way. For instance, the key technology in the solid-phase welding process is a statement knowledge.
- The strategy knowledge is a kind of dynamic knowledge, such as the special models, the arithmetic and the logical reasoning strategy, during the process planning. It is usually used to obtain specific data. For instance, the empirical formula for the strength check of a profiled bar is a strategy knowledge to calculate the strength.
- The ancillary knowledge provides users brief information, such as the technology standard, the selection of machine tools and the work schedule etc.
- The experience knowledge describes a mass of empirical information, such as the personal experience and historical cases etc.

In MPKBS, those four types of knowledge are structured as an organic system which helps push the proper process knowledge at the right time.

2.2 Process Knowledge Organization

Considering manufacturing features, manufacturing technologies can be divided into nine technical fields as stated in Sect. 1. Each technical field is tree-structured and is composed of several sub technical fields, technology orientations, key technologies and development priorities. This five-tier knowledge system defines concepts, characteristics, the application scope and the current development situation of main manufacturing technologies. This system helps build a better integrated manufacturing process

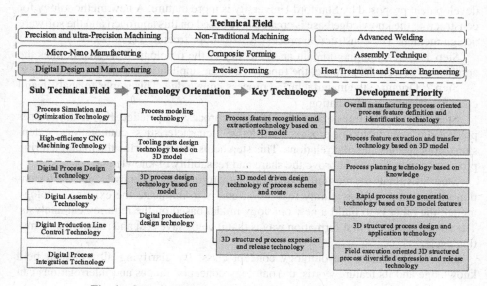

Fig. 1. Organization of the manufacturing process knowledge

knowledge model by illustrating the inheritance, independence, correlation and other horizontal and vertical relations among all technical fields. Figure 1 is a knowledge organization chart of the digital design and manufacturing process.

Based on the knowledge organization method above and the theory of 'metadata', a Manufacturing Process Knowledge Element (MPKE) model is formulated: $MPKE = \{K^L, B^K, P^K, A^E, R\}$ where:

K^L: Knowledge Level defines the organization structure of the manufacturing process knowledge. It indicates a knowledge element's knowledge level, field type, and its father field's and sub field's containing knowledge elements.

B^K: Basic Knowledge represents by $\{B_i^K : i = 1, 2, \ldots, |B^K|\}$ which is a finite set of basic theories, such as key technologies, the current development situation and existing problems etc.

P^K: Process Knowledge refers to the belonging technical field.

A^E: Application Environment illustrates a knowledge element's application scenario and required knowledge background.

R: Resources are related with a knowledge element's explicit and tacit knowledge resource sets, such as technical manuals, design specifications, historical cases and expert review comments etc.

The definition of MPKE model combines the manufacturing process knowledge together with the technical personnel and their knowledge requirements, which forms a multi-level and diversified manufacturing process knowledge system and provides a reference for the formation of a specified knowledge base model.

2.3   A Methodology for Constructing Knowledge Base

Among most theoretical and application researches, an iterative approach to ontology development proposed by Stanford University is more mature. A new methodology for constructing the knowledge base is created here based on this approach and the software design method. The construction process is half-loop structured (Fig. 2).

Step 1: Determine the domain and category of the ontology. This step defines the application object, the purpose, the function and the application scope of the ontology.

Step 2: Organize the manufacturing process knowledge. This step is to analyze and classify technology information.

Step 3: Extract features of the manufacturing process knowledge. Key feature words present the manufacturing process knowledge's characteristics, connotations, extensions, conceptions and interrelations. This step helps better describe the manufacturing process knowledge and improve the share and reusability of knowledge.

Step 4: Evaluate the reusability of the manufacturing process knowledge. The formation of the ontology has mainly two ways: one is to duplicate the existing ontology model, the other is to build a new ontology model based on the requirement analysis. The advantage of the first formation way is that it helps save cost and reduce the formation cycle.

Step 5: Determine the ontology concept class. By clarifying all technical field knowledge and its feature words, the ontology concepts' ranges and interrelations can be well defined.

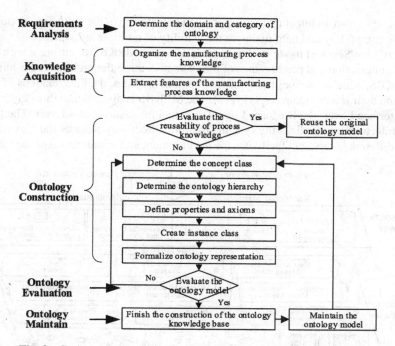

Fig. 2. Construction process of a manufacturing process knowledge base

Step 6: Determine the ontology hierarchy. This step is to organize the manufacturing process knowledge by analyzing relations among ontology concept classes.

Step 7: Define properties and axioms. This step is to reduce the property redundancy and enhance the expression ability of the ontology concept.

Step 8: Create class instance. This step is mainly to define properties for a specified ontology instance.

Step 9: Formalize the ontology representation. By coding with a special language, the ontology model can be recognized and processed by the computer. This step generates specific documents which can be stored and processed later.

Step 10: Evaluate the ontology model. This step is similar to the software testing phase, which takes into account five aspects of the ontology model: integrity, clarity, consistency, compatibility and extensibility.

Step 11: Maintain the ontology model. After the formation of the ontology model, the analysis and maintain work should be down to solve problems during the application of new knowledge.

3 System Implementation

3.1 System Architecture

The MPKBS involves a large range of technical fields, a variety of system users and roles with different operation authorities and a mass of process resources. It needs an appropriate system architecture to guide the concrete design of the software, support the system's complexity and help maintain the stability of multiple subsystems.

C/S (Client/Service) mode is chosen to develop the MPKBS to ensure a high level security, interaction and performance of the system. A three-tier architecture is built for the MPKBS, which describes the system's function modules, the interrelations of logic layers and their interaction modes (Fig. 3). The MPKBS is divided into three layers: the User Interface Layer, the Business Logic Layer and the Data Access Layer. The three-tier architecture standardizes the system structure, effectively reduces the dependency among different layers, and facilitates the development and maintenance of the system.

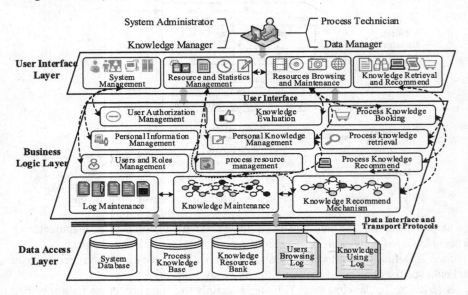

Fig. 3. System Architecture of the Manufacturing Process Knowledge-Based System

3.2 Functions of the System

The MPKBS has four function modules (Fig. 4): the system management module, the knowledge retrieval and recommendation module, the knowledge browsing and maintenance module, and the resources and statistics management module.

The System Management module supports the basic operation and management of the system. The knowledge retrieval and recommendation module mainly supports the user's retrieval and the active recommendation of the manufacturing process knowledge. The knowledge browsing and maintenance module, as the basic function module of the system, is the core module to make full use of the process knowledge. The Resources and Statistics management module is to maintain system resources and improve the human-computer interaction performance by Big Data analysis.

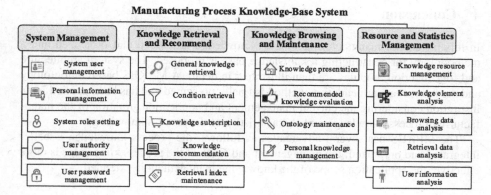

Fig. 4. The function modules of system

3.3   The System Application

The Knowledge recommendation and retrieval mechanism based on the hybrid recommendation method is described in another paper so it is not covered in this paper. Figure 5 shows the main system operation interfaces.

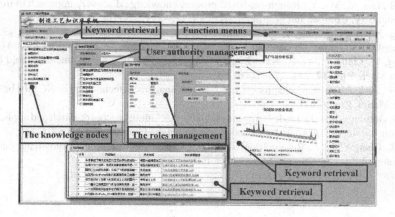

Fig. 5. The function modules of system

This system is used by North Institute of Science and Technology Information. According to the feedback of the institution, the system has following advantages: it has a friendly user interface and is easy to use; the process knowledge is well described and easy to understand; with the high accuracy and relevancy of the knowledge recommendation and retrieval, knowledge requirements are met; user roles and authorities are well defined; and the data has high level of independence, security and manageability.

4   Conclusion

In this paper, the manufacturing process knowledge is defined and organized and a methodology for constructing a knowledge base is proposed. The system architecture and four function modules are then illustrated in detail. A MPKBS based on ontology and the hybrid recommendation method is finally presented and has been applied in an institution considering the current management and application situation of the manufacturing process knowledge and characteristics of the process knowledge.

The MPKBS has several advantages as follows: the process knowledge is better integrated and organized; the management and reuse of the process knowledge is more effective; the application scope of the knowledge management is extended.

Acknowledgements. The project is supported by National Natural Science Foundation of China (no. 51505228).

References

1. Liu, R., Li, P., Zhang, C.: Research and development of the drawing process knowledge database for automobile body. Comput. Integr. Manuf. Syst. **07**, 1613–1619 (2012)
2. Bo, H., Liu, X., Ma, Y.: Rough-set-based process knowledge discovery approach in iron and steel industry. Comput. Integr. Manuf. Syst. **15**, 135–141 (2009)
3. Wang, X., Liu, C., Wang, J.: The manufacturing-oriented process knowledge representation and application for the rubber pad forming. Mech. Sci. Technol. Aerosp. Eng. **01**, 10–14 (2012)
4. Zheng, Y., Liang, P., Yi, P.: Knowledge reuse in manufacturing management of mold & die. China Mech. Eng. **17**, 271–273 (2006)
5. Liu, N., Zeng, Y: Research on process knowledge management technology of NC tube bending. Mod. Manuf. Eng. (2011)
6. Lu, S: Ontology-based knowledge base system for machining process research and application. Nanjing University of Aeronautics and Astronautics the Graduate School (2011)
7. An, A., Chen, Y., Li, F.: Research and development of the drawing process knowledge database for automobile body. Die and Mould Manufacture **8**, 6–10 (2008)

Collaborative Modeling of Manufacturing Processes – a Wiki – Based Approach

Selim Erol[✉]

Industrial and Systems Engineering, TU Wien, Institute of Management Science,
Theresianumgasse 27, 1040 Vienna, Austria
selim.erol@tuwien.ac.at

Abstract. Manufacturing companies face substantial challenges due to a new industrial (r)evolution taking place. The increasing digitalization and intelligentization of manufacturing processes will lead to a higher degree of automation and as well autonomy of production systems. Driven by these developments, model-driven approaches gain increasing attention in the domain of manufacturing. Future manufacturing processes will need to be increasingly adaptive to highly individualized customer needs. Therefore, reengineering of such processes must be supported by a platform that facilitates their quick adaption to changing conditions in an unbureaucratic way. In this paper we describe the design of a collaborative process modeling environment that is based on the principles of wiki-engines and enables quick, easy, concurrent and transparent design of manufacturing processes. Finally, we provide lessons learned from a first large-scale evaluation case-study.

Keywords: Manufacturing · Process modeling · Wiki

1 Introduction

Manufacturing companies face substantial challenges due to a new industrial (r)evolution taking place. The increasing digitalization and intelligentization [1] of manufacturing processes will lead to a higher degree of automation and as well autonomy of production systems. Manufacturing technology will interweave with information and communication technology to form intelligent networks of factories, machines, devices, materials, and workers which fulfills highly individualized customer demand in a highly responsive manner.

Design of such responsive and data driven processes requires adequate methods that support the systematic collection of requirements and the detailed specification of the future manufacturing process. In particular, the sub-processes performed, their logical dependencies, their interfaces and the data objects exchanged. The growing complexity of manufacturing systems will not only require adequate modeling techniques but will as well require adequate protocols for collaboration during different phases of process design. In particular, interdisciplinary and collaborative approaches between experts of different domains are needed to be able to quickly respond to changing conditions of the market and technological developments.

© Springer International Publishing AG 2016
Y. Luo (Ed.): CDVE 2016, LNCS 9929, pp. 17–24, 2016.
DOI: 10.1007/978-3-319-46771-9_3

Software tools for process modeling (e.g. ARIS [2]) have mainly focused on the language aspect whereas protocols for quick and easy collaboration have been neglected. However, many vendors of respective modeling environments meanwhile have included version control and model repositories to provide a minimum of collaboration capability. Though, complexity and closeness of such modeling environments has prevented them to be used in early phases of process design where diverse stakeholders are needed to develop a shared understanding of a process [3].

In this paper we describe the design of a collaborative process modeling environment that is based on the principles of wikis and enables quick, easy, concurrent and transparent design of manufacturing processes. In Sect. 2 we outline the peculiarities of manufacturing processes and specific requirements for modeling and collaboration. In Sect. 3 we will describe our wiki-based approach along with its prototypical implementation and in Sect. 4 we will discuss preliminary learnings from a case-study.

2   Collaborative Modeling of Manufacturing Processes

2.1   Characteristics of Manufacturing Processes

Design of manufacturing processes is driven by a quality and a cost dimension. In other words, a manufacturing process must create value for the customer and at the same time must be efficient. Only if both criteria are met the process is considered competitive and enables a company to generate profit. To ensure competitiveness, processes are engineered from a technological perspective and an organizational perspective. From the organizational perspective, manufacturing processes are analyzed and optimized to ensure global efficiency and effectiveness of multiple locally optimized processes. Throughput time, machine utilization, inventory, and delivery date adherence are indicators that are used to express competitiveness of the whole process.

For organizational process design and evaluation both qualitative and quantitative modeling methods are used. Examples of such methods are Value-Stream Mapping [4] and Six Sigma [5]. In addition, engineers use formal mathematical models for optimization and simulation purposes, e.g. Linear Optimization. A perspective that will be of increasing importance for the design of future manufacturing processes is the information flow perspective [6, 7]. Information flows in production systems are usually taking place in both the horizontal direction – between different sub-processes and related departments – and in the vertical direction – between higher level planning and control activities and the value-adding processes on the shop floor. Well-designed information flows enable a company to close the control loop which in turn ensures responsive ("real-time") manufacturing operations.

In Fig. 1 an exemplary and extremely simplified manufacturing process is illustrated. The process model shows the principal activity flow of a car production. In addition, the material flow and the information flow are shown. The enclosing boxes labeled "PPC" and Production" reflect the organizational units that carry out the tasks. The upper box represents the planning and control activities whereas the lower box represents the value-adding activities. The exchange of information between planning and control activities and manufacturing activities is depicted by the dotted arrows. In the example only two types of information are exchanged: the production order including information such as which type of car to manufacture, the quantity and the scheduled finish date and the completion notification at the end of the process. The flow of material is depicted by dashed lines and boxes that indicate the type of material.

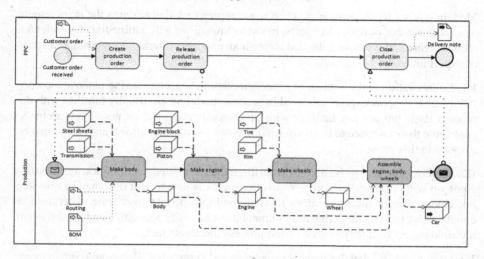

Fig. 1. Exemplary model of a car manufacturing and assembly process

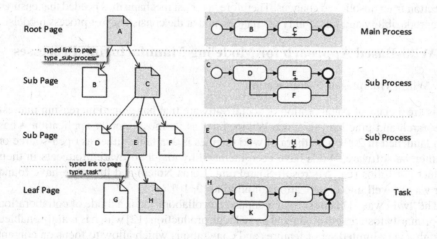

Fig. 2. Wiki page architecture and mapping to process architecture.

Figure 1 shows an extremely simplified manufacturing process of a car. In fact, the actual break-down of a car manufacturing process would reveal several hundreds of tasks, a thousand types of material and a similar number of data objects exchanged, e.g. a tire involves more than 25 different types of materials and about

10 distinct steps of processing. The complexity of the process is again multiplied when a high number of product variants is manufactured.

2.2 Requirements for Collaboration Support

Modeling of such processes in practice is a complex task that requires the involvement of a large number of domain experts. In the following we will outline the most relevant requirements that we have collected through an extensive literature review and a series of expert interviews [7].

R1. Collaboration in the context of process modeling is usually taking place in a corporate setting. Process experts involved in process modeling are usually familiar with the process itself but are not familiar with process modeling techniques. They prefer to contribute their knowledge in an informal manner. Formal workflows and roles must be avoided in this phase.

R2. Experts also like to be able to contribute their knowledge continuously as issues come up with a process. In other words, a process is usually not designed in one step but emerges from multiple interactions of multiple people over time. Therefore, a collaborative process modeling environment must be easily accessible and must support multiple modes of interactions with the process model artifact.

R3. Despite the fact that during idea generation and knowledge elicitation a certain openness is perceived beneficial, process models once enacted need a certain stability and protection from unsolicited changes. Therefore, a robust mechanism is needed that ensures the reproducibility and traceability of changes, and at the consistency of process models.

3 Wiki-Based Approach for Modeling Manufacturing Processes

3.1 Wiki Principles of Collaboration

Wikis are a class of collaboration or social software that has gained increasing interest in research and practice [8]. Since Wikipedia – as its most popular application – has been launched in 2001 a plethora of wiki engines is available either as open-source or commercial software. Wikis have been included by major software producers in their product portfolios (e.g. Microsoft SharePoint, Lotus Notes) and therefore have found their way as well into organizations of all kind [9, 10].

The "wiki way" [11] of software-supported collaboration is a mode of collaboration that primarily fosters self-organized knowledge production [12] which is mainly enabled through a very limited set of features and conventions which allow to focus on content rather than on formalities.

F1. One such feature is the page linking mechanism. In wikis each page (which is the central design artifact of a wiki) is considered a piece of knowledge that complements existing knowledge pieces by linking to them (backlink) and being linked. In a strict sense wikis do not allow unlinked pages which ensures that knowledge evolves as a network. In wikis links do not necessarily need a target page. Rather, a broken link acts as stub for contributing knowledge as it reflects both unfinished work and an encouragement for someone else to join in.

F2. Wiki pages are editable by everyone. This feature is contradicting typical corporate settings where strict access policies prevent contributions from a wider community.

F3. Flat namespace of a wiki. In a wiki pages are organized solely through linking. Every writer is at the same time organizer of the content. The name of a page is at the same time its unique URL. Therefore, page redundancies can be avoided.

F4. For each page a revision history is maintained. Revision histories are transparently accessible and allow pages to be reverted to a former revision. However, in case of concurrent changes taking place the last change wins but can be easily reverted.

3.2 Implementation of Wiki Principles in PWiki

For the purpose of evaluating the suitability of wiki features for process modeling we have extended an open-source wiki-engine[1] with capabilities for process modeling and governance support according to the requirements outlined (see E1, E2, E3).

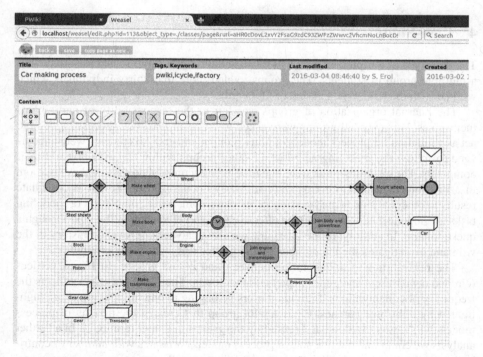

Fig. 3. PWiki page in edit mode showing the model editor component (E1).

---

[1] Weasel, https://launchpad.net/weasel2.

E1. Process model editor. We developed a web-based frontend for process modeling which was subsequently integrated into an existing wiki-engine (see Fig. 3).

E2. Semantic links. We introduced links based on the semantics of the BPMN [13] meta-model. Accordingly, each model element is a candidate for a new wiki page that contains type specific details of the element, e.g. a task element that links to a more detailed specification of its behavior, thus becoming a sub-process in the sense of BPMN. Semantic links foster modeling of deep process architectures in an incremental way (see Fig. 2). The incremental approach is highly relevant for the manufacturing domain where processes or parts hereof are usually automated in a step-by-step manner.

E3. Concurrency handling. We also introduced semi-automated merging of process model revisions. Pages that are concurrently edited by two or more users are compared and subsequently merged if not conflicting, otherwise the user is presented a merging editor. For details see our previous work in [14].

E4. Integration with a Production Planning and Control System (PPCS). We currently are developing a connector for integration with a PPCS and Business Process Engine (BPE). Conceptual process models are transformed into executable processes which can be scheduled and instantiated.

4   Case-Study

The prototype of our process wiki was evaluated through a large-scale case-study with a multiple group of students. The groups totaled more than thirty individuals which worked with the wiki over a period of 18 month.

The internal organization of groups was left to the responsibility of participants themselves. However, all groups were asked to create at least one process model and act as validators for process models of other group members. All students were encouraged to follow the modeling activities of other groups within the wiki and add their comments. The modeling tasks were intended to be accomplished outside the classroom in a distributed manner. Groups were regularly encouraged to present intermediate results to others at a dedicated session in the classroom. After completion of modeling tasks all students had to evaluate the effectiveness and efficiency of the wiki through a questionnaire. In addition to the interview we also analyzed the revision history of the wiki and investigated the interactions within groups and in-between groups.

The results show a collaboration between and across groups. In Fig. 4 vertices (circles) depict users and edges depict collaborations. The weight of edges reflects the frequency of collaborations. Individual users belonging to one original group are highlighted by light blue patches. C1 is a pilot group that created the first set of process models which was extended and reused by the groups in a later term (C2). In a further analysis we could find out that size of process models correlates with number of contributions and frequency of collaborations. We found as well a typical group phenomenon where a small subset of members contributes a relatively large part whereas other contribute only minor parts. This phenomenon could be especially observed in groups

G1, G3 and G5 whereas in groups G2 and G4 collaboration is more balanced. A detailed analysis of link structures (process architecture) shows a maximum tree depth of eight levels and a maximum width of seventeen pages.

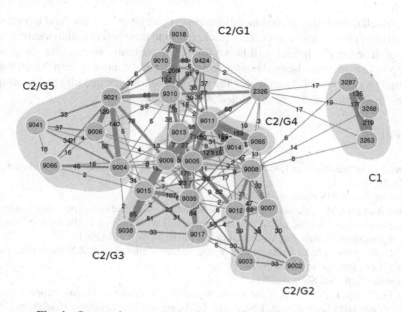

Fig. 4. One-mode network visualization of collaborations in PWiki.

The results from interviews of 22 users revealed a positive tendency towards the effectiveness and efficiency of PWiki. Their overall judgement shows a strong agreement to the effectiveness (13 agreeing versus 4 disagreeing) and efficiency (14 agreeing versus 3 disagreeing). Five participants remain neutral to the statements given.

5 Conclusion

In this paper we proposed a wiki-based approach for collaborative modeling of processes in the manufacturing domain. Given the increasing complexity of manufacturing processes we regard a wiki-based way of collaborative modeling useful in early phases of modeling where a large number of experts needs to be involved in ideation and information elicitation. However, in subsequent stages where high-level process models need to be detailed and unambiguously specified for later automation purpose a certain stability and traceability of changes needs to be ensured.

Through several extensions of an open-source wiki engine we created a prototypical collaborative process modeling environment that proved its usefulness and usability through a large-scale case-study. The case-study with modeling novices showed that the approach chosen is beneficial for open collaboration within and across groups as formal hurdles regarding participation and active involvement are low. We attribute this also to the linking mechanism that facilitates the breakdown of complex processes into sub processes and encourages following up somebody else's work. Given the prototypical state of development we found the results encouraging for further development of the approach.

In particular, for future digital manufacturing scenarios where data and information flows will be of central importance, also quick, easy and transparent collaboration among experts of different disciplines will be vital. We are currently integrating our process modeling wiki with a cloud-based production planning and control system. Thus, mature conceptual process models from within the wiki can be transformed into technical specifications and subsequently are scheduled and instantiated.

References

1. Zhou, J.: Digitalization and intelligentization of manufacturing industry. Adv. Manuf. **1**(1), 1–7 (2013)
2. Software AG, ARIS Platform. Software AG (2011)
3. Nolte, A., Prilla, M., Lukosch, S., et al.: Collaborative usage and development of models and visualizations. In: Proceedings of the 1st International Workshop on Collaborative Usage and Development of Models and Visualizations at the ECSCW 2011 (2011)
4. Rother, M., Shook, J.: Learning to See: Value Stream Mapping to Add Value and Eliminate Muda. Lean Enterprise Institute (2003)
5. Motorola Corp., Six Sigma (2011)
6. Qin, G., Wang, L., Li, Q.: A cloud model for internet of things on logistic supply chain. In: Luo, Yuhua (ed.) CDVE 2015. LNCS, vol. 9320, pp. 93–104. Springer, Heidelberg (2015). doi:10.1007/978-3-319-24132-6
7. Erol, S.: Practical insights into collaborative drafting of organizational processes. In: Proceedings of the 1st International Workshop on Collaborative Usage and Development of Models and Visualizations, ECSCW 2011, pp. 45–51 (2011)
8. Raeth, P., Smolnik, S., Urbach, N., et al.: Towards assessing the success of social software in corporate environments. In Proceedings of the 15th Americas Conference on Information Systems, San Francisco (2009)
9. Bhatti, Z. A., Baile, S., Yasin, H. M.: The success of corporate wiki systems: an end user perspective [WikiSym 2011]. In: Proceedings of WikiSym 2011, Mountain View, California (2011)
10. Voigt, S., Fuchs-Kittowski, F., Gohr, A.: Structured wikis – application oriented use cases. In: Proceedings of OpenSym2014, Berlin, Germany (2014)
11. Leuf, B., Cunningham, W.: The Wiki Way: Quick Collaboration on the Web. Addison-Wesley Professional, Boston (2001)
12. Ren, R.: The evolution of knowledge creation online: Wikipedia and knowledge processes. In: Proceedings of OpenSym 2015 (2015)
13. OMG, "Business Process Model and Notation (BPMN) Version 2.0," OMG (2011)
14. Erol, S., Neumann, G.: Handling concurrent changes in collaborative process model development: a change-pattern based approach. In: 2013 17th IEEE International Enterprise Distributed Object Computing Conference Workshops (EDOCW), pp. 250–257 (2013)

Performance-Matching-Based Resource Selection for Cloud Manufacturing

Li-Nan Zhu[1]([✉]), Yan-Wei Zhao[2], and Guo-Jiang Shen[1]

[1] College of Computer Science and Technology, Zhejiang University
of Technology, Hangzhou 310023, People's Republic of China
{zln, gjshen1975}@zjut.edu.cn
[2] Key Laboratory of Special Purpose Equipment and Advanced
Processing Technology, Ministry of Education, Zhejiang University
of Technology, Hangzhou 310023, People's Republic of China
zyw@zjut.edu.cn

Abstract. Cloud manufacturing is emerged as a kind of networked cooperative manufacturing mode. Under cloud manufacturing environment, the manufacturing resources appear as cloud services, and the amount of their performances is very large, so every cloud service has some sub-modules every one of which also contains many service performance indexes. How to select a suitable cloud service by performance matching is very difficult. In this paper, the authors employ matter-element model to describe the cloud service and user's requirement, and propose a matching method by calculating module similarity with multidimensional extension distance for resource selection. A case study is also provided for illustrating the implementation of the method.

Keywords: Resource selection · Performance matching · Cloud manufacturing · Multidimensional extension

1 Introduction

Cloud manufacturing was put forward in the early 2000s and has gradually risen and become the main direction of manufacturing industry. Cloud manufacturing is a networked cooperative manufacturing process [1], and there are a lot of manufacturing resources that appear as cloud services and cooperatively complete a task. Therefore, performance matching plays an important role in massive resource selection. In previous work, we have proposed a bilayer resource model [2] and a resource selection approach based on service evaluation [3]. In this paper, we will propose a resource performance matching approach based on multidimensional extension theory.

The rest of the article is organized as follows. Section 2 presents the mathematical model of cloud service. The calculation method of similarity for 1-D, 3-D and n-D modules is described in Sect. 3. Section 4 introduces the weight calculation method. A case study is proposed in Sect. 5. Finally, Sect. 6 gives the conclusion and future lines of research.

Y. Luo (Ed.): CDVE 2016, LNCS 9929, pp. 25–33, 2016.
DOI: 10.1007/978-3-319-46771-9_4

2 Mathematical Model of Cloud Service

2.1 Model Assumptions

We describe the cloud service in cloud resource pool as formula (1): *ID* means the flag of cloud service; *RCEID* means the flag of corresponding manufacturing resources in cloud end such as a certain manufacturer or service provider; *BaseInfo* means the basic information set such as name, type, size, and so on; *ServiceInfo* means service performance set such as precision, cost, production time, input temple, output temple, and so on; *AssessInfo* means assessment information set; *StatueInfo* means the working status of the cloud service; *OtherInfo* is other service capability information, added or removed by the provider.

$$ResCloudService = \left\{ \begin{array}{l} ID, RCEID, BaseInfo, ServiceInfo, \\ AssessInfo, StatueInfo, OtherInfo \end{array} \right\} \tag{1}$$

During the process of requirement proposal and resource selection, we make assumptions as follows:

(1) Performance similarity of cloud service is mainly aimed at the match degree of *ServiceInfo* attribute, and has nothing to do with other attributes.
(2) Because of coarse granularity of cloud service, the service performance also has some sub-service performance module which is called as *SerInfo*, and every *SerInfo* also has many service performance indexes which are called as *S*.
(3) Every cloud service has a certain value in every performance index.
(4) In the requirement, there must be an ideal interval F_L and the best value O in every service performance index. So, there must be $O \in F_L$.

2.2 Matter-Element Description of Cloud Service

According to the rules of matter-element description, we can get the matter-element description of cloud service and user's requirement, just like formula (2) and (3).

$$CloudService = (N_s, C_s, V_s) = \begin{bmatrix} CS, & ID, & & & v_{id} \\ & RCEID, & & & v_{rc} \\ & BaseInfo, & & & v_{ba} \\ & & & S_{11}, & v_{se11} \\ & ServiceInfo, & SerInfo_1, & \vdots & \vdots \\ & & & S_{1k_1}, & v_{se1k_1} \\ & & & S_{21}, & v_{se21} \\ & & SerInfo_2, & \vdots & \vdots \\ & & & S_{2k_2}, & v_{se2k_2} \\ & & \vdots & \vdots & \vdots \\ & & SerInfo_i, & S_{i1}, & v_{sei1} \\ & & & \vdots & \vdots \\ & & & S_{ik_i}, & v_{seik_i} \\ & & \vdots & & \\ & & SerInfo_n, & S_{n1}, & v_{sen1} \\ & & & \vdots & \vdots \\ & & & S_{nk_n}, & v_{senk_n} \\ & AssessInfo, & & & v_{as} \\ & StatusInfo, & & & v_{st} \\ & OtherInfo, & & & v_{ot} \end{bmatrix} \tag{2}$$

Here in (2), the service performance *ServiceInfo* contains n sub-service performance module *SerInfo*, every one of which contains k_i service performance indexes S, and v_{seij} is the certain value in the performance index j of sub-service performance module i.

$$CloudDemand = (N_d, C_d, V_d) = \begin{bmatrix} CD, & ID, & & v_{id} \\ & Demander, & & v_{dmr} \\ & & S_{11}, & v_{sd11} \\ & ServiceDemd, & SerD_1, & \vdots & \vdots \\ & & & S_{1k_1}, & v_{sd1k_1} \\ & & SerD_2, & S_{21}, & v_{sd21} \\ & & & \vdots & \vdots \\ & & & S_{2k_2}, & v_{sd2k_2} \\ & & \vdots & \vdots & \vdots \\ & & SerD_i, & S_{i1}, & v_{sdi1} \\ & & & \vdots & \vdots \\ & & & S_{it_i}, & v_{sdit_i} \\ & & \vdots & & \\ & & SerD_m, & S_{n1}, & v_{sdn1} \\ & & & \vdots & \vdots \\ & & & S_{mt_m}, & v_{sdmt_m} \\ & CostDemd, & & v_{co} \\ & TimeDemd, & & v_{ti} \\ & AssessDemd, & & v_{as} \\ & OtherDemd, & & v_{ot} \end{bmatrix} \quad (3)$$

Here in (3), the service performance requirement *ServiceDemd* has the same meaning with *ServiceInfo*, and contains m sub-service performance requirement module *SerD*, every one of which has t_i service performance requirement indexes. But v_{sdij} contains a certain value which is the best value O and an ideal interval F_L. So, there must be $m \le n$, $t_i \le k_i$, *ServiceDemd* $\subseteq$ *ServiceInfo* and *SerInfo*$_i$ $\subseteq$ *SerD*$_i$.

3 Calculation Method of Similarity

The selection of cloud service depends on the matching degree of performance module *ServiceInfo*, which is consist of some sub-service performance modules. Here, we adopt the multi-dimensional extension distance [4] to calculate performance similarity. Assume, there is a cloud service CS, which contains n sub-service performance modules: $CS_1, CS_2, \cdots, CS_i, \cdots, CS_n$, and every CS_i contains k_i service performance indexes. In the requirement, there is an ideal interval F_{Li} and the best value O_i in very service performance index. So, the matching approach is as follows:

Step 1: According the matter-description, we get the coordinates of every sub-service performance module $CS_i\left(x_1^{CS_i}, x_2^{CS_i}, \cdots, x_i^{CS_i}, \cdots, x_{k_i}^{CS_i}\right)$, the best value $O_i\left(x_1^{O_i}, x_2^{O_i}, \cdots, x_i^{O_i}, \cdots, x_{k_i}^{O_i}\right)$, and the ideal interval $F_{Li}\left(x_{1l}^{F_{Li}}, x_{1u}^{F_{Li}}, x_{2l}^{F_{Li}}, x_{2u}^{F_{Li}}, \cdots, x_{il}^{F_{Li}}, x_{iu}^{F_{Li}}, \cdots, x_{k_il}^{F_{Li}}, x_{k_iu}^{F_{Li}}\right)$. Here, $\langle \rangle$ means the ideal interval, it can be open interval ( ), or closed interval [ ], or half open interval [ ) and ( ];

Step 2: Calculate the extension distance between point CS_i to the ideal interval F_{Li} about the best value point O_i: $\rho(CS_i, O_i, F_{Li})$, and the extension distance between point O_i to the ideal interval F_{Li} about the best value point O_i: $\rho(O_i, O_i, F_{Li})$. There must be (4), $Fr(F_{Li})$ means in the frontier of F_{Li};

$$\rho(CS_i, O_i, F_{Li}) = \begin{cases} (0, +\infty), & CS_i \notin F_{Li}, \\ 0, & CS_i \notin Fr(F_{Li}), \\ (\rho(O_i, O_i, F_{Li}), 0), & CS_i \in F_{Li}. \end{cases} \quad (4)$$

Step 3: Establish the correlation function $S(x)$, which reflects the similarity of sub-service performance module x. Calculate the degree of similarity of every CS_i by the formula (5), there must be $S(CS_i) \in [-\infty, 1]$;

$$S(CS_i) = \rho(CS_i, O_i, F_{Li})/\rho(O_i, O_i, F_{Li}) \quad (5)$$

Step 4: With the weight w_i of every CS_i, calculate the degree of similarity of the CS by the formula (6);

$$S(CS) = \sum_{i=1}^{n} w_i S(CS_i) / \sum_{i=1}^{n} w_i \quad (6)$$

According to the quantity of the service performance indexes, the performance module can be named as n-D service performance module (n-DM).

3.1 Similarity Calculation of 1-DM

For 1-DM, showed as Fig. 1, we assume that there is a cloud service CS which has a sub-service performance module CS_i with 1 service performance index represented by the axis D_1, the value of CS_i in this index is p represented by point P; In the requirement, the best value in this index is o presented by point O, and the ideal interval is $\langle a, b \rangle$ presented by line segment AB in the axis D_1. So, there must be $o \in \langle a, b \rangle$.

Fig. 1. The Geometrical Model of 1-DM

According to the computational method of extension distance proposed by Prof. Cai Wen [5], we can calculate the extension distance between point P and line segment AB with the best point O as the formula (7).

$$\rho(P,O,AB) = \begin{cases} a-p, & o \in (a,(a+b)/2) \land p \le a, \\ p-a, & o \in (a,(a+b)/2) \land p \ge o, \\ \frac{b-o}{a-o}(p-a), & o \in (a,(a+b)/2) \land p \in (a,o), \\ a-p, & o = a \land p \le a, \\ p-b, & o = a \land p > a, \\ a-p, & o \in [(a+b)/2,b) \land p \le o, \\ p-b, & o \in [(a+b)/2,b) \land p \ge b, \\ \frac{a-o}{b-o}(b-p), & o \in ((a+b)/2,b) \land p \in (o,b), \\ p-b, & o = b \land p \ge b, \\ a-p, & o = a \land p < b. \end{cases} \quad (7)$$

The distance $\rho(P,O,AB)$ has the following properties: (1) $\rho(P,O,AB) < 0$ *iff* $P \in AB$, and the minimum value is $\rho(O,O,AB)$ when P coinciding with O; (2) $\rho(P,O,AB) = 0$ *iff* $P \in Fr(AB)$; (3) $\rho(P,O,AB) > 0$ *iff* $P \notin AB$. So, the $S_{1-D}(CS_i) = S(P)$ calculated as formula (5) has the following properties: (1) $S_{1-D}(CS_i) \in [0,1]$ *iff* $P \in [a,b]$; (2) $S_{1-D}(CS_i) = 1$ *iff* $p = o$; (3) $S_{1-D}(CS_i) = 0$ *iff* $p = a \lor p = b$; (4) $S_{1-D}(CS_i) \in (-\infty,0)$ *iff* $P \notin [a,b]$.

3.2 Similarity Calculation of 3-DM

For 3-DM, showed as Fig. 2, we assume that there is a cloud service CS which has a sub-service performance module CS_i with 3 service performance indexes represented by the axis D_1, D_2 and D_3, the value of CS_i in the 3 indexes is respectively p_1, p_2 and p_3 represented by point $P(p_1,p_2,p_3)$; In the requirement, the best value is o_1, o_2 and o_3 presented by point $O(o_1,o_2,o_3)$, and the ideal interval is $\langle a_1,b_1 \rangle$, $\langle a_2,b_2 \rangle$ and $\langle a_3,b_3 \rangle$ presented by cuboid $S(AM_1M_2M_3BN_1N_2N_3)$. The crossover points of straight line OP and cuboid S is $P'(p_1',p_2',p_3')$ and $P''(p_1'',p_2'',p_3'')$. So, there must be $O \in S$.

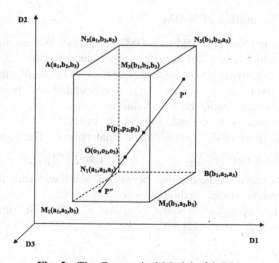

Fig. 2. The Geometrical Model of 3-DM

We calculate the extension distance between P and S with dimensional reduction method as follows:

Step 1: Get p_2', p_2'', p_3' and p_3'' when $p_1' = a_1$ and $p_1'' = b_1$ with formula (8);

$$
\begin{aligned}
p_2' &= \frac{(a_1-p_1)(p_2-o_2)}{p_1-o_1} + p_2 \quad & p_2'' &= \frac{(b_1-p_1)(p_2-o_2)}{p_1-o_1} + p_2 \\
p_3' &= \frac{(a_1-p_1)(p_3-o_3)}{p_1-o_1} + p_3 \quad & p_3'' &= \frac{(b_1-p_1)(p_3-o_3)}{p_1-o_1} + p_3
\end{aligned}
\tag{8}
$$

Step 2: Get p_1', p_1'', p_3' and p_3'' when $p_2' = a_2$ and $p_2'' = b_2$ with formula (9);

$$
\begin{aligned}
p_1' &= \frac{(a_2-p_2)(p_1-o_1)}{p_2-o_2} + p_1 \quad & p_1'' &= \frac{(b_2-p_2)(p_1-o_1)}{p_2-o_2} + p_1 \\
p_3' &= \frac{(a_2-p_2)(p_3-o_3)}{p_2-o_2} + p_3 \quad & p_3'' &= \frac{(b_2-p_2)(p_3-o_3)}{p_2-o_2} + p_3
\end{aligned}
\tag{9}
$$

Step 3: Get p_1', p_1'', p_2' and p_2'' when $p_3' = a_3$ and $p_3'' = b_3$ with formula (10);

$$
\begin{aligned}
p_1' &= \frac{(a_3-p_3)(p_1-o_1)}{p_3-o_3} + p_1 \quad & p_1'' &= \frac{(b_3-p_3)(p_1-o_1)}{p_3-o_3} + p_1 \\
p_2' &= \frac{(a_3-p_3)(p_2-o_2)}{p_3-o_3} + p_2 \quad & p_2'' &= \frac{(b_3-p_3)(p_2-o_2)}{p_3-o_3} + p_2
\end{aligned}
\tag{10}
$$

Step 4: We get 6 crossover points at most: (a_1,p_2',p_3'), (b_1,p_2'',p_3''), (p_1',a_2,p_3'), (p_1'',b_2,p_3''), (p_1',p_2',a_3) and (p_1'',p_2'',b_3). Then, we take the points with their coordinates during the ideal intervals in every dimension, just as P' and P'' showed as Fig. 2;

Step 5: Now, we get the 1-D geometrical model: the best value point $O(o_1,o_2,o_3)$ and arbitrary point $P(p_1,p_2,p_3)$, both of which is in the straight line $P'P''$. Then, we can calculate the distance $\rho(P,O,S)$ and $\rho(O,O,S)$ by the formula (7);

Step 6: Calculate the $S_{3-D}(CS_i) = S_{3-D}(P)$ by the formula (5). So, the $S_{3-D}(CS_i)$ has the same properties with $S_{1-D}(CS_i)$.

3.3 Similarity Calculation of N-DM

We generalized the method of 3-DM to n-DM. For n-DM. We assume that there is a cloud service CS which has a sub-service performance module CS_i with k_i service performance indexes represented by the axis $D_1, D_2, \cdots, D_i, \cdots, D_{k_i}$, the value of the k_i indexes is respectively $p_1, p_2, \cdots, p_i, \cdots, p_{k_i}$ represented by point $P(p_1, p_2, \cdots, p_i, \cdots, p_{k_i})$; In the requirement, the best value is $o_1, o_2, \cdots, o_i, \cdots, o_{k_i}$ presented by point $O(o_1, o_2, \cdots, o_i, \cdots, o_{k_i})$, and the ideal interval is $\langle a_1, b_1 \rangle, \langle a_2, b_2 \rangle, \cdots, \langle a_i, b_i \rangle, \cdots, \langle a_{k_i}, b_{k_i} \rangle$ presented by multidimensional cube S. The crossover points of straight line OP and S is $P'\left(p_1', p_2', \cdots, p_i', \cdots, p_{k_i}'\right)$ and $P''\left(p_1'', p_2'', \cdots, p_i'', \cdots, p_{k_i}''\right)$.

Just like 3.2, we calculate the distance between P and S with dimensional reduction method, and the computational method is as follows:

Step 1: Calculate p_l' and p_l'' when $p_i' = a_i$ and $p_i'' = b_i$ with formula (11). Here, $j = 1, 2, \cdots, k_i$, $l = 1, 2, \cdots, j-1, j+1, \cdots, k_i$;

$$p'_l = \frac{(a_j-p_j)(p_l-o_l)}{p_j-o_j} + p_l \quad p''_l = \frac{(b_j-p_j)(p_l-o_l)}{p_j-o_j} + p_l \tag{11}$$

Step 2: We get $2n$ crossover points at most. Then, we take the points with their coordinates during the ideal intervals in every dimension, at last we get 2 crossover points P' and P'';

Step 3: Now, we get the 1-D geometrical model: the best value point $O(o_1, o_2, \cdots, o_i, \cdots, o_{k_i})$ and arbitrary point $P(p_1, p_2, \cdots, p_i, \cdots, p_{k_i})$, both of which is in the line segment $P'P''$. Then, we can calculate the distance $\rho(P, O, S)$ and $\rho(O, O, S)$ by the formula (7);

Step 4: Calculate the $S_{n-D}(CS_i) = S_{n-D}(P)$ by the formula (5). So, the $S_{n-D}(CS_i)$ has the same properties with $S_{1-D}(CS_i)$.

4 Weight

The weight reflects the importance of every sub-service performance module. Here, we define three categories weight: (1) User-defined weight w_c, which is defined by user when proposing requirement, here we employ tone operator for users; (2) Structure weight w_p, which is defined by domain experts according to the importance during the product lifecycle; (3) Example weight w_r, which is defined with the similarity of every sub-service performance module of cloud services in the cloud service pool. The thinking of determining w_r is that, the more greatly the similarity of the same sub-service performance module in different cloud service varies, the more greatly this module influents the overall performance, and the larger w_r should be, and the smaller, conversely. So, here we use standard deviation to determine w_r.

The final weight of every sub-service performance module w_i is defined with the 3 categories weight above by the formula (12).

$$w_i = \left(w_{ci} \times w_{pi} \times w_{ri}\right) / \sum_{k=1}^{n} \left(w_{ck} \times w_{pk} \times w_{rk}\right) \tag{12}$$

5 Case Study

We take the car tire as an example, the cloud service has 4 sub-service performance modules and 9 performance indexes. Module 'Size' contains 5 indexes (P1–P5); Module 'Deliver Period' contains 2 indexes (P6–P7); Module 'Maintenance' contains 1 index (P8); Module 'Price' contains 1 index (P9). From market survey, we get performance data of 100 resource and 50 users' requirements as well as their w_c, in addition we also get the w_p from domain experts.

Because of the article length limitation, we show a matching result of only 1 user and 12 examples. Table 1 shows the extension distance (E) and similarity (S) of 12 examples. We can see that the example 1, 2, and 5-11 every similarity of which is

Table 1. The Extension Distance and Similarity of Every Example

ID	Module 1		Module 2		Module 3		Module 4	
	E	S	E	S	E	S	E	S
⋮	⋮	⋮	⋮	⋮	⋮	⋮	⋮	⋮
1	0	0	−12	0.35	−500	0.25	−260	1
2	0	0	0	0	−500	0.25	−250	0.96
3	0	0	24	−0.71	−500	0.25	−230	0.88
4	0	0	33.94	−1	−500	0.25	−180	0.69
5	0	0	0	0	−500	0.25	−160	0.62
6	0	0	0	0	−500	0.25	−150	0.58
7	−26.93	0.33	−33.94	1	−500	0.25	−100	0.38
8	0	0	0	0	−500	0.25	−80	0.31
9	0	0	0	0	−800	0.4	−60	0.23
10	0	0	0	0	−1000	0.5	−40	0.15
11	0	0	−33.94	1	−1000	0.5	−30	0.12
12	0	0	−12	0.35	−1500	0.75	20	−0.08
⋮	⋮	⋮	⋮	⋮	⋮	⋮	⋮	⋮

Table 2. The Similarity of Every Suitable Example

ID	1	2	5	6	7	8	9	10	11
S	0.35	0.25	0.17	0.16	**0.49**	0.10	0.10	0.10	0.35

positive is suitable. With the similarity of suitable examples, we can calculate the Example weight w_r. And the similarity of every suitable example is showed as Table 2. So, the example 7 should be chosen.

6   Conclusion and Future Work

Aiming at the coarse grain of cloud service, we have proposed the matter-element description of cloud service. Then we have also calculated the similarity of 1-DM, 3-DM and n-DM by using the extension distance, especially how to change 3-DM and n-DM to 1-DM through dimensional reduction. In order to fully consider the user participation, professional guidance and examples in cloud service pool, we introduce three types of weights, which are calculated to get the final weight of every sub-service performance module. Finally, take the care tire as an example, we show the calculating process in detail. Performance Similarity is just one aspect of resource evaluation, there are also many other aspects under cloud manufacturing environment, such as QoS. In the future, we should research on the characteristic of cloud service QoS, and how to select cloud service according to QoS evaluation.

Acknowledgement. This work was partly supported by the National Natural Science Foundation of China (Grant No. 51275477 and 61572438), the Natural Science Foundation of Zhejiang Province, China (Grant No. LQ15E050006), and the Science and Technique Program of Zhejiang Province, China (Grant No. 2015C31059).

References

1. Garcia-Sabater, J.P., Lloret, J., Marin-Garcia, J.A., Puig-Bernabeu, X.: Coordinating a cooperative automotive manufacturing network – an agent-based model. In: Luo, Y. (ed.) CDVE 2010. LNCS, vol. 6240, pp. 231–238. Springer, Heidelberg (2010). doi:10.1007/978-3-642-16066-0_34
2. Zhu, L.N., Zhao, Y.W., Wang, W.L.: A bilayer resource model of cloud manufacturing services. Mathematical Problems in Engineering, Article ID: 607582, 10 pages (2013)
3. Zhao, Y.-W., Zhu, L.-N.: Service evaluation-based resource selection in cloud manufacturing. In: Luo, Y. (ed.) CDVE 2014. LNCS, vol. 8683, pp. 294–302. Springer, Heidelberg (2014). doi:10.1007/978-3-319-10831-5_42
4. Smarandache, F.: Extenics in Higher Dimensions, Education Publisher, Columbus, Ohio, USA, Chap. 1–4 (2012). ISBN: 978-1599732039
5. Yang, C.Y., Cai, W. Extension Engineering, Science Press, Guangzhou, China, Chap. 1–2 (2007). ISBN: 9787030194732

A Framework for Improving Collaboration Patterns in BIM Projects

Eva-Charlotte Forgues[1], Vincent Carignan[1],
Daniel Forgues[1(✉)], and Samia Ben Rajeb[2]

[1] Department of Construction Engineering, École de Technologie Supérieure,
1100 Notre-Dame West Street, Montreal, QC H3C 1K3, Canada
{eva-charlotte.forgues.1,vincent.carignan.1}@etsmtl.net,
daniel.forgues@etsmtl.ca
[2] LUCID Lab for User Cognition & Innovative Design, University of Liège, Liège, Belgium
samia.benrajeb@ulg.ac.be

Abstract. BIM is often presented as a collaborative platform. However, the core principle of BIM is about sharing data through centralized or distributed platforms. Collaboration is not at the heart of BIM. It is about requiring the actors of the construction project network to reconfigure their patterns of relationships to facilitate the production and exchange of the project data and the information processing using this platform. Organization of work in construction is highly linear and fragmented, and the construction project stakeholders don't have the tools to understand and represent how information is created and processed among them.

This paper presents a collaborative mapping approach that help construction project stakeholders to visualize the existing patterns emerging from their use of BIM. Through a collaborative action-research project, different key stakeholders are invited to participate into the co-construction of a visual mapping of the information processing for the production of the BIM model within the various organizations. The mappings for the whole project were assembled to extract the divergent perceptions and domain-based visions of each participant. The main contribution of this research is a framework for the co-construction of a project process modelling. The aim is to reduce the barriers and conflicts that emerge in a collaborative process.

Keywords: Collaboration · BIM · Barriers · Process mapping · Perceptions

1 Introduction

The AEC (Architecture, Engineering and Construction) industry context is unique and complex. Fragmentation is considered as the main cause to this complexity and uniqueness inducing complications in collaboration, communication and information flows [1]. Building Information Modelling (BIM) challenges this fragmentation by offering a centralized platform of shared information and common models. BIM tools are said to enhance efficiency and productivity and to increase the performance of the building product through multiple usages [2]. The potential of BIM tools is obvious, however,

© Springer International Publishing AG 2016
Y. Luo (Ed.): CDVE 2016, LNCS 9929, pp. 34–42, 2016.
DOI: 10.1007/978-3-319-46771-9_5

the traditional practices and trust-based team practices are strong hindrances to a successful BIM implementation in the industry [3]. Consequently, various studies claim that the BIM promises fall short of expectations [3] and underline the need to reform the traditional practices [3] – [5]. We argue that, to mark the areas of conflicts that impede the transitory process between traditional practices to a new mindset [6], process mapping can be used as a visualization tool to understand and act on redefining collaborative practices around the BIM artefact.

This study proposes a new investigation method based on collaborative research-action developed by LUCID at Université de Liège. This method was adapted to generate project process maps on a BIM project in Quebec. It suggests the collection of data by guiding an actor of the supply chain to model the project process in order to understand and identify their own vision of the collaborative process. The formalization of the mappings will enable comprehension of the visions, semantics, limitations and disparities between the various actors.

This method aims to formalize perceptions through process maps. It takes roots in the theory of collaborative research-action where the research team and the participant co-construct artifacts (in this case, process maps). Afterwards, the development of the protocol of co-construction and the theoretical background will be presented. The data analysis will be centered on isolating in the process maps the gaps and ambiguities in this specific collaborative process.

2   Theoretical Background

2.1   Issues in BIM Collaboration

Miettinen and Paavola suggest that the use of BIM technological tools can deliver their benefits and advantages only if they are fully implemented [3]. Empirical studies have shown that the benefits of BIM implementation are limited by fragmentation of the industry, adversarial relationship between stakeholders, discontinuity in project teams and organizational conditions [3]. In fact, the paradox regarding the so-called collaborative BIM approach is that it excels in finding the coordination problems but it does not support the complexity of solving it through collaboration [7, 8]. A new mindset of collaboration between the different actors is the key to develop optimized process system for BIM implementation [6].

A first issue in collaboration is the quality and the quantity of the information exchanges between the stakeholders. The temporary nature of the building projects and the disparities of the various organizations involved in the different stages results in multiple and scattered pieces of information causing low productivity and ineffectiveness of the construction process [7].

A second issue in collaboration is the lack of a common shared vision of the project across all participants due to the fragmentation between specific domains and perspectives [9]. Each discipline reinterpret the information as variables specific to his domain such as data, tools, languages, perspectives and visions [8]. Furthermore, the comprehension of information can be deformed and reinterpreted individually by the stakeholder based on his own knowledge, role and expertise [10]. A common language between all the stakeholders is primordial to target a successful integration between the human activity processes and the technologies in practice [11].

A third issue hindering collaboration is the lack of understanding of the overall process information flows by the stakeholders. In general, players tend to focus and optimize their own specific work, and to address the interdependencies of the others' tasks in a very ad hoc and reactive way [9]. Each task is completed with the data that reflects the unique perspective of the player, with little integration between the other views creating a large amount of disparate information based on fragmented perspectives. The fundamental way to deal with this complexity is by defining and decomposing the project work into specific tasks and to underline the interdependencies of these activities [9]. Workflows can be used to provide a unifying perspective of the project information exchange, resulting in a common vision and objectives to assure collaboration and efficiency [10].

A fourth issue for collaboration, induced by the introduction of new technology, is the resistance from specialties to evolve their outdated process according to the changes required by the new technological environment. This is characterized by the clash between the market-driven pressure to adjust to rapid technological changes and strong inertia of traditional practices [7]. These transformations in a collaborative project delivery system affect the workflow of actions and mechanisms that are highly dependent on the barriers and organizational constraints [11]. Kiviniemi [6] emphasizes the need to drive efforts in questioning practices and proposing fundamental process changes to enhance collaboration and information exchanges within a centralized platform. Groleau [4] studies contradictions in the traditional practices induced by technological innovation. She suggests that the behavioural opposition to change is mainly caused by sociohistorical barriers. A way to break down these barriers is to expose these contradictions in order to evolve the practices around the new technologies [4].

2.2 Co-construction of Senses and Cognitive Science

Organizational change management linked to the implementation of new technologies such as BIM is based on the group's capacity to comprehend its actual and foreseen situation [12]. A better understanding of its situation allows the group to participate actively in the strategy's development of the new technology's implementation. It also allows the group to adapt itself to its new reality. Collaborative action-research supports this change in every aspect: technological, socio-cognitive and organizational. Collaborative action-research is an interventionist approach that involves the research team as well as the participants from the studied context to collaborate for the collection, processing and analyzing of the research data. [13]. Results are obtained from the co-construction of the same activity by the researcher and the other players, which mark a bold distinction from classical scientific research [14]. This approach is usually used in educational support, leadership development or in the integration of social parameters in urban planning projects. The originality of this work comes from the adaptation of this approach to the construction sector [15].

In this study, the objective is to allow the group of players to pool its BIM activities' knowledge, to share and/or transfer skills [16]. To do so, this paper proposes an adaptation of a retrospective protocol method that comes from cognitive sciences called crossed auto-confrontation [17]. In addition to confronting participants with his perceptions of his own project tasks, this research is also a joint analysis by crossing several snapshots of a common process (between one player and another, but also between a researcher and actor with whom he collaborated for this data collection). Therefore, the memory of the participants is crystallized by the action and not only by a simple individual interview. Consequently, the researcher and the participants can co-model the project development process and its implementation in a BIM context. Moreover, by overlapping different maps produced by each stakeholder, we seek to map the overall flow of activities to identify and expose contradictions which are not visible from the mapping of a single stakeholder.

3   Research Design

This research project is part of a larger one involving two laboratories, the LUCID (ULg) in Liege and the GRIDD (ETS) in Montreal, which aims to develop change management methods focused in the adoption of new collaborative technologies adapted to the peculiar context of construction industry. In this particular study, collaborative research-action method was adapted to design process mapping adding an innovative approach to auto-confrontation.

3.1   The Context of Research

This project was selected because of its legal form and its complexity. As a public-private partnership (PPP) contract, subcontractors are typically invited to participate early in the design phase in order to reduce design errors and facilitate collaboration and communication throughout the whole process. The project consists of a 250 M CAN$ medium-security detention centre composed of 300 individual cells and eighty beds in different dormitories. The complexity of the project stands on the complete unit separation due to security measures. Ergo, all the technical systems are duplicated to feed, as independent systems, the different wings. Considering this particular context, the general contractor paid special attention to the coordination of the mechanical, electrical and plumbing services (MEP) by using a BIM process.

This research aims to illustrate through the process mapping the BIM collaboration between the major participants in the coordination of the MEP during the different phases. The selected participants were the project manager of the architecture firm, the MEP engineering firm and the mechanical subcontractor. The general contractor had a specific employee, called MEP BIM coordinator, who was in charge of all of the MEP coordination between stakeholders in the overall process. The research started when the construction of the prison was ending in order to collect information about the whole process from the early design to the final product.

3.2   The Development of the Protocol

This research protocol was designed to guide the participant to model the various actions and the information exchange between the other stakeholders through the different project stages. To drive this modelling, the project process mapping was co-constructed between the participant and the researcher following a strict protocol. Three major aspects in process modelling were followed:

- The workflow between the various actors;
- The input and output of the information;
- The representation of this information in material objects or documents [10].

To successfully represent these concepts, the research protocol was based on the standard graphic of the Business Process Model and Notation (BPMN) since its notations include the functional aspects of the tasks and activities, the organizational division and the informational entities of documents [18] into an integrated flow. To facilitate this collaborative method of modelling of information flows, our principal objective was to come up with a soft protocol where the participants would feel comfortable and at ease. Therefore, only the basic modelling elements of BPMN were adopted such as event, gateway, activity, sequenced flow and data objects [18].

The protocol aims to extract data about these four main concepts: organizational and role division, tasks and activity, documents output and input and collaboration problems. These aspects were divided in four superposed layers. The first layer, named organization and phase division concern the principal project phases and the different stakeholders. Afterward, the participants combined the sequence of tasks and activities between the various identified actors in a second layer called workflow. They were asked to include gateways to identify the decision-making and the involvement of the different stakeholders. Between the phases, events were added to illustrate the causes of the beginning and the ending of the divided stages [18]. For the third layer dataflow, the participants were requested to specify the different documents as input or output between the activities.

The exercise started with an open discussion on the project to ease the participants and to help them recall the events of the project. Throughout the whole process, the participants were encouraged to explain what they were modelling, to show proofs of documents and to define the emergent conflicts and barriers. As a fifth layer, the problematic zone, the participants were using annotative text and group box [18] to summarize collaboration problems throughout the process map.

Modelling with cross auto-confrontation was a very long and demanding procedure. The intervention per participant was approximately three to four hours. To assure the validity and reliance of the data, the exercises were divided in shorter meeting of approximately one and a half hour. As the participants were getting eased in the process, their involvement and collaboration were increased and thus outbidding further information.

3.3 Data Analysis

As the exercises were fully completed, the process maps were refined and readjusted to fit with a basic BPMN process mapping (example in Fig. 1). The stakeholders' roles were placed in the same order to facilitate comparison between the different maps. To assure the validity of the generated BPMN process map, the participants were invited to comment on the results and to answer further questions emerging from the data analysis of the resulting map. To analyze the data, the different types of information were isolated per layer. The research team focused on isolating the perceptions, the semantic differences, the barriers, the contradictions between the perceptions and the ambiguity throughout the overall process.

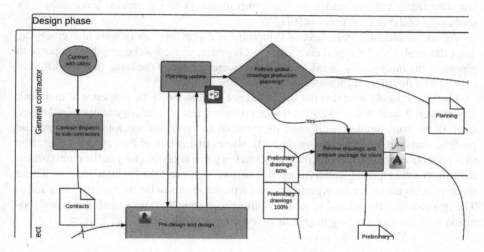

Fig. 1. Partial BPMN processed map by the general contractor

4 The Findings

The comparison of the perceived process maps allowed the researchers to identify numerous problems, barriers and semantics ambiguities. The divergence of perceptions on the overall process was shown to be considerable. Consequently, for the purpose of the article, only the major identified problems to collaboration in this specific project will be presented.

4.1 Workflow and Dataflow Ambiguity

The results show that the participants had a good knowledge of their own activities, but had problems defining the activities of the other players. Consequently, participants could not easily identify which information they generated was used and how it was used by the others in order to complete their tasks. For instance, two players used large activity box tagged "Producing documents" or "Coordination meeting" as the only activities attributed to another player. They were unable to define precisely the corresponding flow of activities that composed this large interpretation. For instance, when questioned on 3D coordination, the architect said: "The 3D field coordination was the sole responsibility of the general contractor. I did not participate in it for the vast majority of the time" meaning that he took for granted that he did not have any good inputs to put forward since 3D field coordination is not his job.

Another player could not precisely tell from whom, between the subcontractor, the general contractor of the public partner, the information he had as input was coming from. His vision of the overall process was limited to the knowledge of his own role as a group member, as if each player was surrounded by an informational "fog of war". As Kiviniemi puts it, the dependencies of tasks and information exchanges in a process are not sufficiently comprehended by the group members and it creates hindrances to a successful collaboration process [6].

As one would anticipate, several symptoms of fragmented work were also emerging from the analysis of the perceived flows. The maps proved to be reliable supports to represent the multiplicity of information that were created at the same time by different players and in different formats.

One could easily note that the actors did not acknowledge the influence of their task on the overall workflow and how it impacted the overall productivity at different stages. Each participant defined a different distribution of work for the four phases. As the professionals put the emphasis on the early phases (using two of four phases to describe the conception phase), the subcontractor and the general contractor put the emphasis on the construction phase, subdividing it into two distinct coordination phases. These discrepancies underline the significance each player grants to his own work and process. The ignorance of the others' processes limits the exchange of information and collaboration by misunderstanding the needs of the other stakeholders.

4.2   Traditional Process Vs BIM Integrated Process

The activity beginning or ending a phase was usually related to a required document that was driving the whole process at that stage (i.e. plans, contracts or 3D models). The participants usually explained the process on how they were working and collaborating to emit the specific requirements for that phase. This type of perception can be related to the underlying problem of the traditional process of information exchange. It rests on requirements of documents for the completion of the design and construction phases and stages and not about the actual information needed [6]. The participants did not question the validity and the need for optimization of the information processing for every step of their traditional process. For example, after a change in the design, the engineer would not communicate with the subcontractors for coordination and was producing directives with sketches, 2D drawings and text. The subcontractor was explaining: "Since we got only 2D drawings from the engineer, we had to integrate the information in our own model". The engineer was following the traditional fragmented and linear process to create uncoordinated information and to transfer it to the next stakeholders as a complete document. The subcontractor was losing a lot of time by remodeling, understanding and coordinating the change. Furthermore, when they were questioned about a task, participants were usually referring to the traditional process in which a specific document requires a specific type of information and activity of work.

4.3 Semantic Ambiguity

Efficiency of collaboration in a group is directly dependent on the capacity of the team to create shared mental models and exchange knowledge fluidly [5] through a common vision and language [9]. However, the different maps based on each stakeholder's perception were showing, when compared, large semantic ambiguities about the actions, mechanisms or data. These epistemic barriers were easily identified: participants did not even use the same taxonomy to make reference to the same information, the same tasks or the same phases. For instance, the architects refer as "conception" the stage of early design for the sketching of the geometry and the space layout. For the general contractor, "conception" is the entire phase of design before bidding. In addition, when the participants were formalizing the flows of other stakeholders, they did not use the same semantic definitions of the actions and mechanisms than the other participants. Such epistemic barriers compromise the successful resolution of conflicts or contradictions resulting from collaborative work.

5   Conclusion and Future Work

This method of collaborative research proposes a new technique to collect data with the use of formalization of processes. Co-construction of the process mapping stimulated the emergence of a shared vision on how the work of the different actors was linked through a complete process modelling. This approach allowed the identification of perception gaps that generate hindrances and conflicts through a collaborative project.

This study was based on a single project case. Hence, the aim of this first exploratory research was to investigate a new participative approach using co-construction process mapping. Since contradictions emerge from the analysis of the process maps, this approach seems to be conclusive. However, more cases should be studied to test the limits of the method.

This paper is a primary investigation in a major research project based on collaborative research action and co-construction of sense. The next step of the study is an optimization and combination of the perceived processes throughout a post-mortem driven by a co-construction method to confront the participants to the emerging contradictions between the traditional and the BIM process. The future research aims to adjust the process map and to suggest an optimized project process that is a step closer to the BIM goal of holistic collaboration.

References

1. Eastman, C., Teicholz, P., Sacks, R., Liston, K., Handbook, B.I.M.: A Guide to Building Information Modeling for Owners, Managers, Designers, Engineers and Contractors. Wiley, New Jersey (2008)

2. Crotty, R.: The Impact of Building Information Modelling: Transforming Construction. Spon Press, Abingdon (2012)
3. Miettinen, R., Paavola, S.: Beyond the BIM utopia: Approaches to the development and implementation of building information modeling. Autom. Constr. **43**(2014), 84–91 (2016)
4. Groleau, C., Demers, C., Lalancette, M., Barros, M.: From hand drawings to computer visuals: confronting situated and institutionalized practices in an architecture firm. Organ. Sci. **23**(3), 651–671 (2012)
5. Forgues, D., Koskela, L., Lejeune, A.: Information technology as boundary object for transformational learning. Electron. J. Inf. Technol. Constr. **14**(March), 48–58 (2009)
6. Kiviniemi, A.: Distributed intelligence in design. In: Distributed Intelligence in Design, L. (ed.), pp. 125–135. John Wiley & Sons, Blackwell Publishing Ltd., Oxford (2011)
7. Kerosuo, H., Miettinen, R., Paavola, S., Mäki, T., Korpela, J.: Challenges of the expansive use of Building Information Modeling (BIM) in construction projects. Production **25**(2), 289–297 (2015)
8. Dossick, C.S., Neff, G.: Messy talk and clean technology: communication, problem-solving and collaboration using Building Information Modelling. Eng. Proj. Organ. J. **1**, 83–93 (2011)
9. Froese, T.: Emerging information and communication technologies and the discipline of project. Intell. Comput. Eng. Archit. 230–240 (2006)
10. Turk, Z.: Communication workflow approach to CIC. Comput. Civ. Build. Eng. **18**, 1094–1101 (2000)
11. Poirier, E.A., Forgues, D., Staub-French, S.: Dimensions of interoperability in the AEC industry. Constr. Res. Congr., 1987–1996 (2014)
12. Heifetz, R.A., Baylor, R., Linsky, M., Grashow, A.: The Practice of Adaptive Leadership: Tools and tactics for changing your organization and the world. Harvard Bussiness Press **87**, 62–69 (2009)
13. Bourassa, M., Philion, R., Chevalier, J.: L'analyse de construits, une co-construction de groupe. Éduc. Francoph. **35**(2), 78–116 (2007)
14. Reason, P., Bradbury, H.: The handbook of action research – introduction. Handb. Action Res. - Concise Paperb., 468 (2006)
15. Ben Rajeb, S., Senciuc, A., Pluchinotta, I.: ShareLab, support for collective intelligence. In: COLLA 2015: The Fifth International Conference on Advanced Collaborative Networks, Systems and Applications, pp. 27–33 (2015)
16. McCall, M.W., Morgan, J., McCall, W., McCall Jr., M.W.: Leadership development through experience. Acad. Manag. Exec. **18**(3), 127–130 (2004)
17. Clot, Y., Faïta, D., Fernandez, G., Scheller, L.: Entretiens en auto-confrontation croisée: une méthode en clinique de l'activité. Education Permanente, 2000. [Online]. Available: http://pistes.revues.org/3833, Accessed 7 Apr 2016
18. Object Management Group (OMG): Business process model and notation (BPMN) version 2.0. Business **50**, 170 (2011)

BIM-Enabled Collaborative Scaffolding Scoping and Design

Jun Wang[1], Hung-Lin Chi[1(✉)], Chongyi Liu[1], and Xiangyu Wang[1,2]

[1] Australasian Joint Research Centre for Building Information Modelling,
Curtin University, Perth, Australia
{jun.wang1,hung-lin.chi,chongyi.liu,
Xiangyu.wang}@curtin.edu.au
[2] Department of Housing and Interior Design, Kyung Hee University, Seoul, South Korea

Abstract. Scaffolding management is critical to construction industries across the oil and gas, building, and infrastructure sectors, where static and ineffective design and planning can lead to low productivity and cost issues. In addition, the requirement analysis of scaffolding scoping seriously relies on the quality of the communication between scaffolding supervisors and owners. To avoid unnecessary disputations, the aim of this research is to develop a Collaborative Scaffolding Scoping and Design Platform (CSSDP) to facilitate the communication among different trades, and engage their expertise to comment, review and improve the design scheme from the end-user perspective. The proposed CSSDP includes three main modules: mobile application, cloud server and management dashboard. In addition, four styles of comments will be embedded into the mobile application, namely, text, voice, image-based sketching, and Building Information Modelling (BIM) model-based sketching. The implementation and evaluation of the user interface and commenting functions have been finished, and the prototype of the application is integrated into the proposed CSSDP. The outcomes of internal workshops conducted through industrial partners show positive responses and further investigations for experimental adaption are expected in the near future.

Keywords: Building Information Modelling · Scaffolding scoping and planning · Mobile application · User interface · Requirement analysis

1 Introduction

Scaffolding is a temporary framework that requires decent design to be established for supporting work crews, equipment and material in a typical construction or maintenance procedure. Scaffolding is made either by a modular of metal pipes or a combination of frames, planks, tubes and braces connected by couplers and bolts [1]. At the structural design aspect, it is crucial to maintain sufficient support strength to satisfy the loading requirement of every work task conducted on the temporary structure, especially when the location of the scaffolding design is located aside complicated structures of buildings (targets).

© Springer International Publishing AG 2016
Y. Luo (Ed.): CDVE 2016, LNCS 9929, pp. 43–50, 2016.
DOI: 10.1007/978-3-319-46771-9_6

In addition, consider the design, shape and location of the target it has to be decided which type of scaffolding is appropriate. The scaffold system that is most adaptable to the contour of the target has to be chosen in order to maximum the serviceability of the following work tasks expected.

In general, 80 % of scaffolding design is straightforward when contours of targets are regular, such as residential buildings with consistent and smooth surfaces. As long as contours of targets become complex, such as refinery plants with irregular pumps, tanks or pipes exposing on site, the designers need to consider more factors in order to avoid inappropriate design solutions below the expected serviceability. Such complex cases usually represent essential construction or maintenance work tasks which influence budgets of projects a lot.

Due to dynamic natures of such cases, the scoping process of scaffolding usually involves scaffolding supervisors and owners in person at site. They will observe the field and discuss together regarding the scaffolding work scope and coming out with consensus. However, most of the cases lack sufficient visualized information, proper documentation, and direct links on the scaffolding cost and inventory situation, to facilitate the communication between each party. The disputes on deviations of expected cost and functionalities would happen and cause further troubles in achieving the certain level of customers' satisfaction.

In order to improve current practice of scaffolding scoping and design, the aim of this research is to develop a Collaborative Scaffolding Scoping and Design Platform (CSSDP) to facilitate communication among different trades, and engage their expertise to comment, review and improve the design scheme from the end-user perspective. Contributions of this paper are as followings:

1. A uniformed user interface and requirement capturing process to be implemented from scaffolding service provider perspective, to facilitate communication during the requirement analysis process.
2. An integrated system for scaffolding scoping and design with the consideration of inventory status of material and detailed geometrical properties of targets, by using Building Information Modelling (BIM) technologies.

2   Related Works

Scaffolding usually represents crucial topics to construction industries across the oil and gas, building, and infrastructure sectors, where static and ineffective design and planning can lead to low productivity and cost issues. Several research topics have been carried out in order to optimize the performance of such activities. Kim et al. [2] proposed a feature lexicon to formalize representation of factors essential to scaffolding planning, which can be used to create a semi-automatic planning generator. Moon et al. [3] highlighted the civil and construction engineers' obligations in oil and gas plant projects with an emphasis on its scaffolding needs.

In addition, many researchers focus on identifying potential safety issues as well as further preventions during the scaffolding construction and operation phases. Many enabling approaches have been investigated and promoted including the fomenting standardization of scaffolding equipment in the construction industry [4], advanced monitoring technologies [5], automatic safety code checking using visualization technologies [6] and so forth.

Among all these research topics, few studies have been made for scaffolding scoping considering the data synchronization in the following design phase. In addition, the requirement analysis process during scoping seriously relies on the quality of the communication between scaffolding supervisors and owners. There is hardly any precise feedback from one specific discipline to another [7]. Few collaborative tools [8] are made for facilitating communication among different trades allowing the engagement of their expertise to comment, review and improve the design scheme from the end-user perspective. Thus, scoping and design tools and methods must bring detailed consideration of all disciplines in the early process. And effective interface of the multiple disciplines demands an appropriate collaborative design process and tool as well [9, 10].

Building Information Modelling (BIM), as a supportive approach, has potentials to address current communication and collaborative issues. BIM technology can extract and process precise geometric and action data in 3D models, which increases consistency and speed in identification of design alternatives for the scaffolding (temporary structures). At present, the construction industry does not leverage advances in BIM for scaffolding scoping and design because it lacks formalization that defines key properties and relationship variables for sharing [11].

This research starts by developing a collaborative platform in order to maximum the benefits of communication and make precise reflections to the design results. It is done by integrating BIM concepts and creating an effective scoping and design platform for scaffolding. The following sections will introduce the details of the platform development in this research.

3   Scaffolding Scoping and Design

The proposed platform for effective scaffolding scoping and design can be seen in Fig. 1. It is divided into three main modules: mobile application, cloud server and management dashboard. They are connected by the data access abilities through Internet. A scaffolding supervisor can utilize the mobile scoping application to communicate with owners to get detailed requirement regarding expected work scenarios of scaffolding. The captured requirement can be transferred and stored in the database. Once the supervisor comes back to the office, the information of the scoping case can be accessed through scaffolding inventory system and design system to do the detailing process.

In order to increase the communication between scaffolding supervisors and owners at site during scaffolding scoping phase, the user interface of the mobile application has been designed to encapsulate common features and general procedures used in a typical scoping activity. For the better interpretation of design scenario, BIM model of the target can be downloaded and viewed through 3D Model Viewer on the user interface of the application. And all the scoping forms are also embedded in the application for supervisors to record the messages coming out from owners. The commenting approach for

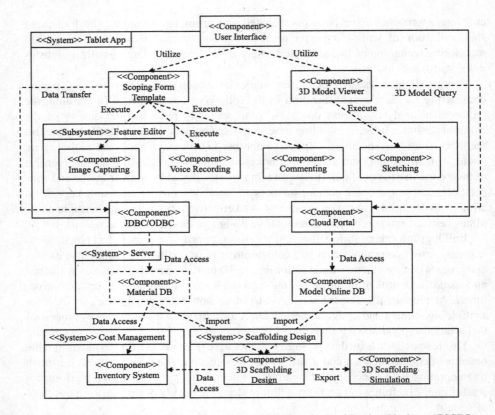

Fig. 1. The architecture of Collaborative Scaffolding Scoping and Design Platform (CSSDP)

scaffolding scoping consists of four styles: Image Capturing, Voice Recording, Commenting and Sketching. Image Capturing utilizes the camera of the mobile devices and help supervisors capture the site image in order to evaluate site situations; Voice Recording is designed to record the discussion and specific requirement raised by owners, so that supervisors can replay the messages when they headed back to offices; Commenting is a regular capturing approach during the requirement analysis process but it has been digitalized and used closely with the other three approaches; Sketching lets supervisors to add arbitrary symbols, markers and annotations onto the specific viewpoints of BIM model, which allows quick annotating and easy to be understood by owners.

Once the owner's requirement has been captured through the four styles of commenting, all the scoping records including expected material lists and annotated 3D models, will be transferred to a database (DB) on a server through Internet. Those data can be accessed by Inventory System and Scaffolding Design System so that the requirement for the material and conceptual design of the scaffolding can be utilized for the following design phase. It allows supervisors to be able to aware if there is a lack of stock situation. In the meantime, every requirement can be completely reserved and easy to be pulled out again on such BIM-based system during the design phase of scaffolding. All these scoping records become one of the design properties reminding designers not to violate specific concerns observed from site. Finally, the final design of the scaffolding can be simulated with scheduled erection timeframe through another BIM system, Scaffolding Simulation System, helping designers and field managers to identify any necessary of re-planning actions when a delay is happened.

4   Implementation

The proposed Collaborative Scaffolding Scoping and Design Platform (CSSDP) has been partially prototyped and described in this section. The first version of the mobile application developed through Android [12] operation system (OS) has been released. As can be seen in Fig. 2, related forms, such as material list (gear list), are fully digitalized in the application by going through an interface design and evaluation process. The user is allowed to input the estimated amount of material based on site observations and discussion results with owners. Such information is directly recorded and transferred through Internet.

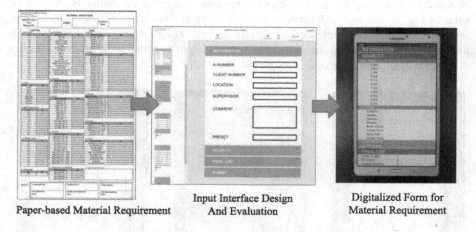

| Paper-based Material Requirement | Input Interface Design And Evaluation | Digitalized Form for Material Requirement |

Fig. 2. The digitalization of a material requirement form

Figure 3 shows the process of utilizing an external program call to pull out 3D model and enable a sketching function on it. The external program is Autodesk™ A360 [13] and each user would have individual account to automatically log in this application and pull out specific parts of 3D models related to design cases. In A360 application, sketching function is built-in one, and the results of sketching can be saved as images then encoded and submitted through A360's web portal to its own cloud servers. The stored images can be accessed anytime as long as the user keeps the account logged in and with Internet capabilities.

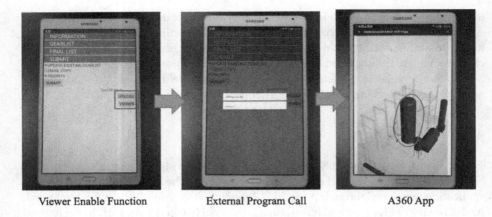

| Viewer Enable Function | External Program Call | A360 App |

Fig. 3. The overview of the 3D model sketching function

The relational database has been implemented to keep all the scoping records from different design cases. The records stored in the database include the details of the material estimations, different styles of comments and related documents. As can be seen in Fig. 4, the user can retrieve scoping records from different cases by simply requesting them through Internet. It helps the user maintain comprehensive information and double check with all the participants involving at scoping phase to avoid further disputes when the final design is generated.

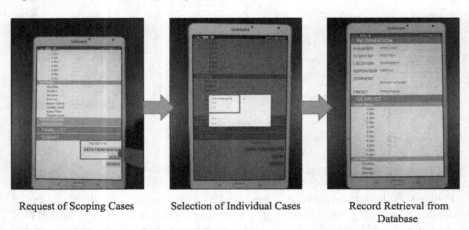

| Request of Scoping Cases | Selection of Individual Cases | Record Retrieval from Database |

Fig. 4. Database synchronization of the mobile scoping application

As for the inventory system in this research, an existing one integrated with industrial partner's ERP system is planned to be integrated through data importing from the database. For the scaffolding design system, the researchers plan to use Autodesk[TM] Auto-CAD's [14] plugin, PON CAD [15], for furthering scaffolding design. The comments from scoping phase, such as 3D model sketching, images, voice records and annotations, can be imported to keep the design intentions on the right track. In addition, Autodesk™ Navisworks [16] is proposed to be used for simulating the final design coming out from PON CAD. Navisworks is a BIM software so all scaffolding and target-related properties, including material information and inventory status, can be added in the 3D model. And the erection process of the scaffolding with time can be simulated by site managers to be able to get further scaffolding planning ideas to optimize the usage of the design.

Internal evaluations (workshops) through the cooperated industrial partners have been conducted and research team has presented the prototype of the platform. The outcomes show positive responses from the partners and further investigations for experimental adaption are expected in the near future.

5   Conclusion

In this research, an integrated collaborative scaffolding scoping and design platform with consideration of visualized information, inventory status and uniform requirement capturing user interface has been designed and developed. Related application, database and plugin for existing management system have been proposed and demonstrated through internal evaluations with scaffolding providers.

At the scoping phase of the scaffolding, a mobile application for tablet is implemented allowing scaffolding supervisors to capture discussion ideas through four styles of commenting: image capturing, voice recording, text documenting and 3D model sketching. The captured data can be stored in the database and further accessed by inventory and scaffolding design system. They allow scaffolding supervisors to check the availabilities of necessary material for fulfilling the design and at the same time help reserve completed design concepts during actual scaffolding design phase.

The demonstration in this paper shows that the developed platform has potentials in enabling better communication and coming out with sufficient information to support the design process. Further evaluations with simulated collaborative design scenarios are needed in order to quantify the benefit of the proposed platform.

Acknowledgement.   This research was undertaken with the benefit of a grant from Australian Research Council Linkage Program (Grant No. LP140100873).

References

1. Zeitzmann, J.: Internal Analysis on Scaffolding. KAEFER Isoliertechnik, Bremen (2006)
2. Kim, J., Fischer, M., Kunz, J., Levitt, R.: Semiautomated scaffolding planning: development of the feature lexicon for computer application. J. Comput. Civil Eng. 29(5), 04014079 (2015)
3. Moon, S., Forlani, J., Wang, X., Tam, V.: Productivity study of the scaffolding operations in liquefied natural gas plant construction: Ichthys project in darwin, northern territory, australia. J. Prof. Issues Eng. Educ. Pract. 4016008 (2016)
4. Rubio-Romero, J., Rubio, M., García-Hernández, C.: Analysis of construction equipment safety in temporary work at height. J. Constr. Eng. Manage. 139(1), 9–14 (2013)

5. Yuan, X., Anumba, C.J., Parfitt, M.K.: Cyber-physical systems for temporary structure monitoring. Autom. Constr. **66**, 1–14 (2016)
6. Kim, K., Cho, Y., Zhang, S.: Integrating work sequences and temporary structures into safety planning: automated scaffolding-related safety hazard identification and prevention in BIM. Autom. Constr. **67**, 1–21 (2016). doi:10.1016/j.autcon.2016.06.006
7. deVries, B., Tabak, V., Achten, H.: Interactive urban design using integrated planning requirements control. Autom. Constr. **14**(2), 207–213 (2005)
8. Selin, C., Kimbell, L., Ramirez, R., Bhatti, Y.: Scenarios and design: scoping the dialogue space. Future **74**, 4–17 (2015)
9. Chalfant, J., Langland, B., Abdelwahed, S., Chryssostomidis, C., Dougal, R., Dubey, A., El Mezyani, T., Herbst, J.D., Kiehne, T., Ordonez, J., Pish, S.P., Srivastava, S., Zivi, E.: A collaborative early-stage ship design environment. In: ESRDC 10th Anniversary Meeting (2012)
10. Andreadis, G., Fourtounis, G., Bouzakis, K.: Collaborative design in the era of cloud computing. Adv. Eng. Softw. **81**, 66–72 (2015)
11. Kim, J., Fischer, M., Kunz, J., Levitt, R.: Sharing of temporary structures: formalization and planning application. Autom. Constr. **43**, 187–194 (2014)
12. Android. https://www.android.com
13. Autodesk^{TM} A360. https://a360.autodesk.com
14. Autodesk^{TM} AutoCAD. http://www.autodesk.com/education/free-software/autocad
15. PON CAD. http://www.meccad.net/software-cad-3d-scaffolding
16. Autodesk^{TM} Navisworks. http://www.autodesk.com.au/products/navisworks/overview

Modeling Temporal Behavior to Identify Potential Experts in Question Answering Communities

Min Fu[1], Min Zhu[1(✉)], Yabo Su[1], Qiuhui Zhu[1], and Mingzhao Li[2]

[1] College of Computer Science, Sichuan University, Chengdu 610065, China
fumin1412@gmail.com, zhumin@scu.edu.cn
[2] RMIT University, Melbourne, Australia

Abstract. Question answering (Q&A) communities are becoming important repositories of crowd-generated knowledge. The success of these communities mainly depends on the contribution of experts, who provide a significant number of high quality answers. Identifying these experts as soon as they participate in a community enables the community managers to nurture and retain experts. However, there is a great challenge to complete this task because lack of enough activities during users' early participation. To take full advantage of users' limited activities, we study the evolution of users' temporal behavior that indicates deeper insights of the activities, both the absolute view and the relative view. Based on our analysis, we propose a Temporal Behavior Model to identify potential experts. Experiments on a large online Q&A community prove that our model can be combined with previous researches to improve the identification performance even further.

Keywords: Q&A community · Potential expert identification · Temporal behavior · Collaborative knowledge creation

1 Introduction

Question answering (Q&A) communities are now popular platforms for online users to exchange knowledge in the form of questions and answers [1]. Those communities often go beyond search engine queries, and offer more desirable answers. As questions become more complex, single question often receives multiple good answers generated by different experts who share distinct aspects of the problem. Thus, knowledge sharing and exchanging becomes a cooperative knowledge-creation process in these communities [2].

As the creation process of crowdsourcing knowledge mainly depends on the participation of experts [4], these Q&A communities employ voting and reputation mechanism to reward experts and recognize members' expertise [7]. The higher the reputation of an expert is, the deeper he or she is trusted. However, accumulating high reputation takes a long time, and users may churn before growing into real experts. So, identifying users that have the potential to become

© Springer International Publishing AG 2016
Y. Luo (Ed.): CDVE 2016, LNCS 9929, pp. 51–58, 2016.
DOI: 10.1007/978-3-319-46771-9_7

experts during their early participation is an important task for community managers. It enables them to improve the community such that these experts can get nurtured and inspired to retain productive. Expert identification in Q&A communities has been studied from several different perspectives. Part of these studies use graph algorithms [13,14,18], while several other studies focus on extracting features from users' activities [3,5,15,17]. However, the activities of users' early participation are limited in most Q&A systems, thus previous models may not perform well in practice.

Understanding the dynamics of users' behavior can gain deep insights in how their activity patterns evolve over time, thus extracts additional information to improve previous researches. To the best of our knowledge, studies exploring evolution of users' activity time for potential expert identification are still lacking. In this paper, we analyze the different temporal activity schemes of users, and observe significant differences between experts and non-experts in the evolution of activity frequency and answer speed. Based on our analysis of temporal behavior schema, we propose a Temporal Behavior Model to identify potential experts on a large domain specific Q&A community, and show that our model can efficiently improve the performance of the state-of-art models.

The rest of the article is organized as follows: Sect. 2 presents our literature survey and Sect. 3 describes the datasets we used. Section 4 analyzes the community members' temporal behavior and proposes our Temporal Behavior Model. Section 5 describes the machine learning models and presents our results. Finally, we draw a conclusion in Sect. 6.

2   Related Work

Expert identification methods can be broadly subdivided into graph based approaches and feature based approaches [10]. The graph based approaches employ graph algorithms or their modifications [13,18] to model the expertise network, and then identify notable nodes (experts). Zhang et al. [17] proposed ExpertiseRank, which analyzed the directed graph of questioners and answerers to explore expertise models. Weng et al. [14] took both the topic similarity and the link structure to measure user's influence rank on Twitter. Instead of finding top-ranked users, feature based approaches [3,5,15] focus on extracting signals of expertise to identify experts. Zhang et al. [17] showed that simple measures based on the number of questions and answers outperformed complex graph algorithms. Studies which identified potential experts are most related to our work. Pal et al. [9–11] proposed a Question Selection Model that captures the selection bias of users based on the questions they choose to answer, and thus identifying potential experts. Movshovitz et al. [8] considered users' contributions such as the number of answers over their early participation to predict long-term contributors. However, these methods rely heavily on the number of users' early activities.

Temporal analysis of users has been used by previous works to identify users' activity patterns, such as blog's weekly evolve behavior [6], knowledge creation process [2], and user churn prediction [12]. Pal et al. [9] argued that models using evolution information of users can be more effective on expert identification. But they only considered the evolution of some statistic features, for example the number of best answer, and they ignored the evolution of users' activity time.

Our work complements previous works by using temporal behavior analysis to present insights into how the time of experts' activity emerges and evolves. We use a user's temporal features to take full advantage of user's early activities, and show that our model can efficiently improve previous works.

3 Data Description

StackOverflow[1] is a technology-focused Q&A community, where people ask specific software engineering and programming questions. We downloaded a complete dataset of actions performed on the community since it was launched in August 2008 until August 2012. The dataset includes 3,453,742 questions and 6,858,133 answers posted by 1,295,620 users.

StackOverflow employs voting and reputation mechanism to quantify users' expertise [8]. We consider one year is long enough to determine whether or not a user is an expert. So we filter the 1.3 million users in our dataset, and leave only those users that have been members for at least one year. From the filtered set, we label the top 1 % of users to be the current experts (13,087 users).

4 Temporal Behavior Exploration

4.1 Characterization of User Temporal Behavior

There are two aspects of a user's temporal behavior in StackOverflow, as the absolute view and the relative view. In this section, we investigate some of the basic principles that reflect users' temporal behavior, and find some early signals for our prediction tasks in the following sections.

Time Gap. For the first aspect, we investigate the absolute time of users' activity series, such as when did a user create a StackOverflow account, when did the user post first answer, second answer, and so on. We use time gaps between the user's activities to capture his or her posting pattern, which indicates the user's activity evolution. In this analysis, we exclude users with reputation 1 that have not performed a single reputation-gaining activity (left 584,488 users). As reputation mainly derived from providing helpful answers, we only consider user's answer behavior.

In our work, time gaps are extracted in day granularity. We group a user's all answers posted in a day as an active unit, and time gaps are time intervals between consecutively active units. Next, we analyze time gaps for experts and non-experts throughout their first 100 gaps.

---

[1] http://www.stackoverflow.com.

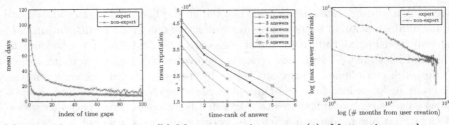

(a) Mean days per time gap (b) Mean reputation versus (c) Max   time-rank   per
                              time-rank   month

Fig. 1. Evidential temporal features, (a) shows the time gaps of experts decrease more rapidly among initial gaps and stabilize at a lower level, (b) shows experts tend to answer early, and (c) shows the evolution of maximum time-rank with a clear difference in both value level and change trend between experts and non-experts.

Figure 1(a) shows the mean time gap distinguishing experts and non-experts, where experts' time gaps decrease rapidly and stabilize at a low level, however non-experts' gaps decrease slowly and stabilize around higher level. This observation is consistent over time and notably over their early participation, supporting our propose that experts can be identified during their early participation.

Time-Rank and Wall-Clock Time. For the relative time, we investigate a user's activity time compared with other co-answerers. To better understand the relative location among other competitors, we take one question together with all its answers as a thread, which is our fundamental unit of analysis. We take both the time-order of answers (time-rank) and the answers' wall-clock time into account, to capture the schemas in which expertise interacts with answer speed.

For the time-rank, it reflects the relative answer speed. There is incentive to answer questions quickly, since many users will accept the first answer that they are satisfied [16]. In Fig. 1(b) we examine how the mean answerer reputation varies with the time-rank of an answer within a thread, especially for questions with a specific number of answers (2–6 answers). We find that the highest-reputation answerers do usually occur earlier in the time-ordering of answers. Reputation clearly decreases with increasing rank, which is evidence of a direct relationship between reputation and answer speed.

Similar with time gaps, we analyze time-rank of community members throughout their lifespan, the time-rank is evaluated over each month of activity of the users. Figure 1(c) shows the mean maximum of the time-rank over experts and non-experts in each month (other metrics such as minimal or average time-rank which show the similar pattern are not plot here due to space constraints). We can observe that experts usually participate in questions that already have many answers, but they tend to become earlier participants over time.

Besides the time-rank of answers, we can also consider wall-clock time to measure answer speed—how fast users of various reputation levels respond to questions.

Different from previous approaches based on answer speed in second granularity, we present a method based on day granularity to find potential experts, and get the same relationship with time-rank.

Following our discussion of the evidences for the time gap, the time-rank and the wall-clock time, we find significant differences between experts and non-experts in terms of their temporal behavior schema, both the value level and the change trend. In following section, we show that features based on this view efficiently improve the prediction performance.

4.2   Temporal Behavior Model

In order to extract insights from the basic principles investigated above, we formulate users' temporal behavior as some specific sequence. All the answers belong to a user are grouped into an activity sequence, which is ordered by the answers' creation time. For each activity, we use time gap, time-rank and wall-clock time to extract users' temporal information. Thus we get three feature sequence—gap sequence, rank sequence and time sequence—to list the feature value for corresponding activity. For a given feature sequence with n items, we define following metrics to extract its temporal insights:

1. **statistics**: Maximum, minimum, summation, mean, standard deviation, variance, quartiles Q1, Q2, and Q3.
2. **distribution**: A histogram represents the discrete probability distribution.
3. **weighted_sum**: Modify the sequential analysis technique "cumulative sum" to capture the overall trend, such as large values in the later part (1, 2, 3) or the front part (3, 2, 1). We gracefully express it as:

$$weighted\_sum = \frac{1}{n} \sum_{i=1}^{n} i * x_i \tag{1}$$

where x_i is the ith item in the given sequence. The later a item lie in this sequence, the more influence it has on weighted_sum. For example the weighted_sum of the sequence (1, 2, 1, 10) is greater than sequence (10, 4, 5, 3).

4. **change_ratio**: Contain two aspects, one is **mean_change_ratio**, it is used to capture the value changing ratio between the mean of the later period and the prior period, it is defined as:

$$mean\_change\_ratio = \frac{(mid+1) \sum_{i=mid+1}^{n} x_i}{(n-mid) \sum_{i=0}^{mid} x_i} \tag{2}$$

where $mid = n/2$, and the i start from 0 for gap sequence, and start from 1 for other sequence. If the value of this metric is large (e.g. larger than 1), the trend of this sequence is likely increase. Another metric is **std_change_ratio**, it is used to capture the trend of the stability between the later period and the prior period of a user's activities. It is defined like the mean_change_ratio, but using standard deviation instead of mean. If the value of this metric is large (e.g. large than 1), the trend of this sequence's stability is likely reduce.

Table 1. Features used in Temporal Behavior Model

Feature	Meaning
gap0	Time gap between account creation and first post
last_gap_change	Ratio between the last post and the post before it
from_last_gap	Time gap between the last post and the observation deadline
weighted_sum list	The weighted_sum of the gap, rank and time sequence
statistics list	The statistics of the gap, rank and time sequence
change_ratio list	The change_ratio of the gap, rank and time sequence
Distribution list	The distribution of the gap, rank and time sequence

Based on our temporal behavior analysis in this section, we propose a Temporal Behavior Model (TBM) to identify potential experts with features in Table 1.

5 Potential Expert Prediction

5.1 Experiment Setup

We examine the activities of StackOverflow users from the moment of creating an account and formulate the predicting task as a classification problem. Given information of a user's activity in the first three months, and classify this user as expert or non-expert. We use stratified random sampling to sample users, and divide them into a training set and testing set with a ratio of 7:3.

5.2 Prediction Results

We compared our model with (1) Pal et al. [10] predict potential experts using a Question Selection Model (QSM), and (2) Movshovitz et al. [8] proposed a User Activity Model (UAM) to predict potential experts.

Table 2 shows the results of Random Forest Classifier for QSM, UAM and our TBM. We report precision, recall, and f-measure for each model. Our model consistently achieves higher recall and higher f-measure, but lower precision than Movshovitz et al. This result is in line with our expectation, as in real-world applications, the cost of maintaining thousands more users is far less than the cost of losing few real experts.

Table 2. Models' performance (testing set)

	QSM	UAM	TBM	QSM+UAM	QSM+TBM	UAM+TBM	QSM+UAM+TBM
Precision	0.770	0.807	0.781	0.798	0.775	**0.811**	0.809
Recall	0.511	0.520	0.533	0.529	**0.541**	**0.543**	**0.546**
f-measure	0.615	0.632	0.633	0.636	0.637	**0.651**	**0.652**

As these three models mentioned above extracting insights from three totally different aspects, we also investigate the performance of composite models, these models all achieve higher performance than any single model. It is interesting to note that, combining our TBM with Movshovitz's UAM can achieve significant improvement than any other model, especially in recall metric. Furthermore, this combination achieves the highest precision, the almost highest recall and f-measure among all models, including the model that combined all the features from three aspects. It shows that our temporal model can sufficiently extract valuable information from the user's early activities, and effectively improve previous models.

6 Conclusion

Q&A communities become valuable crowd-generated repositories which mainly depend on experts contributions. In this paper, we address the problem of identifying potential experts during their early participation, thus enable communities to nurture and retain potential experts. Our main contributions include: (i) Find some interesting temporal behavior schema that can help us to identify potential experts; (ii) Propose a Temporal Behavior Model to identify potential experts, and show that our TBM can efficiently improve previous models' performance.

As further work, we wish to explore several other interesting dimensions to capture the users' behavior in Q&A communities and use these dimensions along with our proposed methodology for the task of discovering potential experts and other interesting users.

References

1. Adamic, L.A., Zhang, J., Bakshy, E., Ackerman, M.S.: Knowledge sharing and yahoo answers: everyone knows something. In: Proceedings of the 17th International Conference on World Wide Web, pp. 665–674. ACM (2008)
2. Anderson, A., Huttenlocher, D., Kleinberg, J., Leskovec, J.: Discovering value from community activity on focused question answering sites: a case study of stack overflow. In: Proceedings of the 18th ACM International Conference on Knowledge Discovery and Data Mining, pp. 850–858. ACM (2012)
3. Bouguessa, M., Dumoulin, B., Wang, S.: Identifying authoritative actors in question-answering forums: the case of yahoo! answers. In: Proceedings of the 14th ACM SIGKDD International Conference on Knowledge Discovery and Data Mining, pp. 866–874. ACM (2008)
4. Cavusoglu, H., Li, Z., Huang, K.W.: Can gamification motivate voluntary contributions?: the case of stackoverflow Q&A community. In: Proceedings of the 18th ACM Conference Companion on Computer Supported Cooperative Work & Social Computing, pp. 171–174. ACM (2015)
5. Jurczyk, P., Agichtein, E.: Discovering authorities in question answer communities by using link analysis. In: Proceedings of the Sixteenth ACM Conference on Information and Knowledge Management, pp. 919–922. ACM (2007)

6. Leskovec, J., McGlohon, M., Faloutsos, C., Glance, N.S., Hurst, M.: Patterns of cascading behavior in large blog graphs. In: SIAM International Conference on Data Mining, vol. 7, pp. 551–556. SIAM (2007)

7. Mamykina, L., Manoim, B., Mittal, M., Hripcsak, G., Hartmann, B.: Design lessons from the fastest Q&A site in the west. In: Proceedings of the SIGCHI Conference on Human Factors in Computing Systems, pp. 2857–2866. ACM (2011)

8. Movshovitz-Attias, D., Movshovitz-Attias, Y., Steenkiste, P., Faloutsos, C.: Analysis of the reputation system and user contributions on a question answering website: stackoverflow. In: IEEE/ACM International Conference on Advances in Social Networks Analysis and Mining, pp. 886–893. IEEE (2013)

9. Pal, A., Chang, S., Konstan, J.A.: Evolution of experts in question answering communities. In: International Conference on Web and Social Media (2012)

10. Pal, A., Harper, F.M., Konstan, J.A.: Exploring question selection bias to identify experts and potential experts in community question answering. ACM Trans. Inf. Syst. **30**(2), 10 (2012)

11. Pal, A., Konstan, J.A.: Expert identification in community question answering: exploring question selection bias. In: Proceedings of the 19th ACM International Conference on Information and Knowledge Management, pp. 1505–1508. ACM (2010)

12. Pudipeddi, J.S., Akoglu, L., Tong, H.: User churn in focused question answering sites: characterizations and prediction. In: Proceedings of the Companion Publication of the 23rd International Conference on World Wide Web Companion, pp. 469–474 (2014)

13. Wang, G.A., Jiao, J., Abrahams, A.S., Fan, W., Zhang, Z.: Expertrank: a topic-aware expert finding algorithm for online knowledge communities. Decis. Support Syst. **54**(3), 1442–1451 (2013)

14. Weng, J., Lim, E.P., Jiang, J., He, Q.: Twitterrank: finding topic-sensitive influential twitterers. In: Proceedings of the Third ACM International Conference on Web Search and Data Mining, pp. 261–270. ACM (2010)

15. Yang, J., Tao, K., Bozzon, A., Houben, G.-J.: Sparrows and owls: characterisation of expert behaviour in stackoverflow. In: Dimitrova, V., Kuflik, T., Chin, D., Ricci, F., Dolog, P., Houben, G.-J. (eds.) UMAP 2014. LNCS, vol. 8538, pp. 266–277. Springer, Heidelberg (2014)

16. Yeniterzi, R., Callan, J.: Analyzing bias in CQA-based expert finding test sets. In: Proceedings of the 37th International ACM SIGIR Conference on Research & Development in Information Retrieval, pp. 967–970. ACM (2014)

17. Zhang, J., Ackerman, M.S., Adamic, L.: Expertise networks in online communities: structure and algorithms. In: Proceedings of the 16th International Conference on World Wide Web, pp. 221–230. ACM (2007)

18. Zhao, Z., Zhang, L., He, X., Ng, W.: Expert finding for question answering via graph regularized matrix completion. IEEE Trans. Knowl. Data Eng. **27**(4), 993–1004 (2015)

Representation in Collective Design: Are There Differences Between Expert Designers and the Crowd?

Darin Phare[1(✉)], Ning Gu[2], and Michael Ostwald[1]

[1] The University of Newcastle, Callaghan, NSW, Australia
Darin.Phare@uon.edu.au, Michael.Ostwald@newcastle.edu.au
[2] The University of South Australia, Adelaide, SA, Australia
Ning.Gu@unisa.edu.au

Abstract. This paper tests if a web-based crowd would, in comparison with an expert benchmark group, exhibit observable differences and similarities when they interact with varying forms of representation. The study uses an adapted online environment to provide the necessary decentralised and open conditions to support collective activity. The methodology uses semiotics to comparatively describe the processes both qualitatively and quantitatively. This paper presents the general findings of an analysis using data collected from a permanently open two-week design session. Comparisons with an expert benchmark group reveal how crowds engage with representational imagery to communicate design information in an openly shared and decentralised web based collective design context.

Keywords: Design · Representation · Crowds · Collective intelligence

1 Introduction

Due to the explosion of web-based technologies that enable mass communication, it is now necessary to revisit more diverse conceptual definitions of mass participation in design. Web-based technologies are increasingly using rich media content to allow large groups or crowds of motivated online individuals to contribute toward solving complex problems [1, 2]. The study of collective human intelligence in design is gaining traction through leveraging web-based outsourcing systems, known as crowdsourcing [3, 4]. The drawback with this approach is that crowdsourcing engages an online 'crowd' in which members work in isolation to a heavily mediated structure of the design process. Such structures require participants to work according to a set of stages that artificially model the design process alone and submit work, often in isolation. Simply stated, crowd members who engage in crowdsourced design function independently of one another and without real-time communication and as a result, the online crowdsourcing structure neglects the premise that design is often characterised as much by its collaboratively social activity [5] as it is by the process of design itself.

Collective intelligence is recognised as a universally distributed intelligence; constantly enhanced and coordinated in real time, resulting in the effective mobilisation of skills [6]. Crowdsourcing rarely provides a platform for members to coordinate their activity in real time. As a result it denies the crowd the social opportunity to freely

Y. Luo (Ed.): CDVE 2016, LNCS 9929, pp. 59–68, 2016.
DOI: 10.1007/978-3-319-46771-9_8

express design meaning independently of the mediated context. Thus, any result of the distributed intelligence is 'collected' and not 'collective' intelligence [4]. Levy [2] argued that one of the critical criteria for successful collective intelligence is real time coordination. Real time coordination is fundamental for social activity where the freedom to express and communicate enables the distributed intelligence to constantly enhance itself. These three criteria alone offer striking parallels to the social activity of design [5]. Through the work of Maher et al. [4] we have a conceptual framework that describes three criteria for design in this collective context; motivation, communication and representation. Motivation and communication have been extensively explored [7, 8], but representation has garnered less attention. Representation is an important vehicle for generating and communicating design meaning [9–14]. What is not so well known is how a universally distributed intelligence would coordinate its use of representation to express and enhance design related knowledge under open, real time conditions.

2   Background

The representation, in design, is often described as a graphic notational object. By exploiting the informational potential of different types of representation the designer has to hand a means to create a vast visual record of ideas and concepts [15]. Fluency with representational artefacts enables designers to effectively communicate design at all stages of the process with other design professionals. Such graphic notational objects are generated by using analogue media (graphite and ink), digital media (3D CAD modeling) or a combination of both [15, 16]. By definition, it is expected that the majority of non-designers do not possess a similar fluency with design notations. However, the ability to exploit the informational potential of various notational signs, including models, maps and pictures, is recognised, designer or not, as a universally human skill. This skill is summarised as pictorial competence [17], which is a sign-based ability that allows us to understand the representational content of "pictures, ranging from the straightforward perception and recognition of simple pictures to the most sophisticated understanding of specialised conventions" [17]. With pictorial competency being a sign based ability, the informational potential of a group of signs can be well accounted for by leveraging semiotic principles. Design and semiotics share several procedures that are directly related to the function of design representations; they both rely on descriptively graphic notation systems to provide functional and generative content, often in simultaneous combination [18].

At its core, semiotic theory is a framework in which three types of sign can be categorised, depending on how they allow for comprehension. These categories include Peirce's semiotic triad (CP 1.369)[1]; Icons, Indexes, and Symbols to identify the leading quality and characteristic of the image itself. The Icon, Index and Symbol provide a

---

[1]   All references for the work of C.S Peirce come from the collected works published by: Peirce, Charles Sanders (1931–58): Collected Writings (8 Vols.). (Ed. Charles Hartshorne, Paul Weiss & Arthur W Burks). Cambridge, MA: Harvard University Press. Any direct reference of the collected papers is written as: CP (collected papers), Vol. number (1 through to 8). This is followed lastly by the entry number (E.g. CP 3:340).

coordinated way of talking about how meaning is expressed via the relationship between Representamen (the form a sign takes), Object (the entity to which the sign points), and Interpretant (the qualities expressed by the Representamen) [19–23]. The use of semiotics in the interpretation of a crowd engaged when in design activity within a web environment is an excellent qualitative approach for dissecting, explaining, and evaluating design meaning. Accounting for imagery in the online design environment by using the Icon, Index and Symbol is the formulation for the analysis presented in this paper.

3 Research Design and Data Collection

There is no universally agreed statistic that defines a 'crowd', but Surowiecki [24] stated that the crowd is best defined by the diversity of its constituent members, which is the adopted approach for this study. Our simulated crowd group consisted of a globally dispersed group of 18 participants. The range of personalities, gender (62 % male) and diverse range of occupations was sufficient to simulate a crowd in a laboratory environment. The expert benchmark group consisted of four highly qualified design participants. The online environment in this study was a shared presentation tool called Prezi, which was selected on the basis of its ability to provide participants with an openly shared online space. The brief was open-ended and required both groups (separately, yet under the same online conditions) to generate ideas for an environmentally friendly approach to modular housing. The session remained open for 14 days. We aimed to report on the experiential differences between the expert and crowd groups and expected that the results of expert participants' design activity within Prezi would provide a baseline dataset sufficient for comparative purposes with the crowd group. The data collected from the experiment was coded using a coding scheme specifically developed for this framework.

Coding Scheme. To review the role of representation in our study, it was necessary to capture the activity involving the representation from the moment it was introduced from an external source into the online design environment. By employing Peirce's semiotic triad of the Icon, the Index, or the Symbol (CP 1.369), it was possible to categorise the initial semiotic value of the image according to its leading semiotic characteristics. This was undertaken for all images used by both groups for the purpose of providing an original general semiotic (coded as Sg) context. The general semiotic context (Sg) provided a starting point from which it was possible to observe and code any subsequent modifications in the semiotic quality beyond the original (Sg) state. Having been introduced into the experimental environment to convey design meaning, the semiotic value became bound to a new design-related context (Semiotics in the design context = $Sd^{(n)}$). The movement between and within these contexts was numerically categorised as transitions ($Tr^{(n)}$). Such changes in meaning can be identified according to the type of semiotic combination they transition ($Tr^{(n)}$) from and to. For example:

$$\text{General to design context} = Sg_{(General\ semiotic)} \rightarrow Sd^{(1)}_{(Semiotic\ value)}$$
$$\text{Design to design context} = Sd^{(1)}_{(Semiotic\ value)} \rightarrow Sd^{(2)}_{(Semiotic\ value)}$$

When meaning in any given image is changed through contextualisation, a shift occurs from what the Icon, Index or Symbol originally signified to a new or additional signified meaning. To understand how representations were used to generate design meaning in our web-based crowd context, it was important to be able to categorise the design-related content of the image. Larkin and Simon [25] and Suwa and Tversky [14] suggested that the pictorial devices for expressing meanings and concepts in design consist of depicted elements, such as objects, spaces or icons, and their spatial arrangements. These summaries of design-related information, conveyed visually, are the distilled result of extensive protocol studies of designers sketching in action, and design theories. In their 1997 study of designers and their sketches, Suwa and Tversky [14] outlined four major informational categories, each containing a number of subclasses of information. These were depicted elements, spatial relations, abstract relations and background knowledge.

In summary, our coding scheme captures the changing semiotic and the informational values according to two contextual shifts. The first is coded as a general to design context and written as:

$$Sg_{(General\ semiotic)} \rightarrow Sd^{(1)}_{(Semiotic\ value)} +(\text{Design Information value})$$

The second contextual shift is the movement that occurs within a design related context. It is written as:

$$Sd^{(1)}_{(Semiotic\ value)} +(\text{Design Information value}) \rightarrow Sd^{(2)}_{(Semiotic\ value)} +(\text{Design Information value})$$

Example:

$Sg_{(icon)}$ (Properties) $\rightarrow Sd^{(1)}_{(index)}$ (Properties)	
Sg - Icon	**$Sd^{(1)}$ - Index**
PHOTO	PHOTO
Properties/Materials - Tyres	Properties /Materials -Tyre as building element

4   Results

To make the following comparison more effective, it was determined that only the first three transitions presented enough data (Sg through to $Sd^{(2)}$) to be reliable. From $Sd^{(2)}$ through to $Sd^{(4)}$ there was not enough data in either group to be able to reliably compare and generalise the activity. As such, the data for transitions $Sd^{(2)}$ through to $Sd^{(4)}$ are omitted. Furthermore, there was a threshold imposed on any data below 5 %. Data falling below this range across the transitions was merged to its nearest semiotic counterpart. The remaining data considered viable for a comparative analysis was reduced to three main transitions (Sg $\rightarrow Sd^{(1)} \rightarrow Sd^{(2)}$).

4.1 Comparison of Representational Distribution

The following analysis is achieved using statistical information and cumulative information drawn from the coded semiotic and informational activity of both groups. From this, the aim was to develop an understanding of the range and scale of the data. To cumulatively describe the construction and movement of design meaning by both groups in a customised online design environment, we employed a combined quantitative, comparative analysis of the semiotic and informational values of the representations, including the combination of semiotic and informational changes over time.

The crowd group uploaded 232 general images from external sources and the expert group uploaded 81 images. In the crowd group, six images of the original 232 images were copied, and subsequently re-used within a new circle by one participant; therefore, the total final image count was 238 images (232 with six duplicates). The expert group did not reuse any images and so their total contribution remained at 81 (Table 1). The number of images uploaded was proportionately different between both groups, with the experts using an average of 6.5 more images per participant than the average crowd member who used 13.7 images per participant (Table 1).

Table 1. Contributions average by group.

	Participants	Images	Average per participant
Expert	4	81	20.2
Crowd	18	232	13.7
		Diff	6.5

Of the 232 images initially introduced by the crowd, 188 were icons and 44 were symbols. No indexical images were provided. Of the 81 images introduced by the expert group, 46 were iconic, one was indexical, and 34 were symbolic (Table 2). The initial use of imagery in the expert group was heavily based on importing the icon, or symbol. In total the expert group introduced 57 % icons and 42 % symbols with 1 % indexes over 14 days. Of these, five were initially then interacted with, followed by another two interactions, with one final interaction based on the same imagery. The initial use of imagery in the crowd group was also heavily based on importing the icon, or symbol.

Table 2. Distribution of semiotics types as introduced.

Sg – Starting point	Crowd		Expert	
	Count	%	Count	%
Icon	187	81	46	57
Index	0	0	1	1
Symbol	45	19	34	42
	232	100	81	100

4.2 Comparison of Informational Distributions

To determine the intended design meaning being engendered into the representation, we adopted the first of Suwa and Tversky's [14] two categories of design-related information (Major categories and Subclass). The major category is divided into: Properties, Spatial, Functional, Technical and Background Knowledge. All images were identified and categorised in association to their closest related major category. Table 3 presents the comparative descriptive statistics for how the images were used to describe design content according to Suwa and Tversky's five main types of design-related information classes [14]. Having applied the developed coding scheme that enables the identification of the static and shifting semiotic qualities, it was then necessary to further clarify the intended design meaning from $Sd^{(1)}$ onwards.

Table 3. Proportions of the major categories of design information.

% CROWD	$Sd^{(1)}$	$Sd^{(2)}$	% EXPERT	$Sd^{(1)}$	$Sd^{(2)}$
Properties	44	15	Properties	–	–
Spatial	4	–	Spatial	–	–
Functional	8	48	Functional	–	–
Technical	23	22	Technical	28	20
Background knowledge	21	15	Background knowledge	72	80

Table 4. Combined design information and semiotic distribution

	%CROWD	$Sd^{(1)}$	$Sd^{(2)}$	%EXPERT	$Sd^{(1)}$	$Sd^{(2)}$
Properties	Icon	6	11	Icon	–	–
	Index	29	4	Index	–	–
	Symbol	–	–	Symbol	–	–
	Icon + Index	1	–	Icon + Index	–	–
Spatial	Icon	1	–	Icon	–	–
	Index	3	–	Index	–	–
	Symbol	1	–	Symbol	–	–
	Icon + Index + Symbol	–	–	Icon + Index + Symbol	–	–
Functional	Icon	2	–	Icon	–	–
	Index	6	48	Index	–	–
	Symbol	4	–	Symbol	–	–
Technical	Icon	1	–	Icon	–	–
	Index	8	11	Index	2	–
	Symbol	14	11	Symbol	23	20
	Index + Symbol	–	–	Index + Symbol	2	–
B/knowledge	Icon	3	–	Icon	1	–
	Index	18	15	Index	40	60
	Symbol	2	–	Symbol	26	20
	Icon + Index	–	–	Icon + Index	4	–
	Index + Symbol	1	–	Index + Symbol	1	–

Table 4 comparatively shows the proportional distribution of the representations' semiotic values within the major categories of design information of both groups. A chi-square test showed that the proportion of images assigned to the five categories (Properties, Spatial, Functional, Technical and Background Knowledge) differed significantly between the expert group and the crowd group, $\chi^{2(4)} = 90.3$, p < .001. Table 4 shows that the majority of the expert group's images are in the Background Knowledge category (72.2 %) and the Technical category (26.7 %), whereas the majority of the crowd images are more widely spread across the Properties category (33.6 %), the Background Knowledge category (23.9 %) and the Technical category (22.8 %).

5 Discussion

Both groups imported iconic imagery that was either scanned (such as book pages), or symbolic drawings personally created by using a variety of traditional and digital media (scanned hand sketches and Adobe Illustrator drawings). Both groups used similar formats such as Graphics Interchange Format (*.gif) or Joint Photographic Experts Group (*.jpeg) images. With these images, both groups exercised pictorial competence in intuitively or intentionally borrowing existing features of iconic imagery to express abstract meaning indexically, such as ideas and concepts. In both groups, the use of the representation therefore was the one commonly shared act in which both groups would engage in order to communicate design meaning within the online design environment. Peirce (CP 5.171) referred to this borrowing of existing characteristics to describe non-existent things or ideas, as abduction; a reasoning process allowing for the visual description of something that does not exist, such as in design.

Abduction is crucial for the creative process because it enables the individual to reason upon elements embedded within existing iconic imagery in order for them to be isolated and borrowed or combined to communicate new concepts. The abductive process of borrowing of qualities was a shared practice in both groups, but it is within each group's abductive processes that there were observable differences in the range of information and the levels of abstraction by which that information was conveyed. Figure 1 is an example of an image used by an expert. The black and white image of exposed concrete steps was used with the main intention of conveying an abstracted consideration based on the receptive qualities of interconnected modular components and construction methods. The crowd member introduced an image of a refurbished shipping container (Fig. 2). The intention was to express a component suitable for modularity; furthermore, the image contained information regarding how such a unit could be furnished.

For the expert group there was a much higher level of abstraction within a narrow informational framework, in contrast to a much lower level of abstraction and a much wider informational framework in the crowd group. The difference in semiotic distributions and the levels of abstractness by which these informational values were conveyed suggests differences in the experts' vs. novices' thinking within the collective design context of this study.

Fig. 1. Expert representational use.   **Fig. 2.** Crowd representational use.

Having generated the information (via the $Sg \rightarrow Sd^{(1)}$ transition), certain participants began to add new interpretations (at varying levels of abstraction) indexically for the sole purpose of contributing new informational variables to the existing design-related meaning of the image. These interactions occurred on an ad hoc basis over different timeframes. All interactions that took place only occurred through indirect means in both groups. This revealed that the movement of design meaning did not occur through normal collaborative processes but by the incremental addition of 'small and discreet chunks' of information applied to existing imagery. This type of interaction is common to collective and web-based systems and is understood as stigmergic collaboration [26]. By comparing the semiotic data of the expert group and the crowd group in the similarities were that the movement of meaning occurred in both groups. Therefore, we can infer that in an openly shared web-based context, such as the environment provided in this study, experts and a crowd alike make use of the representation to generate and express additional design thinking based on existing and already design-contextualised imagery $(Sd^{(n)})$.

6   Conclusion

Emerging from the comparative statistics were two key characteristics: both groups similarly used the iconic image to express index and symbol based content (called Abduction), and informational movement emerged in both groups, as revealed by the semiotic and informational movement of design meaning (transition). The presence of this initial activity was promising because the accumulating representational contributions vindicated the collective laboratory conditions. Moreover, the presence of activity centered on the representation was an important finding because it implies that in employing the representation to communicate design meanings, the image is a pivotal tool for the crowd and the expert alike. This suggests that there is little difference between the crowd and the expert when it comes to the uptake of imagery to express design information. Each participant in both groups demonstrated a capacity for intuitively using icons to creatively build indexical analogies for expressing ideas; this indicated that abductive processes were evident in both groups. However, the difference in semiotic distributions and the levels of abstractness by which these informational values were conveyed suggests differences in the experts' vs. novices' thinking within the collective design context of this study. In addition, the crowd's individual contributions of imagery were prolific, which were consistently added to and interacted with, creating a consistent stigmergic movement of design meaning. This was in contrast to the expert group, whose members traditionally do not design under collective conditions, which might explain the participatory differences between the crowd's consistent activity and the long period of inactivity in the expert group until the last two days of the test period. In summary, both the crowd and the expert group naturally adopted the image as the main carrier of meaning under the provided conditions. However, the engendered meaning was different between the groups.

References

1. Yu, L., Nickerson, J.: Cooks or cobblers? crowd creativity through combination. In: Proceedings of the 2011 Annual Conference on Human Factors in Computing Systems, NY, pp. 1393–1402 (2011)
2. Lévy, P.: Collective Intelligence: Mankind's Emerging World in Cyberspace. Perseus Books, Cambridge (1997)
3. Paulini, M., Maher, M.L., Murty, P.: Understanding collective design communication in open innovation communities. J. CoCreat. Des. Arts **9**, 90–112 (2011)
4. Maher, M.L., Paulini, M., Murty, P.: Scaling up from individual design to collaborative design to collective design. In: Gero, J.S. (ed.) Design Computing and Cognition 2010, pp. 581–600. Springer, Heidelberg (2010)
5. Cross, N., Cross, A.C.: Observations of teamwork and social processes in design. Des. Stud. **16**(2), 143–170 (1995)
6. Ratti, C., Claudel, M.: Open Source Architecture. Thames & Hudson, London (2015)
7. Paulini, M., Maher, M.L., Murty, P.: Motivating participation in online innovation communities. Int. J. Web Based Communities **10**(1), 94–114 (2014)
8. Maher, M.L., Simoff, S., Gabriel, G.C.: Participatory design and communication in virtual environments. In: Cherkasky, T., Greenbaum, J., Mambrey, P., Kabber Pors, J., (Eds.) Proceedings of the Participatory Conference (PDC 2000), pp. 127–134 (2000)
9. Goldschmidt, G.: The dialectics of sketching. Creativity Res. **4**(2), 123–143 (1991)
10. Goldschmidt, G., Casakin, H.: Reasoning by visual analogy in design problem-solving: the role of guidance. Environ. Plan. B Plan. Des. **27**, 105–119 (1999)
11. Goldschmidt, G., Klevitsky, E.: Graphic representation as reconstructive memory: stirling's German museum projects. In: Goldschmidt, G., Porter, W.L. (eds.) Design Representation, pp. 105–126. Springer-Varlag, London (2004)
12. Schön, D.A.: The Reflective Practitioner: How Professionals Think in Action. Perseus Books, New York (1983)
13. Asimov, M.: Introduction to Design. Prentice-Hall, Englewood Cliffs (1962)
14. Suwa, M., Tversky, B.: What do architects and students perceive in their design sketches? A protocol analysis. Des. Stud. **18**, 385–403 (1997)
15. Ari Akın, Ö.: "Simon Says" Design is representation, Arredamento Mimarlık, pp. 82–85 (2001)
16. Arias, E., Eden, H., Fischer, G.: Enhancing communication, facilitating shared understanding, and creating better artefacts by integrating physical and computational media for design. In: Proceedings of Designing Interactive Systems: Processes, Practices, Methods, and Techniques, Amsterdam, August 1997, pp. 1–12. ACM (1997)

17. DeLoache, J.S., Pierroutsakos, S.L., Uttal, D.H.: The origins of pictorial competence. Curr. Dir. Psychol. Sci. **12**, 114–118 (2003)
18. Ashwin, C.: Drawing, design and semiotics. Des. Issues **1**(2), 42–52 (1984)
19. Nadin, M.: Design and semiotics. In: Koch, W.A. (ed.) Semiotics in the Individual Sciences, vol. II, pp. 418–436. Brockmeyer, Bochum (1990)
20. Chandler, D.: Semiotics: The Basics, 2nd edn. Routledge, London (2002)
21. Everaert-Desmedt, N.: Peirce's semiotics. In: Louis, H., (ed.), Signo (2011). http://www.signosemio.com/peirce/semiotics.asp
22. Chapman, M., Ostwald, M.J., Tucker, C.: Semiotics, interpretation and political resistance in architecture, contexts of architecture. In: The 38th International Conference of Architectural Science Association (ANZAScA 2004), Launceston, Tasmania (2004)
23. DeGrassi, M., Giretti, A., Ansuini, R.: Models of design activities: towards effective design scaffolding. In: Zambelli, M., Janowiak, A.H., Neuckermans, H., (Eds.) Browsing Architecture - Metadata and Beyond, pp. 50–65 (2008)
24. Surowiecki, J.: The Wisdom of Crowds: Why the many are Smarter than the Few and How Collective Wisdom Shapes Business, Economies, Societies and Nations. Doubleday Anchor, New York (2004)
25. Larkin, J., Simon, H.: Why a diagram is (sometimes) worth 10,000 words. Cogn. Sci. **11**, 65–99 (1987)
26. Elliot, M.: Stigmergic collaboration: the evolution of group work. M/C Journal 9(2) (2006)

City Probe: The Crowdsourcing Platform Driven by Citizen-Based Sensing for Spatial Identification and Assessment

Yang Ting Shen[1(✉)], Yi Shiang Shiu[2], and Peiwen Lu[3]

[1] Department of Architecture, Feng Chia University, Taichung, Taiwan
yatishen@fcu.edu.tw
[2] Department of Urban Planning and Spatial Information, Feng Chia University, Taichung, Taiwan
ysshiu@fcu.edu.tw
[3] Center of Environmental Studies, National Central University, Taoyuan, Taiwan
peiwenlu@cc.ncu.edu.tw

Abstract. In this paper, we introduce the City Probe, a participatory sensing system that can quantify citizens' perception of places. City Probe recruits citizens to participate in the spatial identification and assessment. It includes the smartphone APP that allows citizens to photo and rate their locational characteristics according to some issues. Their contributions, with latitude and longitude coordinates, would be uploaded and quantified in the City Probe cloud platform and visualized into a weighted map that reveals the collective out-come based on citizens' cooperation. Pilot studies in the campus have been accomplished. The collected geospatial data is represented in terms of the weighted map for disclosure of Information and decision-making supports.

Keywords: Participatory sensing · Crowdsourcing · VGI · Decision support system · Cooperative visualization

1 Introduction

By contributing the development of ICT technologies, many people have become "citizens" of web 2.0 social community; the use of web-enabled mobile devices to upload data gives these devices owners the ability to act as sensors. These advances in mobile phone technology coupled with their ubiquity have paved the way for an exciting new paradigm for accomplishing large-scale sensing, known in literature as participatory sensing [5]. Thus, the term citizens-as-sensors or participatory sensing refers to an interconnected network of people who actively observe, report, collect, analyze, and disseminate information via text, audio, or video messages [27].

Comparing with robotic sensors, citizens have the cognitive ability to perceive the complex events or phenomena such as safe, comfortable, clean, or livable etc. The outstanding perceptions of citizens provide opportunities to reveal and translate cognitive level phenomena into measurable data. In addition, when the participatory sensing integrates the location-based service such as GPS, it can be used to provide useful

Y. Luo (Ed.): CDVE 2016, LNCS 9929, pp. 69–76, 2016.
DOI: 10.1007/978-3-319-46771-9_9

contextual information. This concept sometimes is referred to VGI (Volunteered geographic information). VGI means the widespread engagement of large numbers of private citizens in the creation of geographic information [11]. Following the VGI approach, numerous cooperative citizens are turned into sensors to perceive and locate implicit events or phenomena in the city. This bottom-up approach may reveal context-aware information that can contribute to the urban governance in different levels.

In this paper, we propose a participatory sensing approach to quantify citizens' perception of places in the city. The system called City Probe recruits citizens to participate in the spatial identification and assessment via their mobile devices. City Probe provides the smartphone APP which allows citizens to photo and rate their location characteristics according to some issues. The results with Latitude and longitude coordinates are uploaded and quantified in the City Probe cloud platform. Finally, the visualized and weighted map will reveal the collective outcome based on citizens' cooperation.

The paper introduces the City Probe and its application in practices. It begins by reviewing the current and alternative methods for the assessment of city events or phenomena based on the citizens' participation. The prototype and the experimental studies are addressed in follow. The acknowledgement, theoretical reflections and limits are presented for conclusion.

2   Literature Review

Participatory sensing offers a number of advantages over traditional static sensor networks, particularly in the urban scale [6, 10]. First, participatory sensing leverages existing mobile communication infrastructures, the deployment costs are virtually zero. Second, the mobile phone carriers provide ubiquitous spatiotemporal coverage. Therefore, using mobile phones as sensors not only affords economies of scale, but also facilitates the full-scale deployment [1]. Finally, by including citizens in the sensing loop, it is now possible to build or reveal the implicit information that can assist the decision making process of citizens or governments [13–15, 20].

Several exciting participatory sensing applications have emerged in the recent decade. CarTel [12] is a mobile sensor computing system designed to collect, process, deliver, and visualize data from sensors located on mobile units such as automobiles. The similar idea is used to design Google Maps Navigation service. Comparing with normal GPS navigation system, the most significant feather of Google Maps Navigation is the real-time traffic report. This function is based on traffic users' collective feedback data to increase its accuracy and instantaneity. In addition, some participatory sensing applications engage the power of citizens' perceptibility. Streetscore [17] developed by MIT Media Lab is a scene understanding algorithm that predicts the perceived safety of a streetscape, using training data from an online survey with contributions from more than 7000 participants. Other applications of participatory sensing include the collection and sharing of information about urban air [18] and noise pollution [19], cyclist experiences [9], or consumer pricing information in offline markets [4]. In short, participatory sensing engages crowdsourcing power to compile the implicit urban context into explicit and measurable data.

Singleton (2010) and Goodchild (2010) emphasize scientific information visualization techniques as a way to handle these very large and complex data sets. When we refer to data visualization, especially in urban scale, location and time are crucial context for mobile data gathering. By contributing recent convergence of greater access to web-enabled and GPS-enable mobile devices connections, vast numbers of individuals became able to create and share Volunteered Geographic Information (VGI) [8, 22]. Recent work in geospatial visual analytics has focused on combining visualization, spatial data mining, and statistical methods to these ends [2, 16]. For instance, Casewise Visual Assessment (CAVE) methodology used information visualization to present design options and analyze big data sets from public participation meetings held in urban and regional planning [3]. Currid and Williams [7] applied GIS-based methods for identifying hot spots to large data sets comprised of geo-referenced images. In sum, large geospatial data benefit by geo-visualization methods to reveal the useful information that feedback to citizens and authorities for decision making supports.

3   The Participatory Sensing Approach for Citizens' Cooperation

3.1   The Design of City Probe System

Taking inspiration from mobile network and the trend towards participation of citizens in data collecting and mapping, the system called City Probe is developed for the cooperative identification of place characteristics via citizens' perception [23–26]. The City Probe consists a mobile phone APP and a cloud platform that records citizens' participation for the assessment of place characteristics. Practicing the City Probe include four following steps.

Step 1: defining the issue
Specific issues can be assigned for assessment. The issues of CLEANESS, COMFORT and SAFETY were defined to examine the application. In the Fig. 1 we take the "SAFETY" issue as an example to present our interface design and working process.
Step 2: installing, photo-taking and ranking
Citizens are encouraged to install the APP, to take a place photo and to give a rank of the environment in reflecting to their perceptions (Fig. 1, left). The range of score is from −10 (negative) to +10 (positive). Once the citizens have done the assessment, the APP will upload the records combined with location information to the cloud platform.
Step 3: records and geo-information analysis
All records with longitude and latitude coordinate (in degrees, WGS84) are analyzed and displayed with CartoDB. CartoDB is a software-as-a-service (SaaS) cloud computing platform built on open source PostGIS and PostgreSQL. It enables users to utilize geographic information sys-tem (GIS) and geovisualization mapping for data exploration and decision-making processes. The geo-visualization mapping provides geospatial data analysis through the use of interactive visualization; it also simplifies the display of raw data and facilitates the amateurs to understand the meaning of the data.

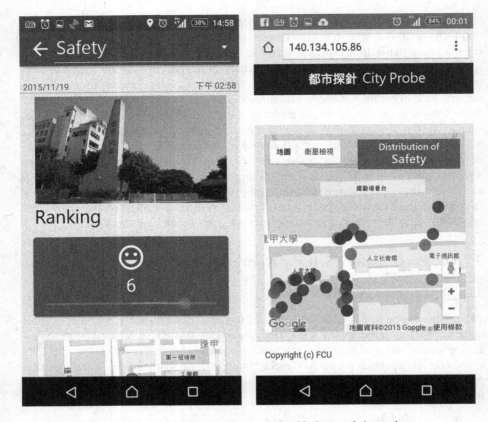

Fig. 1. The identifying interface and identified map of city probe

Step 4: data visualization and representation

Finally, the City Probe system can translate the quantitative data into color code and mark them as dots in the map. The dot with deeper red/blue color means the higher/lower score (Fig. 1, right).

3.2 City Probe as a Cooperative Filed Study Tool

We conduct several filed experiments to test the performance of City Probe applied to identification and assessment of location issues. We choose Feng Chia University campus (Fig. 2A) as our field and engage 31 students to run the pilot study. We initiate 3 issues including CLEANNESS, COMFORT, and SAFETY. After half a year data collection, we receive 448 valid records from 3 issues.

Figure 2(B)–(D) presents visualized results of 3 issues via choropleth map. The visualized maps shows that the most unclear area is near the southwest corner, which is the main entrance of the campus. However, the most comfortable and the safest spots also happen in the same areas. There is the similar spatial concentration of identified dots in each issue.

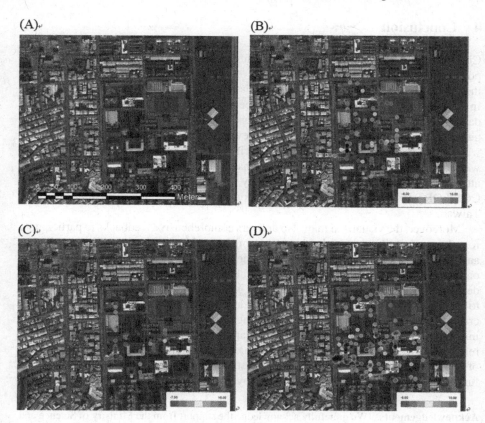

Fig. 2. Geovisualization of cleanness, comfort and security attributes using choropleth map. (A) the campus of Feng Chia University; (B) level of cleanness; (C) level of comfort; (D) level of Safety. The redder parts in each attribute represent the areas with higher ranking, while the bluer parts represent lower ranking. (Color figure online)

We try to inquire the reason of concentration by post-interview of participants. One of the convincing answers is that the southwest area is the most accessible and popular gateway between our campus and nearby markets. Students tend to assess their familiar environments instead of fair distribution. The result suggests that the particular subjects may cause the bias because of their interests or hobbies. To solve this problem, increasing the diversity of subjects may be considerable.

In short, the visualized maps help us to understand the characteristics of campus by crowdsourcing. The distribution, density, and intensity of dots reveal the reliable and quantitative information to assist the decision making of different levels stakeholders. Therefore, the next step we may concentrate on the development of DSS (Decision Support System) based on the City Probe framework.

4   Conclusion

City Probe provides the participatory sensing method to engage citizens' perception power for the identification and assessment of urban places. We can use City Probe as the crowdsourcing tool to survey particular issues and locate their spatial distributions. In addition, the ranking function of City Probe also turns implicit issues into measurable data. The cooperative visualization map based on citizen-generated data reveals the quantitative and statistic information that never existed before. The potential of up to whole citizens' participation to monitor the city environment, to validate global models with local knowledge, and to provide information that only humans can capture is vast and has yet to be fully exploited. A pilot study was provided for the case of CLEANESS, COMFORT and SAFETY places identification and assessment in Feng Chia University, Taiwan.

Moreover, the visualized map also delivers comprehensive feedbacks to participants for advanced decision making supports. Compared with traditional top-down planning and management from authorities, we provide an alternative bottom-up approach based on citizens. In the future, those user-generated information may become the crucial decision making supports for the smart city governance and every individual. In order to realize this vision, the next step will be addressed on how to sustain a human cooperative network at a larger scale and for a longer time than a local and short-term experimentation. The further investigation or research could take advantage of linking social relationships, shared interests or reputation among the participants. Ultimately, the goal of this research is to contribute to our understanding of the city that we have built, and further, build an adaptable and livable city by engaging all citizens' daily living.

Acknowledgements.   We gratefully acknowledge the support from the Ministry of Science and Technology, Taiwan. This research was supported by the Ministry of Science and Technology, Taiwan, under contract MOST104-2221-E-035-024-. We also thank project co-principal investigator Wei-Kuang Liu.

References

1. Aanensen, D.M., Huntley, D.M., Feil, E.J., Al-Own, F., Spratt, B.G.: EpiCollect: linking smartphones to web applications for epidemiology, ecology and community data collection. PLoS ONE **4**, 6968 (2009)
2. Andrienko, G., Andrienko, N.: A visual analytics approach to exploration of large amounts of movement data. In: Sebillo, M., Vitiello, G., Schaefer, G. (eds.) VISUAL 2008. LNCS, vol. 5188, pp. 1–4. Springer, Heidelberg (2008)
3. Bailey, K., Brumm, J., Grossardt, T.: Towards structured public involvement in highway design: a comparative study of visualization methods and preference modeling using CAVE (Casewise Visual Evaluation). J. Geogr. Inf. **5**(1), 1–15 (2001)
4. Bulusu, N., Chou, C.T., Kanhere, S., Dong, Y., Sehgal, S., Sullivan, D., Blazeski, L.: Participatory sensing in commerce: using mobile camera phones to track market price dispersion. In: Proceedings of the International Workshop on Urban, Community, and Social Applications of Networked Sensing Systems, pp. 6–10 (2008)

5. Burke, J.A., Estrin, D., Hansen, M., Parker, A., Ramanathan, N., Reddy, S., Srivastava, M.B.: Participatory sensing. Center for Embedded Network Sensing (2006)
6. Christin, D., Reinhardt, A., Kanhere, S.S., Hollick, M.: A survey on privacy in mobile participatory sensing applications. J. Syst. Softw. **84**, 1928–1946 (2011)
7. Currid, E., Williams, S.: The geography of buzz: art, culture and the social milieu in Los Angeles and New York. J. Econ. Geogr. **10**, 423–451 (2010)
8. Dykes, J., Purves, R., Edwardes, A., Wood, J.: Exploring volunteered geographic information to describe place: visualization of the "Geograph British Isles" collection. In: Proceedings of GIS Research UK 16th Annual Conference GISRUK, pp. 256–267 (2008)
9. Eisenman, S.B., Miluzzo, E., Lane, N.D., Peterson, R.A., Ahn, G.S., Campbell, A.T.: BikeNet: a mobile sensing system for cyclist experience mapping. ACM Trans. Sensor Netw. **6**(1), 6 (2009)
10. Gillmor, D.: We the Media: Grassroots Journalism by the People, for the People. O'Reilly Media Inc., (2006)
11. Goodchild, M.F.: Citizens as sensors: the world of volunteered geography. GeoJournal **69**(4), 211–221 (2007)
12. Hull, B., Bychkovsky, V., Zhang, Y., Chen, K., Goraczko, M., Miu, A., Shih, E., Balakrishnan, H., Madden, S.: CarTel: a distributed mobile sensor computing system. In: 4th ACM Conference on Embedded Networked Sensor Systems, pp. 125–138 (2006)
13. Kim, S., Mankoff, J., Paulos, E.: Sensr: evaluating a flexible framework for authoring mobile data-collection tools for citizen science. In: Proceedings of Conference on Computer Supported Cooperative Work (CSCW 2013), pp. 1453–1462 (2013)
14. Koch, F., Cardonha, C., Gentil, J.M., Borger, S.: A platform for citizen sensing in sentient cities. In: Nin, J., Villatoro, D. (eds.) CitiSens 2012. LNCS, vol. 7685, pp. 57–66. Springer, Heidelberg (2013)
15. Kramis, M., Gabathuler, C., Fabrikant, S.I., Waldvogel, M.: An XML-based infrastructure to enhance collaborative geographic visual analytics. Cartogr. Geogr. Inf. Sci. **36**, 281–293 (2009)
16. Mennis, J., Guo, D.: Spatial data mining and geographic knowledge discovery--an introduction. Comput. Environ. Urban Syst. **33**(6), 403–408 (2009)
17. Naik, N., Philipoom, J., Raskar, R., Hidalgo, C.: Streetscore-predicting the perceived safety of one million streetscapes. In: IEEE Computer Society Conference on Computer Vision and Pattern Recognition Workshops, pp. 793–799 (2014)
18. Paulos, E., Honicky, R., Hooker, B.: Citizen science: enabling participatory urbanism. In: Handbook of Research on Urban Informatics: The Practice and Promise of the RealTime City, pp. 414–436 (2009)
19. Rana, R.K., Chou, C.T., Kanhere, S.S., Bulusu, N., Hu, W.: Ear-phone: an end-to-end participatory urban noise mapping system. In: Proceedings of International Conference on Information Processing in Sensor Networks IPSN, pp. 105–116 (2010)
20. Salesses, P., Schechtner, K., Hidalgo, C.A.: The collaborative image of the city: mapping the inequality of urban perception. PLoS ONE **8**, e68400 (2013)
21. Sandole, T.: Makeshift metropolis: ideas about cities. J. Int. Aff. **65**, 198 (2012)
22. Schade, S., Díaz, L., Ostermann, F., Spinsanti, L., Luraschi, G., Cox, S., Nuñez, M., De Longueville, B.: Citizen-based sensing of crisis events: sensor web enablement for volunteered geographic information. Appl. Geomatics **5**, 3–18 (2013)
23. Shen, Y.T., Chen, P.C., Jeng, T.S.: Design and evaluation of eco-feedback interfaces to support location-based services for individual energy awareness and conservation. In: Kurosu, M. (ed.) HCII/HCI 2013, Part V. LNCS, vol. 8008, pp. 132–140. Springer, Heidelberg (2013)

24. Shen, Y.T., Jeng, T.-S., Hsu, Y.-C.: A "live" interactive tagging interface for collaborative learning. In: Luo, Y. (ed.) CDVE 2011. LNCS, vol. 6874, pp. 102–109. Springer, Heidelberg (2011)
25. Shen, Y.T., Lu, P.W.: Engage the power of social community in the lecture-based learning by using the collaborative tagging system. J. Converg. Inf. Technol. **8**, 485–493 (2013)
26. Shen, Y.T., Lu, P.W.: Learning by annotating: a system development study of real-time synchronous supports for distributed learning in multiple locations. In: 6th International Conference on New Trends in Information Science and Service Science and Data Mining (ISSDM), pp. 701–706 (2012)
27. Sheth, A.: Citizen sensing, social signals, and enriching human experience. IEEE Internet Comput. **13**, 87–92 (2009)

Collaborative Cloud Printing Service

Felix Baumann[✉], Julian Eichhoff, and Dieter Roller

Institute of Computer-aided Product Development Systems,
University of Stuttgart, Universitätsstr. 38, 70569 Stuttgart, Germany
{felix.baumann,julian.eichhoff,dieter.roller}@informatik.uni-stuttgart.de
http://www.iris.uni-stuttgart.de/en.html

Abstract. We develop a small and lightweight cloud based service for the utilization of 3D printer resources enabling users to collaborate on models. Users can collaborate by sharing model files, discussions on aspects of the printing process or using 3D printers as shared resources. This service consists of user, artefact and printer management building on existing web technology. It enables scheduling of printing jobs for artefacts and high utilization of 3D printer resources. This cloud based manufacturing (CBM) system enables 3D printers that are non-native networked to be used remotely by providing easily installable low cost networked computers or installable services. It focuses on the interface between the physical resources and their representation in software to form a cyber physical system (CPS). This service requires smart 3D printers and representation of technical capabilities of physical resources. This work is a research platform for smart machinery or the enhancement of machinery for smart control under the paradigm of Industry 4.0. We discuss the design and concept of this work in progress service and the distinctions from similar systems. Furthermore, the sharing requirements and capabilities of such a service are discussed with a focus on the data integrity and safety for sharing data among users.

Keywords: 3D Printing · Additive Manufacturing · Cloud based service · Cloud based manufacturing · CBM · CPS · Collaborative manufacturing

1 Introduction

3D Printing or Additive Manufacturing (AM) is the process of creating physical objects from digital models usually layer upon layer [9]. Technologies for AM include Fused Deposition Modelling (FDM, trademark by Stratasys Inc., also Fused Filament Fabrication FFF), Laser Sintering (LS), Electron Beam Melting (EBM), Laminated Object Manufacturing (LOM), Stereolitography (SLA) and Electron Beam Freeform Fabrication (EBF). AM technologies differ in the capabilities of processable material and achievable quality. We focus our research on FFF where thermoplastics like Acrylonitrile Butadiene Styrene (ABS) or Polylactid Acid (PLA) are fed from a roll in filament form to a heated extruder that

© Springer International Publishing AG 2016
Y. Luo (Ed.): CDVE 2016, LNCS 9929, pp. 77–85, 2016.
DOI: 10.1007/978-3-319-46771-9_10

heats the plastic to a semi-molten state above the glass-transition temperature and extrudes it through a nozzle mounted on the printing head that is moveable in two dimensions (X-Y plane) by electro motors following a pre-programmed path (Toolpath). With this setup it is possible to trace contours and interiors of an object slice-wise. After completion of every layer, the printing bed is moved in Z-direction, so the following layer can be added on top which makes this technology 2.5 dimensional. For the generation of the toolpath (slicing) it is necessary to segment the original digital model into slices that can be analysed for tool movement along the contours. Various strategies exist for the generation of the toolpath as models are mostly created hollow with a specific infill pattern for reduction of weight and processing time. The initial focus on FFF technology does not limit this research to just this technology as the 3D printing process is the same with alterations due to technology used and parameters adapted. It is our understanding that the following reasons mandate the use of printing services over stand-alone 3D printers at the user's workplace: (a) High cost of printer (dependent upon manufacturer and technology) [21], (b) Potential health risks (e.g., fumes, metal dust) [20], (c) Low utilization for non-shared resources [18], (d) Process knowledge necessary for high quality results [15] and (e) Potential for collaboration and discussion.

Utilizing 3D printing resources in a service enables cooperation on these resources. Users can be enabled to cooperate more in case of failures if the service offers appropriate mechanisms. The 3D printing process consists of five steps (Fig. 1) that start with the design of the product (also see [9]). For this work we propose three research questions: (a) What requirements are necessary to construct a 3D printing service enabling users utilizing existing 3D printer

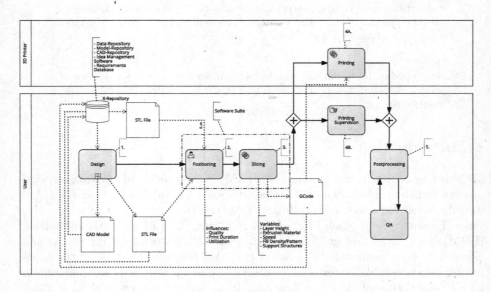

Fig. 1. 3D printing process

resources more efficiently? (b) How can a 3D printing service be enabled to provide an infrastructure for research? (c) How can the security and data integrity problems arising from shared resources be addressed?

This article describes current work in progress and outlines the design and implementation considerations and methodology. This work is an extension to [3] in respect to the collaboration and security aspect. The design phase can be supported by software using CAD (e.g., Autocad[1] or 3D modelling software[2]). The result of this first step is a CAD model that represents the 3D geometry of the object.

Step two of this process is the positioning of the model in the virtual space that represents the 3D printer and its physical restrictions. Positioning can encompass single objects or multiple objects for increased printer utilization. After the print object is positioned it is sliced using slicer software. A variety of slicing software exists and they differ in aspects like speed, precision, quality and strategies for printing support structures.

The following steps include the upload to the printer if it is a networked device or other means like deployment on memory devices (e.g., SD-Card, USB Stick) and the start of the print which can either require manual interaction or be handled from software. Post-processing and Quality Assurance (QA) follow when the object has been printed and influence each other. Those steps are not part of our service.

We provide support for all steps but the design within this work. Post-processing and QA support is limited to the discussion and exchange between users. These are omitted for the following reasons (1) The design process is supported by specialized software and integration is not compatible with our lightweight approach. Recent CAD or other design software for collaboration exists. (2) Post-processing and QA is not reasonable supportable by soft- or hardware as these steps require intensive human interaction. Supporting discussion on this step is beneficial for users to better understanding the influence of parameter selection on the quality of fabricated objects.

The remainder of this article is organized as follows: We display current research in this area in Sect. 2 and derive implementation requirements from established approaches. Then an introduction of the implementation guidelines Sect. 3 for the service is given. This paper concludes with Sect. 4 where we discuss this research and give an outline of future research.

2 Related Work

Similar systems or services already exist in form of closed source commercial services where we will name two of: (a) 3D Hubs[3] (b) 3D Printer OS[4]. As commercial entities their focus is on financial viability without extension

---

[1] http://www.autodesk.com/products/autocad/overview.
[2] https://www.rhino3d.com.
[3] https://www.3dhubs.com.
[4] https://www.3dprinteros.com.

mechanisms for use as a research platform. Contrary to our approach they are not intended as open services. The software octoprint[5] offers remote printing and object management capabilities but does not provide the required collaboration capabilities. Utilizing it as a gateway to connect printing resources to the printing service is feasible. Further research provides proposals from [22] for CBM systems but our system differs from those approaches as our focus is providing a collaborative service for shared resources as well as the sensory upgrade of this technology. From Dong et al. [7] we will implement the video supervision approach for the printing process and its remote error detection. Extensions of CBM in the form of Cloud Based Design and Manufacturing [23] provide further insight into the concept of Hardware-as-a-Service (HaaS) and the connection to the broader concept of flexible manufacturing spanning every phase of product development and involvement of different stakeholders. While the availability of affordable consumer grade 3D printers certainly has helped the progression of research in and distribution of 3D printers the scenario where every individual will own a digital fabricator [14] is unlikely at present as the general direction is to offer and consume services [1]. Van Moergestel et al. [13] proved the concept of Manufacturing-as-a-Service (MaaS) on cheap, distributed and reconfigurable production machines (equiplets) with a focus on interaction in a multi-agent system. Lan [11] names STL viewers as Java applets or other visualization tools as one of the key issues in his review. We employ JavaScript embeddable visualization into the service as to alleviate the dependency on thick clients. Further key issues e.g., (a) Remote control and monitoring (b) Job planning and scheduling and (c) Collaboration of users on models and printing are addressed in our service.

3   Implementation

Our service follows the software framework proposed by Schulte et al. [19] with a focus on the action executioner. It acts as the connector between the printing resources and the printing service in our proposal in contrast to the proposed functionality by Schulte et al. Further foci are the service registry for keeping information on production capabilities and the monitoring data manager that connects the real execution in the 3D printer with the virtual representation. From CloudMan [17] we incorporate the layered service approach but restrict our focus to 3D printers and not manufacturing infrastructure in general. See Fig. 2 for overview of the intended architecture with BPMS supporting the main service controller.

As per the definition of NIST (SP 800-145) [12] of cloud computing, the system is set up to provide a user management system by incorporating available libraries. Besides standard user management information the user is able to store appropriate files[6] in his account. For this we define an interchange format [2] for printing related information consisting of original CAD file(s), resulting STL and

---

[5] http://octoprint.org.
[6] CAD files, STL files, Printing Log files.

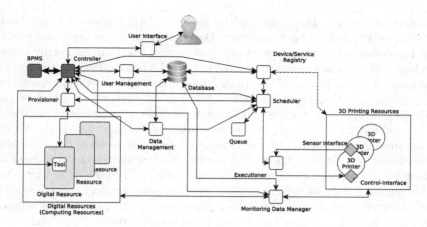

Fig. 2. Abstract architecture for 3D printing service

GCode [8] files, conversion and printing protocols as well as imagery (for quality assessment). The service is accessible in a standard compliant web browser that supports HTML 5[7] and JavaScript, both are necessary for rendering purposes for the phase of positioning. The resources necessary for slicing and preparation of the models are shared amongst the users based on a scheduling scheme that reflects first-come first-serve. As the 3D printer is the limiting resource at present the pooling of the computing resources not regarded as critical. In anticipation of multiple 3D printers controlled by the system the distribution of computing resources for the preparatory tasks is becoming queue based with data stored in associated cloud service storage (e.g., Amazon S3[8]). Users will be informed if the capacity of the 3D printers is depleted and the projected processing time for an object exceeds a defined threshold. The requirement for "rapid elasticity" is severely impaired by the physical restrictions set by the geometry of the object to be printed and the limitations in the speed vs. quality trade-off of a 3D printer. Basic measurements are intended where the user can track the number and nature of printed objects as well as associated information and a full audit trail for research purposes. Utilization of machines and computing resources is measured and associated with respective user accounts. The systems control layer resides in the cloud and is expandable by utilizing proven technology (e.g., Docker[9]) as means of deployment. The interfacing layer consists of gateway computers that interface directly with 3D printers if they do not support network access natively. These interface solutions depend on rapidly deployable, cost sensitive and reliable computer systems. In the first phase these interfaces will allow direct manipulation of 3D printers via the Internet and limited control information backflow. Further iterations extend this system to a broader sensorial back channel ultimately leading to closed

---

[7] http://www.w3.org/TR/html5.

[8] http://aws.amazon.com/s3.

[9] https://www.docker.com.

loop printing systems. Data provided by users as CAD models or other model files are stored in a cloud backed service. Data integrity, file security and privacy are of increasing concern to users [6, 16]. Risks range from untrustworthy service providers, compromised services by third parties (Cybercriminals or Hackers) or governmental spying program. Due to the risks provided the user cannot trust the service provider with safeguarding the submitted data but client-side data protection by encryption is warranted. Common encryption mechanisms can ensure the data submitted by the user is only accessible by the user. The proposed service requires access on parts of the uploaded data for processing (e.g., transformation from CAD file to STL file or for the slicing step) and also for collaboration between users. Approaches to ensure data integrity and privacy exist for the use cases of shared information with partially trusted providers and are described in [5, 10]. This work conceptually builds on these asymmetric encryption schemes to ensure privacy by design. Employing these security mechanisms the service provider still can derive protected information during the necessary decryption but this is indicative of malevolent behaviour. See Fig. 3 where User A is submitting a data file (Model A) to the printing service which the user encrypts locally. The Printing service stores the encrypted Model A in its storage. For slicing the model the user has to submit an access token (Access Token B) that the slicing service uses to temporarily decrypt the file and complete its work. After completion of the work the resulting file is encrypted using the users public key or a key provided with the access token b so only the legitimate user can access the file. For collaborating on a model file or a partial result from intermediary steps the user A provides an access token to the intended user (User B) with specific access permissions. User C as the attacker can only access temporary decrypted files on the computing resources or encrypted information in the service storage system.

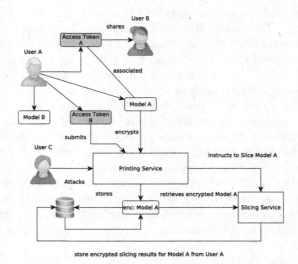

Fig. 3. Information sharing scenario in printing service

We describe the following use case for collaboration in this system. Here, user A has a series of failed prints on a specific machine and can ask other users of the same machine if they experience the same phenomena. For further analysis the users can share all print related information in an aggregated form within the system. Users can also contact the machine operator and issue notes or warnings on machines within the system.

4   Discussion and Future Work

To the best of our knowledge no open source 3D printing service is published yet. Despite a number of publications on CBM, no implementation is available. There are existing solutions that focus on separate parts and provide solutions to different aspects of the 3D printing process or frameworks for CPM services. Our approach is characterized and differs from other approaches by: (a) Focus on 3D printer (b) Focus on communication with manufacturing device (c) Platform for testing BPMN extension (d) Smartifying 3D printer [4] (e) Provides an open source implementation (f) Platform for testing sensor array and (g) Interchange format for print related information. By designing the system security at its core the users are at lesser risk of unauthorized data access. Providing collaboration features like data and model sharing enables the users to quickly adapt to the service. For future work we want to evaluate the acceptance and usability factor for this service. This software service is designed as an open research platform for academic users to embed experiments and utilize distributed resources. Further projects are aimed at 1. providing means of control of 3D printers from within process models as we are writing an BPMN extension, based on the work of [24] tailored for 3D printers, 2. utilize sensors for print status observation and as a means for quality research into 3D printing (see ICRM 2016[10]). 3. implement secure data storage for print related artefacts Those projects are to be incorporated in the umbrella project described in this work. As a related project we develop a BPMN extension for 3D printer integration into BPMN where the hardware resources and data flows can be modelled using the extension. Furthermore we utilize this platform for research on active-control for 3D printers as an additional component. This extension and the active-control are out of scope of this work and published separately.

References

1. Banerjee, P., Friedrich, R., Bash, C., Goldsack, P., Huberman, B., Manley, J., Patel, C., Ranganathan, P., Veitch, A.: Everything as a service: powering the new information economy. Computer 44(3), 36–43 (2011)
2. Baumann, F., Eichhoff, J., Roller, D.: Unified storage file format for additive manufacturing. In: Proceedings of the 2nd international Conference on Progress in Additive Manufacturing, pp. 582–590. Research Publishing, Singapore (2016)

---

[10] http://icrm-aachen.com.

3. Baumann, F., Roller, D.: 3D Printing process pipeline on the internet. In: Proceedings of the 8th ZEUS Workshop, pp. 29–36 (2016)
4. Baumann, F., Roller, D.: Vision based error detection for 3D printing processes. In: 2016 International Conference on Frontiers of Sensors Technologies (ICFST 2016), vol. 59 (2016)
5. Bhaurao, C., Swati, D.: Privacy preservation and secure data sharing in cloud storage. Int. Res. J. Sci. Eng. 3(6), 231–236 (2015)
6. Chabridon, S., Conan, D., Desprats, T., Mbarki, M., Taconet, C., Lim, L., Marie, P., Rottenberg, S.: Collaborative Computing: Networking, Applications, and Worksharing: 11th International Conference, CollaborateCom 2015, Wuhan, November 10–11, 2015, China. Proceedings, chap. A Framework for Multiscale-, QoC- and Privacy-aware Context Dissemination in the Internet of Things, pp. 207–218. Springer International Publishing, Cham (2016)
7. Dong, B., Qi, G., Gu, X., Wei, X.: Web service-oriented manufacturing resource applications for networked product development. Adv. Eng. Inf. 22(3), 282–295 (2008)
8. ISO: 6983–1: 2009 Automation systems and integration - Numerical control of machines - Program format and definitions of address words. Technical report (2009)
9. Kulkarni, P., Marsan, A., Dutta, D.: A review of process planning techniques in layered manufacturing. Rapid Prototyping J. 6(1), 18–35 (2000)
10. Kumar, V., Madria, S.: Distributed attribute based access control of aggregated data in sensor clouds. In: 2015 IEEE 34th Symposium on Reliable Distributed Systems (SRDS), pp. 218–227, Sept 2015
11. Lan, H.: Web-based rapid prototyping and manufacturing systems: A review. Comput. Ind. 60(9), 643–656 (2009)
12. Mell, P., Grance, T.: SP 800–145. The NIST Definition of Cloud Computing. Technical report, Gaithersburg, MD, United States (2011)
13. van Moergestel, L., Puik, E., Telgen, D., Meyer, J.J.: Implementing Manufacturing as a Service: A Pull-Driven Agent-Based Manufacturing Grid
14. Mota, C.: The rise of personal fabrication. In: Proceedings of the 8th ACM Conference on Creativity and Cognition, pp. 279–288. C&C '11, NY, USA. ACM, New York (2011)
15. Petrick, I.J., Simpson, T.W.: 3D printing disrupts manufacturing. Res. Technol. Manage. 56(6), 12 (2013)
16. Potoglou, D., Palacios, J.-F., Feijóo, C.: An integrated latent variable and choice model to explore the role of privacy concern on stated behavioural intentions in e-commerce. J. Choice Model. 17, 10–27 (2015). ISSN: 1755-5345. http://dx.doi.org/10.1016/j.jocm.2015.12.002
17. Qanbari, S., Zadeh, S.M., Vedaei, S., Dustdar, S.: CloudMan: A platform for portable cloud manufacturing services. In: 2014 IEEE International Conference on Big Data (Big Data), pp. 1006–1014, October 2014
18. Ruffo, M., Tuck, C., Hague, R.: Cost estimation for rapid manufacturing - laser sintering production for low to medium volumes. Proc. Inst. Mech. Eng. Part B: J. Eng. Manuf. 220(9), 1417–1427 (2006)
19. Schulte, S., Hoenisch, P., Hochreiner, C., Dustdar, S., Klusch, M., Schuller, D.: Towards process support for cloud manufacturing. In: 2014 IEEE 18th International Enterprise Distributed Object Computing Conference (EDOC), pp. 142–149, Sept 2014
20. Short, D.B., Sirinterlikci, A., Badger, P., Artieri, B.: Environmental, health, and safety issues in rapid prototyping. Rapid Prototyping J. 21(1), 105–110 (2015)

21. Wohlers, T., Gornet, T.: History of additive manufacturing. Wohlers Rep. **2014**, 24 (2014)
22. Wu, D., Rosen, D.W., Wang, L., Schaefer, D.: Cloud-based design and manufacturing: A new paradigm in digital manufacturing and design innovation. Comput. Aided Des. **59**, 1–14 (2015)
23. Wu, D., Thames, J.L., Rosen, D.W., Schaefer, D.: Towards a cloud-based design and manufacturing paradigm: looking backward, looking forward. In: Computers and Information in Engineering Conference, Parts A and B, pp. 315–328. ASME 2012 International Design Engineering Technical Conferences and Computers and Information in Engineering Conference (2012)
24. Zor, S., Schumm, D., Leymann, F.: A Proposal of BPMN extensions for the manufacturing domain. In: Proceedings of the 44th CIRP International Conference on Manufacturing Systems (2011)

Supplier Selection Based on Recommendations

Sylvia Encheva[⊠]

Stord/Haugesund University College, Bjørnsonsg. 45,
5528 Haugesund, Norway
sbe@hsh.no

Abstract. Suppliers' selection is important for any enterprise. Most available approaches for facilitating processes of choosing suppliers from a number of alternatives focus on which criteria are to be used according to a particular business. This implies that the role of a decision maker is to confirm or modify the outcome of an already chosen method. In this work we present a way of incorporate decision maker's opinion along with previous customers experience in the process of suppliers selection.

Keywords: Suppliers · Multi criteria decision making · Recommendations

1 Introduction

The vendor selection problem was presented in [10] as a pair of decisions a firm has to make, i.e. "which vendors to do business with and how much to order from each vendor", [9]. In [8] the vendor selection problem is described as an unstructured, complicated, and multi-criteria decision problem. Vendor selection problem has been treated in [4] "as a fuzzy Multi-objective Integer Programming Vendor Selection Problem, formulation that incorporates the three important goals: cost-minimization, quality-maximization and maximization of on-time-delivery with the realistic constraints such as meeting the buyers demand, vendors capacity, vendors quota flexibility, etc." Decision support systems have been employed for a number of years to assist in the process selecting optimal solutions for choosing vendors.

The model presented in this article gives opportunity to decision makers to incorporate their preferences through the entire selection process instead of just having the final word on the preselected items where the rules remain practically hidden. We also use compensative weighted averaging which "provides an additional parameter that controls the power to which the arguments of aggregation are raised, [2]".

2 Preliminaries

Values $(a_1, a_2, ..., a_n)$ can be aggregated applying a weighting vector w.

© Springer International Publishing AG 2016
Y. Luo (Ed.): CDVE 2016, LNCS 9929, pp. 86–89, 2016.
DOI: 10.1007/978-3-319-46771-9_11

Definition 1. *[1] A compensative weighted averaging (CWA) operator of dimension n is a mapping* $CWA : \mathbb{R}^n_+ \to \mathbb{R}_+$ *defined by arguments* $(a_1, a_2, ..., a_n)$, *an associated weight vector* $\mathbf{w} = (w_1, w_2, ..., w_n)$ *such that* $\sum_{i=1}^n w_i = 1$ *and* $w_i \in [0, 1]$, *and a parameter* $0 \lesssim \lambda \leq, \lambda \neq 1$. *The aggregated value using CWA operator is obtained as* $CWA(a_1, a_2, ..., a_n) = \log_\lambda(\sum_{i=1}^n w_i \lambda^{a_i})$

Examples showing the need of weighted averaging are shown in [5]. Among them is a case where: "several sensors measure a physical property" and since they "may be of different quality and precision, a weighted mean type aggregation is necessary". Another one refers to a "situation when a committee of experts has to assess several candidates or proposals." Then "a weighted mean type aggregation is suitable for reflecting the expertness or the confidence in the judgment of each expert."

For a mapping from one partially ordered set into another unstructured set one can apply methods presented in [6].

3   Main Results

Suppliers are first ranked by consumers who have experience using their products and services. Criteria in Tables 1 and 2 are a subset of the ones listed in [8].

Consider an enterprise which is in a process of selecting suppliers. New ones should be taken into account and existing ones ought to be reevaluated. Apart from using information provided by suppliers of themselves, it is beneficial to incorporate experience of other firms which have had business interactions with them. The latter can be usually obtained via recommender systems. Through such channels one can receive somewhat general ideas about levels of satisfaction with a product or service, where the voter's level of interest in an item remains hidden. In the proposed approach below, we provide an opportunity for decision makers to influence items' choices not only as the final step but also at the point where criteria for purchasing an item are based on what matters most to them.

For this scenario suppliers are first ranked by consumers who have experience using their services or products. Criteria in Tables 1 and 2 are a subset of the ones listed in [8]. For the ranking scale we recommend Likert scale (a five or seven point scale) since a ten point scale often leads to more hesitation. A number of users find large point scales time and energy consuming and very quickly drop the entire ranking. In this work we use positive integers for ranking. If however decision makers prefer nonnumerical terms then they should be converted to numbers.

An entrance in Table 1 indicates the importance of a corresponding item to a decision maker with respect to different criteria. Compensative weighted averaging can be used while implementing decision maker's views.

An entrance in Table 2 can be calculated by f. ex. arithmetic average. This would imply equal influence of all opinions. If previous consumers are identified then one can assign weights to each consumer, as in [7]. Assigning of weights can also be used to signify the time factor, f. ex. several years old opinions might

Table 1. Items

	Quality	Price	Terms	Purchase order reactiveness	Delivery	Technical support
I1	4	5	3	2	4	2
I2	3	4	2	1	5	1
I3	5	3	4	3	2	4
I4	4	4	5	4	5	3

Table 2. Suppliers

	S1	S2	S3	S4	S5	S6	S7	S8	S9
Quality	3	2	5	4	4	5	3	3	4
Price	2	5	3	4	5	2	4	2	3
Terms	4	3	4	2	4	3	5	3	4
Purchase order reactiveness	3	5	2	1	5	4	2	4	5
Delivery	5	4	3	2	4	5	2	5	5
Technical support	2	3	4	1	4	5	4	4	4

not have the same value as the ones that are done several months ago. In both Tables 1 and 2 larger numbers indicate higher level of satisfuction.

The isotone Galois connection λ direct product [3] $I\Delta_\lambda S$ lists all resulting concepts. The extents of $I\Delta_\lambda S$ relate items and suppliers. The amount of thus obtained concepts is definitely unpractical. Here we adopt a filtering technique with three values $\{1, 0.8, 0\}$. The outcome is divided into two sets called first and second choice, respectively. The latter is offered just in case something goes wrong with suppliers listed as first choice.

First choice: item I1 should be ordered from supplier S5, item I2 should be ordered from supplier S9 while items I3 and I4 should be ordered from supplier S6. These recommendations are denoted with 'x' in Table 3.

Second choice: item I1 should be ordered from supplier S3, item I2 should be ordered from supplier S3, item I3 should be ordered from supplier S8, and item I4 should be ordered from supplier S7. These recommendations are denoted with '.' in Table 3. In both first and second recommendations it is not taken into account what will be the outcome if suppliers offer discounts for multiple orders.

Deployment of recommender system with intelligent agents will provide a decision makers with opportunities to customize both Tables 1 and 2 according to decision makers current needs. If opinions are available in text form and or different numerical scales have been used by different data sources a converter has to be applied first and then continue with already described work.

In future research we plan to address some issues related to supplier attributes, f. ex. how many consumers participated in the process of grading suppliers, how current each grading is, and how many suppliers a consumer has business interactions with.

Table 3. Items and suppliers

	S1	S2	S3	S4	S5	S6	S7	S8	S9
I1			.		x				
I2		.							x
I3						x	.		
I4						x	.		

4 Conclusion

The presented approach aims at facilitating suppliers selection processes. It allows adjustments of criteria choices, degrees of influence of each criterion along with opinions of former supplier customers. Assigning weights to recommenders implies that some opinions can be more valuable than others, like f. ex. recommenders that are in a similar situation and or have been previously providing valuable opinions. The alternative is not using weights for recommenders, which means that the system does not distinguish between different sources of information.

References

1. Aggarwal, M.: Compensative weighted averaging aggregation operators. Appl. Soft Comput. **28**, 368–378 (2015)
2. Aggarwal, M.: Generalized compensative weighted averaging aggregation operators. Comput. Ind. Eng. **87**, 81–90 (2015)
3. Kridlo, O., Ojeda-Aciego, M.: CRL-Chu correspondences. CLA **2013**, 105–116 (2013)
4. Kumar, M., Vrat, P., Shankar, R.: A fuzzy programming approach for vendor selection problem in a supply chain. Int. J. Prod. Econ. **101**, 273–285 (2006)
5. Llamazares, B.: Constructing Choquet integral-based operators that generalize weighted means and OWA operators. Inf. Fusion **23**, 131–138 (2015)
6. García-Pardo, F., Cabrera, I.P., Cordero, P., Ojeda-Aciego, M., Rodríguez, F.J.: Generating isotone galois connections on an unstructured codomain. In: Laurent, A., Strauss, O., Bouchon-Meunier, B., Yager, R.R. (eds.) IPMU 2014, Part III. CCIS, vol. 444, pp. 91–99. Springer, Heidelberg (2014)
7. Yager, R.R.: Using trapezoids for representing granular objects: applications to learning and OWA aggregation. Inf. Sci. **178**(2), 363–380 (2008)
8. Yang, J.L., Chiu, H.N., Tzeng, G.-H., Yeh, R.H.: Vendor selection by integrated fuzzy MC decision maker techniques with independent and interdependent relationships. Inf. Sci. **178**, 4166–4183 (2008)
9. Wadhwa, V., Ravindran, A.R.: Vendor selection in outsourcing. Comput. Oper. Res. **34**, 3725–3737 (2007)
10. Weber, C.A., Current, J.R.: A multi objective approach to vendor selection. Eur. J. Oper. Res. **68**, 173–184 (1993)

Kernel Semi-supervised Extreme Learning Machine Applied in Urban Traffic Congestion Evaluation

Qing Shen[✉], Xiaojuan Ban, Chong Guo, and Cong Wang

University of Science and Technology Beijing, Beijing 100083, China
shenqingcc222333@gmail.com, kotrue2015@gmail.com,
banxj@ustb.edu.cn, 1303003723@qq.com

Abstract. In urban transportation assessment system, semi-supervised extreme learning machine (SSELM) can be used to unite manual observed data and extensively collected data and cooperatively build connection between congestion condition and road information. Optimized by kernel function, Kernel-SSELM can achieve higher classification accuracy and robustness. In this paper, Kernel-SSELM model is used to train the traffic congestion evaluation framework, with both small-scale labeled data and large-scale unlabeled data. Both the experiment and the real-time application show the evaluation system can precisely reflect the traffic condition.

Keywords: Kernel-SSELM · Cooperative learning · Traffic congestion evaluation

1 Introduction

Urban road network, is, an integral part of the organic link to achieve mutual coordination for a city. Among them, road traffic congestion is an important indicator to measure the level of road service and traffic capacity. Based on the collection of the floating car data combined with the urban road conditions to achieve urban congestion assessment is the main way of the current study.

Urban Transportation Assessment and Forecast System analyzes the traffic congestion of transportation network in a city of southwest China and shows the evaluation results of the real-time traffic states on the GIS map using different colors.

Seen from the Fig. 1, traffic congestion evaluation system based on floating car data is the fundamental part of core function whose data source consists of road sections information (containing road grades, the number of lanes, the number of neighborhood lanes) and floating car data. We pre-process the floating car data and match the effective floating car speed information to the every road section. Finally, road section traffic flow eigenvalues are calculated.

In previous work of traffic congestion evaluation, the empirical evaluates frameworks [1–3] are adopted to build connection between average speed of floating cars and congestion. The Table 1 shows the road congestion evaluation framework of Beijing. This method is easy to implement and consumes a little system resources. But the

© Springer International Publishing AG 2016
Y. Luo (Ed.): CDVE 2016, LNCS 9929, pp. 90–97, 2016.
DOI: 10.1007/978-3-319-46771-9_12

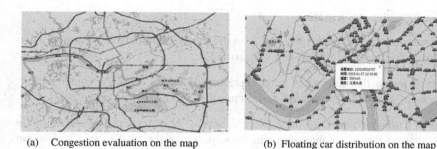

(a)   Congestion evaluation on the map   (b) Floating car distribution on the map

Fig. 1. Traffic congestion evaluation system

empirical evaluation frameworks do not take full consideration of the road information and network conditions and it causes a significant gap between the congestion information on the map and users' experience.

Table 1. Empirical framework based on average speed (km/s)

Congestion	Smooth	Average	Congested
Highway	>65	35~65	<35
Main road	>40	30~40	<20
Minor road & Branch road	>35	25~35	<10

To overcome the shortcomings above, machine learning methods are introduced into the traffic congestion evaluation system such as Random Forest, SVM and etc. However, many approaches such as SVM have deficiencies when applied to huge data and semi-supervised task. First, the reliable labeled data of congestion costs too much on human resources and working time, so that classifiers based upon the supervised learning are ineffective because of the sparse labeled samples. Second, the quantity of data is huge, which results in huge computation cost for many semi-supervised learning algorithms.

Gao Huang et al. [4] proposed the semi-supervised framework of ELM to extend the capacity to deal with unlabeled data with high training efficiency and accuracy. Optimized by kernel function, this model can achieve higher classification accuracy and robustness.

This paper applied Kernel-SSELM in traffic congestion evaluation system to unite small-scale labeled data and large-scale unlabeled data cooperatively, and build connection between congestion condition and road information with high efficiency and accuracy.

2   Traffic Congestion Eigenvalue

Traffic congestion evaluation system takes the road sections as the individual samples. Specifically, a road section demonstrates a portion of a road in a single direction. The traffic congestion evaluation of each road section originates from two sources cooperatively.

2.1   Road Section Information

The first source is the essential information of the road section from the Transportation Department. The following information is extracted:

Number of lanes: the number of lanes represents the road capacity. Under the circumstances of same congestion, the more lanes there is, higher the speed is.

Number of Entrance and Exit: these two numbers are how many lanes the road has in the two adjacent directions that represent the capacity of the road's input and output traffic flow. This capacity has obvious effect on stopping time and speed of cars in the different conditions of congestion.

Number of traffic lights: the number of traffic lights influences the stopping time and average speed of cars on the road, especially at the intersection. Despite of long stopping and low average speed, if cars have a certain velocity the road is clear.

Road grades: roads in the system have four road grades. They are highway, major road, minor road and branch way. This eigenvalue is defined with the numerical value. From branch way to highway the numerical values are 1, 2, 3, 4 in order. The higher the road grade is, the higher road standard speed and maximum speed the road has. The congestion evaluation is also different because of different road grades.

2.2   Speed Information Based on FCD

The second source is the real-time speed information of the road section from the floating car data. In the interval ΔT defined by $\Delta T = 5$ min, the data is calculated and matched to the corresponding road section and is transformed to the following kinds of eigenvalues:

Average speed: first, we calculate the average speed of every car in the interval of ΔT on the road section. Then the average speed of all cars is attained. In the interval of ΔT, the velocity measurement sites of the floating car r on the terminal road section are distributed as shown in the Figure below.

Sequence $\{t_0, t_1, \ldots t_p\}$ and sequence $\{u_0, u_1, \ldots u_p\}$ are the time sequence and speed sequence of floating car r on the road section. The floating car's driving distance S_r is defined by:

$$S_r = \int_{t_0}^{t_p} udt \approx u_0\left(\frac{t_1 - t_0}{2}\right) + u_p\left(\frac{t_p - t_p - 1}{2}\right) + \sum_{i=1}^{p-1} u_i\left(\frac{t_{i+1} - t_{i-1}}{2}\right) \quad (1)$$

Therefore, the average speed of floating car γ can be represented as $U_r = \frac{S_r}{t_p - t_0}$.

If the number of floating cars on the road section at the moment is n, the average speed of all cars on the road section can be written as $\tilde{U} = \frac{\sum_1^n U_r}{n}$.

Table 2. The 5 levels of the speed of floating cars

Speed Grades	1	2	3	4	5
Range(km/h)	<15	15~35	35~55	55~75	>75

Speed distribution: the car speed is distinguished into different levels and the histogram is used to represent the distribution of speed data of all floating cars on the read section. The standard of division is based on the speed distribution of floating cars in the city. Car speed data is mainly no more than 75 km/h except those of highway. Therefore, the car speed is distributed into 5 grades as shown in the Table 2.

Average stopping time: when a car's speed is below 5 km/h, it is identified as a stopped car. The stopping time of floating car r can be represented as $\sum_{i=0}^{p-1} (t_{I+1} - t_i)$ $(u_i < 5)$.

Thus the average stopping time of all cars on the road section can be written as $\tilde{T} = \frac{\sum_{1}^{n} T_r}{n}$.

From all kinds of eigenvalues above, 12-dimensional traffic congestion eigenvalue can be calculated.

2.3   Congestion Value

The work of labeling training samples is completed by 5 experts from the Transportation Department of the city. Through surveillance cameras experts recorded information and gave evaluation of the traffic congestion at that time. Congestion evaluation is divided into three grades: Smooth, Average and Congested. The final label is in the grade which receives the most votes in 5 experts.

We indicate the congestion grades with the 3-dimensional eigenvalue. In each of the evaluation results, each dimension corresponds to a congestion level. The dimension of the corresponding congestion grade is set to 1 and other dimensions are set to 0. Thus congestion evaluation problem is transformed into classification problem. Therefore, the evaluation result is the congestion grade which corresponds to the dimension having the largest value.

3   Kernel-Based SSELM

Gao Huang et al. [4] introduced manifold assumption into ELM [5], and proposed the solution of β in SSELM. For a training data set having l number of labeled samples and u number of unlabeled samples, the output weights β of a SSELM is:

$$\beta = H^T \left(I + \tilde{C}HH^T + \lambda LHH^T \right)^{-1} \tilde{C}\tilde{Y} \tag{2}$$

The formulate is valid when the number of hidden nodes is more than the number of labeled samples l. The $\tilde{Y}$ is the training target including the first l rows of labeled data equal to Y and the rest equal to 0. λ is user-defined semi-supervised learning rate. $\tilde{C}$ is a $(1+u) \times (1+u)$ diagonal matrix with the first l diagonal elements of cost coefficient and the rest equal to 0. $\tilde{C}$ can be calculated as:

$$C_i = \frac{c_0}{N_{p_i}} \quad i = 1, \ldots, l \tag{3}$$

where C_0 is user-defined cost coefficient, and N_{p_i} represents the sample quantity of the pattern of i th sample. L is Laplacian matrix, which can be calculated as $L = D - W$. $W = [w_{i,j}]$ is the similarity matrix of all the labeled and unlabeled samples. D is a diagonal matrix with its diagonal elements $D_{ii} = \sum_{j=1}^{n} w_{ij}$.

G.B. Huang et al. [6] suggested using a kernel function if the hidden layer feature mapping h(x) is unknown. The kernel matrix χ for ELM can be written as follows, where $K(x_i, y_i)$ is kernel function:

$$\chi_{ELM} = HH^T \quad \chi_{ELM_{i,j}} = h(x_i) \cdot h(y_i) = K(x_i, y_i) \tag{4}$$

Then the output function of Kernel-SSELM can be written as:

$$y = F_{SSELM}(x) = h(x)\beta = \begin{bmatrix} K(x,x_1) \\ \vdots \\ K(x,x_n) \end{bmatrix} (I + \tilde{C}\chi_{ELM} + \lambda L\chi_{ELM})^{-1} \tilde{C}\tilde{Y} \tag{5}$$

4   Evaluation Performance

4.1   Experimental Setup

In the experiment, we collect the floating car data from June 15th to Jun 16th 2015, and the quantity is more than 30,000,000. The data is grouped in interval for 5 min and matched to the corresponding road section. Finally we collect 13681 samples. The evaluation of experts is based on the video from surveillance cameras about 30 typical road sections in the city. 537 valid samples were finally collected, and the rest 13144 samples were unlabeled. The experiment was implemented using Matlab R2013b on a 3.40 GHz machine with 4 GB of memory.

4.2   Comparisons with Related Algorithms

For comparison, we tested the empirical rule, SSELM, Kernel-SSELM and state-of-the-art semi-supervised learning algorithms such as TSVM, LDS, LapRLS, and LapSVM. The test set had 100 samples randomly selected from the labeled sample, and the random generation process was repeated 10 times. The cost coefficient C_0 was fixed to 100 and the semi-supervised learning rate λ was chosen from in $\{2^{-20}, 2^{-19}, \ldots, 2^{20}\}$. The kernel function of Kernel-SSELM is Gaussian function with the parameter γ fixed to 1. The number of hidden layer nodes of SSELM was set to 5000.

Table 3. Evaluation result on realistic traffic data

	Empirical rule	TSVM	LDS	LapRLS	LapSVM	SSELM	Kernel-SSELM
Average accuracy	68.9 %	81.3 %	82.2 %	81.4 %	84.8 %	82.6 %	86.2 %
Best accuracy	73.0 %	87.5 %	86.0 %	86.0 %	88.0 %	87.5 %	88.0 %
Training time (s)	–	18437	35334	931	825	41.6	48.2

Table 3 shows that the evaluation model trained by Kernel-SSELM had the highest average accuracy at 86.2%. In addition, Kernel-SSELM only takes 48.2 s for training, which keep the high training efficiency of SSELM. In comparison, the other semi-supervised learning algorithms can also get relatively high accuracy, but the training consumptions are too huge.

Figure 2 shows that with the increase of the proportion of unlabeled data in the training set, the performance of Kernel-SSELM and SSELM get better. In particular, Kernel-SSELM gives a more significant growth when the percentage of unlabeled part is 40% below, and its performance get stable when there are more unlabeled data. By comparison, the performance of SSELM grows slower and is hard to get stable result.

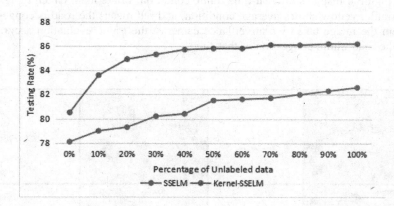

Fig. 2. Evaluation comparison with different percentage of unlabeled data

4.3   Performance Sensitivity on Parameters

Figure 3 shows the Performance Sensitivity. In order to achieve good generalization performance, the cost coefficient C_0 and kernel parameter γ need to be chosen appropriately. The best performance is usually achieved in a very narrow range of cost coefficient C_0, which means the Kernel-SSELM model is very sensitive to C_0. However, when the C_0 is properly chosen, the performance will be not sensitive to the kernel parameter γ. Semi-supervised learning rate λ also significantly affect the performance of Kernel-SSELM. There is an obvious trend that Kernel-SSELM gives lower prediction error with more unlabeled data. However, the best performance is

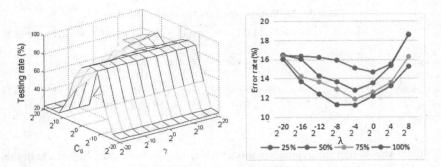

Fig. 3. Performance Sensitivity of Kernel-SSELM on the parameters

achieved in a very narrow range of λ. Moreover, with different number of unlabeled data, the best value of λ varies in a small rage.

4.4 Evaluation on the Realistic Traffic Data

The trained model was used in the Urban Transportation Assessment and Forecast System. Figure 4 displays the real-time traffic condition. In the map, Green represents smooth traffic, yellow shows average condition, and red means the road is congested. Seen from the image taken by surveillance cameras, the traffic evaluation accurately reflects the road traffic congestion at that time.

Fig. 4. Real-time traffic evaluation

5   Conclusion

In this paper, Kernel-SSELM was used to train the evaluation model on the large-scale data set. Both the experiment and the real-time application shows the evaluation system unites small-scale labeled data and large-scale unlabeled data cooperatively, and build connection between congestion condition and road information with high efficiency and accuracy. Extreme learning machine has high training efficiency and is easy to implement. In the case of large data scales, high training speed ensures that despite traffic conditions changes it can still renew training for several times to choose a better model. Kernel-SSELM improves the recognition accuracy of evaluation models by involving unlabeled data in the training. In neglecting the number of hidden layer nodes, the optimization of kernel function improves the stability.

Acknowledgement. This work was supported by National Nature Science Foundation of P. R. China (No. 61272357, 61300074).

References

1. Jie, G.U., Zhou, S.H., Yan, X.P., et al.: Formation mechanism of traffic congestion in view of spatio-temporal agglomeration of residents' daily activities: a case study of Guangzhou. Scientia Geographica Sinica **32**(8), 921–927 (2012)
2. Wen, H., Sun, J., Zhang, X.: Study on traffic congestion patterns of large city in China taking Beijing as an example. Procedia Soc. Behav. Sci. **138**, 482–491 (2014)
3. Liu, R., Hu, W.P., Wang, H.L., et al.: The road network evolution analysis of Guangzhou-Foshan metropolitan area based on kernel density estimation. In: International Conference on Computational and Information Sciences, pp. 316–319 (2010)
4. Huang, G., Song, S., Gupta, J.N., et al.: Semi-supervised and unsupervised extreme learning machines. IEEE Trans. Cybern. **44**(12), 1 (2014)
5. Huang, G.B., Siew, C.K.: Extreme learning machine: RBF network case. In: Control, Automation, Robotics and Vision Conference, ICARCV 2004, vol. 2, pp. 1029–1036 (2005)
6. Huang, G.B., Chen, L.: Convex incremental extreme learning machine, Neurocomputing **70** (16–18), 3056–3062 (2007)

Tablet-Based Synchronous Learning System with Floor-Controlled Multimedia Interaction for Students

Jang Ho Lee[✉]

Department of Computer Engineering, Hongik University, Seoul, Korea
jangho@cs.hongik.ac.kr

Abstract. Previously, we developed a mobile learning system that allowed students to watch an instructor, the slides and annotations using their tablets in real time. Students could ask questions via text chat. Students, however, found the text chat interaction inconvenient and slow. Thus, based on our observation that one student asks a question at any instance of time, we present a tablet-based synchronous learning system that allows only one student with the floor control to ask questions via audio and video that is multicast to all users. A preliminary user survey shows that regarding user interaction, more than half of the users found the proposed system more convenient and faster than the previous one.

Keywords: Mobile learning · Synchronous collaboration · Floor control · Tablet

1 Introduction

The distance learning has its strong merit that enables students to participate in a class from a distance without actually going to the classroom. And as the mobile device and network technology advances and its user population grows over the last decade, researchers have been attracted to mobile learning since it allows students to participate in a class remotely from anywhere with their mobile device [1]. MLVLS [2] is a mobile learning system that allows students to watch video and slides with annotation remotely on their Symbian smartphone in real time. Classroom Presenter [3] is a tablet-based learning system that enables users to share slide and annotation in real time. These systems, however, don't provide the user interaction capability that allows students to ask questions in real time.

Previously, we had developed a mobile learning system that allowed students to watch an instructor and slide with annotation in real time [4]. It also allowed students to interact with the instructor and other students through text chat. The students, however, find it slow and inconvenient to look in the text chat to see the questions and answers between students and the instructor.

Thus, we present a tablet-based synchronous learning system that allows only one student who has the floor control to ask a question via voice and video, which, in turn, is multicast to all the clients. It is based on our observation that most of the time only one student asks a question at any instance of time. Floors are temporary permissions granted dynamically to collaborating users to guarantee mutually exclusive usage of resources such as telepointers or continuous media such as video and audio in networked

© Springer International Publishing AG 2016
Y. Luo (Ed.): CDVE 2016, LNCS 9929, pp. 98–101, 2016.
DOI: 10.1007/978-3-319-46771-9_13

multimedia application [5]. It should be noted that our system doesn't allow voice and video of all the students to be multicast at the same time since it could cause network congestion and server overload.

2 Tablet-Based Synchronous Learning System with Floor-Controlled Interaction

Figure 1 shows the run-time communication architecture of the proposed tablet-based synchronous learning system with floor-controlled multimedia interaction for student.

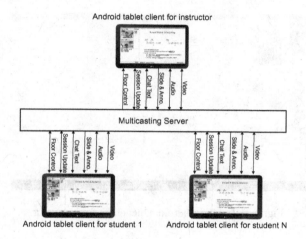

Fig. 1. Run-time communication architecture of the system

The system consists of a multicasting server and multiple tablet clients that are of two types: instructor client and student client. During the lecture, the instructor client encodes the video and audio of an instructor in H.263 and in G.723.1, respectively and sends them to all the student clients through the multicasting server. The student client then decodes them and renders or plays them. When a student takes the floor control, the student client also encodes the video and audio of the student and sends them to the multicasting server. We exploited the floor control to allow only one student's video and audio to be multicast because making all the student clients' video and audio multicast simultaneously would overload the multicasting server as well as cause network congestion. The instructor client sends the slide to the server in pdf format. A series of annotation events made by an instructor are grouped into a packet and sent to the server. When a student client receives these slide and annotation data from the server, it decodes and renders them on the tablet display. A chat text from a client is multicast to all the clients through multicast server. When a client joins or leaves a lecture, it sends the session update to the server, which, in turn, updates its own data and multicasts the update to the clients. When a student gets the floor control, the floor control information such as who just took the floor control, is sent to the multicasting server, which also updates its own data and multicasts it to the clients.

Figure 2 shows the user interface of the Android tablet client for instructor. The instructor starts the lecture by clicking a "Start Lecture" icon in the slide control panel, typing a lecture title and opening a slide file. During a lecture, the instructor can speak and make gestures as well as make annotations on a slide. When a student takes a floor control of asking questions, his/her appearance starts to show in the student video panel. Any student can also ask a question by typing it in the text chat panel. The instructor can answer a question by speaking, making gestures, making annotations on a slide, and/or typing some texts in the chat.

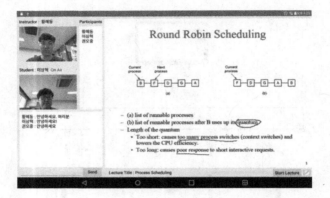

Fig. 2. UI of the Android tablet client for instructor

Figure 3 shows the user interface of the Android tablet client for student. During a lecture, a student can watch the instructor and see the slide, annotation and chat in real time. A student can ask a question via text chat. And one student is also allowed to ask a question via voice and video through floor control. When a student clicks on a floor control button that reads "Speak", other students' buttons except the student's button

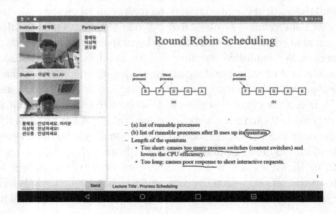

Fig. 3. UI of the Android tablet client for student

become disabled and its text changes from "Speak" to "On Air" so that other students cannot take the floor control. Then, the voice and video of the speaking student is multicast to all the tablet clients. When the speaking student finishes the conversation and clicks on the "On Air" button, the button on all the student clients gets enabled and its text changes from "On Air" back to "Speak", at which time any student can take the floor control and ask a question via voice and video.

Regarding development platform, the client has been implemented in Java using Android Studio IDE with Android SDK and Java SE Development Kit 8. The client runs on the LG G Pad II 10.1 tablet with 10.1 inch display (1920 × 1200) and Android 5.1.1 Lollipop. The multicasting server has been implemented in Java using Eclipse IDE for Java Developers with Java SE Development Kit 8 on Windows 8.1 Pro.

3   Conclusion

We proposed a tablet-based synchronous learning system with floor-controlled multimedia interaction for students. Students can watch an instructor and slide with annotation using their tablets in real time. They can also interact with the instructor with text chat. When a student acquires a floor control, his video and audio is also multicast to users. We conducted a preliminary usability testing by having 7 undergraduate students in our computer engineering department use the prototype system and our previous system without floor-controlled multimedia interaction, for 3 days. In our simple user survey on the student's interaction with the instructor, 4 students (57 %) said they felt that the proposed system is more convenient and faster than the previous one. 2 students (29 %) said they are not sure which one is better. 1 student (14 %) said she preferred the previous system because she didn't feel comfortable with herself being shown to all the users. We are working on the prototype implementation. We plan to conduct detailed empirical study after the implementation is finished.

Acknowledgements.   This work was supported by 2016 Hongik University Research Fund.

References

1. Wains, S.I., Mahmood, W.: Integrating M-learning with E-learning. In: 9th ACM SIGITE Conference on Information Technology Education, pp. 31–38. ACM (2008)
2. Ulrich, C., Shen, R., Tong, R., Tan, X.: A Mobile live video learning system for large-scale learning-system design and evaluation. IEEE Trans. Learn. Technol. **3**(1), 6–17 (2010)
3. Anderson, R., Anderson, R., Davis, P., Linnell, N., Prince, C., Razmov, V., Videon, F.: Classroom presenter: enhancing interactive education with digital ink. IEEE Comput. **40**(9), 56–61 (2007)
4. Lee, J.H.: Synchronous mobile learning system to cope with slow network connection. In: Luo, Y. (ed.) CDVE 2014. LNCS, vol. 8683, pp. 171–174. Springer, Heidelberg (2014)
5. Dommel, H.-P., Garcia-Luna-Aceves, J.J.: Floor control for multimedia conferencing and collaboration. Multimedia Syst. **5**(1), 23–38 (1997)

CIAM Mobile: Methodology Supporting Mobile Application Design and Evaluation Applied on GreedEx Tab

Yoel Arroyo[1(✉)], Christian X. Navarro[2(✉)], Ana I. Molina[1(✉)], and Miguel A. Redondo[1(✉)]

[1] Escuela Superior de Informática, Universidad de Castilla-La Mancha, Paseo de la Universidad, 4, 13071 Ciudad Real, Spain
{Yoel.Arroyo,AnaIsabel.Molina,Miguel.Redondo}@uclm.es
[2] Facultad de Ingeniería Arquitectura y Diseño, Universidad Autónoma de Baja California, Ensenada, Mexico
cnavarro@uabc.edu.mx

Abstract. We have addressed the problem of improving CIAM (*Collaborative Interactive Application Methodology*) in order to support design, modeling and evaluation of collaborative and interactive mobile applications. CIAM Mobile (m-CIAM) is the result of the integration of CIAM with MoLEF (*Mobile Learning Evaluation Framework*), which serves as a basis for an evaluation tool that allows for analyzing characteristics of applications in m-Learning. In this paper, we endeavor to show how to apply m-CIAM to the design of m-Learning applications that were previously developed with the original version of CIAM. The selected application to describe this process is called GreedEx Tab, which is the iPad version of the GreedEx tool. Our objective is to develop a new prototype for the iPad applying m-CIAM as methodological approach and compare the results with the initial version of this application. These results show that we can obtain improved relative values in pedagogical and technological usability.

Keywords: Collaborative mobile systems · Group interaction in mobile systems · Cooperative learning · Mobile usability · m-Learning · Methodology

1 Introduction

Mobile Learning (or m-Learning) came into existence at the end of the 20th Century. It facilitated access to information anytime, anywhere, and enabling a flexible and personalized learning experience in which the context is important. Nowadays, the number of people using mobile phones and using broadband is constantly growing [1]. In 2012, the number of connected mobile phones exceeded world population for the first time in history [2]. Thus, we have an excellent opportunity to improve the collaborative teaching and learning of millions of people around the world if we take advantage of their full potential.

CIAM (*Collaborative Interactive Application Methodology*) is a methodological approach for the modeling and development of groupware applications that takes the

© Springer International Publishing AG 2016
Y. Luo (Ed.): CDVE 2016, LNCS 9929, pp. 102–109, 2016.
DOI: 10.1007/978-3-319-46771-9_14

modeling of work in-group and interaction issues into account [3]. It guides engineers through several modeling stages, starting from the analysis of the context of the group work until obtaining an interactive task model. The final user interface is obtained from the interaction model, applying a semi-automatic method supported by the CIAT-GUI tool [4].

The problem is that CIAM is not primarily focused on the mobile computing paradigm and does not deal directly with evaluation mechanisms and processes of the artifacts produced when this methodology is applied. To solve this problem, we decided to improve it by the proposal of CIAM Mobile (m-CIAM).

m-CIAM is the result of the integration of CIAM with MoLEF (*Mobile Learning Evaluation Framework*). MoLEF is a design and evaluation framework for collaborative m-Learning systems, focused on the support of *Pedagogical Usability* and *User Interface Usability*. These two main features are subdivided in design and assessment of different factors or sub-characteristics [5]. This framework serves as a basis for a design and evaluation tool that allows for analyzing characteristics of m-Learning applications and depicting results in a radar chart. Thanks to this framework and its integration with CIAM, pedagogical aspects can also be considered during the modeling process. These are not taken into account by other proposals for design of collaborative systems, especially in m-Learning contexts [4].

We hypothesize that applying m-CIAM applications with more user interface and pedagogical usability are obtained. Thus, in this paper, we address how to apply m-CIAM to the design of m-Learning applications that were previously developed with CIAM. GreedEx Tab is the application selected to describe this process. It is the iPad version of GreedEx [6]. Our aim is to implement a new prototype for iPad applying m-CIAM as a methodological approach and compare the results with the original version of this application. These results show that we can obtain improved relative values in pedagogical and technological usability.

2   Previous and Related Work

In [4] we introduced CIAM methodology and we mentioned that it is necessary to improve it to deal with the development of collaborative m-Learning applications. In this paper we briefly describe m-CIAM, which is the enhanced version of CIAM integrated with MoLEF.

MoLEF is a design and evaluation framework for collaborative m-Learning systems. It is divided into two main categories: *Pedagogical Usability* and *User Interface Usability*. Pedagogical aspects are considered a key factor for providing a pleasant and rich learning experience in a mobile environment [7], meanwhile user interface usability is fundamental to achieve the acceptance and satisfaction of the students [5]. Each category is organized into several factors and criteria that must be taken into account in the development and evaluation of m-Learning collaborative applications [1]. Thus, *Pedagogical Usability* is divided into *Content, Multimedia, Tasks and Activities, Social Interaction* and *Personalization*; while the *User Interface Usability* is composed of

Design, Navigation, Customization, Feedback and *Motivation* factors. Each of these factors splits further into a series of dimensions. These dimensions and their criteria are described in depth in [5].

The main improvement obtained using m-CIAM is that pedagogical aspects can be considered during the modeling process.

Other authors have addressed similar issues. For example, in [8] a usability framework for the design of m-Learning applications is introduced. In [9] the universal instructional design principles for m-Learning are described. Paper [10] presents pedagogical usability criteria for designing or evaluating m-Learning applications. Finally, [11] describe a design requirement framework. The main aim of m-CIAM is to integrate these important aspects during stages of development: pedagogical and technological usability.

In the following section, we describe how to apply m-CIAM to develop a new prototype of GreedEx Tab in order to improve a previous version and discuss the main differences.

3   CIAM Mobile Vs CIAM on Development of GreedEx Tab

GreedEx Tab v1.0 (*Greedy algorithms Experimentation for Tablets*) [12] is an iPad application developed by the CHICO[1] research group to improve and solve the problems encountered in the previous conventional computer version called GreedEx [6], developed by the University Rey Juan Carlos of Madrid (Spain) within the LITE[2] (*Laboratory of Information Technologies in Education*) research group. GreedEx Tab is an interactive assistant used to learn greedy algorithms. This app takes advantage of the convenience of use and the ability of interaction, visualization, and animation of mobile devices, in order that users learn the behavior of greedy algorithms [12].

In GreedEx Tab, users first select a problem and then interact with it. The statement is immediately shown and then they need to introduce or randomly generate the necessary data to solve it. Next, a simulation can be executed in which users interact with it in real-time. Finally, a small historical summary of the process is shown.

The original version (v1.0) was implemented by applying only CIAM methodology. Our aim in this paper is to design and implement a new iPad prototype (v2.0) using m-CIAM instead and compare the results. In the next sub-sections we briefly introduce the first version implemented and then we explain how to apply m-CIAM. Finally, we comment on some comparative results.

3.1   GreedEx Tab v1.0: CIAM Version

GreedEx Tab v1.0 was developed in its first version using only the CIAM methodology, together with the use of OpenUP [13] as a development methodology and Scrum [14] as an agile management framework.

---

[1] http://chico.inf-cr.uclm.es/cms/.
[2] http://www.lite.etsii.urjc.es/.

We followed all the habitual CIAM steps, such as the generation of the *Sociogram*, the *Responsibilities Model*, the *Process Model*, the *Group Work Task Model* and finally, the *Interaction Model*. The most relevant is the Interaction Model (CTT, Concur-Task-Trees) [15], because of its proximity to the final stages in the definition of the user interface. Using CTT, an interactive task tree is created for each individual task or individual responsibility and for each work in-group task [3]. In the case of collaborative tasks, the interaction model is obtained from the shared context definition [4].

In GreedEx Tab v1.0 we had to generate various interactive task trees using CTTE (*ConcurTaskTrees Environment*) [15] for each of the functionalities extracted from previous requirements and the *Sociogram*, *Participation Table* and *Responsibilities Model* designed. Thanks to this process, developers could improve the cooperative and collaborative interactivity, among other advantages.

In Fig. 1 we can see the appearance of the user interface obtained. One of the main tasks on GreedEx Tab it is to allow students to simulate a problem with the data introduced on their own previously. In Fig. 1, the simulation view can be seen as example of the final user interface of GreedEx Tab v1.0.

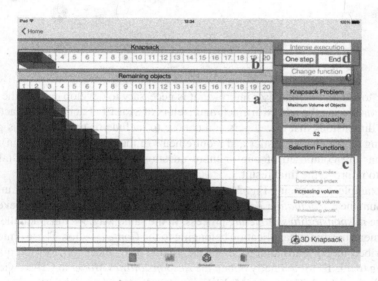

Fig. 1.   Simulation view of GreedEx Tab v1.0

3.2   GreedEx Tab v2.0: CIAM Mobile Version

m-CIAM integrates the CIAM process model and stages with the MoLEF's factors. These stages were described in [4], and this paper addresses how they are applied.

Figure 2 shows the process model and stages of m-CIAM methodology, where "A" (*Content, Multimedia, Tasks or activities, Social interaction* and *Personalization*) corresponds to the factors for evaluation of *Pedagogical Usability* requirements and "B" refers to the evaluation of *User Interface Usability*. In this diagram there are six types of elements which are described in [4]. *Pedagogical Usability* is spread across most stages of CIAM. However, the dimensions of *User Interface Usability* are focused on the *GUI Design* stage because it is applied to the artifacts managed by the process of model-based user interface design (MBUID) that is developed in this stage [16].

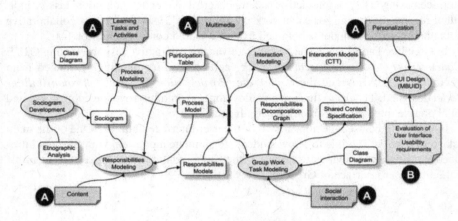

Fig. 2. Process model of m-CIAM

Thus, to obtain the final user interface, it is necessary to develop each of the CIAM models considering the related artifacts and factors of MoLEF. Each of these factors has different dimensions that developers can choose to include or not during this process (depending on the characteristics and requirements of the application to design). These dimensions are composed of one or more questions that developers must take into account to improve the final result.

For example, referencing Fig. 2, to obtain our *Responsibilities Model* we must take into account the *Participation Table* and the *Sociogram* artifacts (previously developed) during the *Responsibilities Modeling* process. In the same way, we must add the appropriate dimensions for our application belonging to the *Content* factor. These dimensions are described in [5]. Furthermore, developers must also select some of the questions pertaining to this factor to finally obtain the *Responsibilities Model* in CIAM with those characteristics added. That is the MoLEF framework is used as a *checklist* that ensures compliance with the requirements of pedagogical and technological (user interface) usability desirable in a collaborative m-learning application.

In Table 1 we show one of these typical *checklists* where developers can detail the accomplishment of the different usability requirements. These questions in particular are related to the *Content* factor and its dimensions selected for the development of our application. In this case, we were able to determine that the content must be organized into modules or units (question C1). In our case, GreedEx Tab has five different and independent problems to solve by the students. However, it is not necessary to organize them according to levels of difficulty (question C5) and users can choose one of them whenever they want.

Table 1. Checklist of accomplishment for the *Content* factor dimensions on GreedEx Tab

ID	Question	Accomplishment
C1	The content is organized into modules or units	Yes
C2	The learning objectives are defined at the beginning of the module or unit	Yes
C3	Disclosed if prior knowledge are required	No
C4	The explanation of the concepts is presented in a clear and concise manner	Yes
C5	The modules or units are organized according to levels of difficulty	No
C6	There are links to external resources related to the content and adapted for mobile devices	No

These steps are followed in each of the typical CIAM processes (*Process Modeling, Responsibilities Modeling, Interaction Modeling, Group Work Task Modeling* and *GUI Design –MBUID-*) to generate the different artifacts (*Participation Table, Responsibilities Models, Interaction Models -CTT-, etc.*) needed to achieve the desired collaborative and interactive mobile interface.

As can be noted, the *Pedagogical Usability* factors are spread across most stages of CIAM. However, the factors of *User Interface Usability* are focused on the *GUI Design* stage because it is applied to the artifacts with evaluative character, i.e., they allow evaluating the user interface during the design process trying to recognize possible problems and intervene in time.

GreedEx Tab v2.0 is a prototype which focuses on the enhancement of the user interface, so some functionalities of GreedEx Tab v1.0 were not implemented (i.e. to show information related with the historical processes or to perform an intensive

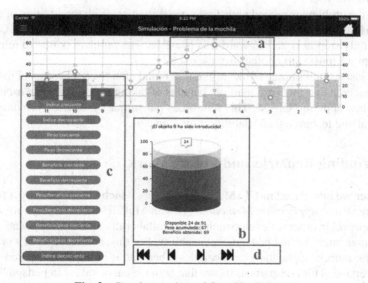

Fig. 3. *Simulation* view of GreedEx Tab v2.0

execution). Nonetheless, as illustrated in Fig. 3, its user interface differs from the first version. The *simulation* view is shown in this figure as in the section before to better comparison.

3.3 Discussion

The main difference between the two versions developed is that pedagogical aspects were not considered in the modeling process of GreedEx Tab v1.0. Nevertheless, user interface usability differences were also found. Thus, some of the most relevant (pedagogical and user interface) are detailed in the next lines, in reference to Figs. 1 and 3 and relying on factors of m-CIAM introduced before.

In "a", we have a *Content* related problem. In GreedEx Tab, we have five problems to choose from. Three of them use weight and profit values, information that must be shown for better comprehension and learning. In GreedEx Tab v2.0 (Fig. 3) this information is shown every time, meanwhile in the original version, it does not appear.

In "b", a *Feedback* problem occurs. Thanks to the new visual metaphor ('barrel'), users are always informed about the situation of the problem (also textual information appears below). Meanwhile, in GreedEx Tab v1.0, this information is shown in a horizontal bar. This bar also has several problems when the information previously introduced has high values (weights and profits), because the knapsack continues growing but graphically these changes cannot be seen.

In "c", we found a *Navigation* problem. The dropdown menu with all the selection functions in the new prototype is more intuitive and when it is pressed, all the information related to it is immediately refreshed. In the original version, users need to select the function using the wheel and then press a button to refresh. Another significant problem is that the button is allocated in a different place than the wheel, so it causes usability problems for the users.

In "d", the problem is related with *Tasks and Activities*. With the addition of the new navigation buttons, step back and rewind functionalities were also achieved. In GreedEx Tab v1.0, only step next and forward it is possible. The problem is that to reinitialize the problem we must start another from scratch.

This is just a small sample of the differences found after the application of m-CIAM. We can conclude that there are multiple benefits of taking the pedagogical aspects into account when applying CIAM. This reinforces our initial hypothesis, providing both pedagogical and technological usability improvements.

4   Concluding Remarks and Future Work

In this paper we introduced m-CIAM, a methodology which integrates CIAM (*Collaborative Interactive Application Methodology*) with MoLEF (*Mobile Learning Evaluation Framework*) in order to develop mobile and collaborative learning applications with enhanced user interface and pedagogical usability. For this, an evolution of a prototype of a specific mobile application has been described and it has been compared with its previous version. This comparison shows that better relative values in pedagogical and technological usability dimensions are obtained when this new approach is applied. Therefore, these results suggest that our initial hypothesis was correct.

In order to generalize our proposal, we also plan to apply this method in other collaborative learning scenarios and applications such as COLLECE (*Collaborative Edition, Compilation and Execution*). COLLECE is a groupware tool that enables users who are located at different workstations to collaborate in real time in the building of a computer program.

Acknowledgments. This research has been partially funded by the Ministry of Science and Innovation through the project TIN2015-66731-C2-2-R, the Thematic Network of CYTED 513RT0481, and the JCCM Project PPII11-0013-1219.

References

1. Navarro, C.X., Molina, A.I., Redondo, M.A.: Towards a model for evaluating the usability of m-Learning systems: from a mapping study to an approach. IEEE (Revista IEEE America Latina) **13**(2), 552–559 (2015)
2. Gedik, N., et al.: Key instructional design issues in a cellular phone-based mobile learning project. Comput. Educ. **58**(4), 1149–1159 (2012)
3. Molina, A.I., et al.: CIAM: a methodology for the development of groupware user interfaces. J. UCS **14**(9), 1435–1446 (2008)
4. Redondo, M.A., Molina, A.I., Navarro, C.X.: Extending CIAM methodology to support mobile application design and evaluation: a case study in m-Learning. In: Luo, Y. (ed.) CDVE 2015. LNCS, vol. 9320, pp. 11–18. Springer, Heidelberg (2015). doi:10.1007/978-3-319-24132-6_2
5. Navarro, C.X., et al.: Framework to evaluate m-Learning systems: a technological and pedagogical approach. IEEE J. Latin-Am. Learn. Technol. (IEEE-RITA) **11**(1), 1–8 (2016)
6. Velazquez-Iturbide, J.A., et al.: GreedEx: a visualization tool for experimentation and discovery learning of greedy algorithms. IEEE Trans. Learn. Technol. **6**(2), 130–143 (2013)
7. Jalil, A., Beer, M., Crowther, P.: Pedagogical requirements for mobile learning: a review on MOBIlearn task model. J. Interact. Media Educ. **2015**(1) (2015)
8. Fetaji, M., Fetaji, B.: Devising m-Learning usability framework. In: 33rd International Conference on Proceedings of the ITI Information Technology Interfaces (ITI). IEEE (2011)
9. Elias, T.: Universal instructional design principles for mobile learning. Int. Rev. Res. Open Distrib. Learn. **12**(2), 143–156 (2011)
10. Nokelainen, P.: An empirical assessment of pedagogical usability criteria for digital learning material with elementary school students. Educ. Technol. Soc. **9**(2), 178–197 (2006)
11. Parsons, D., Ryu, H., Cranshaw, M.: A design requirements framework for mobile learning environments. J. Comput. **2**(4), 1–8 (2007)
12. Ortega, M., et al.: GreedEx tab: tool for learning greedy algorithms on mobile devices. In: Eighth International Conference on Mobile, Hybrid, and On-line Learning (2016)
13. Balduino, R.: Introduction to OpenUP (Open Unified Process). Eclipse site (2007)
14. Schwaber, K., Beedle, M.: gilè Software Development with Scrum (2002)
15. Paterno, F.: ConcurTaskTrees: an engineered notation for task models. In: The Handbook of Task Analysis for Human-Computer Interaction, pp. 483–503 (2004)
16. Molina, A.I., et al.: CIAT-GUI: a MDE-compliant environment for developing Graphical User Interfaces of information systems. Adv. Eng. Softw. **52**, 10–29 (2012)

TerrainVis: Collaborative, Interactive, Visualisation Tool for Engaging Residents in Disaster Preparedness

Dylan Mathiesen[1]($\boxtimes$), Trina Myers[1], Ian Atkinson[2], and Jeremy VanDerWal[2]

[1] Discipline of Information Technology, James Cook University, Townsville, Australia
dylan.mathiesen@my.jcu.edu.au, trina.myers@jcu.edu.au
[2] eResearch Centre, James Cook University, Townsville, Australia
{ian.atkinson,jeremy.vanderwal}@jcu.edu.au

Abstract. Modelling and communicating scientific data are paramount in Disaster planning, yet is not easily communicated and interpreted by non-expert stakeholders. These stakeholders are important to the disaster response planning because they can provide firsthand experience and knowledge not capture by quantitative methods. This project aimed to develop a method for catching the attention of community members and engaging them in disaster preparation discussions around real data. A scale model visualisation tool was developed that allows users to interact with flood levels and visualise the impact on their community. Using an "in the wild" Human Computer Interaction (HCI) field trial approach, we found community members engaged in self-directed discussions with strangers about the mitigation of floods and the current zoning of new housing estates in flood prone areas. TerrainVis has helped residents understand the significance of disaster preparation and changed perspectives on evacuation plans by situating them within the data.

Keywords: User experience · Flood modelling · Visualisation · HCI · Disaster preparation

1 Introduction

Threats from natural disasters including cyclones and flooding are a frequent occurrence for residents of Northern Australia. Preparation for these events has a strong association with successful evacuation [3], coping with trauma and social recovery after events. A major motivating factor of residents in preparation for natural disaster is the perceived personal risk of an event [5]. Communicating the risks and importance of disaster planning and preparation is paramount for ensuring the safety of the wider community.

Emergency service organisations and local governments are already deeply involved in disaster planning, educating stakeholders and residents about risks and the importance of preparation. This communication is based on the wealth of expert and scientific knowledge in forecasting and around the impacts of events.

© Springer International Publishing AG 2016
Y. Luo (Ed.): CDVE 2016, LNCS 9929, pp. 110–117, 2016.
DOI: 10.1007/978-3-319-46771-9_15

However, the communication of this knowledge in a form the public can understand is a barrier to furthering community understanding and preparation. Techniques involving community members in the disaster recovery planning process
have shown an improvement of plan quality and benefits for both planners and
individuals [6]. Tools that can directly communicate complex data, such as output from mathematical models, to the community have the potential to improve
the quality of planning and buy-in of residents.

Technologies that can offer immersive data driven learning experiences to
help communicate spatial properties of the datasets include Virtual Reality (VR)
and Augmented Reality (AR) [7] headsets and 3D simulation [4]. However, each
of these technologies poses barriers to collaborative planning. The VR and AR
technologies are effective but headsets are costly because each concurrent participant needs a separate device. These technologies also present a barrier to entry
as new users require preliminary training on use. As a result VR and AR headsets are often considered infeasible to use as large scale community engagement
tools. 3D visualisations and serious games also offer the potential to make data
easier to interpret, however delivering these in large groups is a complex process.

A new application is presented that allows users to view and interact with
datasets on physical terrain scale models. The focus for this paper is flood visualisations developed for an Australian city in the tropics. A system was developed
to communicate storm surge data and is capable of visualising local and web
based maps. Users can define parameters and make adjustments to the storm
surge level to predict locations that would be prone to flooding. Disaster planners can engage the public around this system and use it as a tool to stimulate
conversations and collect local knowledge from residents to improve their understanding of storm surges. A series of 10 field trials were conducted to refine
the tool and observe how the system can support collaborative planning. The
"in the wild" Human Computer Interaction (HCI) field trials found community
members engaged in their own discussions with strangers about the mitigation
of floods and the current zoning of new housing estates in flood prone areas.

2 Design and Implementation

Storm surges from tropical cyclones pose a flood risk to costal communities. To
manage these risks in the event of a cyclone or storm evacuation zones were
developed. These zones are based on historic data and modelling of likely events
and help emergency services evacuate residents during natural disasters. Evacuation zones are presented to the community as paper maps and the justification
behind these is only available in a large technical report. Residents often express
concerns around the accuracy of the evacuation maps as they are often related to
insurance premiums. A new method is needed to help improve the communities
understanding of the risks from storm surges and justify the evacuation zones in
an easier to interpret format. The idea for this research project centered around
visualising storm surges in an interactive manner to help justify the evacuation
zones to residents. Using an interactive tool will allow users to take control and

build their own understanding. The tool must be accessible to all community members and useable with limited instruction or prior understanding.

2.1   Implementation

The first version of the interactive tool used an AR approach, comprised of a printed map that was projected onto from a projector mounted above the table. A physical marker that represented the high water line of the storm surge could be moved around to adjust the peak of the storm surge. A value is shown that indicates the height above mean sea level required to flood the selected area. Users could see how flood prone a particular area was by moving a physical marker to that area. An initial field trial was conducted with this first prototype where the tracking of the physical marker proved to be imprecise causing frustration or confusion in users. The poor tracking performance was caused by the camera used to track markers being unable expose the image very well in bright or unevenly lit environments. This trial helped to inform the next iteration of the development of the interactive tool that aimed to minimise these limitations. Furthermore users were observed using the markers and surge height to understand the topography of the map, this indicated a need for the visualisation of the height independent of the storm surge model.

The second and third versions of TerrainVis use a 3D physical scale terrain model of the landscape. The model used by the second version was built by an artist, which was difficult to align the projected map to. The third version uses a Computer Numerical Control (CNC) mill to build a scale accurate representation of the landscape. Light Detection and Ranging (LiDAR) data of the city was used to mill a physical terrain model out of a block of foam, which was coated with a matte white paint to improve the projection quality. The elevation in the LiDAR data was exaggerated in the physical terrain model to highlight landmarks and make the coastline and rivers more pronounced. A projector is mounted above the physical model using a light stand and the map is projected onto the physical model (Fig. 1). The projection is aligned to the surface and uses the TerrainVis software to align geospatial data to the physical model.

TerrainVis is built as a Web Application in Node.js using WebSockets for communication, OpenLayers for loading map layers and a custom visualisation library for handling animation of spatial layers. A controller Web Application running on an iPad (Fig. 2) allows users to toggle layers, such as evacuation and population maps, control the water level of flood scenarios or explore historic aerial imagery. To ensure the accessibility of the tool to all community members the controller was designed with the objective of requiring limited instruction yet still providing more technical participants the ability to change advanced settings. The design of both the controller and visualisation went through many revisions based on user feedback and in the field observations throughout the research cycles.

Fig. 1. The TerrainVis software projected onto a CNC milled physical terrain model, showing an (unlikely) storm surge of 11 m in the city of Townsville.

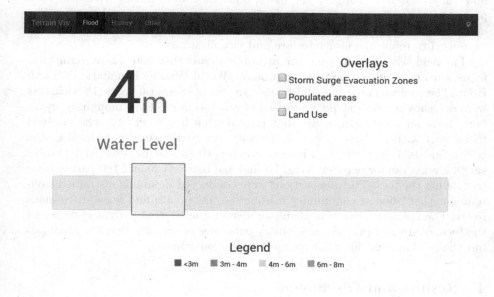

Fig. 2. Tablet controller user interface

3   Methodology - in the Wild Field Trials

Trials and naturalistic deployments of systems have become a core method for investigating user interactions with computing systems. A standard method to test experimental systems within HCI are "in the wild" field trials [1]. This method involves testing new systems with groups of users in settings that are commonly unconstrained and outside of the laboratory. The users can be explicitly or implicitly asked to use the system "naturally". In some cases the users are constrained with set tasks for them to carry out, while other trials avoid controls to encourage "natural" use. Some trials can be a part of a wider experiment, while others adopt a more ethnographic analytic mode [1].

3.1   Methods

This project adopted an observational approach during the field trial where the researcher only interacted with the participants during a preliminary stage. The trial aimed to exploit the unconstrained and unanticipated use of the system "in the wild" to observe actions and reactions of the interplay between groups of random people and how they interact with each other and the system. We observed how people were interacting with the tool, discussions it provoked and how they used it to support the discussions they were having. We also took particular note of any technical problems users ran into using the system. The observations from each session were recorded in a note book and compiled notes were used to refine the user interface and visualisations.

The field trial sessions were run at public events that had an environmental focus, such as a public event run to promote World Wildlife Foundation's Earth Hour. The tool was observed at 10 public events over several years. Participants were not chosen, but instead comprised of random inquisitive community members, from an age demographic that ranged from five to eighty, who stopped to interact with the system out of curiosity. All participants were local to the region and had an interest in how their property would be affected by storm surge. Events ran for between 3 and 7 h and had between 20 and 100 participants controlling the tool. The observations were conducted in an unconstrained environment that allowed community members to enter into and leave discussions freely. The researchers were available to answer questions about the system and the technology and provide preliminary examples of realistic flooding scenarios but the predominant interplay was left to the participants.

4   Results and Discussion

The field trials of the second version of the model generated substantially more interest and engagement of community members than the first. While the first version saw mostly individuals the second version had more groups involved including families and at times large collections of strangers who had joined in. As new groups or individuals would come through, there was often initial

Fig. 3. Community members interacting with the visualisation system at a public event.

hesitation to interact with the display if it was currently not being used. However if it was being used at the time, community members would join in, observing at first and usually asking follow-up questions about the extent of the model and the location of their house. The initial hesitation was easily overcome by the researchers introducing the model with a brief explanation and demonstration of how to interact with it.

At times large groups of participants, up to 15 people, would form on their own (Fig. 3). One of the large groups discussed the vulnerability of their properties and their suburbs. The group also moved on to discuss new housing estates being developed in flood prone areas after one resident shared his aversion to buying a property in a new, low lying, estate. As the discussion developed participants would adjust the model to investigate queries they had and to support their discussion points. Similar discussions developed around the proposal for a new sports stadium and entertainment precinct being developed in areas that are vulnerable to storm surges caused by cyclones.

A trial was conducted at the Mission Beach Cassowary Day using a terrain model of the region developed using the same process. Perspectives of the Mission Beach participants centred on evacuation and the events that would leave their community isolated. This was in direct contrast to the participants in Townsville whose primary concerns were about their personal property and insurance prices.

This difference in the community's perspectives was an unexpected result as both communities have similar issues with roads out of town flooding and are clearly shown on the model. The Townsville residents we pointed this out to were observed adjusting the model to confirm our comments. This seems to indicate an interest of the community members in wanting to learn more about their community and disaster preparation.

4.1   Field Trials

Field Trials of TerrainVis allowed us to test the tool out of a controlled setting and understand how citizens interact with community engagement tools in the real world. Limiting training time was one of the initial requirements for the visualisation tool and this could be easily measured and observed with large numbers of new users each time. The use of such a large participant base wouldn't have been possible with more traditional organised focus groups or observation sessions. Each iteration of the design could be observed and tested with large groups of users all experiencing it for the first time. While the field trials gave an overview of the real world benefits of this tool, more controlled studies are required to refine the delivery process and quantify the value of such an approach.

4.2   Value and Further Applications

During the field trials TerrainVis has received attention from emergency service organisations and several local governments as a tool to support their community engagement efforts. Local councils from the region have already started adopting TerrainVis as a method for engaging the public around their spatial datasets, including storm surge, riverine flooding and urban growth using historic aerial imagery. Furthermore, the planners from these organisations have expressed interest in the value the tool could provide to planning and real-time decision making in their co-ordination centres. Discussions around the tool with planners have provoked novel ideas about how similar tools and technology can be applied to enhance the community engagement activities already undertaken. The visualisation of datasets over a physical model could assist in decision making scenarios where elevation is an important factor in the process.

The findings and software can be applied far beyond simple flood visualisations, for example to urban planning. Urban planning decision-making is based on derived information from a diverse range of requirements but the perspective of the community is not usually integrated in this multifaceted approach. The general public can provide a distinct perspective and firsthand experience at a level not otherwise captured by town planners [2,8]. The use of interactive tools like TerrainVis could enable town planners to uncover community values by allowing community members to experiment and adjust town plans. This interrogation of data by residents will allow them to build a better understanding of plans and assist in the expression of their local knowledge.

4.3   Conclusion

This paper set out to explore the use of interactive, collaborative communication tools to help residents understand the risk of flooding caused by storm surges. Using Field Trials as an exploratory process we developed TerrainVis, a tool that reflected the needs of the users and helped provoke discussions around disaster preparation. The final tool has changed substantially from the outset through the process of observation and analysis. The tool successfully engaged large groups of residents in self-directed discussions and allowed them to investigate the influence of storm surge's on their property and the community. TerrainVis is already enabling local councils to educate and engage residents in disaster planning. Future research into this technology will focus on building a deeper understanding of the potential applications of this tool and identifying best practices for interaction.

References

1. Brown, B., Reeves, S., Sherwood, S.: Into the wild: challenges and opportunities for field trial methods. In: SIGCHI Conference on Human Factors in Computing Systems (CHI 2011), pp. 1657–1666, Vancouver (2011)
2. Corburn, J.: Bringing local knowledge into environmental decision making. J. Plann. Educ. Res. **22**, 420–433 (2003)
3. Dash, N., Gladwin, H.: Evacuation decision making and behavioral responses: individual and household. Nat. Hazards Rev. **8**(3), 69–77 (2007)
4. Lee, E.A.L., Wong, K.W.: Learning with desktop virtual reality: low spatial ability learners are more positively affected. Comput. Educ. **79**, 49–58 (2014). http://dx.doi.org/10.1016/j.compedu.2014.07.010
5. Miceli, R., Sotgiu, I., Settanni, M.: Disaster preparedness and perception of flood risk: a study in an Alpine Valley in Italy. J. Environ. Psychol. **28**(2), 164–173 (2008)
6. Pearce, L.: Disaster management and community planning, and public participation: how to achieve sustainable hazard mitigation. Nat. Hazards **28**(2), 211–228 (2003)
7. Radu, I.: Augmented reality in education: a meta-review and cross-media analysis. Pers. Ubiquitous Comput. **18**(6), 1533–1543 (2014)
8. Yli-pelkonen, V., Kohl, J.: The role of local ecological knowledge in sustainable urban planning : perspectives from Finland. Sustain. Sci. Pract. Policy **1**(1), 3–14 (2005)

Enhancing Design Project Review Board Effectiveness Through a Visual Collaborative Approach

Vasilije Kokotovich[✉] and Catherine P. Killen[✉]

University of Technology Sydney, Sydney, NSW 2007, Australia
{V,Catherine.Killen}@uts.edu.au

Abstract. Organisations with a clear focus on design and development need to carefully and strategically invest in projects. When collaboratively analysing various project proposals, decisions must be made at the macro level using a high-level strategic perspective of the entire portfolio of projects while at the same time considering details at the micro level. It can be difficult for decision makers to absorb the wide range of information about technical, financial, aesthetic, ergonomic, market, and other project factors that need to be considered. Hence, there is a need to better support decision making teams as they collaborate to effectively access and evaluate information. This paper explores the synergies between research and practices in the domain of Project Portfolio Management (PPM) and the disciplines of Design Innovation (DI) and Design Management (DM) to propose a new collaborative visual tool to assist design project review boards in small and medium enterprises (SMEs).

Keywords: Project portfolio management · Design management · Design innovation · Visual collaboration

1 Introduction

The success of design and development organisations pivots on their ability to invest wisely in projects. Decisions must be made at the macro level using a high-level strategic perspective of the entire portfolio of projects, and at the same time at the micro level through design reviews that scrutinise the details of each proposed and existing project. Such design reviews require the evaluation of a range of information about technical, financial, aesthetic, ergonomic, market, and other factors. The difficulty of informing such decisions is compounded when organisations review multiple projects together as a portfolio. The multi-dimensional complexity of design decisions can result in a situation where decision makers 'cannot see the forest for the trees'. Teams of high level decision makers focusing on strategy and overall business outcomes may find it difficult to absorb enough information about individual projects to make the best decisions. In this environment, there is a need to better support decision making teams to effectively access and evaluate information so that they can see both the high level (the forest) as well as the project level (the trees).

We explore the synergies between research and practices in the domain of Project Portfolio Management (PPM) and the disciplines of Design Innovation (DI) and Design

© Springer International Publishing AG 2016
Y. Luo (Ed.): CDVE 2016, LNCS 9929, pp. 118–125, 2016.
DOI: 10.1007/978-3-319-46771-9_16

Management (DM) to propose a new collaborative visual tool to assist design project review boards. Our proposed tool is designed with the needs of small and medium enterprises (SMEs) in mind.

SMEs face extra challenges on two levels. First, their decisions can be particularly multi-faceted as they must make strategic decisions about project investments while also considering project level details that would not be considered at the strategic level in larger organisations. For example such decisions may be tied in and conducted in parallel with detailed design reviews. Second, SMEs do not have the resources or need to justify a fully comprehensive PPM software solution. Such systems are evolving, but are generally large, cumbersome, and expensive and require standardized approaches to most project work that present constraints and barriers that are not matched by benefits in a SME environment.

This paper proposes a tool that aims to provide an enhanced cognitive fit by displaying project information in a manner sympathetic with the problem at hand using network mapping principles augmented by a temporal dimension, and allowing tailored parsing, filtering and synthesis of diverse information. To better understand the context, we now turn our attention to Project Portfolio Management (PPM).

2   Project Portfolio Management (PPM)

Project Portfolio Management is an evolving discipline for the strategic management of a portfolio of projects [1]. By taking a portfolio perspective for decisions about project decisions, organizations aim to achieve the necessary collaborative oversight to increase the overall value of the portfolio. Such group decisions require balancing factors such as risk, return, resources and benefits so that the portfolio as a whole meets the strategic and other objectives.

From a portfolio level, group decisions must be made to select and fund new projects, monitor existing projects and at times to reprioritize projects, including cancelling projects and reallocating resources to projects when better opportunities arise. PPM decisions are often made in stages throughout the project lifecycle with the aim to reduce project and portfolio risk over time. Best practice research shows that such decisions are best made by teams of experienced decision makers [2, 3]. By bringing experienced people together, and providing structures, processes and systems to provide access to information about the decisions at hand, PPM provides a locus for accumulation of a large amount of information about projects (for example about technical, financial, aesthetic, ergonomic, market, and other factors) and a forum for strategic decision making.

The challenge for PPM decision making is how best to capture and analyze such a large amount of information. Multiple research studies attempt to address this problem by proposing computational optimization models that aim to quantify all aspects of the decision problem and use computer algorithms to select the best projects. Such systems are not well adopted by industry amid concerns that the aggregation of information obscures important considerations and complex interactions between aspects are not usually included [4]. Such optimization systems are especially unsuited to the types of multifaceted decisions made in SMEs. However, computers do have a strong role to play in assisting SMEs (and other organizations) manage portfolio information and decision making. The use of computers to generate visual displays of portfolio data assists teams of decision makers and is associated with improved portfolio outcomes, and research indicates that visual displays with high cognitive fit (the design of the display aligns with the nature of the task and the mental models required to evaluate the information) will support better decisions [5, 6]. Systems that provide a visual interface and facilitate human input, allowing for intuition and interaction, have the potential to offer the best of both computer power and human cognitive capability [7, 8].

Portfolio decisions in SMEs generally include high level management and key stakeholders. Managing and balancing risk is a central aspect of portfolio approaches, however a focus on financial concerns can dominate the discussion at the expense of more strategic considerations [9], especially in SMEs. The literature contends we need to be concerned about larger socio-economic, cultural, legal and environmental issues that are dynamically interrelated to technology and science [see: 10–12]. These aspects must be embedded in the decision making processes for PPM.

Given the accelerating rate of change adding to the complexity of PPM decision making, there is equally an accelerated need for tools to assist with complex collaborations within diverse decision making teams drawn from an increasingly large variety of backgrounds, expertise, and domains of knowledge. Moreover, those who are responsible for PPM increasingly work in an extremely intense environment. Yet, in SMEs they still need to make highly detailed and nuanced technical design decisions along with portfolio-level strategic decisions. In such an environment decision makers need to have tools, skills, and experiential knowledge suited to 'extreme' collaborative environments.

The issues highlighted above suggest a need to shape new approaches to support the PPM decision environment. We next turn to the literature in the areas of Design Thinking - Design innovation and Design Management to draw inspiration and understanding of decision processes in uncertain environments to support the development of appropriate tools for operating in a new era of PPM.

3   Design Innovation and Visual Reasoning

Design Innovation [DI] and Design Management [DM] are disciplines for fostering the development of new and successful designs. The design disciplines emphasise the importance of divergent types of information flows and thinking strategies. In many ways DI and DM rely heavily on design thinking methods in order to move projects forward.

The literature surrounding design innovation suggests design is a problem solving activity, and like all such activities requires reasoning. Designers often use drawings (visual imagery) to aid conceptualisations and design reasoning to reason through complex concepts (for example see [13, 14]). Hence design reasoning can be considered synonymous with visual reasoning in that designers may use drawing as a vehicle for reasoning. In point of fact, according to Herbert [15] drawing is considered to be a designer's principle means of thinking. The design process is seen as one in which designers visually reason internally via mental imagery, then draw generating external representations of that imagery, reflect and reason about the external imagery, then draw again. Moreover, this symbiotic relationship between the internal visual imagery and the external visual imagery to reason to a solution is seen by Goldschmidt [13] as a systematic dialectic between the two modes of reasoning.

Essentially the cognitive psychology literature (for example see [16]) views visual reasoning as the use of visual spatial relations in making inferences about corresponding conceptual relations, concluding that external visual representations have special properties which can aid reasoning about higher order abstract concepts. Moreover, the cognitive research focusing on visual reasoning (see for example, [16–21]) has some common themes. While the research mentioned here investigated the resolution of physics problems, economics problems, or biology problems, the overarching view is that diagrams can, and often do, have a significant role in reasoning through problems. Hence, in general when operating across varied domains of knowledge, problem solvers must; (1) identify the underlying nature and structure of the problem (2) generate representations of the problems (i.e. Diagrams) to aid solution discovery, (3) make inferences from these representations which lead to a resolution of the problem. A detailed analysis of the visual reasoning literature reveals these three aspects of reasoning through a problem are seen as interdependent. Fundamentally, abstract knowledge and drawings are thought to mutually influence each other. They are thought to be co-dependent. Indeed, Kindfield [20] argues conceptual knowledge and diagrams co-evolve. These studies are significant here in that their core themes are not unlike those found in the design literature (see for example [22–24]) or indeed the PPM literature.

The above notwithstanding, in the main the visual reasoning research found in the cognitive psychology literature empirically investigates well-defined problems, which have one solution [i.e. solving a physics or chemistry problem]. Conversely, both of the domains of Design and PPM require a capacity to work through complex problems filled with uncertainty. Just as the act of design involves creative visual reasoning about abstract relationships, PPM decision makers also draw upon visual reasoning to make inferences about corresponding conceptual relations. For example, visual representations are commonly used to assist with PPM, for example 2×2 matrix displays are commonly used to help decision makers balance aspects such as risk and reward [25] and network displays provide visual spatial information about interdependencies between projects [6]. Such tools are shown to promote collaborative decisions and are associated with better portfolio outcomes [2, 3] however such existing tools only focus on specific aspects of the decision space. The availability of a more comprehensive visual tool could further assist PPM decision makers and improve portfolio outcomes. Such a tool would employ visual representations with special properties which can aid reasoning about higher order abstract concepts. Given the parallels between the domains of visual reasoning, design, and PPM, it seems prudent to turn our discussions towards a possible collaborative visual reasoning tool.

4 Project Analysis Review Clusters [PARC] and Visual Reasoning

The literature highlights three important aspects that are common to both the PPM and design (DI and DM) decision environments; (1) Decisions are best made in teams by collaboration between experienced people, (2) Decision makers need access to a wide range of information about the projects, and (3) Visual representations of data enable teams of decision makers to better evaluate and discuss relevant information.

Building on these three aspects, we propose a new visual collaborative tool to improve the effectiveness of design project review board decisions. The tool is designed to meet the needs of SMEs by providing groups of decision makers with prompts to consider a wide range of aspects of the problem at hand, and tools to promote and capture discussions and decisions about the specific issues under consideration. As one of the common shortcomings of PPM can be a narrow reliance on financial issues at the expense of more strategic and longer-term consideration, we draw upon the EPISTLE framework [26]. EPISTLE is an acronym for the seven main issues: Economic, Psychological, and so on as shown in Fig. 1 along with symbols used in the Project Analysis Review Clusters [PARC] tool.

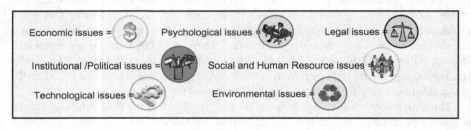

Fig. 1. Symbols representing the EPISTLE framework

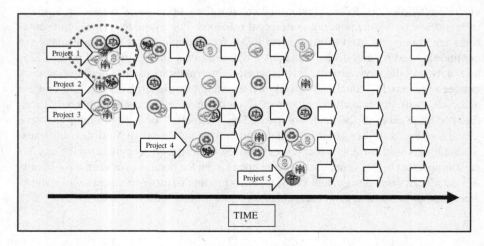

Fig. 2. Project analysis review clustering panel. (Color figure online)

In our proposed tool, decision makers interact with a visual interface providing an overview of projects over time as shown in Fig. 2. Each project is shown on a row, over set time intervals representing the frequency of meetings for design project portfolio reviews. Each column represents one meeting where a number of projects are evaluated and decisions are made, and projects start and end at different times.

The interface prompts the decision making team to consider each of the seven EPISTLE factors for each project at each time period, and provides visual symbols to record team decisions on the factors that are important at each stage. The prompts and the visual display are designed to promote active discussion and collaboration among the decision makers members.

At any one time the column indicates the current issues of concern for the ongoing project decision making. For example the first column (starting on the left) shows the first time period where three projects are discussed by the decision making team, usually in a face-to-face meeting (this tool could also be designed for virtual meetings). The next column represents a new meeting of the decision team in the next time period (which could be each month or quarter for example). The tool enables review of the previous input and prompts identification and discussion of the current issues and their interactions before making decisions.

Figure 3 shows an expanded view that provides more detail about the decision considerations of Project 1 in the first time period (indicated by the red oval in Fig. 2). This expanded view prompts decision makers to consider interactions and relationships between the relevant factors and provides a format to record the information in a visual spatial 'networked' arrangement. In an intuitive display, each arrow indicates an interaction between factors and allows textual or other information to be captured and easily retrieved (see the right side of Fig. 3 for example textual information). At its core this aspect of the tool draws upon an empirical study that demonstrated the utility of non-hierarchical mind-mapping as a visual reasoning tool for ill-structured design problems [27]. Portfolio level design project review decisions are also ill-structured and stand to benefit from such an approach.

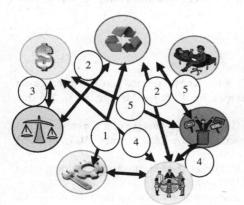

Sample explanatory notes on relationships:
[1] When considering the technical material specification aspects and the associated manufacturing aspects in the development of the proposed product, there is a need to consider the environmental sustainability aspects [2] If we fail to appropriately consider the environmental aspects of the material me are likely to encounter both legal and social problems. [3] Legal problems due to environmental issues may result in a law suit adding unnecessary cost to the project [4] Damage to the social reputation may result in a drop the share value of the company and add costs to the project and may also stimulate action by political institutions. [5] Action by political institutions could result in changes to environmental regulation and affecting all our operations.

Fig. 3. Project 1 detail of cluster for cross project analysis and review.

By eliciting a wider range of considerations and discussions, our proposed tool is designed to enhance collaborative decision making and more effectively draw upon the diverse expertise of the members of the decision team. Furthermore, by providing visual feedback on the status and a visual interface for recording further details of the discussion, the tool is designed to provide easy access to past information to help inform both ongoing and future collaborative decision making.

5   Conclusions

This paper draws upon the domains of PPM, Design, and Visual Reasoning and has identified a number of core themes that have resonance within the three domains. We have proposed a tool that aims to promote collaborative decision making in design project review boards in SMEs.

The tool uses the power of a visual interface that provides access to data and promotes interaction to support decisions at the macro level (using a high-level strategic perspective of the entire portfolio of projects) and at the same time at a micro level (capturing the nuanced relationships between and among the various issues). The tool is designed to prompt decision makers to consider a wide range of factors, and uses network-based, non-hierarchical relationships to allow for capturing the complexity of the situation. In an era of exponential technological change, it is especially important to ensure that decisions are made that consider the larger socio-cultural issues that are dynamically interrelated to technology and scientific advances.

In short, we have proposed a tool to improve decision makers' ability to access the right information, at the right time, in a graphical form. The tool is proposed to enhance collaboration among teams of decision makers so that they see and understand the 'forest' and the 'trees' and are able to make the best decisions to support organisational success. Further work is required in the development of the tool, followed by testing with design project review boards in SMEs. Such research would serve to advance our understanding of the collaborative visualization process while taking a step toward improving PPM in SMEs.

References

1. Killen, C.P., Jugdev, K., Drouin, N., Petit, Y.: Advancing project and portfolio management research: applying strategic management theories. Int. J. Project Manage. **30**(5), 525–538 (2012)
2. Cooper, R.G., Edgett, S.J., Kleinschmidt, E.J.: Portfolio management for new product development: results of an industry best practices study. R&D Manage. **31**(4), 361–381 (2001)
3. Killen, C.P., Hunt, R.A., Kleinschmidt, E.J.: Project portfolio management for product innovation. Int. J. Qual. Reliab. Manage. **25**(1), 24–38 (2008)
4. Frey, T., Buxmann, P.: IT project portfolio management-a structured literature review. In: Paper Presented at the ECIS, pp. 1–26 (2012)
5. Vessey, I.: Cognitive fit: a theory-based analysis of the graphs versus tables literature. Decis. Sci. **22**(2), 219–241 (1991)

6. Killen, C.P.: Visualizations of project interdependencies for project portfolio decision making: evaluation through decision experiments. In: Paper Presented at the Proceedings of the Decision Sciences Institute (DSI) Annual Meeting, Baltimore (2013)

7. Zheng, G., Vaishnavi, V.K.: A multidimensional perceptual map approach to project prioritization and selection. AIS Trans. Hum. Comput. Interact. 3(2), 82–103 (2011)

8. Tergan, S., Keller, T. (eds.): Knowledge and Information Visualisation. Springer, Heidelberg (2005)

9. Raz, T., Shendar, A.J., Dvir, A.: Risk management, project success, and technological uncertainty. R&D Manage. 32(2), 101–109 (2002)

10. Porter, A.L., et al.: A Guidebook for Technology Assessment and Impact Analysis. North Holland, New York (1980)

11. Girifalco, L.A.: Dynamics of Technological Change. Van Nostrand Reinhold, New York (1991)

12. Karamchedu, V.R.: It's Not About the Technology: Developing the Craft of Thinking for a High Technology Corporation. Springer, New York (2005)

13. Goldschmidt, G.: The dialectics of sketching. Des. Stud. 4, 123–143 (1991)

14. Do, E.Y., Gross, M.D.: Drawing as a means to design reasoning. In: Visual Representation, Reasoning and Interaction in Design Workshop Notes, Artificial Intelligence in Design 1996 (AID 1996), 22–27 June 1996. Stanford University (1996)

15. Herbert, D.M.: Architectural Study Drawings. Van Nostrand Reinhold, New York (1993)

16. Gattis, M., Holyoak, K.J.: Mapping conceptual to spatial relations in visual reasoning. J. Exp. Psychol.: Learn. Mem. 22(1), 231–239 (1996)

17. Larkin, J.H.: Simon, H.A: Why a diagram is (sometimes) worth 10,000 words. Cogn. Sci. 11, 65–99 (1987)

18. Larkin, J.H.: The role of problem representation in Physics. In: Gentner, D., Stevens, A.L. (eds.) Mental Models Erlbaum, pp. 75–97. Hillsdale, New Jersey (1983)

19. Tabachneck, H.J., Leonardo, A.M., Simon, H.A.: How does an expert use a graph? a model of visual and verbal inferencing in economics. In: Ram, A., Eislet, K. (eds.) Proceedings of the 16th Annual Conference of the Cognitive Science Society, pp. 842–847. Erlbaum, New Jersey (1994)

20. Kindfield, A.C.H.: Expert diagrammatic reasoning in Biology. In: AAAI Spring Symposium on Reasoning with Diagrammatic Representations, Stanford University, California, pp. 41–46 (1992)

21. Anzi, Y., Yokoyama, T.: Internal models in physic problem solving. Cogn. Instr. 1, 397–450 (1984)

22. Lawson, B.: How Designers Think. The Architectural Press, London (1980)

23. Goldschmidt, G.: On visual design thinking: the viz kids of architecture. Des. Stud. 15(2), 158–174 (1994)

24. Schon, D.A., Wiggins, G.: Kinds of seeing and their functions in designing. Des. Stud. 13(2), 135–156 (1992)

25. Mikkola, J.H.: Portfolio management of R&D projects: implications for innovation management. Technovation 21(7), 423–435 (2001)

26. Kokotovich, V.: Issues in design systemics: the need for dynamic re-framing tools in design and design engineering. In: Digital Proceedings of the Tenth International Symposium on Tools and Methods of Competitive Engineering, Delft University of Technology, Budapest, Hungary, pp. 773–784 (2014)

27. Kokotovich, V.: Problem analysis and thinking tools: an empirical study of non-hierarchical mind mapping. Des. Stud. 29(1), 49–69 (2008)

DataChopin - Designing Interactions
for Visualisation Composition
in a Co-Located, Cooperative Environment

Daniel Filonik[✉], Markus Rittenbruch[✉], and Marcus Foth[✉]

Queensland University of Technology, Brisbane, Australia
{daniel.filonik,m.rittenbruch,m.foth}@qut.edu.au
https://www.qut.edu.au/

Abstract. This article presents our interaction design for *DataChopin*, based on an extensive survey and classification of visualisation for exploratory data analysis. Its distinctive characteristics are the use of a large-scale display wall as a shared desktop, as well as flexible composition mechanisms for incremental and piece-wise construction of visualisations. We chose composability as a guiding principle in our design, since it is essential to open-ended exploration, as well as collaborative analysis. For one, it enables truly exploratory inquiry by letting users freely examine different combinations of data, rather than offering a predetermined set of choices. Perhaps more importantly, it provides a foundation for data analysis through collaborative interaction with visualisations. If data and visualisations are composable, they can split into independent parts and recombined during the analytical process, allowing analysts to seamlessly transition between closely- and loosely-coupled work.

Keywords: Co-located collaboration · Exploratory data analysis · Visualisation composition

1 Introduction

The need for better understanding of abstract data is not new, although it is exacerbated by the growing ease and speed of data acquisition. When automatic methods fail, human background knowledge and intuition are required. Yet as Norman [13] points out, human cognitive abilities are highly constrained and our real ingenuity lies in the ability to devise external aids that enhance them. While our cognitive capabilities for storing and manipulating data may be limited, we have evolved to perform many analytical processing tasks visually. Therefore, a common approach is to devise visual representations of data. However, the choice of representation is not trivial and depends heavily on the task at hand. Consequently, a wide range of visualisation systems have been developed, designed specifically for certain tasks. While such systems with predefined components are typically effective in their intended area of application, they are often too limited for open-ended, exploratory analysis, which requires the ability to manipulate

© Springer International Publishing AG 2016
Y. Luo (Ed.): CDVE 2016, LNCS 9929, pp. 126–133, 2016.
DOI: 10.1007/978-3-319-46771-9_17

and tailor representations based on emerging questions and insights. In order to address this, researchers have systematically studied the structure of graphical representations, along with the rules by which visualisations are constructed. Our proposed system continues this line of research, building on existing theoretical and formal models to arrive at a practical implementation and explore suitable interaction techniques and metaphors for cooperative visualisation specification.

A key promise of novel interaction technologies are better ways for people to work cooperatively. Concepts that were previously only explored in research – such as large-scale environments augmented with interactive capabilities – are becoming technologically feasible. We aim to utilise such technologies to create engaging experiences that put multiple analysts in a shared environment and elicit contextual knowledge from these analysts. The importance of contextual knowledge for the analytical process was already pointed out by Cleveland:

> "Conclusions spring from data when this information is combined with the prior knowledge of the subject under investigation." [6, p. 5]

When multiple analysts join efforts, and are given effective tools to share and communicate their visions, the potential for more diverse and unexpected insights stands to grow accordingly.

2   Related Work

As part of this review, we examine existing systems that allow flexible visualisation specification for exploratory data analysis. Since a multitude of such systems have been developed, we do not attempt to create an exhaustive survey. Instead, we aim to highlight conceptual differences based on notable examples. Furthermore, we identify and categorize the predominant interaction methods, highlighting their commonalities and differences. Since our goal is the design of an interface for ad-hoc end-user composition and collaboration, we place particular focus on how the different conceptual models relate to interface mechanisms and metaphors for visualisation construction.

In order to develop flexible systems for visualisation specification it is necessary to understand the integral components and structure of graphics. The systematic analysis graphical representations, lies at the core of an important set of visualisation theories, sometimes referred to as structural theories of graphics. Much of this research can be traced back to the *Semiology of Graphics* by Bertin [2], which represents one of the first attempts to interpret graphics as a language with formal rules. Another prevalent theoretical model is that of a *visualisation pipeline*, as popularised by Card et al. [5]. This model provides a description of the visualisation process as a sequence of transformation steps.

Depending on the chosen theoretical perspective, certain paradigms for composing visualisations naturally lend themselves. Perhaps the most obvious form of visualisation specification is an imperative algorithm that issues drawing commands to produce graphical primitives. Such specifications provide fine grained control, but require familiarity with programming concepts, such as variables and control flow. However, the approach as its strengths, as evidenced by the popularity of *Processing* [7]. In contrast to imperative algorithms, more recent approaches employ a declarative paradigm, placing emphasis on what to display rather than how to produce it. Such a specification features a description of a graphical scene, and allows connecting data attributes to visual attributes of graphical elements. Libraries based on the *data binding* model are *Protovis* [3] and its successor *D3* [4]. On another end of the spectrum, researchers have created automated presentation tools eliminate the need for a specification entirely. Such research advanced the study of graphic primitives and pioneered key ideas, such as composition algebras for graphical marks [11,14]. Extending further on the ideas of structural theories of graphics, researchers have developed sophisticated graphics grammars [20,21], resulting in specification languages that allow the assembly of statistical graphics from fine-grained, modular units of composition. These ideas also provide the foundation for *Vega* [15], the low-level declarative language behind *Lyra* – as well as *VizQL* [8], the query-based language behind *Tableau*. Meanwhile, the prominence of the visualisation pipeline model has lead to the adoption of a data flow paradigm in many systems. The pipeline structure provides a blueprint for the implementation of reconfigurable visualisation components, such as those in *VTK* [16].

In addition to underlying conceptual models, there are different options for exposing them through graphical interfaces. These aspects are closely related, since a good interface effectively communicates the conceptual model to help users develop their mental model. The following classification aims to characterise the predominant interaction concepts in visualisation software today, including select examples beyond the domain of visualisation as guideposts for future developments.

Chart Typology. Novice friendly programs are often limited to a predefined set of charts, often represented as a catalogue of icons in the graphical interface. However, chart typologies have been heavily criticised by researchers like Wilkinson, who claim that choosing from a limited charts gives "the user an impression of having explored data rather than the experience" [21, p. 2]. This appears problematic especially for exploratory analysis, as it offers no way for users to produce visual representations beyond those explicitly supported by the system.

Text and Preview. A very basic form of graphical support is an environment where text-based specification is accompanied by a preview window. This approach is adopted by software like *Processing Development Environment* [7] and *GPL* [21]. The former employs an imperative programming style, whereas the latter is a proprietary implementation of Wilkinson's graphics grammar. A modified version of the grammar is publicly available in the form of the *ggplot2* [20] module for the R statistical computing environment. While text input is often challenging on touch interfaces, it can be assisted through autocompletion or direct manipulation of the parse tree.

Tokens and Slots. More sophisticated graphical interfaces allow data binding via property sheets, or by dragging and dropping tokens on designated regions of the interface. Such a model is realised in software like *ILOG Discovery* [1], *Polaris* [17], and its successor *Tableau* [8]. These interfaces often incorporate abstract representations of the variables in a data set, which can be manipulated via drag-and-drop gestures. This commonly represents *data binding*, whereby variables are bound to properties of the visual representation. Furthermore, *Polaris* and *Tableau* also inherit ideas from *visualisation grammars*, such as a compositional algebra to specify combinations and nestings of data variables.

Boxes and Wires. Another interaction concept are boxes and wires, also known as the node-link model of visual programming, which is a natural fit for the *data flow* model of visualisation. This approach combines a visual notation with expressive power of text-based specification languages. Complex flows are created by placing processing units that act as operators on the data, and subsequently connecting their inputs and outputs to create a graph. Such a model employed by *VTK* [16] in the form of *VTK Designer*.

Pipeline Stages. Such interfaces are characterised by high-level abstractions focused on the application domain. For example, they might be restricted to pipelines with a limited set of stages, which are directly represented within the interface as text or icons. This style is followed by the *Lark* [18] application, which uses a pipeline with customisation points at three stages: analytical abstraction, spatial layout, and presentation. Furthermore, *LIVE Singapore! Data Browser* [10] and *Datacollider* from MIT's SENSEable City Lab apply similar models. Outside of the visualisation domain, other notable interfaces using very specialised programming models are *Reactable* [9] for musical composition and *Kodu* [12] for specifying simple behaviours in games.

Drawing Canvas. Generally, the interaction model of graphical applications is not a good fit for the task of visualisation specification, as manual manipulation of marks quickly becomes repetitive and tedious. However, paired with facilities for automation and *data binding*, this interaction style can become feasible. In this respect, the web-based *Lyra* [15] application is worth mentioning, as it is inspired by Victor's interface for drawing dynamic visualisations [19]. The users create and arrange visual marks on the canvas through direct manipulation. Subsequently, data variables are dragged onto various anchors in order to bind data to visual properties.

3   Design Process

Based on our review, we assessed the identified interaction concepts for use co-located, collaborative settings. Ultimately, this process informed the design our final artefact, named *DataChopin*. The system was designed from the ground up for co-located, multi-user interactions. Therefore, data sets and visualisations are associated with user accounts. Once a user authenticates with the system, their presence is indicated by a top-level menu element on the shared desktop, which features an avatar and provides access to personal content.

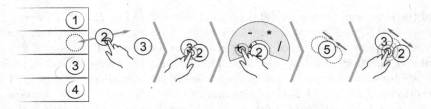

Fig. 1. Selecting and combining data attributes to compose expressions.

Data Interactions. The interaction metaphor for selecting and manipulating data attributes was inspired by poker chips. Our design intuition was that these elements would introduce interesting dynamics to a collaborative analysis process. Poker chips are employed in a variety of tabletop games, enabling playful mechanics and social interactions. They carry associations with collecting, exchanging, and negotiating. Our goal was to capture the affordances of poker chips, while enhancing their digital counterparts with capabilities for data analysis.

Piling tokens on top of each other provides a mechanism for mapping functions over the data, as illustrated in Fig. 1. Tapping on a pile of tokens opens a radial auto-completion menu of applicable functions based on the types of the tokens in the pile. If we limit ourselves to unary or binary functions, we can display the menu as soon as a user drops one token onto another, if there are applicable functions based on their types. If tokens originate from different data sets, they are considered to be incompatible. In this case we can introduce a repulsive force pushing the tokens apart to indicate that they cannot be combined. Once a function is applied, the token pile merges into a single token representing the composite expression. The action can be undone by repeated tapping on a composite token to recover the constituent parts.

View Interactions. The primary interaction mechanism for creating and manipulating graphical marks is through direct interaction with the visualisation canvas, along with a drag-and-drop mechanism for data binding. Interactive elements in the drawing canvas are the *origin*, *axes*, *marks*, and *background*. They are animated to change colour and size as the user drags data tokens to indicate whenever meaningful actions are possible, based on the type of the expression that constitutes the dragged payload. Initially, the visualisation canvas is empty with only the origin visible. Placing a token on any of the interactive elements creates or modifies the mark layer associated with the data set. Dropping tokens on the *origin* spawns new coordinate axes, binding the data attribute to the respective positional component of the marks. Placing tokens on any of the *axes* creates or replaces the existing binding. Dropping on tokens on any of the *marks* binds the data attribute to a visual attribute of the mark as determined by the type. Finally, dropping tokens on the *background* prompts the system to automatically choose an appropriate mapping.

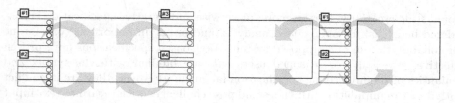

Fig. 2. Collaborative configurations based on arrangements of interface elements.

Cooperative Analysis. The top-level interface elements adopt a classical window metaphor and can be freely positioned in the large-scale, shared-desktop environment. As different users have access to different data sets through their personal profiles, it introduces the need to exchange tokens and work together to achieve the desired visualisation results. The system allows users with different areas of interest and expertise to build personal repertoires of data, and subsequently share and divide responsibilities as they work together.

A common starting configuration is a single data repository and visualisation canvas for each user. This supports a loosely coupled style of cooperation, during which the users mostly work independently on their own canvas. Nevertheless, due to the nature of the shared desktop, even such configurations frequently bring about interactions, such as users glancing over to see other visualisations and asking for instructions. Often times, once users recreate somebody else's visualisation with their own data, they are eager to compare the results.

Another configuration that we explored was a single, shared drawing canvas that multiple users gathered around, as illustrated by Fig. 2a. This configurations supports a closely coupled style of cooperation, and is either based on a single data of shared interest, or on multiple data sets from the repositories of different users, resulting in a combined, layered visualisation. The latter is made possible due to composability being an integral feature of the system. Finally, as a single view can lead to contention, we also experimented with compromises between a single, shared and multiple, independent views. One configuration that appears promising are two drawing canvases, with a number of shared data repositories in between them, depicted in Fig. 2b. That way, two groups can work independently, both having access to the same data sets. If the data used by both groups comes from the same data sets, the visualisations are always compatible, meaning that the groups can interchange and combine parts of their visualisation specifications at any given time.

4   Discussion

Our work lead us to survey the spectrum of conceptual models and interaction concepts for visualisation specification, weighing their associated trade-offs in the specific context of exploratory analysis in collaborative environments. Early on, we ruled out static chart typologies, due to concerns that their rigidity would stifle creativity. Furthermore, piece-wise and iterative specification is considered beneficial for open-ended analysis, and forms an important cornerstone for collaboration in our proposed system. Text-based specifications have proven effective, especially for seasoned users who are familiar with the syntax and semantics of the underlying specification language. However, they are in conflict with direct manipulation principles and pose challenges with regard to text input on touch-based interfaces. While boxes and wires provide a visual notation capable of modelling general-purpose programming languages, their generality comes at the cost of usability. In our experience, we found the domain of exploratory analysis sufficiently constrained to employ a special-purpose abstraction. In our classification, *DataChopin* is a hybrid of tokens and slots, combined with a visualisation canvas for declarative data binding.

So far, we have conducted informal evaluations our system, and our initial experiences have been positive. Cooperating in a co-located setting successfully elicited discussions about the data and participants were quick to share their interpretations. The use of a multi-user, shared-desktop environment was commonly regarded as beneficial. In contrast to the single-user, personal systems that participants were accustomed to, the idea of multiple analysts working in tandem was perceived as empowering. Rather than a single person being in charge and driving the analytical process, the interface enabled them to perform actions in parallel and pursue smaller tasks independently. Therefore, we continue to focus our efforts on placing participants in shared interaction environments, aiming to leverage the implicit and explicit communication channels to stimulate creativity and assist analysis. In future work, we are planning more formal evaluations to assess the expressiveness and effectiveness of the proposed compositional model.

5   Conclusion

Our review has shown that HCI research on cooperative visualisation specification is still lacking. While some systems support distributed, asynchronous collaboration, few focus on co-located, synchronous settings. With the exception of *Lark*, the majority of existing interfaces were designed for single-user, personal environments. This article represents another step towards closing the research gap. We have classified predominant interaction methods for visualisation specification, and derived a design specifically aimed at facilitating cooperation in a shared interaction environment. The result is *DataChopin*, a system for large-scale, shared-desktop environments, based on the premise of composable visualisations. Often, formal visualisation models have been studied in theory and divorced from HCI considerations. In contrast to that, our work presents a practical approach, covering the design and implementation of a working prototype.

Acknowledgments. We would like to thank the Visualisation and eResearch (ViseR) team at QUT for their technical support. Illustrations in this article contain icons by GestureWorks, released under CC BY-SA.

References

1. Baudel, T.: A canonical representation of data-linear visualization algorithms. Technical report, IBM, Software Group, ILOG Products (2010)
2. Bertin, J.: Semiology of Graphics: Diagrams, Networks, Maps. The University of Wisconsin Press, Madison (1983). (Translated by Berg, W.J.)
3. Bostock, M., Heer, J.: Protovis: a graphical toolkit for visualization. IEEE Trans. Vis. Comput. Graph. **15**(6), 1121–1128 (2009)
4. Bostock, M., Ogievetsky, V., Heer, J.: D^3 data-driven documents. IEEE Trans. Vis. Comput. Graph. **17**(12), 2301–2309 (2011)
5. Card, S.K., Mackinlay, J.D., Shneiderman, B.: Readings in Information Visualization: Using Vision to Think. Morgan Kaufmann, San Francisco (1999)
6. Cleveland, W.S.: Visualizing Data. Hobart Press, Summit (1993)
7. Fry, B.: Visualizing Data: Exploring and Explaining Data with the Processing Environment. O'Reilly Media, Sebastopol (2007)
8. Heer, J., Mackinlay, J.D., Stolte, C., Agrawala, M.: Graphical histories for visualization: supporting analysis, communication, and evaluation. IEEE Trans. Vis. Comput. Graph. **14**(6), 1189–1196 (2008)
9. Jordà, S., Kaltenbrunner, M., Geiger, G., Alonso, M.: The reacTable: a tangible tabletop musical instrument and collaborative workbench. In: ACM SIGGRAPH 2006 Sketches, p. 91. ACM (2006)
10. Kloeckl, K., Senn, O., Ratti, C.: Enabling the real-time city: live singapore!. J. Urban Technol. **19**(2), 89–112 (2012)
11. Mackinlay, J.D.: Automating the design of graphical presentations of relational information. ACM Trans. Graph. (TOG) **5**(2), 110–141 (1986)
12. MacLaurin, M.B.: The design of kodu: a tiny visual programming language for children on the xbox 360. In: ACM Sigplan Notices, vol. 46, pp. 241–246. ACM (2011)
13. Norman, D.A.: Things that Make Us Smart: Defending Human Attributes in the Age of the Machine. Basic Books, New York (1993)
14. Radu, V.: Application. In: Radu, V. (ed.) Stochastic Modeling of Thermal Fatigue Crack Growth. ACM, vol. 1, pp. 63–70. Springer, Heidelberg (2015)
15. Satyanarayan, A., Heer, J.: Lyra: an interactive visualization design environment. In: Computer Graphics Forum (Proceedings of EuroVis) (2014)
16. Schroeder, W.J., Lorenson, B.: Visualization Toolkit: An Object-Oriented Approach to 3-D Graphics, 1st edn. Prentice Hall PTR, Upper Saddle River (1996)
17. Stolte, C., Tang, D., Hanrahan, P.: Polaris: a system for query, analysis, and visualization of multidimensional relational databases. IEEE Trans. Vis. Comput. Graph. **8**(1), 52–65 (2002)
18. Tobiasz, M., Isenberg, P., Carpendale, S.: Lark: coordinating co-located collaboration with information visualization. IEEE Trans. Vis. Comput. Graph. **15**(6), 1065–1072 (2009)
19. Victor, B.: Drawing dynamic visualizations. http://vimeo.com/66085662. Accessed 31 Aug 2014
20. Wickham, H.: A layered grammar of graphics. J. Comput. Graph. Stat. **19**(1), 3–28 (2010)
21. Wilkinson, L.: The Grammar of Graphics. Springer, New York (2005)

What Next in Designing Personalized Visualization of Web Information

Shibli Saleheen[1]([✉]), Wei Lai[1], Xiaodi Huang[2], Weidong Huang[3], and Mao Lin Huang[4]

[1] Faculty of Science, Engineering and Technology,
Swinburne University of Technology, Hawthorn, VIC, Australia
{ssaleheen,wlai}@swin.edu.au
[2] School of Computing and Mathematics, Charles Sturt University,
Albury, NSW, Australia
xhuang@csu.edu.au
[3] School of Engineering and ICT, University of Tasmania,
Newnham, TAS, Australia
tony.huang@utas.edu.au
[4] School of Software, University of Technology Sydney,
Ultimo, NSW, Australia
mao.huang@uts.edu.au

Abstract. Current state of the art in personalized visualization of web information is tailored to provide a better view of how the information is resided and connected to each other inside the internet. With the recent enhancement in information and communication technology, users are provided a very large amount of information when they search for a particular information from a specific website. Studies show that, user can perceive the information in a more better way if they are provided the information with visual representation instead of its textual counterpart. However, to be effective to the users, the visual representation should be specific to the need of a particular user. Research is conducted from various viewpoints to make the visual representation (graph-representation of the web information) more user-specific. To achieve this, filtering and clustering techniques have been applied to web information to make large web graphs to compact ones. Besides, user modeling has been applied to infer the user's need for a specific time and context. These tend to make the navigation of web information easy and effective to the end user. This paper discusses the current progress in graph-based web information visualization and also outlines the scopes of improvements that could benefit the user exploring the desired information from the web space effectively and efficiently.

Keywords: Visualization · Webgraph · User model · Clustering

1 Introduction

Websites provide various types of information to their users who have varying needs. Therefore, it is now difficult to present information with an unequivocal

© Springer International Publishing AG 2016
Y. Luo (Ed.): CDVE 2016, LNCS 9929, pp. 134–141, 2016.
DOI: 10.1007/978-3-319-46771-9_18

utility to the users. From the users' viewpoint, finding the interested information is a time-consuming and laborious task. To manage and control the information on the web space, the users use various tools such as web browsers, email clients and search engines. Web browsers facilitate the end users to view and navigate through the web information. Search engines along with web portals retrieve information for user-queries and provide a result list to the users. Search engines generally present the list of information sorted by popularity and relevance of the web content for a specific user query whereas web portals extract information from different sources and represent them in a uniform way. With these lists of information and browser views, the end users can only go forward and backward and consume the web content to check whether these can satisfy their information needs. However, the users do not get an idea of where the information is located in the web space and how the information chunks are related.

Visualization improves the user experience by presenting a pictorial view of the web information. Navigation and searching are improved by web graph visualization because it shows the relationships among the web documents. To achieve this, the web information is processed through several steps from the web data collection to the final visualization. However, to make the visualization more effective, the user interests or preferences need to be incorporated into the web graph generation procedures. The web graph is a widely used tool for visualizing the web information. The web graph shows the relationships between web data so that the users can navigate and explore the information in more effective way.

The web information has to go through several steps before it is displayed in the form of a graph. The steps usually include gathering the information from the web (data collection), removing less important and noisy information (filtering), and connecting the remaining information to form the graph (graph generation). These steps establish the architecture of the web information visualization. Many examples of such architectures start with collecting the information from the web space and end by presenting the visuals to the end users.

The roadmap of the paper is as follows: Sect. 2 describes the existing frameworks for information visualization and their extensions, Sect. 3 describes work related to personalized visualization of web information, Sect. 4 presents the probable extensions of the works for betterment of the visualization, Sect. 5 presents some directions from different view-points which could be beneficial for personalized web information visualization and Sect. 6 concludes the paper.

2   Architectures of Information Visualization Systems

Kamada and Kawai [9] propose a visualization model for translating textual representations into pictorial representation. The translation process presented by them proceeds through four representations. A reference visualization pipeline described by Ward et al. is presented in [16]. The stages of this simple visualization pipeline can be mapped to most other visualization pipelines and systems.

When the dataset is relatively large, it is difficult for a system to produce the visuals. For the end users, these visuals are also difficult to comprehend.

The visualization pipeline developed for datasets like web information includes techniques to reduce the size of the dataset and to compress it. Huang et al. [8] present a framework which applies filtering and clustering techniques to the dataset, before creating the visuals for the users. From the web data they create graph representations which are known as web graphs.

Gao [5] proposes a content-based clustering approach for the web information visualization. The web information can be presented to the visualization module in both clustered and unclustered forms. Gao applies content-based clustering to the structure-based clusters for grouping the web documents based on their semantic similarities. This makes the visualization more beneficial to the users by showing content-based relationships between structurally clustered nodes.

From the above discussion, it is clear that filtering and clustering techniques are very useful in reducing the size of the web graph. However, these approaches are limited (lack effectiveness) because they produce the same web graph (every time for the same data source) for the users with different information needs. To avoid this, the architecture should include the user interests wherever appropriate. The above discussed visualization frameworks do not consider the user interests in their procedures. This calls for the development of a new architecture for the web graph visualization.

3   The Architecture of the UIWG Visualization

The visualization of the user interest-based web information is a system that converts the raw web dataset into a meaningful visual representation for its users. To achieve such visualization, several challenges arise. One of the most important challenges is to decide on the relevant web documents for a user. To accomplish this, the system needs to know the user interests. Another challenge involves the user interest-based representations. To present the web information as a graph, the user interests need to be integrated with the graph construction process. The constructed graph needs to be mapped into visual representation for the user. In addition, a process is needed to keep the user interests updated. In light of the above discussion, the architecture, which is presented in [12] is broadly divided into three processes as presented in Fig. 1:

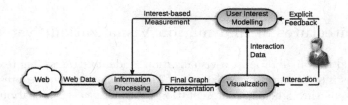

Fig. 1. The High-level architecture of the UIWG visualization

- **User Interest Modelling.** This is responsible for collecting the interests of a user and keeping them updated. This collects the information about the user interests directly from the user and/or from the interaction of the user to the visualization interface. The information is stored in the client device for later usage and is updated according to the user's interactions and further usage. The process is also responsible for assisting the information processing. Because some of the processes need user interest-based measurement scores, this process computes the similarity of the information such as web documents and document-terms to the user interests. For example, calculating the relevancy of a web document for a particular user (comparing with the user interest profile). This assists the system to decide whether the web document is to be filtered out or not. A user model is present in [14].
- **Information Processing.** This process is responsible for collecting the data from the web space and producing the graph representation for visualization. This process also performs the clustering of nodes to make the final graph representation compact. To present the web graph according to the user, interests are incorporated to some of the processes of this process. [14] describes how the user information can be fitted into various phases of the architecture. This architecture incorporates the user interests into the core processes related to web graph generation and in the clustering process.
- **Visualization.** This process is responsible for converting the user interest-based web graph (UIWG) representation into visuals for displaying them to the users. The graph can be mapped to different visual structures depending on the underlying graphics API. This produces an interactive visual so the user can interact with the produced UIWG. This process enables the user to browse and navigate the information. The user interactions are also collected and sent to the *user interest modelling* process to update the user interests.

4   Extension of Current Visualization Strategies

The work described above presents a complete architecture for producing a user interest-based web graph for the users. The work presented in [12–14] paper could be extended further in some areas. Several methods are developed to accomplish the tasks of generating a UIWG and visualizing it. However, there is a scope of extending the work in several directions. These are listed below:

4.1   Extended Approach to Address the Cold-Start Problem

User interest profiles are presented in [12,14] which capture and utilize the user interests during UIWG generation. The user interests are generally entered manually by the user or extracted automatically from the implicit user feedback (by the feedback analyser). As a result, for the first use of the system, the user data may not be present in the system, this is known as the cold-start problem.

This paper handles the above stated cold-start problem by invoking the content-based similarities. However, this can be approached differently. Nowadays, there are many sources in social web, such as 'Facebook', 'Twitter' and

'LinkedIn', which contain information about the user. An initial user interest profile developed from the user information collected from social media and other such sources could address the 'cold-start' problem more effectively. However, it is difficult to quantify the users information from such sources. It is shown in a recent study that only 29 % of new posts of his friends is shown by 'Facebook'. Which means that a lot of user interested information is missed out, despite the user interests being spread across different domains. A recent news article[1] claims that user information in social media can easily be distorted. As a consequence, it is essential to justify the authenticity of the user data.

4.2   Extended User Model

[14] considers only the user interests. However, users generally demonstrate different types of information such as demographic information, location, time, and device usage etc. Utilization of this information could minimize the 'Personae' problem [6]. Consideration of a user's demographic information such as age, eyesight and colour choice are also important in some cases. From the view point of user interests, in addition to the positive interests, the negative interests of a user can also be considered in the user interest profile to better understand the user's information need.

For updating the user interest profiles, [14] uses only *browse* and *expand* interactions from a list of five interactions (refer to Paper [14]). Other interactions on the list can be used to calculate negative interests. For example, the *contract* (putting back the expanded nodes of a cluster into its abstract form) can contribute to the list of negative interests.

4.3   Probabilistic Clustering

Grouping similar information to form an abstract node plays an important role in reducing the size of the web graph. The clustering methods presented in [13] wait for all the web documents to be processed to form the UIWG. This method can be sped up by using probabilistic clustering techniques. Probabilistic topic modelling [1] and probabilistic clustering for uncertain data [10] are among the promising research areas of the IR. Similarly, the approach presented in [13] could benefit from the use of probabilistic clustering which would assign a document to a cluster using a probability function after extracting the document-terms. In such a case, the potential set of clusters could be generated beforehand from the user interests. The probability function could be used to assign a probability score for a document to decide under which cluster it should reside. This whole process could be sped up by using single document term-extractions instead of using the TF-IDF, because TF-IDF needs all the documents for weighting the terms of the documents.

---

[1] http://www.independent.co.uk/travel/news-and-advice/woman-finds-herself-in-southeast-asia-with-a-little-help-from-photoshop-to-satirise-facebook-bragging-972 6396.html- The Independent (UK) - Satirise Facebook Bragging.

4.4   Browser Extensions

Nowadays the most common tools to navigate and explore web information are the web-browsers. The common web-browsers used for exploring web-based information resources do not provide any type of assistance to the users for specific tasks such as researching a subject in a large network of articles [11]. The UIWG visualization interface facilitates the end users in visualizing networks. However, it could be more accessible to the end users if the system can be implemented as a browser extensions. Both the visualization interface and the browser area can be placed side by side. This also provides the opportunity to the users to swap between the visualization and browser interfaces.

4.5   Usability Studies and Extended Prototyping

The work in [12] could be benefited by conducting usability studies, involving real users. Feedback from these users could be helpful to rectify the flaws of the system and improve the suitability of the system. The usability studies could be followed by extensive experimentations and case studies. The result of these experimentations and case studies could also be compared with the existing web graph visualization systems from different aspects such as collecting and analysing the information processing time based on parsing level, analysed words and interests of the user.

The work in the paper [12] does not consider the deep web pages in the prototype for simplicity and privacy issues. However, for better visualization, the deep web pages could be included in the UIWG in some cases. For example, in the websites where this particular user is an authorised user and provides the login information for these websites to the system. Moreover, based on the request of the user, the filtered (based on user interests) web pages could be added in a sub-graph when the user chooses to explore a cluster node of the original UIWG. The extended prototype could also be benefited by use of more customization rules apart from setting the level of parsing or maximum number of pages to be downloaded during crawling.

5   Improvement from Other Directions

5.1   Layout of the Web Graph

UIWG generation and clustering are described in [12]. During the UIWG generation process, the focus remains on how to integrate user interests. However, readability of the UIWG is also an important factor for the end users. The readability of a graph depends heavily on the layout of the visualization. Huang et al. [7] discuss various aesthetics of graph drawing and propose a new algorithm utilizing multiple aesthetics. Consideration of multiple aesthetics contributes to increasing the effectiveness of the graph visualization. Therefore, to increase the readability of UIWG, [12] can be extended by the introduction of the research encompassing web graph layout to choose the optimal layout.

Because the clustering is hierarchical, the initial display of the UIWG can expand the clusters to a certain level (to fit it best on the screen). In a recent study, Gansner et al. [4] present methods to convert a clustered graph into a map presentation which is more accessible to the users. Moreover, the visualization provided to the users could be improved by employing numerous user specific characteristics such as presenting different visualization images of the same graph to various age groups, introduction of meaningful colours, placing the most important nodes in the hot-spot of the screen which is calculated based on the users eye-movement. This paper can also be extended from the above discussed directions.

5.2   UIWG for Portable Computers

The searching of information from the web is experiencing a paradigm shift because of the dominance of smart-phones and personal digital assistants (PDA) over the general purpose computers. These new devices have different types of display sizes and interaction methods. Recall the visualization mantra [15] which speaks for the *overview first and details on demand (Overview+Detail (O+D))* during visualization. Unlike the general purpose computers, the effectiveness of visualization using *Overview+Detail (O+D)* method for mobile devices is yet to be justified [2]. On the one hand, the web information visualization presented in [12] aims to benefit the users. The users, on the other hand, may change the computing platforms. Therefore, to adjust to this change, the visualization should be changed in terms of layout and interaction. To produce a platform independent effective visualization, a study on the UIWG visualization for portable computers needs to be explored.

5.3   Natural Language Processing in Keywords Extraction

Apart from filtering and clustering based on the user interests, the effectiveness of [12] can be improved with the introduction of better techniques to extract keywords from a document. It is very important to address the linguistic ambiguities (mostly occur when the order and relation of the words in a sentence are not considered) during the term or document similarity calculations. A lot of research is currently being conducted in the field of natural language processing which can assist a system to extract the thematic notations from the text. One such work focuses on clustering and diversifying the web search result using graph-based word sense induction [3]. Similarly, the work can be benefit by a keyword extraction technique which considers the order of the words and their relations in a sentence.

6   Conclusion

This paper discusses the current state of the arts of personalized visualization. Although, it is very beneficial for the users to visualize the information that they are searching for, the methods could be benefit from several other directions. This paper summarizes the directions from the view points of effective and efficient personalized web information visualization.

References

1. Blei, D.M.: Probabilistic topic models. Commun. ACM **55**(4), 77–84 (2012). http://doi.acm.org/10.1145/2133806.2133826
2. Burigat, S., Chittaro, L.: On the effectiveness of overview+detail visualization on mobile devices. Pers. Ubiquitous Comput. **17**(2), 371–385 (2013). http://dx.doi.org/10.1007/s00779-011-0500-3
3. Di Marco, A., Navigli, R.: Clustering and diversifying web search results with graph-based word sense induction. Comput. Linguist. **39**(3), 709–754 (2013)
4. Gansner, E.R., Hu, Y., Kobourov, S.G.: Viewing abstract data as maps. In: Huang, W. (ed.) Handbook of Human Centric Visualization, pp. 63–89. Springer, New York (2014)
5. Gao, J.: Structure and content-based clustering for visualization of web network information. Ph.D. thesis, Swinburne University of Technology, Hawthorn, Victoria, Australia (2011)
6. Ghosh, R., Dekhil, M.: Discovering user profiles. In: WWW, pp. 1233–1234 (2009)
7. Huang, W., Eades, P., Hong, S.H., Lin, C.C.: Improving multiple aesthetics produces better graph drawings. J. Vis. Lang. Comput. **24**(4), 262–272 (2013). http://www.sciencedirect.com/science/article/pii/S1045926X11000814
8. Huang, X., Eades, P., Lai, W.: A framework of filtering, clustering and dynamic layout graphs for visualization. In: Proceedings of the Twenty-Eighth Australasian Conference on Computer Science, ACSC 2005, vol. 38, pp. 87–96. Australian Computer Society Inc., Darlinghurst, Australia (2005)
9. Kamada, T., Kawai, S.: A general framework for visualizing abstract objects and relations. ACM Trans. Graph. **10**(1), 1–39 (1991)
10. Lammersen, C., Schmidt, M., Sohler, C.: Probabilistic k-median clustering in data streams. In: Erlebach, T., Persiano, G. (eds.) WAOA 2012. LNCS, vol. 7846, pp. 70–81. Springer, Heidelberg (2013)
11. Lehmann, S., Schwanecke, U., Drner, R.: Interactive visualization for opportunistic exploration of large document collections. Inf. Syst. **35**(2), 260–269 (2010). Special Section: Context-Oriented Information Integration
12. Saleheen, S., Lai, W.: User centric dynamic web information visualization. Sci. China Inf. Sci. **56**(5), 1–14 (2013)
13. Saleheen, S., Lai, W.: An interest-based clustering method for web information visualization. In: Luo, X., Yu, J.X., Li, Z. (eds.) ADMA 2014. LNCS, vol. 8933, pp. 421–434. Springer, Heidelberg (2014)
14. Saleheen, S., Lai, W.: A semi-supervised topic-based user model for web information visualization. In: 11th Asia-Pacific Conference on Conceptual Modelling, APCCM 2015, Sydney, Australia, pp. 43–52, January 2015
15. Shneiderman, B.: The eyes have it: a task by data type taxonomy for information visualizations. In: 1996 Proceedings on IEEE Symposium on Visual Languages, pp. 336–343, September 1996
16. Ward, M., Grinstein, G., Keim, D.: Interactive Data Visualization: Foundations, Techniques, and Applications. A. K. Peters Ltd., Natick (2010)

Isotone Galois Connections and Employees Resource Management

Sylvia Encheva[⊠]

Stord/Haugesund University College, Bjørnsonsg. 45, 5528 Haugesund, Norway
sbe@hsh.no

Abstract. Merging organizations face a number of challenges related to creation of a new establishment. Short deadlines put serious pressure on those, responsible for planning and implementing all possible types of changes. The main issue we direct attention on in this work is concerned with placing employees in new units according to their competencies in a well-organized and controlled way. Isotone Galois connections are used to secure a systematic approach for establishing a correspondence between employees' competencies and units' contents.

Keywords: Employees · Management · Isotone Galois connections

1 Introduction

Every organization has to find a way of assigning the right people to the right tasks. Dynamic changes due to merger of various autonomous entities and restructuring of existing ones is a challenge to leadership on different levels. Let's direct our attention on structural changes in higher education. The tendency is to form larger universities in order to reach the critical mass required for obtaining excellency in both teaching and research, as well as satisfying current and future society needs. In order to facilitate the process of developing new units' structure we propose application of isotone Galois connections. The latter are used to provide a systematic way of establishing a correspondence between people competencies and units' contents.

The rest of the paper is organized as follows. Related work and supporting theory may be found in Sect. 2. The obtained results are presented in Sect. 3. The paper ends with a conclusion in Sect. 4.

2 Related Work

Our initial setting is to consider a mapping $f : A \rightarrow B$ from a partially ordered set A into an unstructured set B, and then characterize those situations in which the set B can be partially ordered and an isotone mapping $g : B \rightarrow A$ can be built such that the pair (f, g) is an isotone Galois connection [11].

© Springer International Publishing AG 2016
Y. Luo (Ed.): CDVE 2016, LNCS 9929, pp. 142–148, 2016.
DOI: 10.1007/978-3-319-46771-9_19

Definition 1. [11]

Given a partially ordered set $\mathbb{A} = (A, \leq_A)$, $X \subseteq A$, and $a \in A$.

- Element a is said to be the maximum of X, denoted $max\ X$, if $a \in X$ and $x \leq a$ for all $x \in X$.
- The downset $a^{\downarrow}$ of a is defined as $a^{\downarrow} = \{x \in A | x \leq_A a\}$.
- The upset $a^{\uparrow}$ of a is defined as $a^{\uparrow} = \{x \in A | x \geq_A a\}$.

A mapping $f : (A, \leq_A) \rightarrow (B, \leq_B)$ between partially ordered sets is said to be

- isotone if $a_1 \leq_A a_2$ implies $f(a_1) \leq_B f(a_2)$, for all $a_1, a_2 \in A$.
- antitone if $a_1 \leq_A a_2$ implies $f(a_2) \leq_B f(a_1)$, for all $a_1, a_2 \in A$.

As usual, f^1 is the inverse image of f, that is, $f^1(b) = \{a \in A | f(a) = b\}$. In the particular case in which $A = B$,

- f is inflationary (also called extensive) if $a \leq_A f(a)$ for all $a \in A$.
- f is deflationary if $f(a) \leq_A a$ for all $a \in A$.

As we are including the necessary definitions for the development of the construction of isotone Galois connections (hereafter, for brevity, termed adjunctions) between posets, we state below the definition of adjunction we will be working with.

Definition 2. Let $\mathbb{A} = (A, \leq_A)$ and $\mathbb{B} = (B, \leq_B)$ be posets, $f : A \rightarrow B$ and $g : B \rightarrow A$ be two mappings. The pair (f, g) is said to be an adjunction between $\mathbb{A}$ and $\mathbb{B}$, denoted by $(f, g) : \mathbb{A} \leftrightharpoons \mathbb{B}$, whenever for all $a \in A$ and $b \in B$ we have that

$f(a) \leq_B b$ if and only if $a \leq_A g(b)$

The mapping f is called left adjoint and g is called right adjoint.

Let y be a vertex of a graph G such that y has exactly three distinct neighbors $\{a, b, c\}$. Let H be the graph obtained from G by deleting y and adding a triangle on the vertices, $\{a, b, c\}$. The graph H is said to be obtained from G by a Y Δ-exchange at y. The inverse operation is called a Δ Y-exchange at (abc). The Petersen family is the set of seven graphs that can be obtained from the Petersen graph by repeated $Y\Delta$- and 2 Δ Y-exchanges, [10]. For further readings on graphs we refer to [1–3]. Importance of human capital is discussed in [4].

Grey theory is an effective method used to solve uncertainty problems with discrete data and incomplete information. The theory includes five major parts: grey prediction, grey relational analysis, grey decision, grey programming and grey control, [5–7] and [9]. Grey numbers are particularly useful for handling information in decision making, [14]. A quantitative approach for assessing the qualitative nature of organizational visions is presented in [12].

3   Human Capital

Consider first a set of all employees and another set of all units in an organization. The question we try to answer is how to allocate people to units based on units descriptions and employees competencies (employees qualifications).

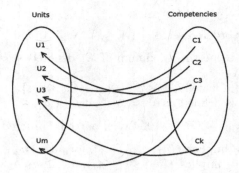

Fig. 1. Units and competencies

In order to establish an optimal placing in organization's units for each person we put forward employment of isotone Galois connections, [11]. The two data sets are to be prepared first. One of them contains a list of all organization's units and competencies required from members belonging to each unit. The other set contains a list of all employees and their corresponding competencies. For obtaining higher level of accuracy both required and available competencies should be represented with agreed upon non binary degrees. A person's competency can be graded depending on f. ex. education, experience and whatever else the organization considers to be important. This can be realized by using linguistic hedges such as 'very', 'rather', 'more or less', etc. as in [8].

An arrow from a competency to a unit implies that a particular unit needs employees with a specific competency, Fig. 1. Unit U3 needs competencies C2 and Ck while competency C3 is needed by units U1 and Um, and competency C1 is needed by unit U2.

An employee has often several skills. In Fig. 2 we observe that:

employees E1 and E2 share skill C1,
employee E3 has two skills C2 and Ck, and
employee En has skill C3.

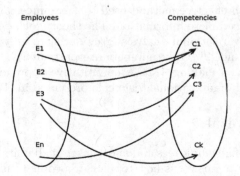

Fig. 2. Employees and competencies

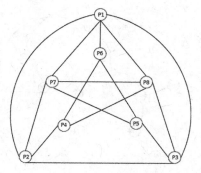

Fig. 3. Several levels of competence

In Fig. 2 a person and a skill are connected without applying non binary degrees for simplicity. If however the number of employees that can be assigned to a particular unit is less than the number of employees that can be potentially assigned to that particular unit, application of non binary degrees to the person/skills connections can be very helpful.

In practice assigning employees to units can be realized by isotone mapping $f : (A, \leq_A) \to (B, \leq_B)$. In this case the employees are elements of the set A and the units are elements of the set B.

Next step is related to assisting leaders in the process of finding an employee formally belonging to one unit that can be called in to work with tasks handled by other units. This can be realized by developing a graphical representation of various competencies shared by the employees.

The diagram in Fig. 3 represents one of the graphs belonging to Petersen family graphs [13]. Vertices represent people and an edge connecting two vertices implies that they share the same qualification. Vertices P1, P2, and P3 represent people with somewhat general qualifications. Vertices P4, ..., P8 represent people with more specific qualifications.

Five disjoint groups

$$(M1, M2, M3, M4),$$
$$(M5, M6, M7, M8),$$
$$(M9, M10, M11, M12),$$
$$(M13, M14, M15, M16),$$
$$(M17, M18, M19, M20)$$

with four members in each group are associated with the Flower snark graph in Fig. 4.

In a group one person is sharing expertise with each of the other three group members and does not share any expertise with members outside of its group. In our notations these members are M1, M5, M9, M13, M17. One member of each group shares two specific skills with two members of two other groups

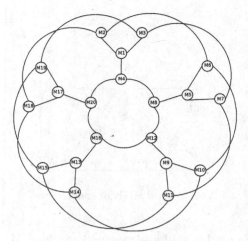

Fig. 4. Flower snark

(the most inner circle composed of members M4, M8, M12, M16, M20). Each of the remaining two members of a group shares two general skills with two members of two other groups (the most outer circle composed of the rest of the members).

The structure in Fig. 4 can also be used to visualize how different skills are related. In this sense a vertex will represent a particular skill and two vertices are connected by a direct line when there is a certain degree of similarity between them. Grey numbers can be used for establishing applicable degree of similarity.

In Fig. 5 a vertex representing an absent member say 'M18' is denoted by red color while the vertices 'M2, M14, M17' representing members sharing a

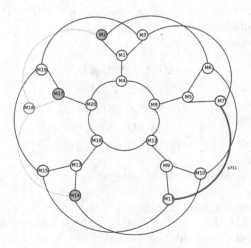

Fig. 5. Member search outcome (Color figure online)

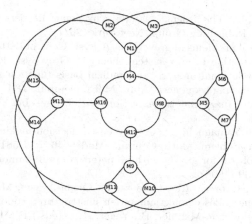

Fig. 6. Graphical configuration illustrating a case where four groups remain in the team

skill with 'M18' are filled by pink color. If a third party is asking for a person with particular expertise one can click on the corresponding edge (provided it is available) and see who can be eventually suggested to do the job. A request for skill 's711' is illustrated in Fig. 5, where the edge representing skill 's711' and the vertices for members 'M7, M11' possessing it are highlighted in dark green.

The principal for constructing Fig. 4 can be used for smaller or larger amount of groups. They will not necessarily be Flower snark graphs but they will serve well for supporting visualization of resources.

Graphical configuration in Fig. 6 is obtained by reducing the number of groups in Fig. 4 by one.

4 Conclusion

Restructuring workforce in a new organization is a difficult and laborious task. Misplacing employees is costly for the organization and for the workers. Success or failure in organizational restructuring very much depend on correct workers placement. In this work we have presented a systematic approach to assign people to different units in an organization and a quick way to find the right people for the right job when a situation calls for it.

References

1. Bollobas, B.: Extremal Graph Theory. Dover, New York (2004)
2. Brinkmann, G.: Generating Cubic Graphs Faster Than Isomorphism Checking, Preprint 92–047 SFB 343. University of Bielefeld, Bielefeld (1992)
3. Brinkmann, G., Meringer, M.: The smallest 4-regular 4-chromatic graphs with girth 5. Graph Theor. Notes NY **32**, 40–41 (1997)

4. Conaty, B., Ram, C.: The Talent Masters: Why Smart Leaders Put People Before Numbers. Crown Publishing Group, New York (2011)
5. Deng, J.L.: Control problems of grey systems. Syst. Control Lett **5**, 288–294 (1982)
6. Deng, J.L.: Introduction to grey system theory. J. Grey Syst. **1**, 1–24 (1985)
7. Hu, Y.C.: Grey relational analysis and radical basis function network for determining costs in learning sequences. Appl. Math. Comput. **184**, 291–299 (2007)
8. Konecny, J.: Isotone fuzzy Galois connections with hedges. Inf. Sci. **181**, 1804–1817 (2011)
9. Li, G.D., Daisuke Yamaguchi, D.: A grey-based decision-making approach to the supplier selection problem. Math. Comput. Model. **46**, 573–581 (2007)
10. Maharry, J.: A splitter for graphs with no petersen family minor. J. Comb. Theor. Ser. B **72**, 136–139 (1998)
11. García-Pardo, F., Cabrera, I.P., Cordero, P., Ojeda-Aciego, M., Rodríguez, F.J.: Generating isotone galois connections on an unstructured codomain. In: Laurent, A., Strauss, O., Bouchon-Meunier, B., Yager, R.R. (eds.) IPMU 2014. CCIS, vol. 444, pp. 91–99. Springer, Heidelberg (2014). doi:10.1007/978-3-319-08852-5_10
12. Rahimnia, F., Moghadasian, M., Mashreghi, E.: Application of grey theory organizational approach to evaluation of organizational vision. Grey Syst. Theor. Appl. **1**(1), 33–46 (2011)
13. Robertson, N., Seymour, P., Thomas, R.: Petersen family minors. J. Comb. Theor. Ser. B **64**(2), 155–184 (1995)
14. Xie, N.-M., Liu, S.-F.: Novel methods on comparing grey numbers. Appl. Math. Model. **34**(2), 415–423 (2010)

Network Visual Analysis Based on Community Detection

Yao Zhonghua[⊠] and Wu Lingda

Science and Technology on Complex Electronic System Simulation Laboratory,
Beijing, China
visworker07@163.com

Abstract. With the rapid increasing size of the network, mining and analyzing the network structure characteristics to enhance network awareness and understanding are facing severe challenges. We use community detection algorithm to obtain the community division. The network nodes are layout by force directed methods to visualize the network structure. At the same time magnifying metaphor method is used to enhance interactively inquiring details to achieve focus-context display. Experimental results show that this can help the network understanding and situation awareness.

Keywords: Community detection · Visual analysis · Force directed algorithm

1 Introduction

This paper aims to analyze network structure characteristics with visualization. Component division and community detection are adopted to obtain the structure characteristics, and then we use force directed algorithm (FDA) to layout network nodes. Nodes within the same community move closer to each other to aggregate in space based on community detection. Quadtree is constructed to reduce the computational complexity during the iteration process to improve traditional FDA. Meanwhile displacement factor is taken into consideration to lower system oscillation and improve system stability in the layout procedure. At last, magnify metaphor by fisheye and enhanced information display by convex hull of concerning provide us contextual information, which contribute to the mining and cognition of network connection mode and structure (Fig. 1).

2 Related Works

Community refers to the internal structure of the network, where internal links within the same community are close while sparse between them. Communities detection divides the network into different group, and the community has many internal edges, and almost no edges exist between communities [1]. It is an important tool to analyze and understand the network structure, and community detection can make large-scale network connection mode that can't easily be directly observed more clearly, thus benefit understanding and awareness of the network structure. Modularity optimization

© Springer International Publishing AG 2016
Y. Luo (Ed.): CDVE 2016, LNCS 9929, pp. 149–156, 2016.
DOI: 10.1007/978-3-319-46771-9_20

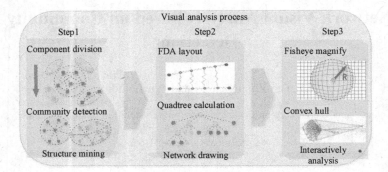

Fig. 1. Visual analysis process of network structural characteristics

method can quantify divided communities, and are efficient, so optimized modularity method by CNM [2] to detect the network community is used in this paper.

Classical FDA (Force Directed Algorithm) [3–7] usually models nodes in the network as charged particles repelling mutually, and edges are modeled as spring with desired length, and elastic spring force applied on the two endpoints is depended on the length of the edge. Significantly accelerating force-directed algorithms have been developed by [8–14], which can generate nice drawings of a big range of large graphs in reasonable time. Some of these methods guarantee a sub-quadratic running time in special cases or under certain assumptions but not in general.

3   Visual Analysis on Network Structure Characteristics

3.1   Communities Detection by CNM

Nodes with the same type are grouped together, and edges between them should have large proportions since connections within the same community are close. Modularity use the proportion of edges connecting nodes in the same type to the value without considering node-type in a random network. When proportion of edges with same node-type is significantly greater than that in random conditions, community division makes sense.

Q is modularity which can measure the quality of community dividing and how tight connections are.

$$Q = \frac{1}{2m} \sum_{vw} \left(A_{vw} - \frac{k_v k_w}{2m} \right) \delta(c_v, c_w) \tag{1}$$

Where A_{vw} is an element of adjacency matrix corresponding to the network, c_v is the community where node v with degree k_v locate, and number of the total edges of network is $m = \frac{1}{2} \sum_{vw} A_{vw}$. To simplify description of the algorithm, we define auxiliary variable e_{ij} to represent the proportion of edges connecting community i and j to total edges number. Auxiliary variable a_i represents the proportion of edges connecting nodes in community i to total edges number, then formulation that calculate modularity Q can be rewritten as below:

$$Q = \sum_i \left(e_{ii} - a_i^2\right) \qquad (2)$$

Higher modularity Q corresponds to better community division, and the optimization process is to choose maximum change during each iteration and merge respective communities. CNM algorithm keeps and maintains incremental matrix ΔQ, in which each element ΔQ_{ij} means the modularity change after merging community i and j. The time that each merging costs is $O((|i| + |j|) \log n)$, then total time cost of the algorithm reaches up to $O(\log n)$ multiplying total degrees of nodes in communities. Assuming that the network is divided into d levels, and sum of all nodes degrees is $2m$, then total time cost is $O(md \log n)$. Real networks are often sparsely connected, so $m \sim n$, and community structures have division depth $d \sim \log n$, then time complexity of the algorithm can be represented as $O(n \log^2 n)$.

3.2   FDA Layout

After getting community structure, layout algorithm will be used to render network drawing, and to keep nodes in the same community close to each other in space. Under the interaction of spring force and repulsion force, the system eventually reaches an equilibrium state when the system has overall lowest energy. During the layout process, forces applied on nodes are continually calculated to update their positions until the system reaches stability. At the same time, repulsion forces between nodes in the same community are weakened and spring forces are reinforced based on community detection, in order to ensure nodes within the community closer to each other. In this way, nodes aggregation forms, facilitating to observe community structure of the network significantly.

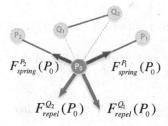

Fig. 2. FDA model schematic diagram

As the diagram shown Fig. 2, network node P_0 is connected to P_1 and P_2, and it get spring forces from adjacent nodes P_1 and P_2, and repulsion forces from non-adjacent nodes Q_1 and Q_2. Among them, the force from adjacent node P_1 is defined as:

$$F_{spring}^{P_1}(P_0) = C_s * \log(\frac{||P_1 - P_0||}{l}) * ||P_1 - P_0|| * (P_1 - P_0) \qquad (3)$$

In which, C_s is community spring factor. The spring force is positively correlate to the distance. Force from P_2 can be obtained similarly.

Repulsion from node Q_1 is defined as:

$$F_{repel}^{Q_1}(P_0) = C_r \frac{P_0 - Q_1}{||P_0 - Q_1||^2} \qquad (4)$$

In which, C_r is community repelling factor, and repulsion force is inversely correlate to the distance, and direction is from Q_1 to P_0. Repulsion force Q_2 can be obtained similarly.

During the iteration, spring forces from adjacent nodes and repulsion forces from all other nodes need to be calculated for any node v, that is:

$$F_{repel}(v) = \sum_{u \in V \setminus v} F_{repel}^u(v) \qquad (5)$$

$$F_{spring}(v) = \sum_{A(u,v)=1} F_{spring}^u(v) \qquad (6)$$

Then resultant forces applied on node v are:

$$F_{res}(v) = \lambda_{repel} * F_{repel}(v) + \lambda_{spring} * F_{spring}(v) \qquad (7)$$

In which λ_{repel} is repelling coefficient and λ_{spring} is spring coefficient. During FDA iteration process, nodes update their positions according to resultant forces to new iteration. Mapping resultant forces directly to nodes' displacements will cause oscillation and jitter, to avoid system oscillations, we define displacement factor $D_f(v, i)$ to adjust displacement $F_{disp}^i(v)$ of node v at i round of iteration.

$$F_{disp}(v) = D_f(v, i) * F_{res}(v) / ||F_{res}(v)|| \qquad (8)$$

$$D_f(v, i) = \begin{cases} \delta * ||F_{res}^i(v)|| , & if \ F_{res}^i(v) < c_{i,v} * ||F_{disp}^{i-1}(v)|| \\ \delta * c_{i,v} * ||F_{disp}^{i-1}(v)|| , else \end{cases} \qquad (9)$$

$$\delta = (MaxIter - i)/MaxIter \qquad (10)$$

In which δ is decay factor, assuming that total iteration rounds is MaxIter. As the increase of the number of iterations, node applied with same resultant get smaller displacement. $\alpha(i, v)$ is the angle between resultant force $F_{res}^i(v)$ and displacement $F_{disp}^{i-1}(v)$ at last iteration, and $c_{i,v}$ is piecewise function of $\alpha(i, v)$:

$$c_{i,v}=\begin{cases} 2, \textit{if } \alpha(i,v) \in [-\pi/6, \pi/6] \\ 3/2, \textit{if } \alpha(i,v) \in (\pi/6, \pi/3] \cup [-\pi/3, -\pi/6) \\ 1, \textit{if } \alpha(i,v) \in (\pi/3, \pi/2] \cup [-\pi/2, -\pi/3) \\ 2/3, \textit{if } \alpha(i,v) \in (\pi/2, 2\pi/3] \cup [-2\pi/3, -\pi/2) \\ 1/3, \textit{other} \end{cases} \qquad (11)$$

As shown Fig. 3, $c_{i,v}$ is 2 if $\alpha(i,v)$ is between $[-\pi/6, \pi/6]$, when node v maintains the main direction of last displacement. And $c_{i,v}$ is limited to 1/3 (without considering decay factor) if $\alpha(i,v)$ is $-\pi$ when node v moves inversely. In this way, displacement factor $D_f(v,i)$ ensure one node to move towards specific direction as much as possible, trying to reducing system oscillations.

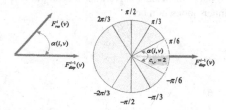

Fig. 3. Piecewise function schematic diagram

During the iteration, calculating repulsion forces cost most time. Consider a network with N nodes. Each node needs to be calculated N times during one iteration, totally $O(N^2)$. To large-scale network, the computation complexity is too high, so one efficient method to reduce complexity is by appropriate division of space, so that nodes located distant can be calculated more efficient. This paper uses Barnes-Hut method to construct quadtree of network nodes, and group distant nodes to single node. Thus calculation can be applied on that single node instead of nodes in the group, in this way, computation complexity in one iteration can be lowered to $O(N \log(N))$.

3.3   Interactively Analysis Technology

Due to the large scale of the network, visual clutter caused by node occlusion and edge cross-cutting issues inevitably arise. To obtain valuable information, interactively analysis technology is needed to provide both overview information (context) and sense of details (focus). Highlighting regions of interest and weakening information display of the rest contribute to gain perception of network structure. Following that principle, this paper provide focus + context [15] details display technology based on Fisheye [16, 17], and uses magnifying glass to provide users with detailed information to explore the region of interest, allowing users to see the overall context observed around the details. And Fisheye can amplify that central region to emphasize the region without losing macro perception. Meanwhile, convex hull of the focus node by interactively selection is highlighted to reduce interference from network redundancy information.

4 Case Analysis

Dataset consist of 260,000 connections from network layer, and network topology is built from the IP connections. During the data processing stage, connections with the same origin and destination are merged to one edge, thus 6281 nodes and 9068 edges are obtained. After component division, 981 independent components are gained, 99.8 % of which are "isolated islands" with less than 20 nodes. Thus the two biggest scale component are selected for community analysis, one with 3704 nodes, another with 500 nodes as shown in the following Table 1 in bold dark.

Table 1. Distribution of component scales

Component Scale (inner nodes number)	Number of components
2	911
3	49
4	12
5	2
6	1
7	2
11	1
19	1
500	1
3704	1

115 communities are gained by CNM communities detection algorithm, and scales of communities differs vastly. The biggest community owns 976 nodes while the smallest owns only 2 nodes, and communities with scale less than 5 count for 61.7 % of all nodes. To avoiding color confusion, top 20 communities are encoded by different colors, and small scale ones are colored the same. As shown Fig. 4, communities with ellipse shaded are colored, and nodes in the same community has the same color and positioned close in space due to community adjust factor.

Users can analyze the network at different scale extent, when zooming to a concerning node in community at the left part as shown Fig. 5, the center node outlined by

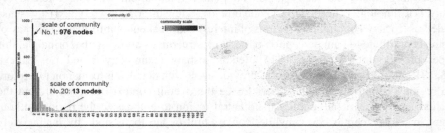

Fig. 4. Components scale distribution (left) and network topology structure diagram (right)

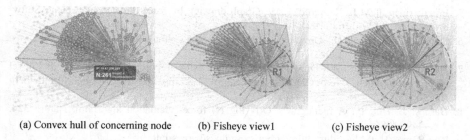

(a) Convex hull of concerning node   (b) Fisheye view1   (c) Fisheye view2

Fig. 5. Interactively analysis by convex hull and fisheye view (Color figure online)

red with IP 10.67.220.221. It belongs to community 4 which has 775 nodes, and has 261 adjacent nodes, and most of them belong to the same community. Connections of that node are highlighted, and other nodes and connections are weakened. At the same time, convex hull of the connections is calculated and encoded with the same color of that center node to identify community attribute and attract user focus.

When visual clutter seriously influences network understanding, fisheye view can magnify central area. As shown above in Fig. 5(b), circular shadow with radius R1 is an enlarged area to enhance contrast with surrounding area of the region of interest. Scale extend and fisheye radius can be adjusted for further interactively analysis. As shown in Fig. 5(c), magnifying area with radius R2 is enlarged, bigger than that with R1, making it available to analyze connection modes in larger scale.

5   Conclusion

This paper mined network structure characteristics by component division and community detection, and improved traditional force directed algorithm. Case analysis revealed that this algorithm improves the stability of layout and help to understanding and perception of network structure. Magnifying tool and convex hull display were provided to enhance interactively analyze detail information, and contribute to obtain network connection modes. This paper mainly focuses on static structure, mining on dynamic characteristics method to reduce visual clutter needs further research, and this paper has limitation in cooperative visualization

References

1. Newman, M.: Networks: An Introduction. Oxford University Press, Oxford (2010)
2. Clauset, A., Newman, M.E.J., Moore, C.: Finding community structure in very large networks. Phys. Rev. E **70**, 66111 (2004)
3. Eades, P.: A heuristic for graph drawing (1984)
4. Kamada, T., Kawai, S.: An algorithm for drawing general undirected graphs. Inf. Process. Lett. **31**(1), 7–15 (1989)

5. Fruchterman, T.M.J., Reingold, E.M.: Graph drawing by force-directed placement. Softw. Pr. Exp. **21**, 1129–1164 (1991)
6. Davidson, R., Harel, D.: Drawing graphs nicely using simulated annealing. ACM Trans. Graph. **15**, 301–331 (1996)
7. Hachul, S., Jünger, M.: Drawing large graphs with a potential-field-based multilevel algorithm. In: Pach, J. (ed.) GD 2004. LNCS, vol. 3383, pp. 285–295. Springer, Heidelberg (2005)
8. Barnes, J., Hut, P.: A hierarchical O(N log N) force-calculation algorithm. Nature **324**, 446–449 (1986)
9. The Barnes-Hut Algorithm: http://arborjs.org/docs/barnes-hut
10. Gajer, P., Goodrich, M.T., Kobourov, S.G.: A multi-dimensional approach to force-directed layouts of large graphs. In: Marks, J. (ed.) GD 2000. LNCS, vol. 1984, pp. 211–221. Springer, Heidelberg (2001)
11. Harel, D., Koren, Y.: A fast multi-scale method for drawing large graphs. In: Marks, J. (ed.) GD 2000. LNCS, vol. 1984, pp. 183–196. Springer, Heidelberg (2001)
12. Quigley, A., Eades, P.: FADE: graph drawing, clustering, and visual abstraction. In: Marks, J. (ed.) GD 2000. LNCS, vol. 1984, pp. 197–210. Springer, Heidelberg (2001)
13. Tunkelang, D.: JIGGLE: java interactive graph layout environment. In: Whitesides, S.H. (ed.) GD 1998. LNCS, vol. 1547, pp. 413–422. Springer, Heidelberg (1999)
14. Walshaw, C.: A multilevel algorithm for force-directed graph drawing. In: Marks, J. (ed.) GD 2000. LNCS, vol. 1984, pp. 171–182. Springer, Heidelberg (2001)
15. Card, S.K., Mackinlay, J.D., Shneiderman, B. (eds.): Readings in Information Visualization: Using Vision to Think. Morgan Kaufmann Publishers Inc., San Francisco (1999)
16. Sarkar, M., Brown, M.H.: Graphical fisheye views of graphs. In: Proceedings of the SIGCHI Conference on Human Factors in Computing Systems, pp. 83–91
17. Tory, M., Moller, T.: Human factors in visualization research. IEEE Trans. Vis. Comput. Graph. **10**, 72–84 (2004)

Evaluating Overall Quality of Dynamic Network Visualizations

Weidong Huang[1]([⊠]), Min Zhu[2], Mao Lin Huang[3,4], and Henry Been-Lirn Duh[1]

[1] University of Tasmania, Hobart, Australia
{tony.huang,henry.duh}@utas.edu.au
[2] Sichuan University, Chengdu, China
zhumin@scu.edu.cn
[3] Tianjin University, Tianjin, China
mao.huang@uts.edu.au
[4] University of Technology Sydney, Ultimo, Australia

Abstract. Visualizing dynamic networks is a challenging task. One of the challenges we face is how to maintain visual complexity and overall quality of visualizations at a reasonable and sustainable level so that the information about the network embedded in the visualization can be effectively comprehended by the viewer. Many techniques and algorithms have been proposed and developed to facilitate the discovery of changing patterns. Much research has also been done in investigating how visualization should be constructed to be effective. However, how to measure and compare the quality of visualizations of a changing network at different time points has not been well researched. In this paper, we report on a preliminary work towards this direction. In particular, we apply an existing multi-dimensional overall quality measure in a user study data of different networks and found that the measured quality is positively correlated with user task performance regardless of network size.

Keywords: Cooperative visualization · Quality metrics · Evaluation · Visualization · Dynamic networks

1 Introduction

Cooperative visualization of dynamic networks, such as social networks and biological networks, is often seen in practice. For a given network and at any given time, some actors leave while new ones join the network. Accordingly, relationships among these actors also change. These dynamic features make visualization of these networks a challenging task [8]. Much research has been done on how dynamic networks can be better visualized while many tools are available to assist practitioners and researchers in making sense of this type of networks. In visualizing dynamic networks, one criterion that is commonly adopted is to preserve layout stability or mental map so that layout changes in a series of individual visualizations are kept to the minimum when possible [9]. Although empirical evidence for its positive effect is not conclusive [11], it is commonly

© Springer International Publishing AG 2016
Y. Luo (Ed.): CDVE 2016, LNCS 9929, pp. 157–162, 2016.
DOI: 10.1007/978-3-319-46771-9_21

believed that keeping node positions unchanged across the visualizations will reduce the effort that is otherwise needed for a viewer to look for the same nodes in their new positions and refresh/rebuild their relationship patterns. This in turn will allow him/her to focus more on knowledge discovery and network comprehension while the network changes over a time period.

Although it may be an important factor for viewers to understand change patterns of a dynamic network quickly, maintaining mental map could be counterproductive as it can also have a negative effect on overall quality for individual visualizations. To explore this effect in the context of dynamic networks, as a first step towards this direction, we conducted a preliminary research into the method of measuring overall quality of networks of different sizes. More specifically, we took an existing quality measure of static networks [3] and apply it on an experimental data of dynamic networks. We examined whether the quality measure was correlated with the task performance.

In what follows, we first briefly review related work on quality metrics of network visualization, followed by the report on this preliminary research. The paper finishes with a short summary and our plan for future work.

2   Related Work

Dynamic networks are commonly visualized in the format of animation or a collection of static node-link diagrams [7]. For static graph drawings, aesthetics, such as minimum crossings and maximum crossing angles, are used to define layout for readability [5]. For dynamic networks, mental map has been widely accepted as an important criterion in judging the quality of layout. Much research has been done to develop visualization principles, tools and algorithms for both static and dynamic networks. For example, Friedrich and Eades [6] derived a set of criteria and measures for a good visualization of dynamic networks when animation is used. The criteria include uniform movement and symmetrical movement while measurements include minimize temporary edge crossings and maximize structured movements. Diehl et al. [12] developed an algorithms that is able to preserve mental map while the underlying graph structure changes. Animation also has implications on attention, memory and learning process which has been investigated in different domains [4,10,14].

While mental map requires that layout be changed as little as possible when the underlying graph is changed, aesthetics imply that different layouts should be used for different graphs. As a result, it is important to understand possible interactions between aesthetics and mental map in the context of dynamic networks. And measuring overall quality should help toward this goal. Different approaches have been proposed in the literature to measure visualization quality from different perspectives. Eades et al. [2] proposed a set of new shape-based quality metrics for large graphs, while Janicke and Chen [1] proposed a quality metric for visualization based on visual salience that can quickly guide the viewer's attention to the most relevant part of the image. Huang et al. [4] proposed an overall quality measure that takes into consideration performance gain in relation the cognitive cost devoted during the task performance.

Recently, Huang et al. [3] proposed an overall quality measure that aggregates z scores of individual quality metrics in a formula that outputs a single numeric value. The formula is as follows:

$$O = -z_{cross\#} + z_{crossRes} + z_{angularRes} - z_{uniEdge} \qquad (1)$$

In this formula, $cross\#$ is the number of crossings in the visualization; $CrossRes$ is the minimum crossing angle. $AngularRes$ is the minimum angle formed by any two neighboring edges. $uniEdge$ is the standard deviation of all edge lengths. The authors also conducted a user study in which the measurement was tested on different visualizations of a same static network. The study demonstrated the sensibility and predictability of this measure with statistical significance, indicating its validity in measuring overall quality. In our study of exploring the possibility of measuring quality of different visualizations of a dynamic network, this formula is used. The details of the study are described in the following section.

3   Experiment

Visualizations of a dynamic network can be considered as visualizations of a series of static networks. Therefore, to examine the validity of formula 1 in measuring overall quality of dynamic networks, we applied it on visualizations, or drawings, of different networks (or graphs). We wanted to know whether this measure was still sensitive enough to predict task performance when different graphs were used. We used part of the experimental data of Huang et al. [5] for this purpose.

3.1   Data

There were 100 graphs, which were randomly selected from popular benchmark test suits: Rome graphs [13]. Rome graphs were a graph collection that were collected from real world applications in the field of software engineering, and have been widely used in graph drawing for testing purposes. The selected graphs were of different sizes, ranging from 15 to 50 ($Mean = 33.63$, $StDev = 6.47$). These graphs were drawn using a force-directed algorithm, resulting in 100 drawings in total.

The drawing stimuli were displayed one by one by a custom-built system. Forty-three subjects participated in the study. They were asked to find the shortest path between two pre-specified nodes in each drawing. Task completion time, responses to the task and mental effort were recorded. Visualization efficiency [4] was also computed afterward based on the recorded data. Therefore, the dependent variables for the study were time, effort, accuracy and efficiency. Overall quality, the predictor, was computed for each of these drawings using formula 1. Figure 1 shows three drawing examples that were of different graphs, but had close overall quality valued at 2.70, 2, 74 and 2.80 from left to right,

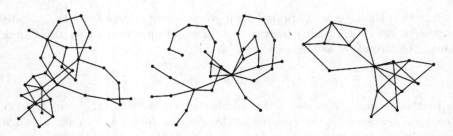

Fig. 1. Three drawings with close overall quality. The left drawing has 34 nodes and 42 edges, the middle drawing has 33 nodes and 37 edges, and the right drawing has 15 nodes and 24 edges

respectively. To test its predictability, we first looked at the scatter diagrams, and then regressed each dependent variable on overall quality. The results are reported in the next sub-section.

3.2   Results

The scatter diagrams are shown in Fig. 2. It can be seen that there was a general trend between each dependent variable and overall quality.

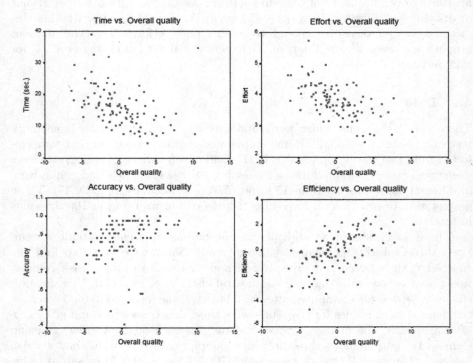

Fig. 2. Scatter diagrams between dependent variables and overall quality

Table 1. Results of simple linear regression tests

Dependent Var.	Predictor	β	F-statistics	R^2
Time	overall quality	-0.568	46.777 ***	0.323
Effort	overall quality	-0.610	58.072 ***	0.372
Accuracy	overall quality	0.279	8.242 **	0.078
Efficiency	overall quality	0.597	54.310 ***	0.356

Notes: **: $p < .01$; ***: $p < .001$

The results of simple linear regression tests are shown in Table 1. The overall regression test of time was significant, $F(1, 98) = 46.777$, $p < 0.001$. Time was negatively correlated with overall quality, $\beta = -0.568$. Overall quality accounted for 32.3 % of the variance in time. Similarly, overall regression tests of effort, accuracy, efficiency were also significant with $p < 0.01$, or $p < 0.001$.

4   Discussion

The results of our data analysis indicated that the overall quality measure (formula 1) was significantly correlated with each of the dependent measures with a medium or large effect size. In other words, the overall quality measure has significant predictive capacity for the performance of human graph comprehension with graphs of different sizes.

This finding indicates that the measure can be used to compare the overall quality of different visualizations, regardless of the size of the underlying networks and their internal structures. Being able to compare overall quality without having to hold the underlying graph constant makes the measure more widely applicable. For example, given a large graph dataset, interaction techniques are often used to show one part of the graph at one time to facilitate the human graph reading process. However, designing and implementing an interaction method can be time-consuming. Even if it has been implemented, there is still a need of knowing whether the interaction method in consideration is actually effective or not by conducting more time-consuming user studies. By applying the overall quality measure on the layout of the whole graph and the intended layouts of its sub-graphs, the visualization designer can quickly decide whether the proposed interaction method is effective, without having to go through the whole implementation process as required otherwise.

Further, in visualizing dynamic networks, it is often desirable to keep positions of nodes unchanged in order to preserve mental map. However, empirical research on dynamic visualization has so far not been conclusive in supporting this practice [11]. Being able to compare the overall quality of snapshots of an evolving graph, the measure of formula 1 may offer us new insights into visualizing dynamic networks and explaining the current research results on mental map.

It should be noted that our study had limitations. For example, only one specific path-search task was used and further, this task might not be generally related to comprehension of dynamic networks in practice.

5 Summary

In this paper we presented an initial study that is part of our effort of investigating how preserving mental map and at the same time maintaining overall quality at a reasonable level can be balanced for visualization of dynamic networks. We applied an existing overall quality metric that is an aggregation based measure on a number of visualizations of different networks. The results showed that the quality measure was significantly correlated with the user task performance, indicating its validity for the purpose of measurement. For future work, more comprehensive studies with various types of benchmark datasets, use cases and tasks should be conducted to test the validity of the measurement.

References

1. Janicke, H., Chen, M.: A salience-based quality metric for visualization. In: Proceedings ofthe 12th Eurographics/IEEE - VGTC Conference on Visualization (EuroVis 2010), pp. 1183–1192 (2010)
2. Eades, P., Hong, S.-H., Klein, K., Nguyen, A.: Shape-based quality metrics for large graph visualization. In: Di Giacomo, E., Lubiw, A. (eds.) GD 2015. LNCS, vol. 9411, pp. 502–514. Springer, Heidelberg (2015). doi:10.1007/978-3-319-27261-0_41
3. Huang, W., Huang, M.L., Lin, C.-C.: Evaluating overall quality of graph visualizations based on aesthetics aggregation. Inf. Sci. **330**, 444–454 (2016)
4. Huang, W., Eades, P., Hong, S.-H.: Measuring effectiveness of graph visualizations: a cognitive load perspective. Inf. Vis. **8**(3), 139–152 (2009)
5. Huang, W., Eades, P., Hong, S.-H., Lin, C.-C.: Improving multiple aesthetics produces better graph drawings. J. Vis. Lang. Comput. **24**(4), 262–272 (2013)
6. Friedrich, C., Eades, P.: Graph drawing in motion. JGAA **6**(3), 353–370 (2002)
7. Moody, J., McFarland, D., Bender-DeMoll, S.: Dynamic network visualization. Am. J. Sociol. **110**, 1206–1241 (2005)
8. Bender-deMoll, S., McFarland, D.: The art and science of dynamic network visualization. J. Soc. Struct. 7(2) (2006)
9. Misue, K., Eades, P., Lai, W., Sugiyama, K.: Layout adjustment and the mental map. J. Vis. Lang. Comput. **6**(2), 183–210 (1995)
10. Minamoto, T., Shipstead, Z., Osaka, N., Engle, R.: Low cognitive load strengthens distractor interference while high load attenuates when cognitive load and distractor possess similar visual characteristics. Attention Percept. Psychophys. **77**(5), 1659–1673 (2015)
11. Archambault, D., Purchase, H.: The map in the mental map: experimental results in dynamic graph drawing. Int. J. Hum. Comput. Stud. **71**(11), 1044–1055 (2013)
12. Diehl, S., Gorg, C., Kerren, A.: Preserving the mental map using foresighted layout. In: VisSym, pp. 175–184 (2001)
13. di Battista, G., Garg, A., Liotta, G., Tamassia, R., Tassinari, E., Vargiu, F.: An experimental comparison of four graph drawing algorithms. Comput. Geom. Theory Appl. **7**(5–6), 303–325 (1997)
14. Ng, H.K., Kalyuga, S., Sweller, J.: Reducing transience during animation: a cognitive load perspective. Educ. Psychol. **33**(7), 755–772 (2013)

An Ingredient Selection System for Patients Using SWRL Rules Optimization and Food Ontology

Chakkrit Snae Namahoot[1(✉)], Sakesan Sivilai[1], and Michael Brückner[2]

[1] Department of Computer Science and Information Technology, Faculty of Science,
Naresuan University, Phitsanulok, Thailand
chakkrits@nu.ac.th, sakesan@psru.ac.th
[2] Department of Educational Technology and Communication, Faculty of Education,
Naresuan University, Phitsanulok, Thailand
michaelb@nu.ac.th

Abstract. This paper presents research on the design and development of an ontology to represent knowledge about food and nutrition for patients and on the development and optimization of SWRL (Semantic Web Rule Language) rules to select suitable ingredients for patients. Emphasis was placed on optimizing search response times by testing different rule processing approaches to achieve the fastest processing time. According to the effort on seeking the way to optimize SWRL inference rules for recommending the most appropriate ingredients to the patients, it was found that the particular rule pattern can be processed faster than the previous rules designed for the original structure at an average of 35 %.

Keywords: Ontology · Semantic Web Rule Language · Rule optimization · Dietary knowledge representation · Knowledge management · Algorithm

1 Introduction

Dietary requirements are second only in importance to medical treatment for hospital in-patients. Nutritional principles and suitable ingredients that take into account the patients' medical condition, particular illness and physical conditions are essential and contribute to the relief of the patient's illness and to the continuing rehabilitation of the patient. This is particularly the case for many specific diseases, diabetes, high blood pressure, coronary artery disease, gallstones, gout and cancers [1]. Consumption of inappropriate food and foods to which the patient has an allergy will exacerbate and prolong the medical condition of the patient. Hospitals have to manage numerous and diverse groups of patients; specific disease conditions and allergies as well as social, ethnic and religious food preferences and prohibitions must be catered for. All of these factors create a complicated and time consuming process in hospitals.

To overcome these problems, the application of a technology-driven solution of an automated dietary planning system is suggested. This system is responsible for managing ingredient selection for a suitable diet for each particular patient. The proposed ingredient selection system is based on a food ontology developed with SWRL. The system uses SWRL rules optimization of ontology reasoning to find and rank the most appropriate

© Springer International Publishing AG 2016
Y. Luo (Ed.): CDVE 2016, LNCS 9929, pp. 163–171, 2016.
DOI: 10.1007/978-3-319-46771-9_22

nutrients. An important aspect of such a system is to be user friendly and provides timely information to the users, as well as being sufficiently comprehensive.

2   Literature Review

In general, it can be said that a food ontology provides automatic food recognition capability. Within the contemporary information technology environment, these automated food recognition methods can connect to a cloud-based lookup database comprising data, food and plate images, food item barcodes, previously classified Near Infrared (NIR) spectra of food items, and as many other aspects of food preparation, nutrition information and ingredient composition as may be required, and provides the ability to match and identify a scanned food item, and report the results back to the user. However, these methods remain of limited value if we cannot reason with the identified ingredients and quantities/portion sizes in a proposed meal in various contexts; i.e., to understand from a semantic perspective food types, properties, and interrelationships in the context of health conditions and preferences [2].

The development of special knowledge ontologies has been discussed previously. The food ontology presented in [3] is appropriate to, for example, elderly users, when recommending meal plans. Other researchers have proposed diet planning systems for diabetes patients using ontology and SWRL. In [4] a recommendation system based on domain ontology and SWRL for anti-diabetic drugs selection with a knowledge base developed by experts in a Taiwan hospital, which is based on the American Association of Clinical Endocrinologists Medical Guidelines for Clinical Practice for the Management of Diabetes Mellitus (AACEMG). These ontologies are used to store knowledge about drugs and patient's condition, and the SWRL is used to create rules for choosing the most appropriate medication regarding the physical condition of patients. The system is implemented using the Java Expert Systems Shell (JESS). In [5] an ontology based system for predicting disease uses SWRL rules. Our system, reported in [2] included a web-based food menu recommender system for patients with diabetes. All of these examples show the successful application of ontologies.

The current proposed system discussed here manifests a significant processing difference. In the systems identified in our literature review and mentioned above, the SWRL rules have not been optimized. This means that if the semantics of the data are very large it can be very time consuming to generate the output from JESS, rendering these system less than optimal for the users. Timeliness of response is almost always a key factor in system acceptability. To overcome this significant problem, we have designed and developed an ontology to represent the knowledge about food and nutrition for patients with a novel technique to optimize the SWRL rules using JESS, thereby substantially increasing the speed of response and reducing the time taken for the SWRL rules to arrive at a conclusion. In our research, we first constructed the SWRL rules and then iteratively modified, varied and tested the rules to achieve optimal processing time. The main outcome of this part of the research is a new technique for optimizing SWRL rules used in the suitable ingredient selection system.

3   Methodology

3.1   Ontology Design

We reused the FOODS ontology [6] and redesigned it for patient dietary and menu planning. The new food ontology includes classes providing knowledge about restrictions when specific medical disorders are present.

The ontology is divided into fourteen classes, including Regional Cuisine, Religious preferences (Nationality), Foods, Patient, Gender, Preparation Method, Types of Diet, particular Meal components, Specific Dishes, Seasonal considerations, Ingredients, Nutritional information, Body Organs, and Disease information. A class tree includes classes further divided into up to a further three levels of sub-classes depending on the suitability of the information for actual use.

Data about nutrients and ingredients was retrieved from The USDA National Nutrient Database for Standard Reference which is a database published by the United States Department of Agriculture [7]. We have comprehensively analyzed and regrouped the ingredients, such as meats, cereals, vegetables, fruits, dairy products, beverages, and spices and seasonings in order to make it appropriate for the meals provided by hospitals in Thailand. It is suggested that the ontology is appropriate for any country but the data can be reconstructed or otherwise modified according to local cuisine and cultural norms.

3.2   SWRL Rules Development

The SWRL rules have been designed and developed in selecting the suitable ingredients for the patient according to the design principles of SWRL [8] which consists of (Table 1): (1) Atom: symbol used to represent classes, properties or variables within the rules such as food: Diseases (? X) represents the class form, food: essentialNutrients

Table 1. An example of the SWRL rule construction for Gout disease (original rule)

	Rule 1 Atoms	Atom Description
1	food:Diseases(?x) ^	Access Diseases class for finding diseases
2	food:hasDiseaseName(?x, "Gout")^	Find disease name which is Gout disease
3	food:essentialNutrients(?x, ?ess) ^	Find essential nutrients from Gout disease
4	food:avoidNutrients(?x, ?avoid) ^	Find avoiding nutrients from Gout disease
5	food:Ingredients(?ine) ^	Access Ingredients class for finding ingredients with essential nutrients for Gout
6	food:Ingredients(?ina) ^	Access Ingredients class for finding ingredients with avoiding nutrients for Gout
7	food:hasNutrients(?ine, ?ess) ^	Find ingredients with essential nutrients
8	food:hasNutrients(?ina, ?avoid) ->	Find ingredients with avoiding nutrients
9	food:shouldConsume(?x, ?ine) ^ food:shouldNotConsume(?x, ? ina)	Display results: Ingredients should and should not consume

(? x, ? ess) represents a property format and ?x or ?ess represents variables. (2) Classes: the concept of knowledge or information, such as food: Diseases (? X) presents concept or knowledge of the disease. (3) Properties: the property of the class, such as food: essentialNutrients (? X, ? Ess) is a class of property Diseases, and (4) Variables: is used to represent a variable in classes or properties such as food: Diseases (? X) where ? X is a variable represents any diseases in class.

Table 1 is the example of the forty SWRL rules developed for selection of ingredients that should and should not consume for patients with Gout disease. The SWRL rules were developed and tested via JESS [9]. An example of an original rule of selecting the most suitable ingredients for Gout disease which consists of 9 Atoms: Atoms 1 to 8 as Processing Atoms, and Atom 9 is a Result Atom. There is only ever one Result Atoms for a Rule. Each Rule has the same set of Atoms but a different 'variable' in each Rule.

4   SWRL Rules Optimization and System Architecture

Our objective was to optimize the SWRL rules to achieve the fastest possible rule processing time that still produced a complete and correct result. In this part, we show how to optimize the SWRL rules and test for the best rule that gives the least processing time. The terminology appropriate here is that each SWRL rule comprises 8 'processing' atoms, and 1 'results' atom. The ontology consists of 40 rules in total. One data preparation process (Sect. 4.1) and a technique of alternating pairs of atoms for the best position (Sect. 4.2) were used and tested for finding the optimal SWRL pattern to be used in the system.

4.1   Data Preparation

This section consists of two processes as follows:

(1)   Test original rules (Table 1) to get processing time and Table 2 (atom order 0) shows the results of the processing time of the original rules.

Table 2.   An example of the possible pairs of swapped atoms with the processing time

Atom order	Swapped Atom pair	Processing time (second)			
		Gout	Gastritis	Liver cirrhosis	Average
0	original rule	3.48	3.73	3.78	3.66
1	5 -> 8, 8 -> 5	3.48	3.62	3.64	3.58
2	7 -> 8, 8 -> 7	3.51	3.65	3.67	3.61
3	3 -> 5, 5 -> 3	3.46	3.70	3.76	3.64
4	1 -> 6, 6 -> 1	3.45	3.75	3.79	3.66

(2)   The pair swapped atoms with Combinatorics

This section has adopted the Combinatorics [10] used in preparation for the pair swapped atoms process without duplicate data using $C(n, r) = n!/(n - r) * r!$, where the

C(n, r) represent the possible pairs of swapped atoms without duplicates, n is the number of processing atoms and r is the number of atom pairs.

For example, the SWRL rule processing uses 8 processing atoms (n = 8) to switch atom pairs (r = 2); therefore, C (n, r) = 8!/((8 − 2)!2!), which has 28 possible pairs of swapped atoms as presents in Tale 2 ordered by the processing time (three examples of rules based on Gout, Gastritis, and Liver cirrhosis were analyzed to get an average time).

4.2 Alternating Pairs of Atoms for the Best Position

Part of the process is to compare possible pairs of swapped atoms (Table 2) against the time for the original processing. The distinct pairs of atoms that give the minimum processing time to form new rule patterns consist of 1 pair swapping, 2 pairs swapping, and 3 pairs swapping of atoms. The fastest rule is chosen to be used. The alternating pairs of atoms for the best position technique process can be described as follows:

1. Compare and choose the pairs of atoms with the combinatorics that takes less processing time than the original rules (Table 2).
2. Find all possible pairs of alternating atoms to be constructed with the new rule pattern.
3. Compare the processing time of the possible pairs from 2.
4. Choose the optimal rule with the fastest processing time from 3.

The selection of these pairs is gained by alternating pairs of atoms with the best position technique, as described in the process stated above in Sect. 4.2. Table 2 shows that the atom pairs 1–3 are better than the original rule in terms of processing time.

The best atom pair swapping that gives the least processing time (less than the original rule) is the atom swapping between 5 -> 8 and 8 -> 5 (average 3.58 s). Therefore, the first new rule of 1 atom pair swapping is constructed by swapping the atom pair 5 -> 8), resulting in a new atom order of 1, 2, 3, 4, 8, 6, 7, 5. For 2 atoms pair swapping rule construction we use atom order no. 4 and swap the pairs 5 - >8 and 1 -> 6), resulting in the atom order of 6, 2, 3, 4, 8, 1, 7, 5. The reason we did not use atom order no. 2 (7 -> 8, 8 -> 7) and 3 (3 -> 5, 5 -> 3) was that atom 8 and 5 were already used in atom no 1. Also if we consider a rule of 3 atom pair swapping we would have the distinct atom order no. 5 included (switching pair 3 -> 4, 4 -> 3) as 6, 2, 4, 3, 8, 1, 7, 5. As can be seen from Table 3 the 3 atom pair swapping (6, 2, 4, 3, 8, 1, 7, 5) gives the least processing time (3.53 s) to be used in the system.

Table 3. Result of processing time from atom swapping

Rule no. and pattern	Detail	Time (second)			
	Techniques	Gout	Gastritis	Liver cirrhosis	Average
(1) 1, 2, 3, 4, **8**, 6, 7,5	1 Pair swapping 5 -> 8	3.48	3.62	3.64	3.58
(2) **6**, 2, 3, 4, 8, 1, 7,5	2 pairs swapping (5 -> 8 and 1 -> 6)	3.46	3.62	3.66	3.58
(3) **6**, 2, **4**, 3, 8, 1, 7, 5	3 pairs swapping (5 -> 8, 1 - >6 and 3 -> 4)	3.50	3.58	3.63	3.53

4.3 Ingredient Selection System

The process of Fig. 1 can be described as follows:

1. Retrieve patient information from a database of Personal Health Record (PHR), which consisted of weight, height, age, sex, type of disease, food allergies, etc.
2. Analyze and summarize the number of cases of the disease and calculate the nutritional needs of patients per day.
3. Retrieve the ingredients that should and should not be consumed for patients with the diseases from optimal SWRL rules (SWRL Rules Optimization) via Jena API and SPARQL.
4. Select and rank the suitable ingredients for the patient by calculating and ranking appropriate ingredients in each nutritional category using worthiness algorithms.
5. The results of suitable ingredient selection for patients which can be divided into 7 nutritional categories: flour, meat, fruits, fats, vegetables, milk and spices.

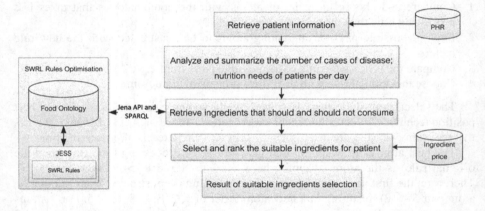

Fig. 1. Process of the ingredient selection system for patients

The algorithm for ranking the most suitable ingredients uses $W_i = N_i * TN/P_i$, where W_i is worthiness of ingredient, N_i is number of nutrition needs in ingredient, TN is total amount of nutrition in ingredient and P_i is ingredient price:

- Take the suitable ingredient list (take out the list of ingredients that should not consume out from the list of ingredients that should consume) and calculate worthiness of ingredients using the above equation
- Rank result of suitable ingredients from the highest to lowest values for each category of ingredients. Sort the number of ingredients in each category in descending.
- Recommend the suitable ingredients with the first two or three with highest values (depending on user defined) of each ranking category.

An example of the worthiness calculation of flour and cereals category is presented in Fig. 2. The corn and egg noodles can be selected for suitable ingredients since they are ranked with the highest worthiness 34.2 and 15.75, respectively, according to the calculation above.

Ingredient types	Ingredient name	Ni	TN	Pi	Worthiness(Wi)	Ranking
Flour and Cereals	Corn	19	27	15	34.20	1
	Egg noodles	21	30	40	15.75	2
	White rice	17	25	30	14.17	3

Fig. 2. An example of the worthiness calculation of flour and cereals category

5   Testing and Result

This section shows the result of optimal SWRL rule with processing time on the system and the result of suitable ingredient selection system with the optimized rules.

First, we took the 40 optimized rules from the process in Sect. 4.2 and tested with original rules using the suitable ingredients selection system. The result shows that the rules which have been optimized still gives the faster processing time (8.72 s on average) than the original rules (13.48 on average). From the experiment results, the gain on processing time on the system is not substantial. However, it provides a huge difference in user's experience since the faster result generating better ingredient selection adjustment can be achieved by nutritionist which is around 35 % faster $((13.48-8.72)/13.48) \times 100 = 35.31$.

Second, we discuss the results of the system testing for patients in hospitals. The testing process uses simulated patient data to obtain a sufficient number and variety, which consisted of 120 patients divided into 83 male and 37 female admitted with total 40 diseases, (equal to the number of SWRL rules construction) containing 26 general diseases and 14 specific diseases.

Figure 3 shows the most suitable ingredient selection with nutritional categories for all diseases, which consists of three parts: (1) the ingredients identified as suitable for individual patients, (2) ingredient prices (baht per kilogram), and (3) the cost saving summary. In the category of flour and cereals, the system selects two kinds of ingredients: corn and egg noodle with have the highest worthiness. In the category of meat, the system selects two kinds of ingredients: Pangasius and Tilapia which have the lower worthiness than the first five ingredients (egg yolk, egg, duck egg, chicken meat and chicken drumstick). These top five ingredients cannot be consumed by patients with diseases such as gout disease (cannot consume poultry). Therefore, the system selects ingredients that can be consumed for all patients with the highest worthiness and are not in the ingredient prohibited. From this result, the system separates ingredients for general and specific diseases since this provides better results in terms of food consumption and cost savings as shown in Fig. 4.

An Ingredient Selection System for Patients

Ingredient types	Select	Ingredient name	Price(B)/Kg.	Ingredient types	Select	Ingredient name	Price(B)/Kg.
Flour and Cereals	☑	Corn	15	Vagetables	☑	Cabbage	9
	☑	Egg noodles	40		☑	Okra	12
Meats	☐	~~Egg yolk~~	~~60~~		☑	Eggplant	12
	☐	~~Egg~~	~~60~~	Fruits	☐	~~Mango~~	~~10~~
	☐	~~Duck egg~~	~~70~~		☐	~~Grape~~	~~12~~
	☐	~~Chicken meat~~	~~60~~		☑	Papaya	15
	☐	~~Chicken drumstick~~	~~76~~		☑	Pineapple	18
	☑	Pangasius	57				
	☑	Tilapia	75				

Display more nutritional categories

Number of patients: **120** | Budget per day: **12,000B** | Total cost per day: **8,760B** | Save: **3,240B**

Fig. 3. Result of the ingredient selection system for all diseases

An Ingredient Selection System for Patients (General diseases)

Ingredient types	Select	Ingredient name	Price(B)/Kg.	Ingredient types	Select	Ingredient name	Price(B)/Kg.
Flour and Cereals	☑	Corn	15	Vagetables	☑	Cabbage	9
	☑	Egg noodles	40		☑	Okra	12
Meats	☑	Egg yolk	60		☑	Eggplant	12
	☑	Egg	60	Fruits	☑	Mango	10
					☑	Grape	12

Display more nutritional categories

Number of patients: **71** | Budget per day: **7,100B** | Total cost per day: **3,194B** | Save: **3,906B**

An Ingredient Selection System for Patients (Specific diseases)

Ingredient types	Select	Ingredient name	Price(B)/Kg.	Ingredient types	Select	Ingredient name	Price(B)/Kg.
Flour and Cereals	☑	Corn	15	Vagetables	☑	Cabbage	9
	☑	Egg noodles	40		☑	Okra	12
Meats	☑	Pangasius	57		☑	Eggplant	12
	☑	Tilapia	75	Fruits	☑	Papaya	15
					☑	Pineapple	18

Display more nutritional categories

Number of patients: **49** | Budget per day: **4,900B** | Total cost per day: **3,585B** | Save: **1,315B**

Fig. 4. Result of the ingredient selection component for diseases

Figure 4 shows that the system recommended the most suitable ingredients for 71 patients with 26 general diseases and 49 patients with 14 specific diseases. For general diseases, patients can consume all ingredients with the first two or three ingredients ranked, such as corn and egg noodle, egg yolk, and mango and grape in the category of flour and cereals, meats, and fruits, respectively. For specific diseases, the result of suitable ingredient selection is the same as in Fig. 3 but it differs in terms of cost savings due to the number of patients.

As can be seen in Figs. 3 and 4 the system both shows nutrient values and cost savings. Regarding the 120 patients from the example, the budget per day and patient was 100 baht per person/day, amounting to 12,000 baht in total per day. However, the ingredients suggested by the system used for all diseases had cost 8,760 baht in total per day and therefore, the saving was up to 3,240 baht in total. Similarly, in case of using the system separately for general and specific diseases (Fig. 4) the saving would was up to 5,221 baht (3,906 baht for general diseases and 1,315 baht for specific diseases). Consequently, the effective use of the system would save a substantial amount of money for ingredients each fiscal year.

6   Conclusion

This paper has presented the results of a design-and-create research leading to an optimized set of SWRL rules for knowledge representation relating nutritional data considering health conditions and food preferences of individual patients. The resulting system can be used by hospitals to improve their dietary service processes and optimize processing times. The research shows that it is possible to speed up the search through changing an order of evaluation of atoms within the rules. In such a way a collection of rules becomes better "adjusted" to a pre-defined collection of queries. For a given collection of queries it has achieved 35 % improvement in time of the selected queries. Further work will be carried out to identify a set of techniques to arrange the atoms of knowledge representation in an optimized order to further improve the performance of the selection process.

References

1. Sivilai. S., Namahoot, C.S., Brückner, M.: SWRL rules optimization for an in-patient diet planning system (DIPS). Inf. J. **19**(7), 3031–3038 (2016)
2. Boulos, M.N.K., Yassine, A., Shirmohammadi, S., Namahoot, C.S., Brückner, M.: Towards an "Internet of Food": food ontologies for the internet of things. Future Internet **7**, 372–392 (2015)
3. Sivilai, S., Snae, C., Brückner, M.: Ontology-driven personalized food and nutrition planning system for the elderly. In: The 2nd International Conference in Business Management and Information Sciences, Phitsanulok, Thailand (2012)
4. Chen, R.C., Huang, Y.H., Bau, C.T., Chen, S.M.: A recommendation system based on domain ontology and SWRL for anti-diabetic drugs selection. Expert Syst. Appl. **39**, 3995–4006 (2012)
5. Thirugnanam, M., Thirugnanam, T., Mangayarkarasi, R.: An ontology based system for predicting disease using SWRL rules. Int. J. Comput. Sci. Bus. Inf. **7**(1), 1–15 (2013)
6. Snae, C., Brückner, M.: FOODS: a food-oriented ontology-driven system. In: The 2nd IEEE International Conference on Digital Ecosystems and Technologies (DEST 2008), Phitsanulok, Thailand, pp. 168–176 (2008)
7. USDA. National nutrient database for standard reference. http://www.nal.usda.gov
8. SWRL: A Semantic Web Rule Language Combining OWL and RuleML. http://www.w3.org/Submission/SWRL/
9. Jess: the Rule Engine for the JavaTM Platform. http://www.jessrules.com/
10. Roberts, F., Tesman, B.: Applied combinatorics. Chapman and Hall/CRC, London (2009)

A Web Based Cooperation Tool for Evaluating Standardized Curricula Using Ontology Mapping

Chayan Nuntawong[1], Chakkrit Snae Namahoot[1,2(✉)], and Michael Brückner[3]

[1] Department of Computer Science and Information Technology, Faculty of Science,
Naresuan University, Phitsanulok, Thailand
chayan@nsru.ac.th, chakkrits@nu.ac.th
[2] Center of Excellence in Nonlinear Analysis and Optimization, Faculty of Science,
Naresuan University, Phitsanulok, Thailand
[3] Department of Educational Technology and Communication, Faculty of Education,
Naresuan University, Phitsanulok, Thailand
michaelb@nu.ac.th

Abstract. In this paper, we present HOME 2.0, an improved version of an ontology mapping tool that can create subject ontologies from subject curricula. To illustrate the design and test of the system we use a computer science curriculum. The semantic data of standard computer science topics can be created using synonyms of topics that are categorized in Wikipedia for mapping improvement of the relevant topics. The tool generates the curriculum data automatically into a course ontology with instances and properties, then finds the correspondences with a standard curriculum ontology using a combination of instance-based and structure-based ontology mapping techniques. The test results with sample data show that the tool works sufficiently and shows improved performance regarding results.

Keywords: Ontology mapping · Knowledge management · Semantic representation · Information-integrated collaboration · Web application

1 Background and Problems

Standardization of curricula and teaching approaches across all universities is a matter for higher education management to consider. In practice, however, the process to improve and standardize curricula is difficult and time consuming. Moreover, approaches to compare a given subject curriculum with a standardized curriculum is a complex and tedious task. Automated methods would be of great help but they should be easy enough to be used by technically inexperienced staff, e.g. educational administrators. Some technology-based approaches to decision-making in the area of curriculum standardization and teaching practice have been developed previously, but they have not been able to successfully and accurately support the decision-making process due to lack of standardization in their data content, lack of comprehensive content and complicated algorithms and language.

© Springer International Publishing AG 2016
Y. Luo (Ed.): CDVE 2016, LNCS 9929, pp. 172–180, 2016.
DOI: 10.1007/978-3-319-46771-9_23

The purpose of our study was to create a software tool that has processing techniques that are easy-to-use and understand, allowing the construction of a comprehensive, standard set of data, relevant to the subject of the curricula using Wikipedia essentially as a Thesaurus of terms, their synonyms and definitions, and SKOS features to make accurate and efficient terminology comparisons.

The rest of this paper is structured as follows: after an overview of related work we detail the design of the ontology and the process steps of the system: preprocessing, matching and instance-based/structure-based mapping of the ontologies. Section 4 shows an overview of the tests and results before conclusions are drawn and an outlook on further work is given.

2   Related Work

There are several ontology mapping techniques used to evaluate the standards of curricula. Nuntawong et al. [1] have developed the TQF: HEd ontology with the semantic-based ontology mapping tool that can find similarity of words, which relate to the same meaning in course descriptions (computer science context) by extending Wu & Palmer's algorithm. However, there was no standard of evaluation and the semantic technique seemed to give unrelated words in computer science contexts. Subsequently, Nuntawong et al. [2] presented the HOME tool, a combination of semantic-based and structure-based ontology mapping techniques. The standard curriculum data in computer science has been developed using SKOS, which is a semantic data language defined by W3C. The advantage of the structure-based ontology mapping technique is to determine the correctness of the body of knowledge categories sufficiently. However, the semantic–based technique was still time consuming in the process and the results of similar words matching by Wu & Palmer [3] and WordNet need to be improved in term of the meaning of words that can related to the similar computer science contexts especially long words.

An instance-based ontology mapping technique is also applied, especially to consider the relationship of instance, property, or both [4]. Instance is like a record in a database and can be used to map the relational data, such as in Octaviani et al. [5], who presented the tool D2RQ for mapping the relational educational data using instance or property from various DBMS's (e.g., MySQL, PostgreSQL or Oracle). Jin et al. [6] introduced PROMPT-V applying an instance-based mapping technique which can create visual instances from all ontology nodes. Natural Language Processing and Vector Space Model are used in the virtual instance mapping process. The results of this mapping show that PROMPT-V gives a better performance against such string matching techniques as COMA [7] and PROMPT [8]. Zheng et al. [9] presented ontology mapping techniques based on structure and instances. The similarity of the instance mapping was calculated using Bayesian analysis and used the structure based to consider the mapping. Singh and Cheah [10] presented an approach for ontology mapping using a library of ontology mapping algorithms to produce a composite algorithm. The F-measures for each ontology mapping module are calculated and form a chromosome in a genetic algorithm; then a fitness value is used to determine the optimal ontology mapping technique (single or combination) to employ.

From the literature review above, the instance-based ontology mapping seemed to be simple and well-used. So, we combined the instance-based and structure-based techniques into our new tool, which we call HOME 2.0. We also improved the standard curriculum data relating computer science by generating the synonyms from that domain in the Wikipedia for solving unrelated meanings of words.

3   Methodologies and System Design

3.1   Ontology Design

Many state-of-the-art matching systems apply internal matching processes and rely only on the knowledge stated in the ontologies to match. Systems using such external knowledge sources as dictionaries and synonym lists apply external matching processes. HOME 2.0 is a system with external matching processes. Three ontologies were used in the development and test of this tool, TQF: HEd ontology (O_{TQF}), curriculum ontology (O_{CC}) and SKOS ontology with synonym (SOS_{CC}) for knowledge management and information-integrated collaboration.

We modified some class levels from the TQF: HEd ontology (O_{TQF}) described in [1] for better performance in the mapping process. The O_{TQF} contained classes of all "Knowledge Area", e.g. Intelligent Systems, Software Engineering, Operating Systems, etc. Each knowledge area class contained the "Body of Knowledge" class. For example, the "Intelligent Systems" knowledge area must contain "Fundamental Issues", "Basic Search Strategies" and "Knowledge Based Reasoning". The example of O_{TQF} can show in Fig. 1.

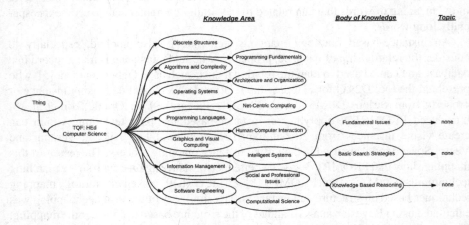

Fig. 1. The example of O_{TQF} in Intelligent Systems knowledge area

The tool can generate the curriculum ontology (O_{CC}) for each curriculum automatically. This ontology contained the classes that categorized by subject, such as "Required

Subject", "Selective Subject", etc. Each subject class contained instances and properties that generated when input the curriculum data. In each instance of subject must have the datatype property: "hasSubjectName", "hasSubjectID", "hasDescription" and the object property: "hasCredit" and "hasLecturer". Figure 2 shows the example of O_{CC} classes and some instance of subject, and instances as detail of Artificial Intelligence (AI) subject.

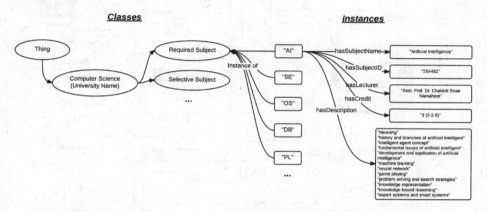

Fig. 2. An example of O_{CC}, some instances of subject, and detail of AI subject

The tool needs the standard data for the computer science curriculum to check the correctness of the mapping process. In this work, we created the SKOS ontology with the synonym (SOS_{CC}) using data from the standard curriculum data in computer science ($SKOS_{CC}$) designed by [2] that uses data from the Computer Science Curricula 2013 [11] defined by the joint task force of ACM and IEEE, and use synonyms generated from Wikipedia (see Sect. 3.2). Figure 3 shows knowledge areas in SOS_{CC} and the Intelligent Systems concepts, such as the body of knowledge and synonyms of topics.

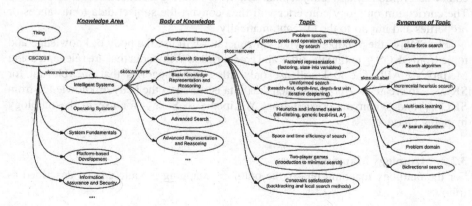

Fig. 3. An example of SOS_{CC}

3.2   System Architecture

Figure 4 shows the system architecture. It illustrates the two phases; the preprocessing phase and the ontology mapping phase.

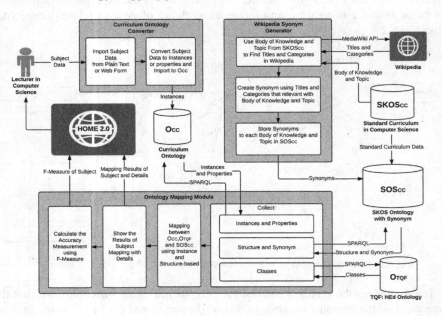

Fig. 4. The system architecture

3.2.1   Preprocessing Phase

A lecturer in computer science will input the subject data, such as course syllabus or course description by uploading a plain text file or entering the data through a web form. The curriculum ontology converter will then convert the subject data to instances or properties and import to the O_{CC} automatically.

For SOS_{CC}, the Wikipedia synonym generator will use the body of knowledge and topic from $SKOS_{CC}$ to find the titles and categories in Wikipedia that are relevant, using MediaWiki API. The tool will use only titles and categories that are relevant for $SKOS_{CC}$ to create as synonyms, then that data is stored as the body of knowledge from $SKOS_{CC}$ and synonyms created from Wikipedia to SOS_{CC} for use in the ontology mapping phase.

3.2.2   Ontology Mapping Phase

For the ontology mapping phase, the ontology mapping module can be described as follows:

- Collect the instances and properties of each subject from the O_{CC}, classes from O_{TQF}, and structures and synonyms from SOS_{CC} using SPARQL queries.

- Create a mapping between the O_{CC} and O_{TQF} using the combination of instance-based and structure-based ontology mapping techniques (see Sect. 3.2.3).
- Show the results of the subject mapping and details, such as the topics from the subject with matches and mismatches.
- Calculate the accuracy measurement using F-measure and present in the summary of mapping.

3.2.3   Instance-Based and Structure-Based Ontology Mapping

Now we present the combination of the two ontology mapping techniques: instance-based and structure-based techniques [2]. The methodology of the mapping technique can be described as follows:

- First, the tool will check the correspondence of each instance in the O_{CC} and each class in O_{TQF} that matches with each body of knowledge or synonyms from the specific knowledge area in SOS_{CC}.
- If the correspondence is found, the tool will continue to check the position of the instance and class using the structure levels received from SOS_{CC}.
- But if the instance is not found in this knowledge area, that may be because the course description is not relevant to this knowledge area. Then the tool will check with all the body of knowledge classes, topics and synonyms in SOS_{CC} because that particular body of knowledge or topic may cross-reference with other knowledge areas.
- But if the instance is still not found to correspond to all concepts in the SOS_{CC}, the tool decides that this instance is not relevant to the O_{TQF} (and also with SOS_{CC}).

4   Testing and Results

We developed HOME 2.0 as a web based cooperation tool and users can view the mapping results from both SOS_{CC} and O_{TQF}. Both show the topic harnessing the course description that matches within each body of knowledge, matches another body of knowledge as a cross-reference (in case it occurs). It also shows mismatched topics that the user can edit to improve future accuracy, and the weight value for each body of knowledge that represents the teaching objectives of the respective subject. The test process consists of two main parts: mapping with standard curricula SOS_{CC} and mapping with standard curricula TQF. When users import the course description of the AI subject into HOME 2.0, the system separates each section of the course description using the comma separator (,) and compares all these descriptions (instances) with SOS_{CC} (mapping with standard curricula SOS_{CC}) based on the class name, the body of knowledge, topic and synonyms of each topic that comes from Wikipedia synonyms. Figure 5 shows an example of the mapping using test data from a course description in the Artificial Intelligence (AI) domain matched with five bodies of knowledge: Fundamental Issues, Basic Search Strategies, Basic Knowledge Representation and Reasoning, Basic Machine Learning, and Advanced Machine Learning. As an example, for the first body of knowledge, Fundamental Issues, the system found that there are three matching course descriptions: the "intelligent agent concept" matches with

"Intelligent agent" by synonym of "Problem characteristics" (Wikipedia synonym), "fundamental issues of artificial intelligent" matches with the "Fundamental Issues" topic, and "development and application of artificial intelligence" matches with the "AI applications" topic. The system then calculates the average of each course description correspondences to the body of knowledge to allow users to see the importance of content in body of knowledge, called weight values. The weight values indicate how much the course of AI has stressed the importance of content in teaching in each body of knowledge, e.g. Fundamental Issues is a very important piece of knowledge due to the highest weight value of 25 % (number of course description matched in each body of knowledge divided by total number of course description in AI, which is $(3/12) \times 100 = 25\%$).

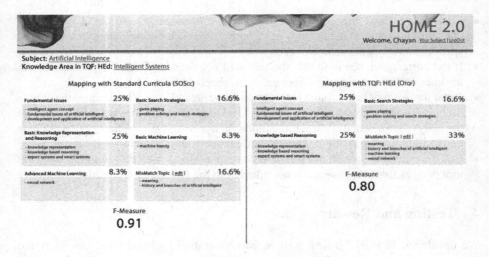

Fig. 5. The interface of HOME 2.0 test with AI subject

Finally the system calculates the f-measure, which indicates the accuracy of the HOME 2.0 calculation, and in this example of the AI subject f is equal to 0.91. The testing process repeated the mapping with standard curricula TQF and revealed that the mismatch topic has the highest weight value at 33 %, and the f-measure is 0.80. This test shows that the body of knowledge in SOS_{CC} covers almost all topics because SOS_{CC} has more body of knowledge classes than O_{TQF}, which may be due to the O_{TQF} using the standard reference from the computer science curriculum which is older than the newer version used by SOS_{CC}. This difference or discrepancy can be illustrated by such terms as "machine learning" and "neural network" which are relatively new terms. These mismatches limit the accuracy of the results.

In this research, examples of five subjects in a computer science course from a university in Thailand, with course descriptions written in English, were tested. These were Artificial Intelligence (AI), Software Engineering (SE), Operating Systems (OS), Database Systems (DB), and Fundamentals of Programming (PL). The F-measure was used to evaluate the accuracy of the HOME 2.0 with SOS_{CC} and to compare with three other techniques identified in the literature: semantic with Ext. WUP [1], HOME [2], HOME 2.0 with O_{TQF} and other mapping algorithms that use WordNet as the standard data such as PROMPT-V [6], and COMA [7]. The results of our evaluation using F-measure are presented in Table 1.

Table 1. The tool evaluation and comparison using F-measure against sample subjects

| | Semantic with Ext. WUP [1] | HOME [2] | PROMPT-V [6] | COMA [7] | HOME 2.0 | |
					with O_{TQF}	with SOS_{CC}
AI	0.67	0.80	0.82	0.80	0.80	0.91
SE	0.63	0.70	0.85	0.80	0.87	0.96
OS	0.55	0.77	0.57	0.55	0.77	1.00
DB	0.31	0.84	0.77	0.72	1.00	1.00
PL	0.56	0.92	0.92	0.64	0.92	0.96
AVG	0.54	0.81	0.78	0.70	0.87	0.97

The F-measure of HOME 2.0 with O_{TQF} is 0.87 and with SOS_{CC}, 0.97, which indicates that HOME 2.0 provides greater accuracy than both Semantic with Ext. WUP [1] and HOME [2]. The F-measure of the semantic with Ext. WUP is quite low (0.54) due to the descriptions of the subjects in the O_{TQF} not including many topics. This was especially so in the DB subject. This means that certain topics in the DB subject are not relevant to the O_{TQF}, resulting in many mismatches. We found that the semantic with Ext. WUP, HOME and HOME 2.0 with O_{TQF} failed to match the topics in OS and PL. For example, the topics "inter-process communication" should appear in OS and "recursive functions" should appear in PL. However, these topics were matched using HOME 2.0 with SOS_{CC} and this increased the F-measure score. We used HOME 2.0 to test with O_{TQF} and SOS_{CC} to allow us to see the difference between the body of knowledge represented in both ontologies, using our technique. The body of knowledge in SOS_{CC} was found to be more up-to-date than the O_{TQF} in terms of the variety of topics and the extent of the body of knowledge. Furthermore, the F-measure of PROMPT-V and COMA provide lower accuracy than the HOME2.0. Since, the algorithms use WordNet as the standard data in word mapping process which some words were not relevant with the subject data.

5   Conclusions and Further Work

In this paper, we present an improved curriculum evaluation tool (HOME 2.0) for the computer science curriculum and academic body of knowledge and demonstrate improvements for the standard data content and extent on computer science by generating synonyms of each body of knowledge and topics from Wikipedia that are relevant to our domain. We use a combination of instance-based and structure-based ontology mapping techniques which has achieved better accuracy and correctness than the techniques developed previously.

Limitations are: the data and synonyms used in our tests may not be fully authoritative and reliable, being generated from Wikipedia, but this data was sufficiently extensive and correct for our testing purposes.

This work will be continued to find improved algorithms to check and update the synonyms of standard data recorded in our ontology to achieve greater relevance of content. We will increase the features of the tool to analyze all subjects in a comprehensive body of knowledge for different subject courses, and use more ontology mapping techniques that may improve the correspondence between terms. Test data from other universities in other countries will be incorporated to ensure better results.

References

1. Nuntawong, C., Namahoot, C.S., Brückner, M.: A semantic similarity assessment tool for computer science subjects using extended Wu & Palmer's algorithm and ontology. In: Kim, K.J. (ed.) Information Science and Applications. LNEE, vol. 339, pp. 989–996. Springer, Heidelberg (2015)
2. Nuntawong, C., Namahoot, C.S., Brückner, M.: HOME: hybrid ontology mapping evaluation tool for computer science curricular. The Jurnal Teknologi, Malaysia (2016, to be published)
3. Wu, Z., Palmer, M.: Verb semantics and lexical selection. In: Proceeding of 32nd Annual Meeting of the Association for Computational Linguistics (ACL), Las Cruces, pp. 133–138 (1994)
4. Liu, X., Cao, L., Dai, W.: Overview of ontology mapping and approach. In: 4th IEEE International Conference on Broadband Network and Multimedia Technology (ICBNMT), 28-30 October 2011, pp. 592–595 (2011)
5. Octaviani, D., Pranolo, A., Othman, S.: RDB2Onto: an approach for creating semantic metadata from relational educational data. In: International Conference on Science in Information Technology (ICSITech), pp. 137–140 (2015)
6. Jin, T., Fu, Y., Lin, X., Liu, Q., Cui, Z.: A method of ontology mapping based on instance. In: 3rd International Conference on Intelligent Information Hiding and Multimedia Signal Processing, Kaohsiung, pp. 145–148 (2007)
7. Do, H. and Rahm, E.: COMA - A system for flexible combination of schema mapping approaches. In: Proceedings of the 28th VLDB Conference. pp. 610–621 (2002)
8. Noy, N. F., Musen, M.A.: Anchor-PROMPT: using non-local context for semantic mapping. In: Proceeding of Ontology and Information Sharing Workshop, IJCA (2001)
9. Zheng, C., Shen, Y., Mei, L.: Ontology mapping based on structures and instances. In: International Conference on Machine Learning and Cybernetics, vol. 1, Qingdao, pp. 460–465 (2010)
10. Singh, S., Cheah, Y.: Hybrid approach towards ontology mapping. In: International Symposium on Information Technology, vol. 3, Kuala Lumpur, pp. 1490–1493 (2010)
11. ACM and IEEE. Computer Science Curricular (2013). http://www.acm.org/education/curricularecommendation

Co-creation of a Digital Game to Support Language Revitalisation

Dianna Hardy[✉], Elizabeth Forest, Zoe McIntosh, Janine Gertz, and Trina Myers

James Cook University, Townsville, Australia
{dianna.hardy,elizabeth.forest,zoe.mcintosh,janine.gertz,
trina.myers}@jcu.edu.au

Abstract. Many Aboriginal languages are becoming extinct due to lack of fluent speakers. Computer games offer a way to help teach these languages in a fun and engaging way. However, computer games like all technology objects are based in the culture of their creators. In this paper we describe a project where we co-designed a language application for mobile phone with the Gugu Badhun, an Aboriginal community from north Queensland Australia. The participatory action research process allowed our Aboriginal partners to embed their own culture in the games, leading to a product that supported their goals and aspirations for language renewal. This collaboration has not only provided a way to sustain their language, but also added capacity to their community in ICT development.

Keywords: Participatory action research · Game based learning · Cooperative design · Indigenous research methods

1 Introduction

Every day, ICT professionals are required to bridge the communication divide that exists between technologists and everyday users of technology [1, 2]. When the research team is working with members of marginalised cultures such as Indigenous peoples, this requirement becomes more challenging [3]. Much of the previous research conducted with Aboriginal people has provided little benefit to the communities involved [4], and so any new projects must ensure positive outcomes for Aboriginal people for the time they invest in the research [5].

This paper describes a participatory action research project conducted with members of the Gugu Badhun (an Australian Aboriginal language/community group). The purpose of the project was to develop a smart phone based language teaching game that both children and adults of the group could use to learn their original language in order to aid its preservation.

The language game is an Android application created using Android Studio. The game contains a login screen, a dictionary with audio pronunciation of words, a game demo, and 34 levels which contain 270 words in all. The android application developed was created using Android Studio with Java SE 8's JDK targeting Android 4.0.3 (Kit Kat) to Android 5.0 (Lollipop). A SQLite database was used to store the dictionary of language words, the user's details, and any other data.

© Springer International Publishing AG 2016
Y. Luo (Ed.): CDVE 2016, LNCS 9929, pp. 181–184, 2016.
DOI: 10.1007/978-3-319-46771-9_24

The main features of the game are the dictionary and the levelling system. The dictionary contains all of the language words used in the application and their English translations. Further information can be discovered about each word, such as the words definition and an audio example of the pronunciation. The application is broken into 34 levels, with each 5th level a revision level. In order to 'Level Up' the user must achieve 100 % on the match-a-word game using the level specific words. As the user progresses through the levels they will acquire badges to emphasise certain achievements (Figs. 1 and 2).

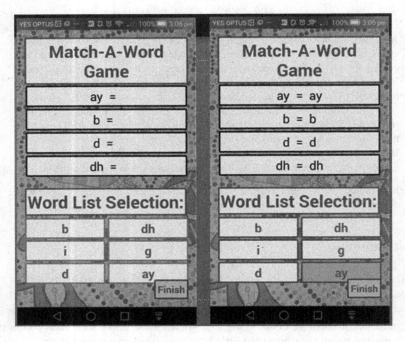

Fig. 1. Match a word functionality in game

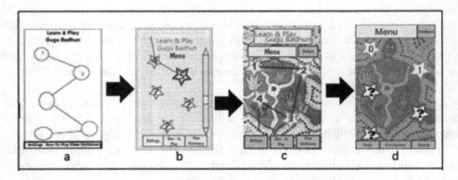

Fig. 2. Development process from sketches through high fidelity application Findings

2   Methods

Information from interviews with the participants was used to create two paper prototypes which were then evaluated by the group. After analysis of the playtesting with the
paper prototypes, a high fidelity version of the game was created and tested by the group.
The final product developed was a small android game, which taught users a few words
at a time and re-enforced this knowledge with a word-match game. Once a black and
white storyboard showing potential functionality was approved then two paper prototypes were developed and then presented to the group. The best aspects of each paper
prototype were combined in a final version of the game.

The participants were particularly concerned that the game not be tokenistic or
contribute to further misunderstanding about their culture. Through the use of co-design
methods such as sketching, paper prototypes and short iteration cycles the researchers
were able to focus on aspects of the game that were of the most interest to the participant.
One of the primary outcomes of the research (other than the creation of the game) was
a kindling of interest in the community to develop further games which might be of a
more immersive aspect. A further outcome was the realization that making the game
available via Google Store or other public mechanisms might restrict the group's ability
to control who has access to the intellectual property embodied in the game. To this end
the group decided to make the game only available by USB installation.

3   Conclusion

Digital games, like all other technology objects reflect the culture of their creators. Salen
and Zimmerman [8] emphasize that "games are culture...The Sims is not merely a
simulation of suburbia, but a representation of cultural interaction that relies on an ideo-
logical reality located beyond the scope of actual game play" (p. 507). By involving a
group in the design of a game that reflects their culture, we help ensure that the underlying norms of that culture are embodied within it [9]. Co-making a game with a cultural
focus, i.e. a game that focuses on the culture of a given group avoids the problem of
stereotypical representation in the larger non-indigenous society. Indeed, Shaw suggests
that while complete non-representation in the video game market is better than stereotypical representation this lack of presence leads to the increasing invisibility and lack
of voice in the wider gaming community [9]. Facilitating Indigenous partners to create
games that reflect their own culture, gives them increased "voice" and presence in the
dominating culture.

References

1. Stappers, P.J.: Designing for other people's strengths and motivations: Three cases using
   context, visions and experiential prototypes. Adv. Eng. Inf. **23**(2), 174–183 (2009)
2. Koskinen, I., Battarbee, K., Mattelmäki, T. (eds.): Empathic Design. IT Press, Helsinki (2003)
3. Madden, D., Cadet-James, Y., Watkin-Lui, F., Atkinson, I.: Healing through ICT: enhancing
   wellbeing in an Aboriginal community. J. Trop. Psychol. **2**, 1–9 (2012)

4. Smith, L.T.: Decolonizing methodologies: Research and indigenous peoples, 2nd edn. Zed Books, New York (2012)
5. Bull, J.R.: Research with aboriginal peoples: authentic relationships as a precursor to ethical research. J. Empirical Res. Hum. Res. Ethics Int. J. 5(4), 13–22 (2010)
6. Sutton, P.: Gugu-Badhun and its neighbours: A Linguistic Salvage Study. (MA Master Thesis), Macquarie University, Sydney (1973)
7. Van Rijn, H., Stappers, P.J.: Motivating users in a codesign process. In: Participatory Design Conference (2008)
8. Salen, K., Zimmerman, E.: Rules of play: game design fundamentals. MIT Press, Cambridge (2004)
9. Shaw, A.: Putting the gay in games: cultural production and GLBT content in video games. Games Cult. 4(3), 228–253 (2009)

Design and Evaluation of an Integrated Collaboration Platform for Secure Information Sharing

Jane Li[1(✉)], John Zic[2], Nerolie Oakes[2], Dongxi Liu[2], and Chen Wang[2]

[1] CSIRO Health and Biosecurity, Marsfield, Australia
Jane.Li@csiro.au
[2] CSIRO Data61, Marsfield, Australia
{John.Zic,Nerolie.Oakes,Dongxi.Liu,Chen.Wang}@csiro.au

Abstract. This paper presents the design and evaluation of a collaboration platform which enables secure information sharing and interaction across professional and organizational boundaries in the biosecurity domain. The platform integrates shared digital workspace and eAuthentication and eAuthorisation technologies in a multi-display environment. It aims to support the diagnosis and decision making meetings between committee members working in different laboratories and organizations in their cooperative work of emergency response on animal diseases. Results from a user study on the security features of the platform show that the integrated platform can provide the basis of trustworthy information sharing, particularly real-time information from laboratory instruments.

Keywords: Collaboration · Authentication and authorization · Evaluation

1 Introduction

Collaboration technology has been used to support individuals and teams from diverse disciplines to coordinate their work and share information across organizational boundaries. With technology advances there has been a trend of expanding the context of collaboration, such as large-scale initiatives for health related collaborations and crisis management and emergency response [1, 2]. These changes have broadened the scope of collaboration settings and introduced challenges in technology design.

We have explored the design of a secure collaboration platform to support multi-organizational collaborations in emergency response on infectious animal diseases. The outbreak of animal diseases, such as foot-and-mouth disease and Hendra virus, can potentially impact on animal welfare and cause enormous economic consequences. A strong national biosecurity management infrastructure for emergency animal disease has been developed by the Australian government. One component of the initiative is the establishment of national Consultative Committee for Emergency Animal Disease (CCEAD) and its associated subcommittees. Each committee is essentially a distributed set of representatives that collaboratively analyse information and discuss the strategies for monitoring and controlling of emergency animal diseases. Committee members are geographically dispersed across Australia and distributed teleconferencing meetings are held during the outbreak of an emergency animal disease. A challenge faced by these

© Springer International Publishing AG 2016
Y. Luo (Ed.): CDVE 2016, LNCS 9929, pp. 185–193, 2016.
DOI: 10.1007/978-3-319-46771-9_25

committees is to collaborate across multiple locations and groups to share and discuss information in a timely manner. Information security is of high priority due to the confidentiality of the information in managing disease outbreaks. An effective secure collaboration platform has been identified as one of the potential tools to enhance the information sharing in their collaborative meetings.

This paper describes our work in designing and evaluating a secure collaboration platform for the collaborations in this particular biosecurity application. We present the collaboration and security requirements that have guided the design of the platform. We provide an overview of the design and report on a user study which aimed to understand the appropriateness of the integrated access control technology.

2 Background and Challenges

We have engaged with members of CCEAD and conducted workplace studies to understand their collaborations [3]. The use case we explored during the design of the secure collaboration platform is the work of LSC-CCEAD (Laboratory Subcommittee CCEAD). LSC-CCEAD is formed immediately following emergency animal disease laboratory findings to facilitate coordination among laboratories involved. It consists of members from the Australian Animal Health Laboratory (AAHL), jurisdictional animal health laboratories at all states, and Department of Agriculture, Fishery and Forestry (DAFF). The work of the LSC-CCEAD is essentially analysing information from multiple sources to provide technical advice to CCEAD. AAHL takes the lead in the diagnostic services based on its expertise and advanced containment facilities.

The challenges in this context relate to supporting real-time information sharing across different organizations [1, 3]. Information is disseminated within and between different organizations through different channels. The data-centric diagnosis meeting is for experts from different disciplines (e.g. microscopy, antigen detection, veterinary) to get together to discuss data from various resources, such as laboratory information systems and databases that can only be accessed by particular workgroups. Email and audio-based teleconferencing are not efficient in supporting the sharing and visualisation of complex data in the diagnosis meetings between LSC-CCEAD members.

The collaboration may involve sensitive information, such as occurrence of a new animal disease. The secure access and sharing of information is important to build shared understandings and support the actions carried out by different members [2]. In addition, a particular challenge in this biosecurity context relates to the sharing of real-time information from scientific instruments. Collaboration systems supporting scientific data analysis need to address three core capabilities: linking people with people, linking people with information and linking people with facilities [4]. These pose specific access control requirements in interacting with instrument applications, such as expensive and sensitive microscopes, since remote participants may be inclined to manipulate devices that they do not know how to operate. These requirements have led to our investigation of secure, trustworthy collaboration infrastructure allowing real-time information exchange and interaction, while preserving confidentiality and privacy.

Balancing the competing goals of collaboration and security represents a multidimensional challenge in collaboration system design. Collaboration systems allow groups of users to share and interact with information in real-time, whereas information security seeks to ensure information availability, confidentiality and integrity while providing it only to those with proper authorization [5, 6]. As the demand of collaboration application increases, diverse access control solutions for sharing resources across organizations have been investigated [7, 8]. Researchers argue that access control in collaborative systems needs to be simple and user-friendly, ease of administration, adaptable to changes, and tailored to the particular work practice [5]. We are interested in contributing to this body of research by exploring the design and evaluation of a secure collaboration platform in a challenging collaboration setting.

3   Integrated Collaboration Platform

Our ultimate goal is to enable information from various data resources to be shared and interacted by experts and officers who work in different organizations. The proposed solution is to introduce a secure collaboration platform which has workstations over multiple sites for distributed workgroups. There are two broad requirements that needed to be met. The first is information sharing and interaction, and the second is access control for information security.

The integrated collaboration platform is built on our prior work of Biosecurity Collaboration Platform (BCP) which supports the first requirement [9]. The BCP workstation has four high-resolution large displays and supports shared interaction with various resources, such as computer screens, documents and applications, via its Shared Workspaces (Fig. 1). It also enables telepresence video-conferencing. Two BCP workstations have been installed at AAHL, one inside the containment area and the other outside the containment area. The workstations have been used regularly to support the internal collaboration across the containment barrier within AAHL. The underlying BCP has three components: the workstations themselves (one per site), Shared Workspaces which generally run as VNC servers, and a central unit that controls login and distributes configuration information.

Fig. 1. The BCP workstation

Our work in supporting the second requirement is the design of access control technology that has been integrated into the BCP and tested in the biosecurity use case. The eAuthentication and eAuthorization technology allows users to log into the platform using their individual access card, rather than a single user typing in user name and password. Meeting participants are not only authenticated to use their respective workstations, but also authorised to join in the distributed meetings and interact with data resources that they are entitled to access. It also addresses the particular requirement in the collaboration by allowing participants at different sites to share instrument operation. Figure 2 shows the architecture of secure collaboration platform and major components. We use XACML to specify the security policies protect individual resources within the collaboration. The user interfaces will be described in Sect. 4.1. How the key components work together to manage the accesses of disease-specific meetings, participants, resources are described below.

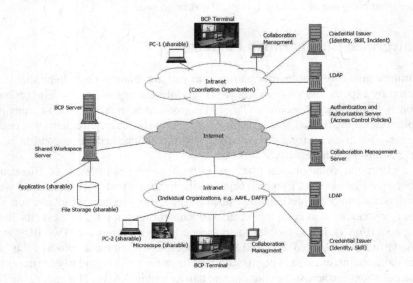

Fig. 2. Integrated secure collaboration platform architecture

The Authentication and Authorisation server enforces an attribute-based access control mechanism. Before a staff of an organization joins a distributed meeting or accesses shared resources, the BCP servers request from the security service whether this access can be permitted. The Authentication and Authorisation server checks the permission of the staff based on their attributes which are encoded in cryptographic credentials issued by their organisation. This access control mechanism is driven by the dynamic and multi-organizational feature in emergency response meetings. The Authentication and Authorisation server simply makes judgements based on the signature of the organizations without concerning the details of the staff.

To support this level of trust, each organisation has a Credential Issuer which issues credentials to certify the staff attributes, including staff name, organization and skills (e.g. microscope expert). In addition, the Credential Issuer at the Coordination organization issues separate disease-specific credentials for each organizations involved. This is because of the need to manage the accesses for different incident meetings which have different requirements in terms of expertise and resources. The Credential Issuer at the

Coordination organization works together with each organizational LDAP server which checks the validity of the staff members in an organization to ensure that particular staff can take part in particular meetings dealing with particular disease incidents.

The data resources involved and the associated access control policies are configured at each organization by using the Collaboration Management component in the platform. The access control policies are then stored in the Authentication and Authorisation server. The Collaboration Management component at the Coordination organization manages the schedules of specific disease incident and the participants involved. The overall resource configuration descriptions and meeting schedules are stored at Collaboration Management server.

4 User Study of the Secure Collaboration Platform

We have conducted a user study to evaluate the prototype of the integrated collaboration platform, focusing on the Authentication and Authorisation component, in supporting emergency response meetings. Due to the unpredictable and confidential nature of the CCEAD meetings, it was difficult to conduct the study in the actual meetings. The study was conducted with actual users by using a mock-up scenario and in a workshop format. The workshop was designed to allow participants to experience the security functionalities and provide feedback as part of the iterative design process. The mock-up collaboration scenario required participants to use the workstation to interact with and discuss various protected data resources (Fig. 3). Participants were given different access cards which contained ID, skill and organization details to log in/out of the system and acted on specific roles to exercise the interaction as realistically as possible.

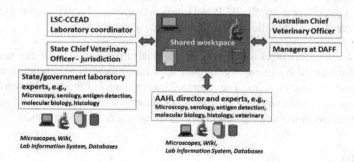

Fig. 3. The organisations, distributed participants and data resources in the scenario

We focused on AAHL staff since their work covers a range of activities in disease diagnosis and LSC-CCEAD. We recruited staff who were familiar with the existing BCP at AAHL. We carried out three workshops. Each audio-video recorded workshop lasted 1.5 h and had three participants. The nine participants included three microscopy scientists, one veterinary leader, one veterinary diagnostics scientist, two veterinary virologists and one epidemiologist. The questions asked in the workshop focused on the appropriateness of the access control technology, usability, areas of improvement and potential technology extensions. The audio recordings of the discussion sessions were transcribed and the transcriptions were analysed using thematic coding.

4.1 Technical Setting

In each workshop a point-to-point connection was set up between the workstation at AAHL where the participants were located and the workstation in our lab. Two researchers of our team facilitated the workshop at the AAHL site and two researchers attended from our lab. Settings of data access and interfaces are described below.

Protected Resource. Three protected resources from AAHL were made available for the participants to use during the workshops. Each protected resource had its own access policies. Participants could access protected resources through the interface designed on the Shared Workspace toolbar. These resources included:

- AAHL Lab Information System which is the AAHL diagnostic web portal
- A microscope running a VNC server and accessed through a VNC Viewer
- A personal computer running a VNC server and with specific application opened inside to access to specific databases

Roles and Access Cards. Authentication and authorization cards were prepared before the workshops. These RFID access cards contained data of staff attributes to allow the testing of the access policies. For example, the electron microscope was accessible to anyone with the skill of microscope expert; the Lab Information System was accessible to anyone with one or more skills of microscope expert, serology expert, molecular expert, histology expert, antigen detection expert and veterinary investigation leader. A card reader was connected to the BCP workstation computer. Each registered user could swipe their cards to access the system if they were assigned to.

Policy Creation. Access control policies for instruments and data resources were created and managed by using a graphical user interface that simplified the use and understanding of these policies. The interfaces were demonstrated in the workshops to illustrate how an administrator from the Coordination organization could set up and manage the access control for different organization users and resources.

4.2 Results

There was broad consensus in the workshops that the overall solution of the prototype had the capabilities to support secure information sharing in LSC-CCEAD type of collaborations. The key results are summarized below.

Enhanced Microscopy Collaboration. The importance of supporting secure access to microscope and other laboratory instruments was highlighted by the participants. All participants believed that the real-time and secure access to laboratory instruments would be particularly useful in certain technical-driven meetings. One of the future work pointed out by the three microscopy scientists was the fine-grained access control which would involve the development of access control rules to define different types of users when accessing certain functions on the microscope application.

Log In/Out Card.   There were positive responses to the use of the eAuthentication cards to replace the existing user name and password login mechanism. Some of the CCEAD meeting sites have more than twenty meeting participants and most of them are observers. The workshop participants commented that the protocol of everyone swiping card to attend a meeting could provide necessary access control for all meeting participants and maintain a record of participation in a large group.

Interaction.   When we asked "Does this access control technology constraint the flow of interactions with your remote collaborators when using the platform", most of the participants responded that it would not be an issue as long as the security technology were robust and ease of use.

Usability.   The usability was assessed in terms of transparency, ability to define security policy, ease of learning and ease of use. We differentiated two types of users: normal user and access control administrator. The participants were satisfied with the usability for normal users in terms of log in/out and access to different data resources in general. The administrator management component was introduced as a guided use only during the workshop to allow the security policies to be explained thoroughly to the participants. Thus, the participants had limited hands-on experience on this and their responses were just neutral. They expressed their willingness to assess this component in the future.

Potential Extensions.   Supporting mobile users emerged as one of the important requirements. Quite often, members of the CCEAD travel or work in the fields and need to join the meetings by using mobile communications. The integration of mobile devices into the overall secure collaboration platform has been highlighted as one of the future directions. Similarly, the need of a desktop solution was also mentioned since the multi-display type of collaboration workstation may not be always available to some meeting participants and some of them prefer to join the meeting from their offices.

Implementation.   The veterinary investigation leader at AAHL suggested that a pilot trial in informal meetings would be helpful before introducing the technology into the real meeting practices. Workshop participants also pointed out that the requirements for different situations would be vary and the design would need to address the flexibility need to support different forms of collaborative activities and contexts.

5   Discussion and Conclusion

The priority of improving information sharing in this biosecurity collaboration setting is not to support a shared data repository across organizations but rather to develop technologies to support collaboration during the analysis and interpretation process. The data is distributed in various repositories with different access requirements. The Shared Workspace in a multi-display environment supports simultaneous visualization of multiple data resources and synchronous interactions. However the Shared Workspace in itself will not solve all the information sharing requirements. Access control for sharing a range of resources is critical for the accomplishment of the collaborative tasks, particularly when discussing real-time information results from instruments.

The integrated collaboration platform we developed entails eAuthentication and eAuthorisation at a distributed platform level and provides security support for the collaborations between various types of experts in different organizations. Protection of information resources in this application addresses more complicated security requirements than those for the traditional single-user environments [5, 6]. In our design, access rights can be easily configured and managed to meet the particular needs of the cooperative work. Importantly, our work has demonstrated that a collaboration platform can be extended by facilitating transparent access control for multi-organizational users in a flexible manner that does not constraint real-time distributed collaboration.

The findings of the user study indicate several directions worthy of further exploration. One is to incorporate mobile solutions. We have a long-standing interest in the area of integrating mobile interaction technologies into a collaboration platform, for example using iPad to interact with large displays [10]. The integration of mobile devices and the implementation of associated security mechanisms will be explored. A second direction is to evaluate the technology design in a real collaboration environment. It will be valuable to observe the real use of the platform to understand how it can be designed to fit well with the work practices and contexts.

In sum, we have investigated the design of a secure collaboration platform to support real-time information sharing in a biosecurity use case. Cross-organizational eAuthentication and eAuthorisation are integrated into the collaboration platform and issue accesses to well-defined meeting participants based on their respective organizations, skills and capabilities. Positive responses have been received from the user study. We believe our explorations have broader implications for supporting multi-organizational collaborations in other domains where secure information sharing is important.

References

1. Fitzpatrick, G., Ellingsen, G.: A review of 25 years of CSCW research in healthcare: contributions, challenges and future agendas. J. CSCW **22**, 609–665 (2013)
2. Pipek, V., Liu, S.B., Kerne, A.: Crisis informatics and collaboration: a brief introduction. J. CSCW **23**(4–6), 339–345 (2014)
3. Li, J., O'Hara, K.: Understanding distributed collaboration in emergency animal disease response. In: Australasian Conference on Computer-Human Interaction, pp. 65–72 (2009)
4. Finholt, T.A., Olson, G.M.: From laboratories to collaboratories: A new organizational form for scientific collaboration. J. Psychol. Sci. **8**(1), 28–36 (1997)
5. Tolone, W., Ahn, G.J., Pai, T., Hong, S.P.: Access control in collaborative systems. J. ACM Comput. Surv. **37**, 29–41 (2005)
6. Baïna, A., Deswarte, Y., Abou El Kalam, A., Kaaniche, M.: Access control for cooperative systems: a comparative analysis. In: Third International Conference on Risks and Security of Internet and Systems, pp. 19–26 (2008)

7. Demchenko, Y., Gommans, L., Tokmakoff, A., Buuren,R.V.: Policy based access control in dynamic Grid-based collaborative environment. In: International Symposium on Collaborative Technologies and Systems, pp. 64–73 (2006)
8. Lv, B., Wang, Z., Huang, T., Chen, J., Liu, Y.: Virtual resource organization and virtual network embedding across multiple domains. In: International Conference on Multimedia Information Networking and Security, pp. 725–728 (2010)
9. Li, J., Robertson, T., Muller-Tomfelde, C.: Distributed scientific group collaboration across biocontainment barriers. In: International Conference on Computer Supported Cooperative Work, pp. 1247–1256 (2012)
10. Cheng, K., Li, J., Müller-Tomfelde, C.: Supporting interaction and collaboration on large displays using tablet devices. In: International Working Conference on Advanced Visual Interfaces, pp. 774–775 (2012)

Securing Shared Systems

Mandy Li$^{(\boxtimes)}$, Willy Susilo, and Joseph Tonien

Centre for Computer and Information Security Research,
School of Computing and Information Technology,
University of Wollongong, Wollongong, NSW, Australia
{ml414,wsusilo,joseph_tonien}@uow.edu.au

Abstract. With increasing reliance on new and interactive technologies, a challenge producers face is the requirement of a secure system to control users of their cooperative designs or applications to reap economic benefit. An authentication code is the series of letters and numbers, often disclosed after purchasing a product or service and that allows access for that user. This paper provides insight into the generation and verification of existing authentication codes and proposes a new scheme, which uses cryptography to embed mathematical structure within the codes to better protect cooperative applications. The proposed method uses a changing key based on a secret key and a random number, and symmetrical block cipher.

Keywords: Cooperative applications · Security · Cryptographic design · Authentication

1 Introduction

In an age in which there is increasing demand in computer technologies and growing interaction in digitalised areas, providers of cooperative products and services face a problematic issue - in order to remain useful or profitable, they must protect their products or services to only be accessible to certain user groups. Authentication codes are used in diverse applications and this method of proof by possession can be adapted to be also relevant for cooperative applications. The authentication generation and verification must be efficient and secure to be effective. If the process is not efficient then the end user may become frustrated and dissatisfied, and if the codes are not secure then unlicensed codes could be generated and the application is prone to piracy. It is therefore vital for these two conditions to be met, to an extent, in operational authentication code systems. Security in cooperative applications is not extensively researched or explored, but this paper proposes a new scheme using cryptography becoming a valuable method of securing cooperative operations.

There are many different circumstances where authentication codes are or can be implemented for the security of cooperative applications. Computer gaming and other digital services that connect users through internet, network connection or multiplayer gaming from the same computer, utilises the authentication

© Springer International Publishing AG 2016
Y. Luo (Ed.): CDVE 2016, LNCS 9929, pp. 194–201, 2016.
DOI: 10.1007/978-3-319-46771-9_26

code approach to ensure only those who register or purchase the application can download the program. These, however, are currently not very advanced systems, with the example of StarCraft using a simple checksum with the last digit [1]. The verification checks the 13th digit is true in relation to the other 12 digits, providing very little security with an attacker able to change the last digit ten times until guaranteed entry. A stronger cryptosystem will be more beneficial for these gaming companies.

Verification codes can also used to protect online resources intended for specific user groups, an example is a restricted website provided by a school or company to access internal information, or an online quiz that must be completed at a certain time and only when the access code is disclosed allowing controlled entry into the site. A textbook is another example, where buyers can be given access to additional online collaborative learning support on a given website by entering a specified unique code. The authentication code can be stored under a scratch card in the cover of the textbook and those who have purchased the book will have access to interactive resources or forums for correspondence and interactions with other students to learn collaboratively.

In an alternate way, the produced access code can be incorporated into the URL of web-based cooperation tools such as Google Docs to share private documents. By generating access codes to be inserted within the URLs, only those who have the correct URL will be able to access the documents and any adversary trying to access documents will be very unlikely to randomly guess an accepted code.

Authentication codes may be printed on the bottom of receipts allowing customers of a business to provide feedback and rate in-store experiences. It provides a unique code to enter at a specified website. Fast food restaurants such as KFC and departments stores such as Big W all use the authentication code method to ensure only customers who have purchased their items are able to return feedback. The collection of collaborative feedback from customers allows the businesses to adapt and improve.

Other major uses of authentication codes are to licence software and to activate software to prevent piracy. Many software companies use product keys including Windows XP [3], Microsoft, Kaspersky Internet Security, SolidWorks products [8], and on CDs and Antiviruses. Windows XP uses cryptography techniques in their activation and verification processes to ensure the buyer has a product key that is unique and valid. The process begins when a customer purchases Windows XP and receives a product key. This product key is verified using a digital signature and an installation ID is produced allowing the user to register their product online or over the phone to prevent piracy [3]. Similarly, any software supporting concurrent design, collaborative editing, or multiple location collaborative design can be protected using this method.

Protocol. This paper introduces a new method to generate and verify authentication codes, where the generation of codes involves one entering the secret key and the number of desired codes into the developed program and it will output the specified number of unique codes of length 30. These are then distributed or sold for economic benefit. The users have the code verified by entering the 30 characters in an indicated space, whether it is on a website or in a dialogue box. The code and the embedded secret key are entered into the verification program and an output of true or false is provided. This designates whether the user is granted access or not and directly causes the product or service to become more valuable. The necessity in this method is to have the key embedded and unable to be obtained by the general public otherwise codes may be forged. The proposed program generates codes with mathematical structure rather than comparing to those stored in a database, allowing the program to have more structure, have the ability to operate offline if required, be more efficient, secure and reliable. This program will be effective for cooperative software, restricted website or gaming use, and other cooperative applications.

Related Work. The Data Encryption Standard [7] was a cryptographic algorithm that protected sensitive digital data. With the advancement in technology, it has been deemed insecure and withdrawn as a standard. The basis is still however relevant where the Feistel cipher is an effective cryptography technique that can be applied to the generation and verification of authentication codes. The Feistel scheme involves splitting a 64-bit plaintext into two halves where the halves undergo 16 rounds of encryption with a secret key to obtain a ciphertext. Verification of the ciphertext has the same structure. Michael Luby and Charles Rackoff proved the original plaintext becomes a pseudorandom permutation with three rounds of the system [4]. The downside to the standard was the key size, which was too small to be secure and is amended in our scheme [7]. Gerhard de Koning Gans and Eric Verheul proposed a method of generating and verifying activation codes called Best Effort and Practice Activation Codes that similarly incorporates a Feistel network. A combination of a hash function with Feistel is believed to satisfy both authenticity and confidentiality. The activation code scheme produces a text combining a hash of a plaintext and the plaintext, which is encrypted using the Feistel network to create a ciphertext. The ciphertext is verified by undergoing the reverse of the encryption [2]. The Windows Product Activation process also requires code verification with the use of a digital signature as well as the Feistel system in the process. The product key is 25-characters long, roughly 115-bits and 15 bytes when stored in little endian byte order. Of the 15 bytes, four bytes contain the raw product key and eleven contain the digital signature of the raw product key, verified using hard-coded public key. An installation ID is then formed from the user's computer hardware and the product key involving Feistel to prevent pirating. The software is then registered and activated for the device [3].

2   Scheme Selection

Definition 1 ([6]). *Symmetric cryptography refers to an encryption system in which the sender and receiver of a message share a single, common key that is used to encrypt and decrypt the message.*

Let p be a plaintext in which there is an encryption rule e_K based on a key K that produces c, where c is ciphertext. Let there be a decryption rule d_K that is applied to c to return to p, where d_K is the inverse of e_K [10].

The process involves creating an algorithm with mathematical structure to determine if the code belongs to an allowed user. All authentication codes have the same plaintext, however, the key will change depending on a random number r and the secret key. Using symmetrical cryptography, codes are generated using e_K, transforming p to c, where c along with r is used as the given authentication code. When verifying user-entered codes, d_K is applied to c, revealing p. p is tested causing a true or false result, determining whether the code is accepted or declined. This identifies allowed users.

To produce the codes, input variables into the program: $f(k_S, n) = codes$, where k_S is a chosen key and n is the number of codes required. The algorithm uses symmetric encryption, so to check user-entered codes, input variables into the program: $g(k_S, code) = T/F$, where the code is entered by the user and the key is embedded, outputting a true or false answer.

1. choose a $k_S \in K_S$
2. select a $n \in Z^+$
3. compute $C = f(k_S, n)$
4. distribute C
5. verify using $ans = g(k_S, c \in C)$
6. if $ans = true$ then

   allow access (success)

   else if $ans = false$ then

   deny access (failure)

2.1   Setup

The proposed scheme can be seen in Fig. 1, where encryption is based upon the Feistel network [11]. Two equal halves of the 120-bit plaintext are inputted and undergo 16 rounds of encryption using the key to output a ciphertext. The key is specific to each produced code and is generated from the combination of the 18-character secret key and a 10-digit random number. The secret key is unique to every different product or service using the program to ensure entered codes are only valid for the expected product. The random number is coupled with the ciphertext to produce the authentication code. This authentication code is distributed to allowed users and verified in reverse.

The authentication code uses the following alphabet:

$$A \; B \; C \; D \; E \; F \; G \; H \; J \; K \; M \; N \; P \; R \; T \; U \; V \; W \; X \; Y \; Z \; 2 \; 3 \; 4 \; 6 \; 7 \; 8 \; 9 \qquad (1)$$

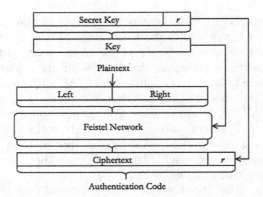

Fig. 1. Scheme

The system is a five-tuple (r, k_S, p, c, n) where:

1. r is a finite set of possible random numbers
2. k_S is a finite set of possible secret keys
3. n is the number of required codes
4. For each $r \in R$ and each $k_S \in K_S$, there is a $c \in C \mapsto p \in P$.

2.2   Generation

The number of codes and the unique secret key is entered into the program to generate authentication codes. p is a common binary code of 120-bits of 1s, yet all different applications of the program require a unique k_S. For each code, a different r is chosen and subsequently a c can be produced. K for the particular c is 120-bits in length and is made from converting the 18-character hexadecimal k_S to 90-bits of binary combined with the 30-bit r converted from the 10-digit decimal. The K is divided and used in subkeys [9] in the Feistel Network to encrypt p to c. A subkey is an allocated 60-bit portion of K specific to each round, where one round of the network is described as:

$$L_i = R_{i-1} \qquad R_i = L_{i-1} \oplus f(R_{i-1}, K_i)$$

The entire Feistel Network contains 16 rounds of the encryption, and after the 16th round, the ciphertext is outputted in 120-bits of binary. This, in combination with 30-bits of r, gives 150-bits of binary, where finally it is converted to 30 characters of hexadecimal from the allowed alphabet characters (1) to reveal the authentication code. The process is repeated n times with different values for r, resulting in a different K and a different c.

2.3   Verification

The authentication code is entered into the program on a given website or in a dialogue box and undergoes the following verification. The first step in verification involves checking the length of the code and the characters to ensure the

entered access code contains the correct number of characters and only characters specified by the allowed alphabet (1). The 30 character hexadecimal code
is converted into 150-bits of binary code. The last 30-bits are combined with
the binary conversion of k_S to create K. The remaining 120-bits of binary are
decrypted using the Feistel Network converting c back to p. The decryption has
the same structure as in encryption, however reversing the order of the subkeys:

$$L_i = R_{i-1} \oplus f(L_{i-1}, K_i) \qquad R_i = L_{i-1}$$

After the 16th round of decryption, p is obtained. Since the required p is
known as 120 1s, it can be easily identified whether the p that is obtained
matches the required p. If no 0s are in the final p, the authentication code is
accepted and the user is allowed access, however, if there contains one or more
0s, the authentication code is rejected and the user is denied access.

2.4 Example

This method of authentication code generation and verification can be very practical when it comes to profiting from cooperative learning resources by restricting
access to only those who have purchased a specific textbook. In this example,
students studying a certain course in high school can interact with others in
the same course both in their school and in other high schools by accessing the
online collaborative resources protected by an authentication code. The authors
and publishers of the textbook generate a number of authentication codes using
the proposed system and distribute the codes in the back cover of the textbook
behind a scratchcard. Those who purchase the textbook can then enter the given
code on the specified website, where the code and the embedded secret key are
verified using the method described in this paper. The student will either be
accepted or denied into the website depending on whether the code is valid. If
the student is allowed access, they will be prompted to register and then given
entry to collaborative learning support and forums restricted to only those who
are in the same subject.

2.5 Analysis

The proposed system of generating and verifying authentication codes ensures
efficiency and reliability. Security is ensured due to a number of features including the structure of the encryption and the complexity in the key. The system
relies upon the Feistel Network, where two halves undergo rounds of encryption
functions and exclusive or logical operations [11]. This symmetrical cipher has
been greatly experimented with, especially in regards to DES, and theoretical
work is continuously conducted to prove the Feistel cipher to be quite secure,
where three rounds have been proven to create a pseudorandom permutation [4].
The proposed system uses a key that is constructed from two sources, a secret
key and a random number, where in each round the key is split into different
subkeys. A different secret key is used for every different product or service that

requires a group of codes and a different random number is generated for every single code generated, and so the key is different for every code.

In terms of protection against unauthorised users, the 30-character authentication code and the 28-character alphabet (1) allows for 2.6×10^{43} code possibilities. Every random number maps to an accepted code and thus with a 10-digit random number, 10 billion codes are considered allowed and there is only a 3.8×10^{-34} chance of an adversary entering a random allowed code. The secret key is 18-characters long, ensuring the secret key is, again, very unlikely to be guessed. The security of each set of authentication codes is reliant on the protection of its secret key. The program's coding can be revealed to adversaries, yet the secret key must be kept hidden and embedded into the website or disc in which the verification occurs.

There are, however, some negatives identified in the proposed system. The size of the random number determines the number of available codes and so this number must be large enough to allow for the possibility of requiring large amounts of codes, however, it must small enough to ensure the chance of guessing a code is very little. The random number may also be re-chosen when producing a new code, however this is quite unlikely when producing a small number of codes. Another issue arising is the program does not have the means to prevent a code from being accepted multiple times as it is not an online system. A solution is to employ an online registration system in conjunction with the code verification such as in Windows Product Activation [3] or in the example.

The proposed scheme is superior to related authentication code generation and verification methods such as DES [7], Windows Product Activation [3], BEPAC [2] and the database system mostly due to its efficiency and reliability comparatively. It has the ability to run offline, the structure is less complex and doesn't employ techniques that take extensive time to run, for example public-key encryption [5] and HASH functions.

By implementing the described authentication security system for cooperative applications, these resources can identify allowed users though proof by possession and accordingly accept or decline access. Methods for protecting collaborative resources are not greatly researched and so the proposed system is aimed at introducing a new authentication scheme that is relevant, specifically, for these applications. It can be applicable in collaborative learning, multiplayer gaming, sharing documents, collaborative design software and many others. The proposed system includes many arbitrary values which have been set and can be easily modified with little change to the entire system. This allows the program to be very flexible and customisable.

3   Conclusion

Authentication codes are very widely implemented and are important in gaining the benefits of developing a commercial computer program. The proposed scheme combines the symmetrical encryption of the Feistel network with randomly selected numbers to produce a system that can generate and verify access codes and allow the codes to contain mathematical structure, hosting a range of benefits. The design is very flexible and can be altered to meet different requirements. In comparison to several other authentication systems, the described is effective, efficient and secure. A notable difference from many modern authentication code schemes is the change from asymmetrical encryption to symmetrical encryption, which is much more efficient, where public key encryption systems, such as Windows, are effective but lack efficiency.

The proposed system has many advantages and can be very revolutionary to the authentication of cooperative digital designs. Currently, there is little research in the development in the security of applications that promote collaboration, yet the proposed authentication code approach is a successful system combining the needs of the program creator and the user. It is quite simple for a user to enter the given code, however, in this way the intellectual property of a cooperative product or application is protected. Cooperative applications are becoming increasingly more prevalent in today's society and thus it is vital to employ schemes for these applications to ensure higher digital security.

Acknowledgments. The first and third authors would like to thank the Faculty of Engineering and Information Sciences for the Start-Up Funding 231050500.

References

1. Cullen, D.: Product Keys and Hashing (2010). https://bnetdocs.org/?op=doc&did=20
2. de Koning Gans, G., Verheul, E.R.: Best effort and practice activation codes. In: Furnell, S., Lambrinoudakis, C., Pernul, G. (eds.) TrustBus 2011. LNCS, vol. 6863, pp. 98–112. Springer, Heidelberg (2011)
3. Licenturion: Inside Windows Product Activation, Germany (2001). http://www.licenturion.com/xp/
4. Luby, M., Rackoff, C.: How to construct pseudorandom permutations from pseudorandom functions. SIAM J. Comput. **17**(2), 373–386 (1988)
5. Penton: Symmetric vs. Asymmetric Ciphers (2016). http://windowsitpro.com/security/symmetric-vs-asymmetric-ciphers
6. Quinstreet Enterprise: Symmetric-key Cryptography (2016). http://www.webopedia.com/TERM/S/symmetric_key_cryptography.html
7. Rouse, M.: Data Encryption Standard (DES) (2014). http://searchsecurity.techtarget.com/definition/Data-Encryption-Standard
8. SolidWorks Corporation: English EULA (2016). https://www.solidworks.com/sw/support/1090_ENU_HTML.htm
9. Staggs, B.: Implementing a Partial Serial Number Verification System in Delphi (2007). http://www.brandonstaggs.com/2007/07/26/implementing-a-partial-serial-number-verification-system-in-delphi/
10. Stinson, D.R.: Cryptography Theory and Practice. CRC Press Inc., Boca Raton (1995)
11. Tutorials Point: Feistel Block Cipher (2016). http://www.tutorialspoint.com/cryptography/feistel_block_cipher.htm

NetflowVis: A Temporal Visualization System for Netflow Logs Analysis

Likun He[1], Binbin Tang[1], Min Zhu[1]($\boxtimes$), Binbin Lu[1], and Weidong Huang[2]

[1] College of Computer Science, Sichuan University, Chengdu 610065, China
likunhe@gmail.com, shangshuiweihan@gmail.com, zhumin@scu.edu.cn
[2] University of Tasmania, Newnham, TAS 7248, Australia
Tony.Huang@utas.edu.au

Abstract. Netflow logs record the interactions between host pairs on both sides of the monitored border, and have got more attention from researchers for security concerns. Such data allows analysts to find interesting patterns and security anomalies. Visual analytics provides interaction and visualization techniques that can support these tasks. In this paper, we present a system called NetflowVis to analyze communication patterns and network abnormalities from netflow logs. This system consists of four views, including the communication trajectories view, the traffic line view, the snapshot view and the protocol view. The communication trajectories view is a composite view that dynamically describes the communication trajectories. This view combines a link-node tree and an improved ThemeRiver. The protocol view is designed to display statistical data of the upstream and downstream traffic on different protocols, which is an improved radial view based on an area filling strategy. The system provides a multilevel analysis architecture for netflow cognition. In this paper, we also present a case study to demonstrate the effectiveness and usefulness of our system.

Keywords: Network security visualization · Netflow logs · Temporal visualization · Traffic trajectory

1 Introduction

Netflow logs, as a kind of temporal data, describe the real-time hosts status and network traffic on different protocols. Detecting network events and communication patterns from the netflow data is a critical task. This task is challenging because of the complexity of events and the large amount of hosts. As it combines visual schemes and interaction, providing an effective way for users to make sense of massive datasets, visual analytics has been widely used for various analytical purposes, including netflow analysis [2]. However, much of the current research for netflow analysis focuses on specific parts of data, lacks overall network analysis with static analysis and has poor interaction.

In this paper, we present the NetflowVis system, which supports communication patterns discovery and network abnormalities analysis from netflow logs.

© Springer International Publishing AG 2016
Y. Luo (Ed.): CDVE 2016, LNCS 9929, pp. 202–209, 2016.
DOI: 10.1007/978-3-319-46771-9_27

The system shows the overall network states through interconnected views and interactions between them to support dynamic multi-granularity analysis. Our system consists of four views:

Communication trajectories view shows connections between clients and servers. It provides an overview of the dynamic network. In order to avoid visual clutter, IP segmentations are used to describe these connections.

Traffic line view describes upstream and downstream traffic dynamically. The traffic is a significant feature for network status.

Snapshot view catches anomalies and records some parameters. A series of snapshots are used to record the anomalies and their conditions for further analysis.

Protocol view displays traffic distribution on different protocols. Traffic distribution on different protocols and traffic ratios always indicate unusual activities.

2   Related Work

2.1   Traffic Visualization

Network traffic data is important to study network security. If the amount of traffic exceeds a certain range, or there is a mutation in a normal traffic flow, then it is highly likely there is an anomaly, such as DDoS(Denial of Service Attack), SYN Attack, etc.

Many innovative approaches for visual analytics have been proposed in the literature [4]. Among them, visualization tools have been specifically developed to detect anomalies. For example, NVisionIP [7] displays data records of netflow logs to detect class-B network abnormal events by a hierarchical manner. It can find DDoS, Port Scan, etc. However, it can not simulate communication tracks in real-time.

VisFlowConnection [11] uses the parallel axes view with interaction mechanisms for the analyst to find anomalous traffic patterns between networks. Stoffel et al. [10] use time-series visualizations together with similarity modelling so that correlations and anomalies in large data sets can be easily detected for security-related events. Promrit and Mingkhwan [9] provides an approach to show abnormalities and normal communication activities, and helps analysts to find possible causes of a network malfunction. Although these methods are able to effectively visualize the network status, they often do not scale well with the complexity of data sets. More specifically, if the data used increases in complexity, visual clutters become unavoidable in the final traffic visualization as a result of edge crossings, thus undoing the benefits of visualization in assisting analyst with detecting anomalies.

2.2   Multi-dimensional Visualization

Many techniques have been developed to visualize multivariate data, such as Parallel Coordinates [5], Andrews curves [1], and Star Coordinates [6]. Promrit and Mingkhwan [9] use parallel coordinates to display the SIP (source IP), Sport, Time, DIP (Destination IP), Dport and Size (Packet Size), which allows users to see the shape and distribution of these dimensions information. Lu et al. [8] proposed a concentric-circle method for visualization of multi-dimensional network data. This method uses polycurves instead of polylines to link dimensional values. With some additional visual features, this method was shown to be effective in recognizing network attacks, such as DDoS attack. However, these methods can not show real-time network status.

3   Visual Design and Implementation

Our NetflowVis system was developed to dynamically display network status. The system consists of four views: Communication trajectories view, Traffic line view, Snapshot view and Protocol view.

The Traffic line view dynamically depicts upstream and downstream traffic in the selected period, which helps users to analyze the changes of traffic. The Snapshot view contains a series of snapshots which record the anomalies and their conditions for further analysis. To analyze more details in different granularity, users can reset the whole system to any specific moment. We describe the remaining two views in more detail in the sub-sections that follows.

3.1   Communication Trajectories View

In this paper, we explore 7 aspects of netflow: timestamp, source IP, destination IP, port, protocol, upstream traffic and downstream traffic. As a large number of clients/servers can easily cause visual clutter, to avoid this, raw data is divided into client groups and server groups according the type of IP. Client groups are clustered into different subnets. Figure 1 shows the visual design and implementation.

The structure of Fig. 1(a) is a virtual tree, which is drawn by link-node layout algorithm. The positions of nodes depend on the radius and the angle, which is calculated according to the total number of nodes. We utilize edge clustering and curve smoothing methods to avoid waste of space. Every node in the tree represents a server or a subnet. The two parts are connected together by lines which display the trajectory of the communication. The color of lines indicates the type of the current communication protocol. If a malicious host scans the entire network for the same port, this view would appear as asymmetric so that the anomaly can be easily detected.

Figure 1(b) is an improved version of ThemeRiver [3], which takes asymmetric plotted strategies. It displays upstream traffic and downstream traffic on different protocols. The baseline is a timeline, traffic on different protocols is accumulated along the vertical coordinate. Each ribbon in this view corresponds to a special protocol. We control the width of each ribbon by a certain ratio to avoid disorder of the size of different areas. To make the stack flow diagram visually appealing, we use Bezier curves.

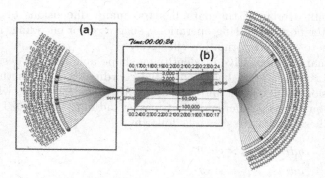

Fig. 1. Fusion views. (a) radial layout view represents the path from server groups to client groups. (b) Improved ThemeRiver displays upstream and downstream traffic. The color of the path corresponding to special protocol. (Color figure online)

The changes of the traffic trend in a short period are described by animations. In a normal status, the ribbons usually have a gentle trend and a small vibration amplitude. We can get the distributions and trends of the upstream and downstream traffic on different protocols within a specific time window.

3.2 Protocol View

While the communication trajectories view dynamically depicts connection trajectories at a specific time, the protocol view displays traffic statistics on different protocols. Protocol view analyzes the protocol distribution of upstream and downstream during a longer period of time, which helps users to understand network security incidents, such as DDoS and Worms. The view is an improved dimensional radial coordinates visualization method. It displays upstream and downstream traffic trends in real-time. The size of the block represents the total traffic on different protocols under the current time window.

As shown in Fig. 2, in the traditional radial coordinates method, each axis corresponds to an attribute and each closed polygon represents an object. It will

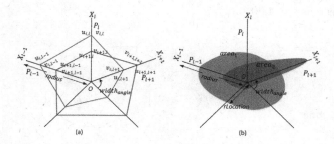

Fig. 2. Radial coordinates: (a) the traditional method, (b) our improved method.

cause segments overlap if the data has too many dimensions or distributes unevenly. After post-processing operations, such as color encoding, it would be more difficult to obtain information effectively.

Since humans are sensitive in identifying shape and size, we design an area filling visualization method based on radial coordinates. This method maps a multi-dimensional data point into an area with a specific color, which makes the comparison between different objects easier and more efficient. The drawing formulas of these points are shown as following:

$$x_i = radius_{server} \times \cos \theta_i \tag{1}$$

$$y_i = radius_{server} \times \sin \theta_i \tag{2}$$

$$\theta_i = \pi - \left[\frac{width_{angle}}{n} \times (i-1) + (1 + (-1)^i) \times \frac{width_{angle}}{4n} \right] \tag{3}$$

Bezier curve equation is used to smooth curve in this view.

4   Case Study

We use the data provided by 2015 ChinaVis Challenge to conduct our experiments. The data ranges from 23th April to 30th April, with 24th and 25th of April being weekends.

4.1   Discovery of Distribution and Pattern

Figure 3 shows that April 25th has a similar communication pattern to 24th, but its overall traffic is lower than 24th. Moreover, the activities of 24th covered a wide communication protocol, and most of which were web access. As shown in Fig. 4, daily network communication patterns in a week were "rise - steady - drop". Frequent communication happens between servers in the network every day around 2:00 am, which appears as a peak traffic. We can presume that there was a data backup task between the network servers at that time. The web access traffic reached its peak between 8:00 am and 4:00 pm. During this period, the traffic of upstream and downstream was relatively stable and the protocols were mainly http or http_proxy (normal web activity). Overall network traffic started to decrease at 4:00 pm.

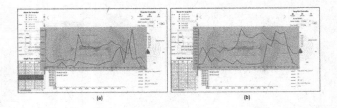

Fig. 3. Traffic statistics line chart in day mode. (a) 24th, April (b) 25th, April

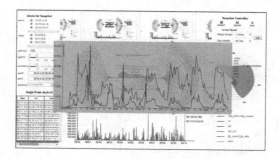

Fig. 4. Traffic statistics line chart in week mode.

For each period, the overall network traffic of weekends was much smaller than the weekdays had, and the general trend changed in a more moderate and stable manner.

4.2 Network Status Analysis

On the traffic level, network anomalies generally have the following features:

1. The proportion of upstream and downstream traffic is normal, but upstream traffic increases sharply.
2. The proportion of upstream and downstream traffic is not balanced. The downstream traffic is significantly greater than the upstream traffic, and has a continuous feature.
3. The proportion of upstream and downstream traffic is normal, but they keep at the same level, and exist local steep and dips characteristics.

To demonstrate the strength of NetflowVis for identification of network anomalies, we analyzed the abnormal network status by looking at the four views of the system in combination with the underlying network structure characteristics.

First, we selected the time period [15:00, 18:00] of 24th. The changes in traffic on different protocols are shown in Fig. 5. As can be seen, there were frequent data operations during [15:00, 17:30], which contain a lot of uploading and downloading activities. The traffic rose with web accesses based on the http protocol that became more frequent at 15:30. By observing the traffic evolution on different protocols, we can find that database operations reduced and web connections based on http_connect rose around 17:45, as shown in Fig. 5(a). To identify whether this period was abnormal, the time window was set to 1 s in the period from 17:35 to 17:45, and the vertical scale was set to 80, 000 bytes.

The upstream traffic periodically reached the peak before 17:42, while the downstream traffic stayed at around 4, 000 bytes or below. From 17:43 on, a large number of connections based on http_connect appeared, which kept the upstream traffic in the peak state. Communications mainly occurred between the server 10.26.52.169 and the client group 10.59.X.X. Such status matches the

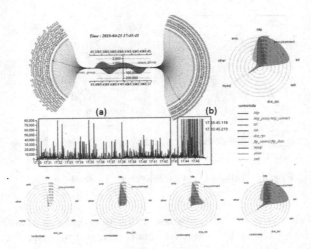

Fig. 5. A downloading activity is abnormal: (a) normal traffic, (b) abnormal traffic.

DDoS attack pattern, which starts with periodical illegal SYNs, followed by a large number of high-frequency network connections, and resulted in network congestion.

As shown in Fig. 6, most of the protocols were http_proxy/http_connect and ssl. The Traffic line view shows that the distribution of upstream traffic has an obvious pattern, which has constant peaks. However, downstream traffic kept at a low level. This phenomenon indicates that clients only sent requests to servers but hardly received messages. Therefore, it can be safely concluded that the network was under SYN attack at that time.

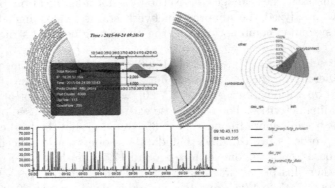

Fig. 6. Network communications during [9:00, 9:30].

5   Conclusion

NetflowVis provides four interconnected views for analysts to interact with the system and understand the characteristics of network status. The intuitive interfaces of the system provide users with information about communication objects, traffic and protocols. The effectiveness of our system has been demonstrated in a case study. In summary, our system is effective in analysis of network activities, particularly for identification of network anomalies.

For future work, we plan to extend our system to be used in other domains. Further, we will improve it to deal with on-line analysis of netflow logs.

References

1. Andrews, D.F.: Plots of high-dimensional data. Biometrics, pp. 125–136 (1972)
2. Chen, S., Guo, C., Yuan, X., Merkle, F., Schaefer, H., Ertl, T.: Oceans: online collaborative explorative analysis on network security. In: Proceedings of the Eleventh Workshop on Visualization for Cyber Security, pp. 1–8. ACM (2014)
3. Havre, S., Hetzler, B., Nowell, L.: Themeriver: visualizing theme changes over time. In: Proceedings of the IEEE Symposium on Information Vizualization 2000, pp. 115–123 (2000)
4. Huang, M., Huang, W. (eds.): Innovative Approaches of Data Visualization and Visual Analytics. IGI Global, 464 pages (2014)
5. Inselberg, A., Dimsdale, B.: Parallel coordinates: a tool for visualizing multi-dimensional geometry, San Francisco, pp. 361–375 (1990)
6. Kandogan, E.: Star coordinates: a multi-dimensional visualization technique with uniform treatment of dimensions. In: Proceedings of the IEEE Information Visualization Symposium, vol. 650, p. 22. Citeseer (2000)
7. Lakkaraju, K., Yurcik, W., Lee, A.J.: NVisionIP: netflow visualizations of system state for security situational awareness. In: Proceedings of the 2004 ACM Workshop on Visualization and Data Mining for Computer Security, pp. 65–72. ACM (2004)
8. Lu, L.F., Zhang, J.W., Huang, M.L., Fu, L.: A new concentric-circle visualization of multi-dimensional data and its application in network security. J. Visual Lang. Comput. **21**(4), 194–208 (2010)
9. Promrit, N., Mingkhwan, A.: Traffic flow classification and visualization for network forensic analysis. In: IEEE 29th International Conference on Advanced Information Networking and Applications (AINA), pp. 358–364. IEEE (2015)
10. Stoffel, F., Fischer, F., Keim, D.A.: Finding anomalies in time-series using visual correlation for interactive root cause analysis. In: Proceedings of the Tenth Workshop on Visualization for Cyber Security, pp. 65–72. ACM (2013)
11. Yin, X., Yurcik, W., Treaster, M., Li, Y., Lakkaraju, K.: VisFlowConnect: netflow visualizations of link relationships for security situational awareness. In: Proceedings of the 2004 ACM Workshop on Visualization and Data Mining for Computer Security, pp. 26–34. ACM (2004)

Rigid Body Sampling and Boundary Handling for Rigid-Fluid Coupling of Particle Based Fluids

Xiaokun Wang, XiaoJuan Ban[(⊠)], YaLan Zhang, and Xu Liu

University Science and Technology Beijing,
Beijing 100083, People's Republic of China
{wanglxiao2kun3,xuliu213}@163.com, banxj@ustb.edu.cn,
602980797@qq.com

Abstract. We propose an efficient and simple rigid-fluid coupling scheme employing rigid surface sampling and boundary handling for particle-based fluid simulation. This approach samples rigid bodies to boundary particles which are used for interacting with fluids. It contains two steps, sampling and relaxation, which guarantees uniform distribution of particles using less iterations. We integrate our approach into SPH fluids and implement several scenarios of rigid-fluid interaction. The experimental results demonstrate that our method is capable to implement interaction of rigid body and fluids while mainly ensuring physical authenticity for rigid-fluid coupling simulation.

Keywords: Physically-based simulation · Surface sampling · Boundary handling · Rigid-fluid coupling

1 Introduction

Physically-based fluid simulation is a popular issue in computer graphics while has a huge research and application demand in virtual reality. Two major schemes are used for animating fluids, the grid-based Eulerian approach and particle-based Lagrangian approach. Eulerian method is particularly suited to simulate large volumes fluid, but it is restricted by time step and computing time for small scale features. In contrast, Lagrangian method are suitable for capturing small scale effects such as spindrift, droplet. Among various Lagrangian approaches, Smoothed Particle Hydrodynamics (SPH) is the most popular method for simulating fluid due to computational simplicity and efficient.

In reality, rigid-fluid interaction widely exists in many scenarios. As a result, the interesting fluid behavior emerges when rigid objects are added to fluid simulation. While coupling of particle-based fluids with rigid objects seems to be straightforward, there are still several issues not well resolved. For one thing, rigid bodies must be sampled to particles in order to interact with particle-based fluids, but only a few rigid boundary sampling methods can be directly employed in rigid-fluid coupling simulation. For another thing, boundary handling method for rigid-fluid coupling is considerable. To cope with the increasing demand for more detailed fluids, we present

© Springer International Publishing AG 2016
Y. Luo (Ed.): CDVE 2016, LNCS 9929, pp. 210–218, 2016.
DOI: 10.1007/978-3-319-46771-9_28

integrate rigid sampling and boundary for rigid-fluid coupling and design a practical and easy animation simulation scheme of rigid-fluid interaction.

2 Related Work

Monaghan's simulating free surface flows with SPH [1] serves as a basis for SPH fluid simulation. Muller et al. [2] proposed using gas state equation with surface tension and viscosity forces for interactive applications, which also bring compressibility issue. Becker et al. [3] proposed WCSPH which reduces compressibility with Tait Equation. It significantly increased realistic effects but the efficiency is limited by time step. As incompressibility is time-consuming, many improved algorithms were addressed to enhance the efficiency. Solenthaler et al. presented PCISPH [4] using a prediction-correction scheme which significantly improved efficiency. Ihmsen et al. addressed IISPH [5], which carefully constructs pressure poisson equation and solves it using Relaxed Jacobi, which has a great improvement in stability and convergence speed. Recently, Bender and Koschier [6] proposed a promising approach for impressible SPH. It combines two pressure solvers which enforces low volume compression and a divergence-free velocity field. It allows larger time steps which yields a considerable performance gain since particle neighborhoods updated less frequently.

For boundary handling and rigid-fluid coupling, distance-based penalty methods with boundary particles have been commonly used [7, 8]. However, these approaches require large penalty forces that restrict the time step meanwhile particles tend to stick to the boundary due to the lack of fluid neighbors. The sticking of particles is avoided with frozen and ghost particles based models [9]. In order to ensure non-penetration, the positions of penetrating particles should be corrected [10]. However, handling two-way interaction is problematic in these approaches since the elevated density on one side of a boundary particle affects potential fluid particles on the other side. For this reason, Ghost SPH scheme [11] resolves this with a narrow layer of ghost particles and Akinci et al. employed boundary particles to correct the calculation of fluid density [12]. Due to Ghost SPH is time-consuming, we employ Akinci's boundary handling method which is simple and easy to achieve in this paper.

For rigid surface sampling, Turk used repelling particles on surfaces to uniformly resample a static surface [13]. Witkin and Heckbert employed local repulsion to make particles spread uniform [14]. Cook addressed stochastic sampling of Poisson-disk distributions with blue noise [15]. Blue sampling has the ability to generate random points and get uniform distribution of sampling points. Hence, the following sampling methods always have blue noise characteristics. Corsini et al. sampled triangular meshes with blue noise [16]. Dunbar et al. [17] modified Poisson-disk sample using a spatial data structure. Bridson [18] simplified Dunbar's approach with rejection sampling and extending it to higher dimensions. Then Schechter [11] modified Bridson's approach and employed it to Ghost SPH. Inspired by Schechter's approach, we address a sampling method which is more efficient and easy to implement.

3 Particle-Based Fluid Simulation Framework

In the Lagrangian description, flow controlled equations of Navier-Stokes for fluids can be expressed as

$$\frac{d\rho_i}{dt} = -\rho_i \nabla \cdot v_i \tag{1}$$

$$\rho_i \frac{D\mathbf{v}_i}{Dt} = -\nabla p_i + \rho_i g + \mu \nabla^2 \mathbf{v}_i \tag{2}$$

Where $\mathbf{v}_i$ is the velocity, ρ_i is the density, p_i is the pressure, μ is the viscosity coefficient and g represents the external force field. Eq. (1) is mass equation and Eq. (2) momentum equation.

The SPH theory is to utilize the form of discrete particles to characterize the successive fields and use integration to approximate the fields. For particle i at location x_i,

$$\langle A(\boldsymbol{x}_i) \rangle = \sum_j m_j \frac{A_j}{\rho_j} W(\boldsymbol{x}_i - \boldsymbol{x}_j, h) \tag{3}$$

Where m_j and ρ_j represent particle mass and density respectively, $W(\boldsymbol{x}_i - \boldsymbol{x}_j, h)$ is the smoothing kernel and h the smoothing radius.

Applying Eq. (3) to the density of a particle i at location x_i yields the summation of density

$$\rho_i = \sum_j m_j W(\boldsymbol{x}_i - \boldsymbol{x}_j, h) \tag{4}$$

Thus, forces between particles including pressure $\mathbf{f}_i^p$ and viscous force $\mathbf{f}_i^v$ can be represented as

$$\mathbf{f}_i^p = -\sum_j m_j \left(\frac{p_i}{\rho_i^2} + \frac{p_j}{\rho_j^2} \right) \nabla W_{ij} \tag{5}$$

$$\mathbf{f}_i^v = \mu \sum_j m_j \frac{\mathbf{v}_{ji}}{\rho_j} \nabla^2 W_{ij} \tag{6}$$

In this article, we employ Tait equation [3] to calculate the pressure and use the method in literature [12] to compute viscous force.

4 Boundary Handling for Particle-Based Fluids

Considering influence of boundary particles, density formula of fluid particles in (4) need to introduce weighted summation influence of boundary particle [12], that is

$$\rho_{f_i} = \sum_j m_{f_j} W_{ij} + \sum_k m_{b_k} W_{ik} \qquad (7)$$

Where f_j, b_k denotes fluid particle j and boundary particle k respectively. This formula can overcome boundary defects in SPH fluid simulation to some extent.

The density of fluid particles is incorrect and instability when the setting of boundary particle mass is unreasonable or distribution of boundary particles is uneven. Hence, using the contribution of boundary particles to a fluid particle through taking the volume of boundary particles into account as

$$\Psi_{b_i}(\rho_0) = \rho_0 V_{b_i} \qquad (8)$$

With ρ_0 denotes rest density of fluid, V_{b_i} is the estimation value of boundary area volume of corresponding boundary particles. Applying $\Psi_{b_i}(\rho_0)$ replace the boundary particle mass can guarantee the stability.

Therefore, Eq. (7) can be written as

$$\rho_{f_i} = \sum_j m_{f_j} W_{ij} + \sum_k \Psi_{b_k}(\rho_{0i}) W_{ik} \qquad (9)$$

The pressure acceleration generated by boundary particles to fluid particles is

$$\frac{dv_{f_i}}{dt} = -\frac{kp_{f_i}}{\rho_{f_i}^2} \sum_k \Psi_{b_k}(\rho_{0i}) \nabla W_{ik} \qquad (10)$$

Where $p_{f_i} > 0$ takes $k = 2$. When $p_{f_i} < 0$, boundary particles and fluid particles attract each other, then we can adjust parameter $k(0 \le k \le 2)$ to realize different adsorption effects, we choose $k = 1$ in our experiment.

To simulate the friction between fluid and rigid body, we have to compute the friction between boundary particles and fluid particles. The friction consults from artificial viscosity, that is

$$\frac{dv_{f_i}}{dt} = -\sum_k \Psi_{b_k}(\rho_{0i}) \Pi_{ik} \nabla W_{ik} \qquad (11)$$

Where $\Pi_{ik} = -v\left(\frac{v_{ik}^T x_{ik}}{x_{ik}^2 + \varepsilon h^2}\right)$, $v = \frac{2\alpha h c_s}{\rho_k + \rho_j}$.

Then we can get the forces of boundary particles using Newton's third law. The forces generated by fluid particles to boundary particles is

$$F_{b_k} = \sum_i \left(\frac{kp_{f_i}}{\rho_{f_i}^2} + \prod_{ik}\right) m_{f_i} \Psi_{b_k}(\rho_{0i}) \nabla W_{ik} \qquad (12)$$

where i denotes the fluid neighbors of boundary particle k. It is the counter-acting force of Eqs. 10 and 11.

For a rigid body, the total force and torque need to be calculated. It can be separately written as

$$F_{rigid} = \sum_k F_{b_k} \tag{13}$$

$$\tau_{rigid} = \sum_k \left(x_k - x_{rigid}^{cm}\right) \times F_{b_k} \tag{14}$$

Where x_k denotes the location of boundary particle k, x_{rigid}^{cm} is the mass center of a rigid body. The total force and torque will be transmitted to the physics engine to handle the motion of rigid bodies.

5   Rigid Boundary Sampling

In order to optimize the position of sample points, reduce noises and get a uniform distribution set of sampling points, we propose a sampling method with a surface relaxation step. For rigid objects sampling, boundary particles is used to sample the surface of rigid objects, which has several merits. For one thing, using particles can derive a rigid model which can handle different shapes even with complex geometry structure. For another thing, the use of boundary particles successfully alleviates sticking artifacts and makes sampling uniform. As shown in Fig. 2, we first sample the surface of rigid object using the sampling method in [11], then we improve it with surface relaxation (Fig. 1).

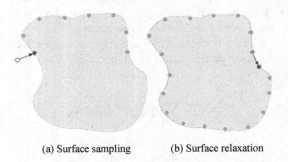

(a) Surface sampling   (b) Surface relaxation

Fig. 1. Surface sampling and relaxation. Black points: newly added points. Gray points: Surface sampling points. White points: exterior points before projected to the surface.

Surface relaxation algorithm is presented in Algorithm 1. Unlike using random testing way in [11], we compel particles move by density gradient. It makes particles move to sparse aera, which insures uniform distribution of particles. It starts with the initial sample obtained by surface sampling. Then it computes density $\rho_i(t)$ and density gradient $\nabla\rho_i(t)$ of each surface particles, using deviation of $\rho_i(t)$ and average density

$\overline{\rho_i(t)}$ as a coefficient to tune distance d. Next it employs $d \cdot \nabla \rho_i(t)$ t o adjust particle locations. Surface sample candidates are additionally projected to the surface of the level set and merely reserved which satisfies the Poisson disk criterion. Particle's density gradient using SPH gradient formula which is $<\nabla \rho_i> = \sum_{j=1}^{N} m_j \nabla W(|\mathbf{x}_i - \mathbf{x}_j|, h)$, while projection formula is $\mathbf{p}^{new} = \mathbf{p} + d \cdot \nabla \rho_i(t) - \nabla \phi(\mathbf{p}^{new})$.

Algorithm 1 Surface Relaxation

Input: sample set S , Level set ϕ , radius r , count t , constant f
Output: relaxed sample set S
1: **for** each t **do**
2:   **for** each $p_i \in S$ **do**
3:     compute density $\rho_i(t)$, average density $\bar{\rho}(t)$
4:     compute density gradient $\nabla \rho_i(t)$
5:     $d \leftarrow r \cdot \left| \dfrac{\rho_i(t) - \bar{\rho}(t)}{\bar{\rho}(t)} \right| \cdot f$
6:     $p^{new} \leftarrow p + d \cdot \nabla \rho_i(t)$
7:     if p^{new} outside ϕ or came from surface sample
8:       Project p^{new} to surface of ϕ
9:     if p^{new} satisfies the Poisson Disk criterion in S
10:       $p \leftarrow p^{new}$

We compare our method to fast Poisson disk method [11] in a 2 dimension experiment. We randomly generate 100 points in a 0.1×0.1 square and relax it using our method and fast Poisson disk method respectively. Figure 2 shows the relaxation results, the first row is our method and the second row is fast Poisson disk. The column (a) reveals the distribution of points after relaxation and the red point means it do not satisfy Poisson disk condition. Each algorithm iterates 100 times, while column (b) illustrates the number of points that do not satisfy Poisson disk conditions each iteration. It is obvious that our method get a better results with a slight concussion. Besides, our method is more efficient, in matlab environment our method takes 2.44691 s while relaxation fast Poisson disk method costs 56.44153 s for 100 iterations.

6 Implementation and Results

We implemented our method to rigid-fluid coupling animation system and verified the validity of our method. The simulation is performed on an Intel 3.50 GHz CPU with 4 cores. Bullet is used for simulating rigid objects and OpenMP is used for parallelize particle computations. We reconstruct fluid surface using anisotropic kernels [19]. Images were rendered with Blender.

In order to demonstrate the validity of fluid-rigid coupling simulation system, we designed a scene of water shock sculpture using 873 k fluid particles. The experimental

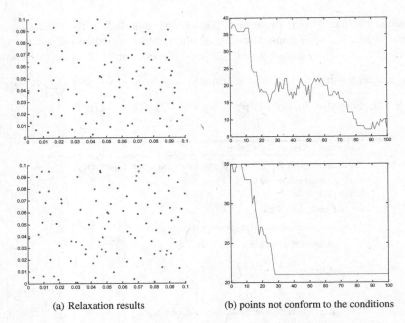

(a) Relaxation results   (b) points not conform to the conditions

Fig. 2. Relaxation results comparison of our method with fast Poisson disk.

results are displayed in Fig. 3. In this scenario, the breaking dam of water hit the sculpture which is knocked down and pushed for some distances due to kinetic energy of water. The motions of sculpture are in line with expectations which proved the simulation and calculation of fluid-rigid coupling system accord with physics laws.

The experiments proved our method can implement vivid fluid-rigid coupling animation simulation system with high realistic effects. It can be expected that this animation system can be used to virtual reality domain, special effects in film and game.

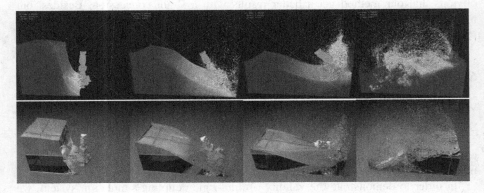

Fig. 3. Water shock sculpture. Top: simulation in particle view; Bottom: rendering results.

7 Conclusion

We proposed an efficient and simple rigid-fluid coupling scheme for particle-based fluid simulation. Our approach samples the surface of rigid bodies with boundary particles that interact with fluids. It insures uniform distribution of particles which requires less iterations. In addition, we combine rigid bodies sampling with boundary handling for rigid-fluid coupling. The scheme is implemented in rigid-body coupling scene which has a good sense of visual reality. Overall, our sampling and coupling method can be applied to other particle-based simulation or relevant approaches. Future work would be extending the method to IISPH and large-scale scenarios.

Acknowledgements. This work was supported by National Natural Science Foundation of China (No. 61272357, 61300074, 61572075).

References

1. Monaghan, J.J.: Simulating free surface flows with SPH. J. Comput. Phys. **110**(2), 399–406 (1994)
2. Muller, M., Charypar, D., Gross, M.: Particle-based fluid simulation for interactive applications. In: Proceedings of the 2003 ACM SIGGRAPH/Eurographics symposium on Computer animation. Eurographics Association, pp. 154–159 (2003)
3. Becker, M., Teschner, M.: Weakly compressible SPH for free surface flows. In: Proceedings of the 2007 ACM SIGGRAPH/Eurographics symposium on Computer animation. Eurographics Association, pp. 209–217 (2007)
4. Solenthaler, B., Pajarola, R.: Predictive-corrective incompressible SPH. ACM Trans. Graph. (TOG) **28**(3), 40 (2009)
5. Ihmsen, M., Cornelis, J., Solenthaler, B., et al.: Implicit Incompressible SPH. IEEE Trans. Vis. Comput. Graph. **20**(3), 426–435 (2014)
6. Bender, J., Koschier, D.: Divergence-free smoothed particle hydrodynamics. In: ACM SIGGRAPH/ Eurographics Symposium on Computer Animation, pp. 147–155. ACM 2015
7. Muller, M., Schirm, S., Teschner, M., Heidelberger, B., Gross, M.: Interaction of fluids with deformable solids. Comput. Animation VirtualWorlds **15**(34), 159–171 (2004)
8. Monaghan, J.J., Kajtar, J.: SPH particle boundary forces for arbitrary boundaries. Comput. Phys. Commun. **180**(10), 1811–1820 (2009)
9. Hu, X., Adams, N.: A multi-phase SPH method for macroscopic and mesoscopic flows. J. Comput. Phys. **213**(2), 844–861 (2006)
10. Ihmsen, M., Akinci, N., Gissler, M., Teschner, M.: Boundary handling and adaptive time-stepping for PCISPH. In: Workshop on Virtual Reality Interaction and Physical Simulation, pp 79–88. The Eurographics Association (2010)
11. Schechter, H., Bridson, R.: Ghost SPH for animating water. ACM Trans. Graph. **31**(4), 611–618 (2012)
12. Akinci, N., Ihmsen, M., Akinci, G., et al.: Versatile rigid-fluid coupling for incompressible SPH. ACM Trans. Graph. (TOG) **31**(4), 62 (2012)
13. Turk, G.: Generating textures on arbitrary surfaces using reaction-diffusion. In: ACM SIGGRAPH Computer Graphics, vol. 25(4), pp. 289–298. ACM (1991)

14. Witkin, A.P., Heckbert, P.S.: Using particles to sample and control implicit surfaces. In: Proceedings of the 21st Annual Conference on Computer Graphics and Interactive Techniques, pp. 269–277. ACM (1994)
15. Cook, R.L.: Stochastic sampling in computer graphics. ACM Trans. Graph. (TOG) 5(1), 51–72 (1986)
16. Corsini, M., Cignoni, P., Scopigno, R.: Efficient and flexible sampling with blue noise properties of triangular meshes. IEEE Trans. Visual Comput. Graph. 18(6), 914–924 (2012)
17. Dunbar, D., Humphreys, G.: A spatial data structure for fast Poisson-disk sample generation. ACM Trans. Graph. (TOG) 25(3), 503–508 (2006)
18. Bridson, R.: Fast poisson disk sampling in arbitrary dimensions. In: ACM SIGGRAPH, p. 5 (2007)
19. Wang, X.K., Ban, X.J., Liu, X., et al.: Efficient extracting surfaces approach employing anisotropic kernels for SPH fluids. J. Vis. 19(2), 301–317 (2016)

A Density-Correction Method
for Particle-Based Non-Newtonian Fluid

Yalan Zhang, Xiaojuan Ban$^{(\boxtimes)}$, Xiaokun Wang, and Xing Liu

University of Science and Technology Beijing, Beijing 100083, China
yalan.zhang920503@gmail.com, banxj@ustb.edu.cn,
wanglxiao2kun3@163.com, ustbdante@gmail.com

Abstract. We propose a novel non-Newtonian fluid simulation method for SPH. The variable viscosity under shear stress is achieved using a viscosity model known as Cross model. By adopting a density-correction scheme, larger time step is available for simulation. The achieved results show that both Newtonian fluid and non-Newtonian fluid could be achieved by our model. Furthermore, density-correction scheme improves the stability and efficiency of simulation significantly.

Keywords: Physically-based animation · Non-Newtonian fluid · SPH

1 Introduction

Lagrangian fluid simulation is a popular topic in computer animation. Currently, physics-based fluid animation research has focused on homogeneous incompressible Newtonian fluids with linear physical characteristics, while non-Newtonian fluids is rarely involved. However, the non-Newtonian fluid is widely present in the chemical industry, oil industry, mining engineering, biomedical, food processing and many other fields, such as pit filled paste, the body of blood, melted chocolate, mud (Fig. 1), etc. Since non-Newtonian fluid have the properties of solids and fluids both [1], it is pretty difficult to simulate non-Newtonian fluid realistically. In recent years, Smoothed particle hydrodynamics [2] (SPH) has become an important particle-based methods for computer animation.

There are several approaches to simulate Non-Newtonian fluid. In 2004, Goktekin et al. [3] proposed a quasi linear plastic model to control the change of viscosity in the process of a solid turn into a Non-Newtonian fluid gradually. This model obey the von Mises's yield condition. Losasso et al. [4] modeled fluid with different viscoelasticity and density unified by extending the particle level set. Bergou et al. [5] proposed a method based on discrete differential geometry to simulate one dimensional linear viscous fluid. This approach can simulate one dimensional phenomenon vivid, but distortion often appears when the flow layer become more and more thicken. Batty et al. [6] simulate viscous thin layer by dimensionality reduce technology. This approach can achieve the physical properties of viscous thin layer preferable, such as bend and drape.

© Springer International Publishing AG 2016
Y. Luo (Ed.): CDVE 2016, LNCS 9929, pp. 219–226, 2016.
DOI: 10.1007/978-3-319-46771-9_29

Fig. 1. Non-Newtonian fluid (mud)

Müller et al. [7] simulate fluid with High elasticity and high plasticity by structuring an animation modeling method based on point. He combined continuum mechanics with von Mises's yield condition, and calculated the displacement and the velocity by using moving least squares. [8] modeled non-Newtonian fluid by General Newtonian Fluid model. It implemented the process of the heated non-Newtonian fluid with high viscosity melting for low viscosity fluid. [9] proposed a SPH method applying to free surface. This method can apply to Newton fluid and viscoplastic fluid, and implement the blend phenomena of the viscous fluid. [10] implemented the unified molding of viscous Newtonian fluid and shear thinning non-Newtonian fluid. However, this method can only simulate fluid with low viscosity, unstable phenomenon will appear when the time step is larger.

In recent years, the density-corrective method has been used widely. Predictive - corrective algorithm was first proposed by [11], the core idea is to predict the fluid state without pressure, then use pressure on their conduct correction. Solenthaler and Pajarola [12] proposed an implicit SPH method through the relationship between density and velocity in the next time step, and then adjust the density by pressure. [13] proposed a divergence-free velocity method, which prevents volume compression and enforces a divergence-free velocity field formulation of the physical laws.

We present a density-correction method for SPH Non-Newtonian Fluid. In order to capture the viscous behavior, the viscosity of Newtonian fluid and non-Newtonian fluid flows is achieved by using Cross model. Larger time step is achieved by density-corrective method, which corrects density error by pressure and predictive intermediate velocity.

2   The Non-Newtonian Model

2.1   Governing Equations

In the Lagrangian formulation [14], the governing equation of non-Newtonian fluid should be written as follow:

$$\frac{d\mathbf{v}}{dt} = -\frac{1}{\rho}\nabla p + \frac{1}{\rho}\nabla \cdot \boldsymbol{\tau} + \mathbf{g} \qquad (1)$$

where t denotes the time, $\mathbf{v}$ the velocity field, ρ the density, p the pressure, $\mathbf{g}$ the gravity acceleration vector and $\boldsymbol{\tau}$ the shear stress tensor.

Lagrangian formulation of Eq. (1) represents the acceleration of a particle moving with the fluid flow. The term $-\frac{1}{\rho}\nabla p$ is related to particle acceleration due to pressure changes in the fluid. While, the term $\frac{1}{\rho}\nabla \cdot \boldsymbol{\tau}$ describes the viscous acceleration due to friction forces caused by particles with different velocities, which plays a key role in non-Newtonian fluid animation.

2.2 Cross Model

For our simulation, we use the Cross model [15] to build a unified model for Newtonian fluid and shear thinning non-Newtonian fluid. The Cross model can not only realize the physical properties of non-Newtonian fluid, but also suit for low viscosity Newtonian fluid simulation. In particular, for non-Newtonian fluids, the shear stress $\boldsymbol{\tau}$ is a nonlinear function of the rate-of deformation tensor $\mathbf{D} = \nabla\mathbf{v} + (\nabla\mathbf{v})^T$ as follows:

$$\boldsymbol{\tau} = \rho\upsilon(D)\mathbf{D}, \text{ with } D = \sqrt{\frac{1}{2}\cdot trace(\mathbf{D})^2} \qquad (2)$$

For shear-thinning non-Newtonian fluid, the fluid's viscosity decreases with increasing of the local shear rate D, thus the kinematic viscosity υ is defined as a function of D:

$$\upsilon(D) = \upsilon_\infty + \frac{\upsilon_0 - \upsilon_\infty}{1 + (KD)^n} \qquad (3)$$

where K and n are positive parameters to control the viscosity of the fluid and usually positive, υ_0 and υ_∞ are the limiting values of the viscosity at low and high shear rates.

2.3 Smoothed Particle Hydrodynamics

In the Lagrangian setting, the density at location x_i: is to approximated as:

$$\rho_i = \sum_j m_j W_{ij} \qquad (4)$$

where $W_{ij} = W(x - x_j, h)$ is the kernel function with h the particle radius, j iterates all the neighbors.

For simplicity, we use equation of state proposed by [13] to compute the pressure:

$$p_i = k(\rho_i - \rho_0) \qquad (5)$$

where k is a gas constant that depends on the temperature, ρ_0 is the rest density. The value $\rho_0 = 1000$ kg/m^3 is tuned out to be suitable for all experiments.

The pressure acceleration is computed as following:

$$-\frac{1}{\rho_i}\nabla p_i = -\sum_j m_j \frac{p_i + p_j}{\rho_j}\nabla W_{ij} \tag{6}$$

In order to compute the shear stress τ_i at particle i, we adopt the same SPH approximation as [16] for the deformation tensor $\mathbf{D}_i = \nabla\mathbf{v}_i + (\nabla\mathbf{v}_i)^T$ with:

$$\nabla\mathbf{v}_i = \sum_j \frac{m_j}{\rho_j}(\mathbf{v}_i - \mathbf{v}_j) \otimes \nabla W_{ij} \tag{7}$$

After updating shear stress at all particles, the viscous acceleration is approximated by:

$$\frac{1}{\rho}\nabla \cdot \tau_i = \sum_j m_j \left(\frac{\tau_i}{\rho_i^2} + \frac{\tau_j}{\rho_j^2}\right)\nabla W_{ij} \tag{8}$$

3 Density-Correction Method

To avoid the time step restriction, we propose to use a density-correction scheme based on the SPH algorithm. In this work we introduce a new solver which set a separate stiffness parameter k_i for each fluid particle i to satisfy local incompressibility.

The pressure force of particle i caused by pressure acceleration is determined by:

$$\mathbf{F}_i^p = -m_i \frac{1}{\rho}\nabla p = -k_i \frac{m_i}{\rho_i}\sum_j m_j \nabla W_{ij} \tag{9}$$

We consider the pressure forces $\mathbf{F}_{j\leftarrow i}^p$ that act from particle i on the neighboring particles j. According to $\mathbf{F}_i^p + \sum_j \mathbf{F}_{j\leftarrow i}^p = 0$, we can get:

$$\mathbf{F}_{j\leftarrow i}^p = k_i \frac{m_i}{\rho_i} m_j \nabla W_{ij} \tag{10}$$

Using a semi-implicit Euler scheme for position and velocity update, the velocity can be rewritten as: $\mathbf{v}_i(t + \Delta t) = \mathbf{v}_i(t) + \Delta t \frac{\mathbf{F}_i^{adv}(t) + \mathbf{F}_i^p(t)}{m_i}$ with unknown pressure forces $\mathbf{F}_i^p$ and known non-pressure forces $\mathbf{F}_i^{adv}(t)$ such as gravity, surface tension and viscosity. We consider intermediate velocities $\mathbf{v}_i^*$:

$$\mathbf{v}_i^* = \mathbf{v}_i(t) + \Delta t \frac{\mathbf{F}_i^{adv}(t)}{m_i} = \mathbf{v}_i(t) + \Delta t \cdot \mathbf{g} + \Delta t \cdot \frac{1}{\rho}\nabla \cdot \tau_i \tag{11}$$

According to [13], the intermediate density resulted by predicted velocity is:

$$\rho_i^* = \rho_i(t) + \Delta t \sum_j m_j \left(\mathbf{v}_i^* - \mathbf{v}_j^*\right)\nabla W_{ij} \tag{12}$$

We now search for pressure forces to resolve the deviation from the rest density $\Delta \rho_i$:

$$\Delta \rho_i = -\frac{k_i}{\rho_i} \Delta t^2 \left(\left(\sum_j m_j \nabla W_{ij} \right)^2 + \sum_j \left(m_j \nabla W_{ij} \right)^2 \right) = \rho_0 - \rho_i^*$$

Solving for k_i yields:

$$k_i = \frac{\rho_0 - \rho_i^*}{\Delta t^2} \alpha_i, \quad \text{with } \alpha_i = \frac{\rho_i}{\left(\left(\sum_j m_j \nabla W_{ij} \right)^2 + \sum_j \left(m_j \nabla W_{ij} \right)^2 \right)} \quad (13)$$

Algorithm 1.simulation

1. **for** all particles i **do**
2.   find neighborhoods N_i
3.   compute time step size Δt
4. **end for**
5. **for** all particles i **do**
6.   update ρ_i, α_i
7. **end for**
8. **for** all particles i **do**
9.   update $\nabla \mathbf{v}_i$, $\boldsymbol{\tau}_i$
10. **end for**
11. **for** all particles i **do**
12.   update $\mathbf{v}_i^*$
13. **end for**
14. **while** ($\rho_{avg} - \rho_0 > \eta$)**or** *iter* < 2 **do**
15.   **for** all particles i **do**
16.   update ρ_i^*, k_i
17. $\rho_i^* = \rho_i^* + \dfrac{k_i}{\alpha_i} \Delta t^2$
18.   **end for**
19. **end while**
20. **for** all particles i **do**
21. $\mathbf{v}_i(t + \Delta t) = \mathbf{v}_i^* - \Delta t \sum_j m_j \left(\dfrac{k_i}{\rho_i} + \dfrac{k_j}{\rho_j} \right) \nabla W_{ij}$
22. $\mathbf{x}_i(t + \Delta t) = \mathbf{x}_i(t) + \Delta t \cdot \mathbf{v}_i(t + \Delta t)$
23. **end for**

4   Implementation and Results

All timings are given for an Intel 3.50 GHz CPU with 4 cores. The simulation and surface reconstruction are actualized with C++ language and multi-threading technology. Images were rendered with Blender. The density fluctuation is set to 0.01.

Figure 2 shows the Newtonian fluid and non-Newtonian fluid in particle state according to our method. When $K = 0$ the non-Newtonian fluid model is simplified to a Newtonian fluid with constant kinematic viscosity (Fig. 2, left). When the fluid touches the container in the bottom of scene, the fluid particles interact with container splash upward. In contrast, the non-Newtonian fluid particles (shown in Fig. 2, right) won't splash when they couple with container due to their viscosity.

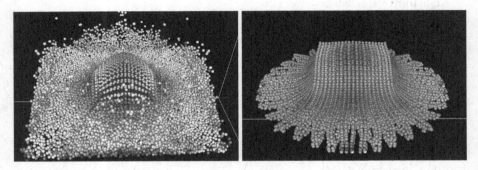

Fig. 2. Comparison between the Newtonian fluid (left) and the non-Newtonian fluid (right)

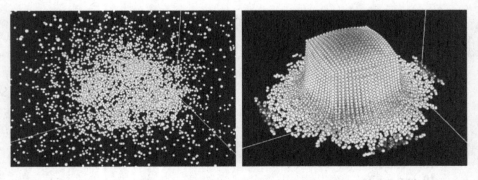

Fig. 3. Test for stability. Fluid particles scattered in all directions without predictive-corrective step (left), while the algorithm still run with predictive-corrective step (right).

During the experiment, we found that, when the scene is small or the fluid particles move gently, it takes more running time for the algorithm with density-corrective step, which consumes storage space and computing time. Take the experiment shown in Fig. 2 as an example. Figure 2 shows a free falling non-Newtonian fluid column with 13671 particles, $v_0 = 2$, $v_\infty = 0.2$, $K = 1$, $n = 0.5$. When the time step is set to 0.2 ms, it takes 53.3 ms for every time step without density-corrective step, while it takes 83.4 ms with density-corrective step. However, when the scene is large or the fluid particles intense collide, the non-Newtonian fluid will be unstable with larger time step. As shown in Fig. 3 left, when the time step is set to 0.3 ms, fluid particles scattered in all directions without predictive-corrective step, while the algorithm still run with predictive-corrective step (Fig. 3, right).

5 Conclusion

This paper presents a novel SPH-based technique for animating non-Newtonian fluid. The technique relies on the SPH approximation of a non-Newtonian fluid, where the variable viscosity is ruled by the Cross model. A predictive-corrective method is proposed to avoid tensile instability and numerical instability. Furthermore, we suggested an adaptive time-stepping method which increases and decreases the required time step according to the state of the simulation.

Acknowledgment. This work was supported by National Natural Science Foundation of China (No. 61272357, 61300074, 61572075).

References

1. Ellero, M., Tanner, R.I.: SPH simulations of transient viscoelastic flows at low Reynolds number. J. Non Newton. Fluid Mech. **132**(1), 61–72 (2005)
2. Müller, M., Charypar, D., Gross, M.: Particle-based fluid simulation for interactive applications. In: Proceedings of the 2003 ACM SIGGRAPH/Eurographics Symposium on Computer Animation, Eurographics Association, pp. 154–159 (2003)
3. Goktekin, T.G., Bargteil, A.W., O'Brien, J.F.: A method for animating viscoelastic fluids. ACM Trans. Graph. **23**(3), 461–466 (2004)
4. Losasso, F., Shinar, T., Selle, A., et al.: Multiple interacting liquids. ACM Trans. Graph. **25**(3), 812–819 (2006)
5. Bergou, M., Audoly, B., Vouga, E., et al.: Discrete viscous threads. ACM Trans. Graph. **29**(4), 157–166 (2010)
6. Batty, C., Uribe, A., Audoly, B., et al.: Discrete viscous sheets. ACM Trans. Graph. **31**(4), 13–15 (2012)
7. Müller, M., Keiser, R., Nealen, A., et al.: Point based animation of elastic, plastic and melting objects. In: ACM SIGGRAPH/Eurographics Symposium on Computer Animation, Eurographics Association, pp. 141–151 (2004)
8. Afonso, P., Fabiano, P., Thomas, L., Geovan, T.: Particle-based viscoplastic fluid/solid simulation. Comput. Aided Des. **41**(4), 306–314 (2009)
9. Paiva, A., Petronetto, F., Lewiner, T., et al.: Particle-based non-Newtonian fluid animation for melting objects. In: 2006 19th Brazilian Symposium on Computer Graphics and Image Processing, pp. 78–85. IEEE (2006)
10. Rafiee, A., Manzari, M.T., Hosseini, M.: An incompressible SPH method for simulation of unsteady viscoelastic free-surface flows. Int. J. Non Linear Mech. **42**(10), 1210–1223 (2007)

11. Andrade L.F.D.S., Sandim, M., Petronetto, F., et al.: SPH fluids for viscous jet buckling. In: Graphics, Patterns and Images, pp. 65–72. IEEE (2014)
12. Solenthaler, B., Pajarola, R.: Predictive-corrective incompressible SPH. ACM Trans. Graph. **28**(3), 341–352 (2009)
13. Ihmsen, M., Cornelis, J., Solenthaler, B., et al.: Implicit incompressible SPH. IEEE Trans. Vis. Comput. Graph. **20**(3), 426–435 (2014)
14. Bender, J., Koschier, D.: Divergence-free smoothed particle hydrodynamics. In: Proceedings of the 14th ACM SIGGRAPH/Eurographics Symposium on Computer Animation, pp. 147–155. ACM (2015)
15. Becker, M., Teschner, M.: Weakly compressible SPH for free surface flows. In: ACM SIGGRAPH/Eurographics Symposium on Computer Animation (SCA 2007), San Diego, California, USA, pp. 209–217, August 2007
16. Morris, J.P., Fox, P.J., Zhu, Y.: Modeling low Reynolds number incompressible flows using SPH. J. Comput. Phys. **136**(1), 214–226 (1997)

Areas of Life Visualisation: Growing Data-Reliance

Jesse Tran[1(✉)], Quang Vinh Nguyen[1], Simeon Simoff[1], and Mao Lin Huang[2]

[1] MARCS Institute and School of Computing, Engineering and Mathematics,
Western Sydney University, Penrith, Australia
{jesse.tran,q.nguyen,s.simoff}@westernsydney.edu.au
[2] School of Software, Faculty of Engineering and IT, University of Technology,
Sydney, Australia
mao.huang@uts.edu.au

Abstract. This paper presents a framework to mine and identify the areas of life and the way they are perceived, understood cognitively, and effectively using visualisation and machine learning. We provide an overview of the network of users including their activity and connections as well as zoom and details on demand of each individual areas of life. This research identifies the factors of each area of life which are significant on the user's social media profile in relation to information associated with each user such as time and location, including dynamic social behaviours. It aims to identify the key psychological factors and salient behaviours in order to find out the psychological factors of the user, and other overheads that can be portrayed in an image.

Keywords: Data visualisation · Areas of life · Social networks · Psychology · Dynamic social behaviours · Twitter · Machine learning

1 Introduction

Analysis of large-scale network datasets using visualisation is a trend of growing importance. This is true for social networks as more of our daily lives are recorded onto our online profiles. Examples of events that trigger users to post on social networks include being at a particular venue, to communicating with other people from their workplace, vent out emotional discomforts, and to express to the world their relationship statuses. There are no set number areas of lives as different theory concludes with different numbers of areas of lives. Henrique proposed eight areas of life [1]. Martin argues that there can exist more than eight, and instead of seeing each area as equal, they can be different and are interlinked with each other [2].

A number of psychology information can be extracted from social networks. It is stated that narcissism can exist on social networks, where the messages and photos a user posts are taken into account [3]. Many users tend to have more than one profile on different websites to display their peer groups more than themselves [4]. Personality traits are related to who these users present themselves. Self-efficacy was reflected by their number of friends, the amount of details in their profile, and the photo they have [5]. Research also discovered that the mean rating for each subject was different from the subjects with lowest personality scores [6]. Extravert people used the internet for

© Springer International Publishing AG 2016
Y. Luo (Ed.): CDVE 2016, LNCS 9929, pp. 227–234, 2016.
DOI: 10.1007/978-3-319-46771-9_30

researching, and extraverts did not use the internet for socialising [7]. Social networking can lead to better personal development as a whole and also better psychological well-being and improved skills [8].

Available network visualisation techniques often rely only on automation. However, these tools could face challenges of creating meaning, clear representations and high user acceptability. While there are many research works on predicting and visualising personalities on social networking websites such as Facebook and Twitter, limited research has been done on the areas of life of each user. Areas of life refer to the different matters in our lives – such as work, family, and entertainment – and how they relate to each other. Research has shown that for a person to be satisfied with their life, these areas of life must be in a balanced equilibrium.

The visualisation can be used to provide an overview of the network of users including their activities and connections with other users, as well as the ability to zoom in and retrieve detail on demand for each user's node and their areas of life. It allows the analyst to get the optimum display of the system by shifting different modules into different areas, which as a result. Attributes can be also used to portray extra information such as if there are any friends within the network, and how many, as well as interpreting how of much their profiles have been dedicated to each area of life to give a birds eye view of each user in general and also common nature of the entire network.

This paper introduces a system that mines and identifies the areas of life and the way they are perceived, understood cognitively, and affectively, by the use of machine learning and other psychological theories to output them into a meaningful visualisation. In our research, we are focusing on Twitter network, however the process can be applied to any social network. The system includes algorithms for accessing Twitter API and processing the data into a systematic way. It then interprets the data and presents in an interactive visualisation that allows the analyst to interact with the system, and consistently update the display after each interaction.

2   Related Work

Several visualisation tools already exist for social networks. Crimson Hexagon [9] allows users to listen to online conversations posted on social media websites including Twitter and Facebook. The algorithm known as BrightView, is used to track and calculate the most highly influential users based on certain hashtags and mentions. Analyst can use IntelliViz [10] to browse through users within a connection of a certain hashtag and shows their number of friends and followers, and how many of them have also mentioned the same hashtag. Clarabridge [11] collects data from popular sites like Facebook and Twitter, as well as Trip Advisor and Booking. A visualisation is then shown using social management software such as Radian6 [12] and Sysomos [13] in the forms of pie charts, line graphs, and bar charts.

There are many ways in which social networking data are mined and analysed but one of the most popular one includes using n-grams, and has been proven to be able to show opinions [14] and emotions [15] of users making the posts. The results have then been used to detect stock market results and subjects related to money and finance [16].

In addition to this, using a dictionary with machine learning has also been beneficial [17]. A language detection research has been carried out using decision trees as the machine learning technique that also uses n-grams [18], This same technique has also been used to classify users into groups based on ethnicity, political orientation and behaviour [19] and classify latent users attributes [20].

Research has shown users are able to understand hints displayed in graphical user interfaces placed in order to teach them how to use the system, but not a lot of research has been applied to text-based user interfaces [21]. Most often, immersive virtual reality is used, and uses software not optimised for large data sets [22]. The English usage should be simple, have domain knowledge and natural [23]. Five aspects that need to be considered includes awareness, collaboration, interaction, creativity and utility [24]. When creating meaningful personal visualisations, there should be two types of features when classifying data queries: filtering and browsing. There is, however, no classification that merges the two together [25].

The issues arising when a system contains a large set of data and how the visualisation can be generated because the way a user interacts with the visualisation remained unchanged regardless how much data there was. But because of the large number of data, complex compression, deeper deaths and sophisticated hierarchy, the system was unable to process what the user was asking for despite what they did were the same for every dataset [26].

3   Framework

Our system contains several phases to analyse the social behaviours of users and relate them to their appropriate areas of life as illustrated in Fig. 1.

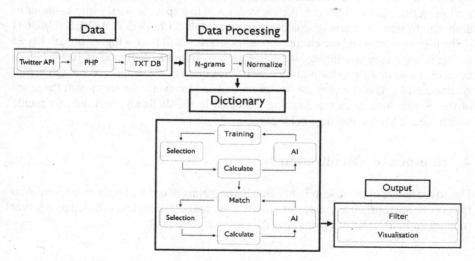

Fig. 1.   Framework of our system.

The *Data* process utilises the Twitter API with Javascript and PHP to collect all messages posted by a user, along with further details including time, followers and location. In most cases, a hashtag is inputted to mine data from a network of users that have mentioned the hashtag. The data are stored in a text file and processed to have certain words changed, such as typos and other internet acronym into more familiar wordings that will be understandable by our system. Symbols and emoji are removed. Extra processing is carried on for two of the areas of life which depends on the information already collected. The first is the "Friends and Family" area of life, which counts the number of messages exchanged between users through mentions and retweets. The second is the "Physical Environment" area of life where geometrical details from each message are taken into account in our calculation.

The *Data Processing* process organizes each message into n-grams. Several numbers of n-grams are used, starting at 1, and reaching to the total number of words in the message. In the *Dictionary* process, machine learning using a decision tree decides which area of life each post falls into. Before this process can be fully automated, it must be trained by the analyst. Each n-gram is matched with a n-gram in a dictionary, which is a database, containing predetermined n-grams from our literature review, as well as new ones resulted by the analyst training the machine.

Each of these n-grams in the dictionary are assigned with a score/likelihood of it falling into a certain area of life. For example, the phrase "I LOVE YOU" may have the likelihood of 70 % being in the Relationships area of life, and 10 % being in the Career area of life. Because Relationships has the highest likelihood, the n-gram will be assigned as Relationships. The likelihood of all of the areas of life are compared, and the match with the highest score/likelihood will take the title of that area of life.

The longer the n-gram, the higher the score is assigned to it for its corresponding area of life, which before being normalised, will have a score of 100 %. This is because the longer the n-gram, the more likely it is devoted to a specific area, while a shorter n-gram can fit into more ambiguous areas. For example, "I LOVE YOU VERY MUCH -" the n-gram containing the entire number of words – will have a higher probability of falling into the area of relationship (therefore assigning it a likelihood of 100 % before normalization) more than the n-gram, "I" (0 % regarded as not significant enough before normalization). These scores are finally normalized by averaging them with the score of the n-gram already in the database, reflected in the dictionary and used to decide which area of life the message belongs to.

4   Interactive Visualisation

Due to the nature of our research dwelling in the realms of online data, a web application is the most appropriate to create our visualisation upon. The system is based on a server running on PHP, extended from IntelliViz's framework [10].

4.1 Layout and Visualisation

We applied a spring force algorithm based on work created by Dwyer and Jakobsen's work which makes the movements of the nodes abide to the law of physics [27]. Quadratic programming techniques are used to ensure that the spacing between each node is equal by making sure the gravity forces between each node matches the equilibrium. We use a JSON call to retrieve the data from our database. In the visualisation, each user is represented as a circular node whose size is proportional to the number of followers that are also following them. On other social network, this can be referred as friends as the term 'friends' does not exist on Twitter. The thickness of the ring around each node represents the number of followers. The visualisation shows relationships that the user has with other users on the network by the colour of its node. A grey node represents the user having no connections present in the network while a blue one represents otherwise. Figure 2 illustrates a visualisation corresponding to different attributes. In this Figure, the smallest node has 5 friends where the largest has 15. The thinnest ring has 5 followers where the largest has 15. The thickness of the lines between nodes indicates the number of private messages exchanged.

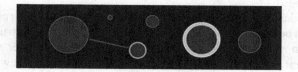

Fig. 2. Visual property of the visualisation.

Edges indicate connections between friends in the same network. The thickness of the lines represents the amount of communication between both users. If they have not communicated before, the line will be defaulted at 1px thickness. In terms of Twitter, this was calculated by the number of mentions, however on other social networking websites, this could be the total number of comments left and private message sent if

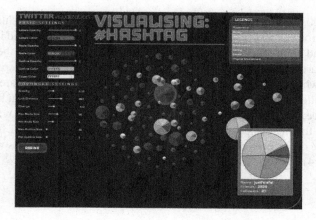

Fig. 3. Layout of user interface of visualisation. (Color figure online)

the information can be extracted via an API. As it loops through each user and calculate their customised areas of life, a pie chart is created and fills the centre of each user's node (see Fig. 3). The pie charts are designed using a colour palate that is also suitable for colour blindness. Together with these attributes, the influence of each user can be seen such as the journey in which a message is posted by a user with a lot of friends and followers, and then the way it gets retweeted and mentioned into the greater community until it turns into a trending topic.

4.2   Interaction

We update the spring force layout so that the analyst is able to adjust each node using their mouse or touch screen. As soon as a node is altered, the user will have the option to have the node escape the algorithm's gravity that positions it in a way where the spaces between each of the nodes around it are equal. The opposite is also possible. The advantages of the first is that the links between nodes can be better seen, and since it will not return into its initial layout proposed by the algorithm, the adjusted nodes would stand out from the rest of the nodes that are in the spring force layout, giving it better attention to when it is needed.

To get additional information, the pie chart that represents the areas of life contained in each node can be enlarged by clicking on it. A new window will pop up, showing the enlarged version with some accompanying details of their number of friends and followers. Several filtering options are available to let the analyst view optimal information based on their intentions. One includes hiding nodes that have no connections so that the analyst will only see what is useful to them, in this case, nodes only with connections. This is done by labelling each node with a class type, and adding styles to each class depending on the filter. Another option is to allow labels, which are the usernames displayed beside each node, to be hidden, and the visualisation to be shown in full screen without the physical interferences of the user interface.

4.3   Case Studies

We collected 20,848 tweets from 150 users who had mentioned the hashtag, "#deals." This resulted around 250,000 n-gram entries being generated and entered into our database, which had common stop words filtered out. In the visualisation, the majority of the user pie charts inside each node had the "Career" taking most of the space. This can be confirmed when all nodes not showing "Career" as the dominating area of life was hidden. The following most popular areas of life, judging only what can be seen, were ego, appearance, money, fun, relationship, environment and health. It was also interesting to learn that it seemed everyone had around the same number of followers and friends, and the differences between the influential levels from both ends were not very wide (see Fig. 4).

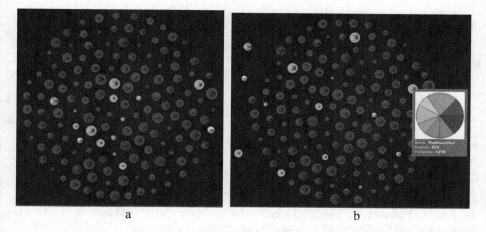

a   b

Fig. 4. Figure 4a shows the visualisation of the network. The nodes are scattered randomly across the canvas, and are all around the same sizes. The coloured nodes with a teal outline are users with friends in the network. The grey nodes are users with no friends. Figure 4b indicates that one of the most influential people in the network came by the name of "TheWoundGod". Further inspection on the profile reveals that the user hosts an online radio with several retweets proving their popularity. (Color figure online)

5   Conclusion

We have presented a system that retrieves and visualises psychological and general networking data from a social network. We introduced the idea of using rules to measure certain social behaviours from literature and machine learning with the use of n-grams and a dictionary. Data obtained from each user in the network, based on a certain hashtag, are automatically categorised for the user to use to train the machine learning to decide which area of life the messages are most likely belong to. After the initial training, the machine learning will then be able to decide on its own the areas of life automatically. We have also contributed a simple pie chart with colours to reflect the different areas of life that fill the centre of each node, and can also be enlarged when clicked on.

References

1. Henriques, G.: A Vision for psychological check-ups. Psychology Today (2014). https://www.psychologytoday.com/blog/theory-knowledge/201405/vision-psychological-check-ups
2. Martin, F.: Perceptions of links between quality of life areas: implications for measurement and practice. Soc. Indic. Res. **106**(1), 95–107 (2012)
3. Buffardi, L.E., Campbell, W.K.: Narcissism and social networking web sites. Pers. Soc. Psychol. Bull. **34**(10), 1303–1314 (2008)
4. Kluemper, D.H., Rosen, P.A.: Future employment selection methods: evaluating social networking web sites. J. Manag. Psychol. **24**(6), 567–580 (2009)
5. Livingstone, S.: Taking risky opportunities in youthful content creation: teenagers' use of social networking sites for intimacy, privacy and self-expression. New Media Soc. **10**(3), 393–411 (2008)

6. Wilson, K.F.: Psychological predictors of young adults' use of social networking sites. Cyberpsychology, Behav. Soc. Networking **13**(2), 173–177 (2012)
7. Yu, A.Y., Tian, S.W., Vogel, D., Kwok, R.C.W.: Can learning be virtually boosted? an investigation of online social networking impacts. Comput. Educ. **55**(4), 1494–1503 (2010)
8. Jin, L.,, Wen, Z.: An augmented social interactive learning approach through Web 2.0. In: 33rd Annual IEEE International Computer Software and Applications Conference (COMPSAC 2009), pp. 607–611 (2009)
9. Crimson Hexagon (2015). http://www.crimsonhexagon.com/
10. Tran, J., Nguyen, Q.V., Simoff, S.: IntelliViz- a tool for visualizing social networks with hashtags. In: Bebis, G., et al. (eds.) ISVC 2014, Part II. LNCS, vol. 8888, pp. 894–903. Springer, Heidelberg (2014)
11. Clarabridge (2015). http://www.clarabridge.com/
12. Radian6 (2015). https://radian6.com/
13. Sysomos (2015). https://sysomos.com/
14. Pak, A., Paroubek, P.: Twitter as a corpus for sentiment analysis and opinion mining. In: International Conference on Language Resources and Evaluation, pp. 1320–1326 (2010)
15. Agarwal, A., Xie, B., Vovsha, I., Rambow, O., Passonneau, R.: Sentiment analysis of twitter data. In: The Workshop on Languages in Social Media, pp. 30–38 (2011)
16. Bollen, J., Mao, H., Zeng, X.: Twitter mood predicts the stock market. J. Comput. Sci. **2**(1), 1–8 (2011)
17. Marafino, B.J., Davies, J.M., Bardach, N.S., et al.: N-gram support vector machines for scalable procedure and diagnosis classification, with applications to clinical free text data from the intensive care unit. J. Am. Med. Inform. Assoc. **21**(5), 871–875 (2014)
18. Häkkinen, J., Tian, J.: N-gram and decision tree based language identification for written words. In: 2001 IEEE Workshop on Automatic Speech Recognition and Understanding (ASRU 2001), pp. 335–338 ((2001))
19. Pennacchiotti, M., Popescu, A.M.: A machine learning approach to twitter user classification. ICWSM **11**(1), 281–288 (2011)
20. Rao, D., Yarowsky, D., Shreevats, A., Gupta, M.: Classifying latent user attributes in twitter. In: Proceedings of the 2nd International Workshop on Search and Mining User-Generated Contents, pp. 37–44. ACM, October 2010
21. Krämer, N.C., Winter, S.: Impression management 2.0: The relationship of self-esteem, extraversion, self-efficacy, and self-presentation within social networking sites. J. Media Psychol. **20**(3), 106–116 (2008)
22. Donalek, C., Djorgovski, S. G., Cioc, A., et al.: Immersive and collaborative data visualization using virtual reality platforms. In: 2014 IEEE International Conference on Big Data (Big Data), pp. 609–614 (2014)
23. Scholtz, J.: Beyond usability: evaluation aspects of visual analytic environments. In: 2006 IEEE Symposium on Visual Analytics Science and Technology, pp. 145–150 (2006)
24. Nafari, M., Weaver, C.: Query2Question: translating visualization interaction into natural language. IEEE Trans. Visual. Comput. Graphics **21**(6), 756–769 (2015)
25. Mizuno, H., Mori, Y., Taniguchi, Y., Tsuji, H.: Data queries using data visualization techniques. In: 1997 IEEE International Conference on Systems, Man, and Cybernetics, Computational Cybernetics and Simulation, pp. 2392–2396 (1997)
26. Wong, P.C., Shen, H.W., Johnson, C.R., Chen, C., Ross, R.B.: The top 10 challenges in extreme-scale visual analytics. IEEE Comput. Graphics Appl. **32**(4), 63 (2012)
27. Dwyer, T.: Scalable, versatile and simple constrained graph layout. Comput. Graphics Forum **28**(3), 991–998 (2009)

Discovering the Social Network and Trust Relationship in a Networked Manufacturing Environment

Tingting Liu[⊠] and Huifen Wang

Nanjing University of Science and Technology,
Nanjing 210094, Jiangsu, China
liutingting@mail.njust.edu.cn

Abstract. The aim of this paper is to apply the trust relationship in a social network to support access control policy development in a NME. Considering that social relations and their trust feature between users in a NME are associated with the roles these users assume, we first classify the social network in a NME into three types. Then, an extended markup language (XML) schema is proposed as the access control mining format to support a unified representation of system logs. Based on the scheme, we discuss the factors affecting the trust intention, analyze the trust relation types, and propose trust intention calculation algorithms.

Keywords: Access control · Social network · Trust relation · Trust intention

1 Introduction

A Networked Manufacturing Environment (NME) is a distributed, highly dynamic, and collaborative network environment [1, 2]. Access control in a NME is closely related to the users and organizations. The social relations of users within the collaborating organizations have a direct impact on the development, application, and implementation of the access control strategy, and furthermore, affect safety management. A social network refers to the relatively stable system of relations formed by interactions between social individual members and is concerned with the interactions between people. As a virtual form of a social network, relations in a NME have many similarities with those in a social network and it is a good idea to define the access control model and strategies based on the social network.

From the viewpoint of the social network, interactions between people are based on relationships of trust and understanding. "Trust" derives from a concept in sociology and can be expressed as the subjective expectation an agent has about another's future behavior based on the history of their encounters [3]. As the NME involves a large number of enterprise organizational affairs and collaborative project related information resources, and at the same time contains some private information distinguished from the general distributed application environments, trust relations in a NME have their own particularity, which is mainly reflected in the organizational business correlation and project co-correlation. An employee in a NME not only needs to be involved in the

© Springer International Publishing AG 2016
Y. Luo (Ed.): CDVE 2016, LNCS 9929, pp. 235–244, 2016.
DOI: 10.1007/978-3-319-46771-9_31

enterprise/departmental affairs, but must also be involved in some collaborative projects across the enterprises and sectors. In these two different types of work domain, trust relationships between the employees have different characteristics, properties, and nature. For example, assume Tom and Jack are colleagues in the same department and have close contacts in the business. Now Tom is involved in project X whereas Jack has no connection with X. Therefore, in this case, the trust relationship strength between Tom and Jack is high in the sub-environment related to enterprise/departmental affairs. On the contrary, the strength of the trust relationship is low in the sub-environment related to project X.

The trust management concept was originally proposed in 1996 by Blaze et al. [4]. It adopts a unified approach for describing the security policies, security credentials, and trust relationships for direct authorization of security-critical operations. As a result, it helps minimize risk and assures the network activity of benign entities in distributed systems [5], improves the accuracy and security of the authorization, and reduces the complexity of authorization [6]. In recent years it has been introduced into distributed network systems as an emerging technology in the data security field [7].

Although certain aspects of trust management are dealt with satisfactorily by existing services in some distributed systems, the trust management problem in a NME has not previously been investigated, particularly as the basis of an access control policy. Owing to the complexity of trust relationships in a NME, existing trust research does not apply to NMEs. It is our thesis that a coherent trust model is needed for the study of access control in a NME. Our idea is to mine the social networks in a NME to establish a resource-type-oriented trust model for different types of resources.

2   Resource Classification in NMEs

If the numbers of users and data resources in a NME are very large, a huge amount of work is required to develop and manage security policies. If the social network of a NME can be identified automatically, it can provide preliminary strategies to support access control strategy development and application.

Assume an actual scenario as shown in Fig. 1. User A is an employee of the production department in an enterprise with users E and D in the same division. User A is undertaking a task in project P together with users B, C, and other staff. Now, as an employee in the production department, user A may submit production data, daily reports, and production planning to the NME server; he may need to share project Power-point with team members of project P after he has completed a project report; in addition, certain private pictures may be uploaded to his personal space. The access control requirements of these data are given in Table 1. At the same time, while performing a project task, such as planning a new plant assembly line for a new product model, user A may need to access task-related resources from similar projects.

From Table 1, we see that the access control requirements are closely associated with the social relations of the access subject and source owner. Moreover, the social relations and their trust feature between users in a NME are associated with the roles assumed by these users. Because we wish to discover the social relations of user A in order to manage and control the distribution of his daily report, the main characteristics we should be focusing on are possibly departmental structure, working relationships, and sector members. However, if we are concerned with the project Power-pointer preliminary program of project tasks introduced in Table 1, the main issues we should consider are project division, project process, and cross-project management methods. The issue of trust is particularly relevant; user A may trust D when it comes to the daily report, however, A should not trust D in relation to the project Power-pointer. Further more, the trust strength between users A and B is higher than that between users A and C because users A and B are in one sub-team. That is, the relation between users A and B is different from that between users A and D. Thus, we can say that the social relations between users are not unified in a NME.

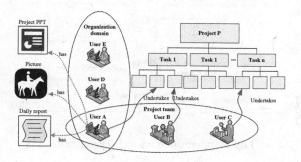

Fig. 1. An actual scenario

Table 1. Access control requirements of the data produced by user A

Sequence	Data	Why the data is submitted	Data owner	Access control requirements
1	Project PPT	To exchange the implementation of the project task with project team members	User A	Can be accessed by all project members
2	Preliminary program of project tasks	The program needs to be discussed in the forthcoming sub-team meeting	User A	Can only be accessed by closely related sub-team members
3	Private picture	Stored on the server	User A	Can be accessed by good friends
4	Daily report	During or after completion of the day-to-day work, he needs to submit work information	User A	Can be accessed by work-related employees and the department head

According to the above analysis, we divide the NME into three sub environments: a Daily-Affairs Environment (DAE), Collaborative Project Environment (CPE), and Personal Social Environment (PSE). In the DAE, the company's organizational structure is relatively stable, and organizational affairs generally have good repeatability and great regularity. In a CPE, the collaborative project team is configured according to the scope, time, and cost of each project, the project team structure is usually not the same, and the roles of the team members are usually one-time and time limited. In a PSE, social relations are random and subjective, and do not follow any fixed rules.

A further division can then be carried out, that is, information resources in a NME can be divided into three categories: organizational information, project-related information, and private information, as shown in Fig. 2.

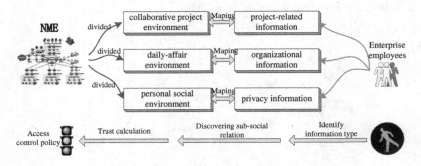

Fig. 2. Information resource classification

Organizational information refers to a series of transaction information from each organizational level produced during the day-to-day operations and management of enterprises. This information only has a bearing on the staff's role within the organization through out its life cycle, is not directly related to the specific tasks of various projects, and usually includes daily production information, site management information, and logistics information, amongst others.

Project-related information refers to the information generated in the planning and implementation of project tasks. This information is only associated with the project (task) roles, is not directly involved in organizational affairs, and usually consists of planning information, progress information, execution information, and so on.

Private information refers to the individual's personal privacy and is not involved in daily work or projects, for example, holiday travel photos.

3   Modeling Logs Based on XML: Access Control Mining Format

Almost all computer systems record and store logs. Web logs record a variety of original information, such as received and handled client requests and run-time errors, while Windows logs record the hardware, software, and system information and monitored system events. Most WFM, ERP, CRM, SCM, and B2B systems record transactions in a systematic way. To discover the social network for NME access control, an XML schema is proposed (Fig. 3) specifying what data need to be extracted from the log. XML provides a unified approach to describe and exchange structured data independent of the application or system platform. Van der Aalst et al. proposed an XML schema for a workflow mining format. Here we also use the XML schema to describe the access control mining format. The difference between our research and that of Van der Aalst et al. [8] is that we mainly focus on the factors affecting access control policies.

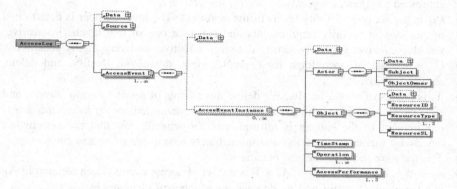

Fig. 3. An XML schema for discovering social networks for NME access control

Our schema has the AccessLog element as the root element with Data, Source, and AccessEventas elements. The Source element contains information about the net-worked system used to record the log, for example, ERP and MES. The AccessEvent element represents the access events occurring in the system and each AccessEvent may contain many access instances, which map to the access control history. An AccessEvent Instance is the core element of our schema, including mainly Actor, Object, Timestamp, Operation, and AccessPerformance. Actor refers to the persons involved in the access control event, including Subject (the user who submitted the access request) and Object-Owner (to whom the accessed resource belongs); Object refers to the relevant information concerning the accessed resource, composed of ResourceID, ResourceType, and ResourceSL; Timestamp is a description of the time of the event in a standard format; Operation denotes the behavior access the subject executed (such as view or modify); while the AccessPerformance element refers to the access result of this access event. Like the schema proposed by van der Aalst et al., to make the format more expressive, we also define a Data element, which other elements can use as a sub tag. If users wish to specify more information than the basic elements, they can record the additional information using the Data element.

Based on the schema, we define the formal concepts of discovering social networks and trust calculations as follows:

- $L = \{l_1, l_2, \ldots l_N\}$ denotes the set of all logs; setting $n_L = |L|$ gives the number of logs in the current environment.
- $S = \{s_1, s_{2,\ldots,}s_M\}$ denotes the set of access control subjects.
- $O_w = \{w_1, w_2, \ldots, w_K\}$ is the set of resource owners (that is, to whom the accessed resource belongs).

- $A_R = S \times O_w = \{ar_1, ar_2, \ldots, ar_J\}$ denotes the relations between S and O_w involved in access control events, where ar_j is a binary relation between s_m and w_k. This means s_m accessed some resource w_k owns, which is expressed as $ar_j = (s_m, w_k) j \in [1, J]$. Setting $n_r = |A_R|$ gives the cardinality of A_R.
- R_T is the set of resource types in the NME, of which there are three: daily production information, site management information, and logistics information, expressed as *Affair, Project,* and *Social,* respectively.
- R_{SL} is the set of sensitivity levels of the resources. The level number is determined by the system security requirements and can take one of five levels: insensitive, weakly sensitive, generally sensitive, highly sensitive, and very highly sensitive.
- O_p is the set of operations; for example, view, download, modify, and delete, amongst others.
- A_p is the set of access results. We define three kinds of results: *Permit, Reject,* and *Suspend. Permit* means the access requirement is permitted; *Reject* means the access requirement of the subject is refused; and *Suspend* implies that the system has detected a malicious intrusion and immediately terminates its access connection.
- T is the time the access event occurred.
- $A_E = S \times O_w \times R_T \times R_{SL} \times A_p \times T$ is the set of access events. Each element in A_E is a six-element vector and n_E denotes the number of elements in A_E.

4   Trust Relation and Calculation in a NME

Definition 1: A trust relationship refers to the trust intensity between the access subject and source owner for a specific trust type.

As previous defined, S is the access subject, O_W is the source owner, and R_T is the sub-environment type. Let V_T be the trust intensity, then T_R can be expressed as:

$$T_R = S \times O_W \times R_T \times V_T = A_R \times R_T \times V_T.$$

4.1   Factors Affecting Trust Intensity

If we consider the access history in a system, a recent visit is more trust worthy than an earlier access. This means trust has a time decaying characteristic. There are two common time decay functions: the exponential decay function (Eq. 1) and reciprocal decay function (Eq. 2).

$$f(t) = e^{-\alpha t}, t \geq 0, \alpha \geq 0 \tag{1}$$

$$f(t) = \frac{1}{\alpha t + 1}, t \geq 0, \alpha \geq 0 \tag{2}$$

In Eqs. (1) and (2), α is the attenuation coefficient. It shows that the decay rate of the exponential decay function is faster than that of the reciprocal decay function. In access control, we need to ensure data security and prefer to take a more recent visit event as the foundation of the trust relationship. So here the exponential decay function is adopted to describe the time characteristic of the trust relation in a NME.

In addition to the time factor, a visitor's subjective intention should be taken into account. Typically in a computer system an access request is accepted and handled based on the preset access control policy, with the access result recorded in the system log. The result may be success or failure, with the latter result usually caused by one of the following reasons: (a) The access request is rejected owing to the access requestor's low rights. In this case, the requestor perhaps does not clear the purview and performs some routine operations. (b) The access requestor tries to access certain system resources through an illegal attack with malicious intent. Obviously, failure owing to the former access behavior can be regarded as the requestor's misjudgment of his/her rights and the access event will not have a negative impact on the trust relation between the requestor and resource owner. However, once a requestor tries to access certain system resources through illegal means, the system needs to pay special attention to the visitor's behavior and he/she cannot be trusted by the resource owner. Considering the visitor's subjective intention, feedback operator β is used to describe the access result-trust relation. Table 2 gives the values of β for different access statuses. In Table 2, *Permit* means the access requirement is passed in an access event, *Reject* means the access requirement is declined, and *Suspend* means the requirement is monitored to be illegal.

Table 2. Values of for different access statuses

Access result	β
Permit	1
Reject	0
Suspend	$-\propto$

Table 3. Sensitivity index operator δ

Sensitivity level	Sensitivity value
L1	0.2
L2	0.4
L3	0.6
L4	0.8
L5	1.0

In real life, if an owner allows a visitor to see very important data, it means that the owner has a high level of trust for the visitor. In a NME, some data is very important, while other data can possibly be ignored. So if some successful access has happened, the degree of importance of the accessed resource can reflect the trust level of the visitor from the perspective of the resource host. Then the sensitivity index operator δ can be used to describe the importance degree of the accessed resource.

Considering the time, the nature of the historical access incident, and the data sensitivity level, the trust value of a single access event $e_i = (ar_i, rt_i, rs_i, ap_i, t_i)$ can be expressed as

$$v(e_i) = V_r \cdot V_p \cdot e^{-t^* \cdot t_g}, \ i \in [0, n_E].$$

In the above formula, the values of $V_r = \delta(rs_i)$ and $V_p = \beta(ap_i)$ are given in Tables 2 and 3, respectively. Here t_g is the interval between the current time and event time, and t^* is the time attenuation coefficient. The larger the value of t^* is, the faster v_i attenuates.

4.2   Trust Strength Calculation

Trust relations can be divided into two types: direct trust relationship (DTR) and recommendation trust relationship (RTR), as shown in Fig. 4. For A and B, if a direct interaction exists from A to B, i.e., A visited B's resources directly, we say there is a DTR from A to B. If no direct interaction exists between A and B, but there is a credible body or trusted group C who can provide B with the interaction history between A and C, then we assume there is an RTR from A to B.

Obviously, a DTR directly reflects the interactive relationship from A to B, while an RTR reflects an indirect relationship from A to B.

If the trust strength from A to B needs to be evaluated, the direct interaction history can be applied to assess the strength in the case that a DTR exists from A to B, or the indirect interaction history can be applied based on the social network in the case that only an RTR exists from A to B.

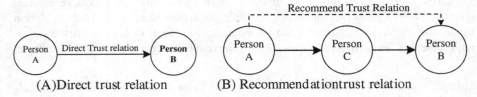

(A)Direct trust relation   (B) Recommendationtrust relation

Fig. 4. Direct and recommendation trust relations

In Algorithm 1, the input parameter t_w is the access event number for a specific defined time period. In a NME, information interactions occur frequently and the number of events in the NME log is huge. So if all the elements in A_E are considered as the foundation of the trust strength, the complexity of the calculation is enormous. Taking into account the smaller effect of earlier access events on the trust relationship, a time window can be used to limit the number of access events.

Algorithm 1: DTR intensity from subject to source owner

    Input: $ar_j = (s_m, w_k)$, rt_n, t_w

    Output: $direct\_v_{ar_j}^{rt_n}$

    Step1: Traverse all the elements $e_i, i \in [0, n_E]$ in A_E, input element e_i into a new set $A_E' = \{e_1', e_2', e_3', ...\}$ where $ar_i = ar_j, rt_i = rt_n (i \in [0, n_E])$;

    Step2: Set $n_E' = |A_E'|$. If $n_E' = 0$, then $direct\_v_{ar_j}^{rt_n} = 0$; otherwise, go to next step;

    Step3: If $0 < n_E' \leq t_w$, set $A_E'' = A_E'$; otherwise, set $A_E'' = \{e_1, e_2, ..., e_{t_w}\}$;

    Step4: Traverse all the elements in A_E'' and calculate $v(e_i)$ for each element $e_i, i \in [0, n_E'']$;

    Step5: $direct\_v_{ar_j}^{rt_n} = \frac{\sum_{i=1}^{n_E''} v(e_i)}{n_E''}$

Algorithm 2: RTR intensity from subject to source owner

Input: $ar_j = (s_m, w_k)$, rt_n, trust relation network $TN = \{tn_B, tn_M, tn_P\}$

Output: indirect_$V_{ar_j}^{rt_n}$

Step1: Traverse all the elements $e_i, i \in [0, n_E]$ in A_E, input element e_i into a new element set $B_E' = \{e_1', e_2', e_3', \ldots \ldots\}$ where $rt_i = rt_n$;

Step2: Establish trust relation sub-network S from B_E', search the path and set $Route$ from s_m to w_k, and set $n_{Route} = |Route|$;

Step3: Calculate $direct\_V$ for every two adjacent nodes;

Step4: $indirect\_v_{ar_j}^{rt_n} = \dfrac{\Sigma_{route_i \in Route}(\prod direct\_V)}{n_{Route}}$

Based on the above two algorithms, we express the strength of the trust from s_m to w_k as:

$$V_T = \begin{cases} indirect_v = \dfrac{\Sigma_{route_i \in Route}(\prod direct_V)}{n_{Route}}, if\ DTR\ doesn't exist \\[3mm] direct_v = \dfrac{\Sigma_{i=1}^{n_E''} v(e_i)}{n_E''}, \quad if\ DTR\ exists \end{cases}$$

5 Conclusion

In this paper, we used social network discovery and a trust relationship calculation to support access control policy development in NMEs. Considering that access control requirements are closely associated with the social relations of the access subject and source owner, a NME can be classified into three types, namely, DAE, CPE, and PSE. Based on the classification, we used XML to standardize the system logs, and presented a trust strength calculation method.

An NME is a very broad concept and a variety of access control models can be applied in an NME. However, irrespective of which access control model is applied, social network discovery and trust relationships can be used in two ways. In the first method the trust strength value is placed between the subject and object owner as the basis for access control decisions. The second method uses the social network as an auxiliary tool to assist in the access decision. Future work involves incorporating an access control scheme into the current study.

Acknowledgements. This work is funded by Defense Basic Research Program A2620132010.

References

1. Yushun, F.: Connotation and key technologies of networked manufacturing. Comput. Integr. Manuf. Syst. **9**(7), 576–582 (2003). (in Chinese)
2. Shuzi, Y., Bo, W., Chunhua, H., et al.: Network manufacturing and enterprise integration. China Mech. Eng. **11**(1–2), 45–48 (2000). (in Chinese)

3. Mui, L., Mohtashemi, M.: A computational model of trust and reputation. In: Proceedings of the 35th Annual Hawaii International Conference on System Sciences, pp. 2431–2439 (2002)
4. Matt, B., Joan, F., Jack, L.: Decentralized trust management. In: Proceedings of IEEE Conference on Security and Privacy, Oakland, CA, USA, pp. 164–173 (1996)
5. Huaizhi, L.I., Mukesh, S.: Trust management in distributed systems. Computer **40**(2), 45–53 (2007)
6. Luhmann, N.: Trust and Power. Wiley, Chichester (1979)
7. Hao, F., Min, G., Lin, M.: MobiFuzzyTrust: an efficient fuzzy trust inference mechanism in mobile social networks. IEEE Trans. Parallel Distrib. Syst. **25**(11), 2944–2955 (2014)
8. van der Aalst, W.M.P., Reijers, H.A., Song, M.: Discovering social networks from event logs. Comput. Support. Coop. Work **14**, 549–593 (2005)

Evaluating the Economic Effect of the Delayed Differentiation in the Customized Product's Supply Chain Network

Zhiliang Wang[✉]

School of Mechanical Engineering,
Nanjing Institute of Technology, Nanjing 211167, China
wwangzzll@njit.edu.cn

Abstract. Employing delayed differentiation in the customization product supply chain network (CPSCN) can bring customers more opportunities for personalized products, but bears the cost pressure. As to assemble CPSCN, on the basis of building the cost model, considering the changes of the fixed investment and product cost at transferring standard production to customization production, this paper proves firstly, the fixed investment has economy threshold and diseconomy threshold. When the real fixed investment is less than economy threshold (or greater than diseconomy threshold), the production cost of the supplier decreases (or increases) with the increase of postponement degree. When the real fixed investment is between the two thresholds, postponement degree has a threshold; if the actual postponement degree is less or more' than this threshold, the production cost decreases or increases with the increase of postponement degree. Secondly, by deducing relationship between the total costs of CPSCN and the fixed investment, and the postponement degree, it is proved that, the economy of the supplier's delayed differentiation directly decides the economy of CPSCN's delayed differentiation; the impact of different supplier on the total cost of CPSCN is different. Finally, the conclusions have been verified through the simulation. The economy analysis provides the measurement tools, identification criteria and decision foundation for evaluating CPSCN's delayed differentiation.

Keywords: Mass customization · Postponement · Supply chain · Product differentiation · Cost model · Economy

1 Introduction

Under mass customization, the customization product manufacturer chooses several customized modules according to the customer needs; and these customized modules are produced by suppliers which have corresponding customization capability. Under postponement manufacturing, the entire manufacturing process of each customized module is divided into standard production process and customization production process by customer order decoupling point (CODP) [1]. As the module is not differentiated until the customization production stage, call this differentiation the delayed differentiation in the paper.

© Springer International Publishing AG 2016
Y. Luo (Ed.): CDVE 2016, LNCS 9929, pp. 245–256, 2016.
DOI: 10.1007/978-3-319-46771-9_32

As to CPSCN consisting of several customized module suppliers and a customization product manufacturer, if some standard production are transferred into customization production, this transferring inevitably brings the change of production equipment and technological process, which augments the fixed investment, and therefore the customized module suppliers will consider whether the delayed differentiation is carried, which postponement strategy shall be taken if postponement has to be employed; in other words, economic problems of module's delayed differentiation must be taken into account. Meanwhile, the customization product manufacturer which is the leader of the supply chain must consider from the CPSCN how to choose appropriate customization modules, which postponement strategies the customization product family should possess to fulfill the diversified demands of customers; in another word, economic problems of CPSCN's delayed differentiation must be taken into account [2]. This paper will expand the previous research [3], focuses on the impact of the delayed differentiation on supplier cost and the supply chain network cost, and valuates the economic effect of the delayed differentiation.

2 The Cost Model of CPSCN

2.1 The Cost Model of Suppliers Sub-Network

The total cost of suppliers sub-network consisting of customized module suppliers should be the sum of all customized modules cost. As to each customized module, operation cost can be made up of two parts, the product cost of semi-finished goods and the product cost of customization process.

2.1.1 The Product Cost of Semi-finished Goods

Under the centralized strategy, according to the orders of customers, customization product manufacturer will transfer the total demand rate D, and corresponding variance σ_D^2 to each customized module supplier; and also give cycle service level (CSL). Assuming that a manufacturer assembly production cycle is Ts, the ordering cycle shall be Ts. Hence the demand is $Q = Ts * D$ in production cycle Ts.

Assuming that customization products contain M customized modules; the k th customized module has $mv(k)$ variants and an integer variable " v" represents its v th variant; the customer's choice rate for the v th variant of customized modules k is $fd(k,v)$, $\sum_{v=1}^{mv(k)} fd(k,v) = 1$; The variety number of products is $N = \prod_{k=1}^{M} mv(k)$; demand rate and variance of the i th customization product is respectively $d(i), \sigma(i)^2$ [3].

The total production time, the standard production time and the customization production time of a k th module are denoted as $S(k)$, $St(k)$ and $Sd(k)$ respectively (ignoring the small differences between variants). Considering the uniform productivity, we can define the postponement degree as $L(k) = Sd(k)/S(k), L(k) \in [0,1]$, thus $St(k) = (1 - L(k)) \times S(k)$, $Sd(k) = L(k) \times S(k)$.

Define that $ht(k)$, $htw(k)$ – average inventory holding cost rates of semi-finished goods and WIP respectively, $Mt(k)$ –unit manufacturing cost of semi-finished goods.

$Tt(k)$, $Td(k)$ – the total time of standard production and customization production respectively when order quantity is Q. As the average inventory costs of WIP at the ordering cycle Ts are $\frac{Q \times Tt(k)}{Ts} \times htw(k)$, and semi-finished product's safety stock $ss(k) = \Phi^{-1}(CSL) \times \sqrt{Tt(k)+1} \times \sigma_D$ while the safety factor is $\Phi^{-1}(CSL(k))$ [4, 5], manufacturing cost per period of the customized module k at standard production and at ordering cycle Ts is $Ct(k)$:

$$Ct(k) = D \times Mt(k) + \frac{Q \times Tt(k)}{Ts} \times htw(k) + [\frac{1}{2}\frac{Q \times Tt(k)}{Ts} + \Phi^{-1}(CSL) \times \sqrt{Tt(k)+1}$$
$$\times \sigma_D] \times ht(k)$$

$$(1)$$

Considering that each supplier adopts the parallel move method in the process of production, $Tt(k) = St(k) + (Q-1) \times tr(k)$, $Td(k) = Sd(k) + (Q-1) \times td(k)$, here $tr(k)$ and $td(k)$ is respectively the longest working procedure time of a part at standard stage and at customization stage.

After standard production, semi-finished products are transferred to the customization production and each of them will be processed into multiple variants of this customized module by the delayed differentiation.

2.1.2 The Cost Model of Customization Process

Let $hd(k)$, $hdw(k)$ –the average inventory holding cost rate of customized modules k' finished goods in customization production and WIP, $pd(k)$ –the production rate, $Td(k)$ –the customization production time. Hence, there are inventory costs: $Q \times (Ts - Td(k)) \times ht(k)$; when all variants of module k are delivered to manufacturers as a whole after the delayed differentiation, the finished goods inventory costs of module k is $D \times Ts \times Td(k) \times hd(k)/2$.

Considering the changeover cost $Ad(k, v)$ required to switch to the variant v's production from other variants' production, the customization average production cost $Md(k)$, and the inventory costs of WIP $Q \times Td(k) \times hdw(k)$, the manufacturing cost $Cd(k)$ of customized module k in Ts by expanding the previous research [3] is:

$$Cd(k) = D \times (Ts - Td(k)) \times ht(k) + \frac{1}{Ts}\sum_{v=1}^{mv(k)} Ad(k, v)$$
$$+ D \times Md(k) + D \times Td(k) \times hdw(k) + \frac{1}{2}D \times Td(k) \times hd(k)$$

$$(2)$$

After each supplier finishes the production of customization module respectively, these customized products will be delivered to manufacturers.

2.2   The Cost Mode of Customization Product Manufacturer

After the manufacturer orders and receives each customized module (variants), the manufacturer will organize customization products assembly production. Thus at this stage, the total cost consists of the ordering cost and the assembly production cost.

2.2.1   The Manufacturer's Ordering Cost Model

The manufacturer orders the required finished products of (customized module k's) variants from its supplier at once. We may define that average order price of customized module k as $Cp(k)$, average inventory holding cost rate is $hg(k)$ and the order start-up cost is $Ag(k)$ when the order quantity is Q, according to Economic Ordering Quantity, the order cost per period in ordering cycle Ts is:

$$Cg(k) = \frac{1}{Ts}Ag(k) + \frac{1}{2}Q \times hg(k) \tag{3}$$

2.2.2   The Manufacturer's Assembly Production Cost Model

As to the manufacturer's assembly cost [6]. While an approximate optimal production sequence is obtained by the heuristic algorithm of customization production [7], and assuming that the customization products' assembly operating costs is Mz per unit, the optimization model of assembly cost per period in ordering cycle Ts is:

$$Cz = \frac{1}{Ts}\sum_{j=1}^{N} Az(j) + Mz \times D + \frac{1}{2}Ts \times \sum_{j=1}^{N} hz(j) \times d(j) \times [1 - \frac{d(j)}{p(j)}] \tag{4}$$

In formula (4), $Az(i)$, $hz(i)$, $d(i)$, $p(i)$ respectively are customization products changeover cost, inventory cost rate, demand rate and productivity; therefore, the first term, the second term and the third term on the right side represent changeover costs, production costs, and inventory costs respectively.

2.3   The Total Cost Model of CPSCN and Parameter Analysis

2.3.1   Suppliers Cost Model and Parameter Analysis

The lot cost of the supplier in the ordering cycle Ts can be expressed as:

$$STC(k) = Ct(k) + Cd(k)$$

$$= D \times Mt(k) + D \times Tt(k) \times htw(k) + [\frac{D}{2}Tt(k) + ss(k)]ht(k) + D \times (Ts - Td(k))ht(k)$$

$$+ \frac{1}{Ts}\sum_{v=1}^{mv(k)} Ad(k, v) + D \times Md(k) + D \times Td(k) \times hdw(k) + \frac{1}{2}D \times Td(k) \times hd(k)$$

$$\tag{5}$$

Then the total lot cost of suppliers sub-network's in the cycle Ts becomes:

$$ATC = \sum_{k=1}^{M} STC(k) \qquad (6)$$

Without loss of generality, assuming that each production process of customized module has linear cost function, and the production cost increases by linearity mode, production cost per unit at standard and at customization stage can be written as:

$$Mt(k) = (g(k) + \frac{q(k)}{Q}) \times St(k) = (g(k) + \frac{q(k)}{Q})(1 - L(k)) \times S(k), Md(k)$$
$$= (u(k) + \frac{z(k)}{Q}) \times L(k) \times S(k)$$

Here, $g(k)$, $u(k)$ represent the same module variable costs per unit respectively from two aspects of the standard production and customization production; $q(k)$, $z(k)$ represent the fixed investment of the standard production and customization production respectively, as the standard production and customization production may need different equipment and tooling, both of them can be different.

Let I –return rate on capital per period, $hy(k)$ –raw materials inventory holding cost rate, thus the inventory holding cost rates of the semi-finished goods and WIP at standard stage are $ht(k) = hy(k) + I \times Mt(k)$, $htw(k) == hy(k) + I \times Mt(k)/2$ respectively. The inventory holding cost rates of the finished goods and WIP at customization stage are $hd(k) = ht(k) + I \times Md(k)$, $hdw(k) = ht(k) + I \times Md(k)/2$.

2.3.2 The Manufacturer Total Cost Model and Parameter Analysis
The total cost of customization products' manufacturer can be expressed as:

$$MTC = \sum_{k=1}^{M} Cg(k) + Cz \qquad (7)$$

After the suppliers have finished customized module production, considering certain cost margins, transportation costs, inventory holding cost and administration cost of logistics, suppliers will provide customized modules to the product manufacturer. In this paper, $pr(k)$ has been used as the increasing rate of unit price.

When the cost of raw materials is $mc(k)$, the unit price for customized module after the customization production is $cp(k) = mc(k) + STC(k)/D$. Thus, inventory cost rate at replenishment can be expressed as $hg(k) = pr(k) \times cp(k) \times I$.

Usually, the order start-up costs can be considered as a percentage of stock value, we denote this percentage by $ra(k)$; therefore, the order start-up cost for a batch is $Ag(k) = ra(k) \times cp(k) \times Q$. Inventory cost rate of assembly operation becomes:

$$hz(j) = \sum_{ik=1}^{M} hg(ik) + \sum_{ik=1}^{M} Ag(ik) \times I/Q = \sum_{ik=1}^{M} hg(ik) + [\sum_{ik=1}^{M} ra(ik) \times cp(ik)] \times I$$

2.4   The Total Cost Model of Customization Product

The average total cost per period in the ordering cycle Ts can be expressed as:

$$TC = ATC + MTC = \sum_{k=1}^{M} STC(k) + [\sum_{k=1}^{M} Cg(k) + Cz] \tag{8}$$

Substitute $ht(k)$, $htw(k)$, $hd(k)$, $hdw(k)$ into the formula (8) and then substitute $Mt(k)$, $Md(k)$ into this expression; expand and merge similar items. Let

$$ss(k) = \Phi^{-1}(CSL) \times \sqrt{(1 - L(k)) \times S(k) + (D \times Ts - 1) \times tr(k) + 1} \times \sigma_D$$

$$f(L(k)) = [hy(k) + I \times \left(g(k) + \frac{q(k)}{D \times Ts}\right) \times (1 - L(k)) \times S(k)] \times ss(k)$$

$$a(k) = \frac{1}{2}S(k)^2 \times D \times I \times \left(g(k) + \frac{q(k)}{D \times Ts}\right) + S(k)^2 \times D \times I \times \left(u(k) + \frac{z(k)}{D \times Ts}\right)$$

$$b(k) = -S(k) \times D \times hy(k) + \{-D - \frac{3D}{2}S(k) \times I - (tr(k) + \frac{1}{2}td(k)) \times (D \times Ts - 1) \times D \times I$$
$$- D \times Ts \times I\} \times \left(g(k) + \frac{q(k)}{D \times Ts}\right)S(k) + \{D + (D \times Ts - 1)td(k) \times D \times I\} \times \left(u(k) + \frac{z(k)}{D \times Ts}\right)S(k)$$

$$c(k) = \{\frac{3}{2}[S(k) + (D \times Ts - 1) \times tr(k)] \times D + D \times Ts + \frac{D}{2}(D \times Ts - 1) \times td(k)\}$$
$$\times hy(k) + \{D + [S(k) + (D \times Ts - 1) \times tr(k)] \times D \times I + D \times Ts \times I$$
$$+ \frac{D}{2}(D \times Ts - 1) \times td(k) \times I\} \times \left(g(k) + \frac{q(k)}{D \times Ts}\right) \times S(k) + \frac{1}{Ts} \sum_{v=1}^{mv(k)} Ad(k, v)$$

Then, we get $STC(k) = a(k) \times L(k)^2 + b(k) \times L(k) + c(k) + f(L(k))$.

3   The Economic Analysis Based on Deterministic Demand

Based on deterministic demand, in this section we are going to explore the delayed differentiation influence on the cost respectively from the suppliers and CPSCN.

3.1   The Impact of the Delayed Differentiation on Suppliers' Cost

Proposition 1: For a customized module supplier, the fixed investment for the delayed differentiation possesses two thresholds. When the real fixed investment is less than the lower one, the production cost of the supplier decreases with the increase of postponement degree. When the real fixed investment is more than the higher one, the production cost of the supplier increases with the increase of postponement degree.

When the real investment is between the two thresholds, the production cost of the supplier has a minimum point in the range of postponement degree; if the actual postponement degree is less or greater than the minimum point, the supplier's production cost decreases or increases with the increase of postponement degree; if the actual postponement degree is greater than the minimum point, the supplier's production cost increases with the increase of postponement degree.

Proof: under the deterministic demand, safety stock $ss(k) = 0$, hence $f(L(k)) = 0$.

(i) When $-b(k)/2a(k) \leq 0$, because $a(k) > 0$, $b(k) \geq 0$ and $STC(k)$ is a convex function. By substituting expressions of $b(k)$ into $b(k) \geq 0$, we get

$$z(k) \geq \left\{ \frac{hy(k) + \{1 + \frac{3}{2}S(k) + (tr(k) + \frac{1}{2}td(k))(D \times Ts - 1) + Ts \times I\}(g(k) + \frac{q(k)}{D \times Ts})}{1 + (D \times Ts - 1) \times td(k) \times I} - u(k) \right\} \times D \times Ts$$

Denote the right side of the inequality by $z1^*$, hence $z(k) \geq z1^*$.

On the other hand, as postponement degree $L(k) \in [0, 1]$, the range of $L(k)$ is at the right side of the convex function $STC(k)$'s symmetric axis $L = -b(k)/2a(k)$.

Therefore, while the fixed investment for the delayed differentiation is greater than $z1^*$, $STC(k)$ increases with the increase of $L(k)$ (see curve 3 in Fig. 1). Obviously, the delayed differentiation is not economical (it can be taken as delayed differentiation diseconomy, and $z1^*$ as diseconomy threshold).

(ii) When $-b(k)/2a(k) \geq 1$, substituting $a(k)$ and $b(k)$, we get:

$$z(k) \leq \left\{ \frac{hy(k) + \{1 + \frac{1}{2}S(k) + (tr(k) + \frac{1}{2}td(k))(D \times Ts - 1) + Ts \times I\}(g(k) + \frac{q(k)}{D \times Ts})}{1 + 2 \times S(k) \times I + (D \times Ts - 1) \times td(k) \times I} - u(k) \right\} \times D \times Ts$$

Denote the right side of the inequality by $z3^*$, hence $z(k) \leq z3^*$.

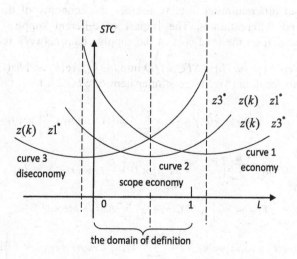

Fig. 1. The total cost trend of customized module

On the other hand, $L(k) \in [0,1]$, viz. the range of $L(k)$ is at the left side of the convex function $STC(k)$'s symmetric axis $L = -b(k)/2a(k)$.

Therefore, while the fixed investment for the delayed differentiation is less than $z3^*$, $STC(k)$ decreases with the increase of $L(k)$ (see curve 1 in Fig. 1). Obviously, the delayed differentiation is economical (It can be taken as delayed differentiation economy, and $z3^*$ as economy threshold).

(iii) When $0 \le -b(k)/2a(k) \le 1$, $z3^* \le z(k) \le z1^*$, the fixed investment is between the economy threshold and the diseconomy threshold, let $L^* = -b(k)/2a(k)$, and it is a minimum point of the convex function $STC(k)$. When $0 \le L(k) \le L^*$, this range of $L(k)$ is at the left side of the convex function $STC(k)$'s symmetric axis, $STC(k)$ decreases with the increase of $L(k)$. When $L^* \le L(k) \le 1$, $STC(k)$ increases with the increase of $L(k)$ (see curve 2 in Fig. 1).

Therefore, $L^* = -b(k)/2a(k)$ is the postponement degree's threshold by which to judge if the delayed differentiation is economical. Only when the postponement degree is in the scope of this threshold, the delayed differentiation is economical, we say here the delayed differentiation has economy of scope (It can be taken as delayed differentiation scope economy). □

Above all, the proposition 1 provides two kinds of identification criteria about the economy analysis and evaluation of the supplier's delayed differentiation: The fixed investment for the delayed differentiation has both critical values, economy threshold and diseconomy threshold;while the delayed differentiation has economy of scope, and the postponement degree has a critical value.

3.2   The Delayed Differentiation's Impact on the Cost of Supply Chain Network

Proposition 2: As to the customization product supply chain network, the economy of a supplier's delayed differentiation directly decides the economy of the supply chain network's delayed differentiation; The impact of different supplier at employing delayed customization on the total cost of the supply chain network is different.

Proof: substitute $cp(k) = mc(k) + STC(k)/D$ into $hg(k)$, $Ag(k)$ and $hz(j)$ and then take three of them into formula (8). Merge similar item of $STC(k)$, let

$$w1(k) = \left\{ 1 + \left[ra(k) + \frac{I}{2} Ts \times pr(k) \right] + \frac{1}{2} Ts \times \sum_{j=1}^{N} \left[(pr(k) + ra(k)) \times \frac{I}{D} \right] \times d(j) \times [1 - \frac{d(j)}{p(j)}] \right\}$$

$$w2(k) = \sum_{n=1}^{M,n \ne k} STC(n) + \sum_{n=1}^{M} \left\{ ra(n) \times mc(n) \times D + \frac{D}{2} Ts \times pr(n) \times mc(n) \times I \right\}$$

$$+ \sum_{n=1}^{M,n \ne k} \left\{ ra(n) + \frac{I}{2} Ts \times pr(n) \right\} \times STC(n) + \frac{1}{Ts} \sum_{j=1}^{N} Az(j) + Mz \times D$$

$$+ \frac{Ts}{2} \times \sum_{j=1}^{N} \left\{ (pr(k) + ra(k)) mc(k) \times I + \sum_{n=1}^{M,n \ne k} [hg(n) + ra(n) \times cp(n) \times I] \right\} d(j) [1 - \frac{d(j)}{p(j)}]$$

Then, we get:

$$TC = w1(k) \times STC(k) + w2(k)$$
$$= w1(k) \times [a(k) \times L(k)^2 + b(k) \times L(k) + c(k) + f(L(k))] + w2(k) \qquad (9)$$

Therefore, the total cost of supply chain network is a function of the postponement degree $L(k)$ of module k, and of the fixed investment by parameters $a(k)$, $b(k)$.

Using the similar method and process of customized module suppliers' cost analysis, when the demand is deterministic, the total cost of the supply chain network TC is quadratic parabolic function of $L(k)$, too; and we can gain the similar conclusion as the Sect. 3.1.

In addition, for different customized modules k, each coefficient of the variable $L(k)$ in section (9), i.e. $a(k)$, $b(k)$, $c(k)$, $w1(k)$, $w2(k)$ and $f(L(k))$ is different, hence the impact from the different supplier when it takes the delayed differentiation on the total cost of the supply chain network is also different. ☐

When the manufacturer has learnt the two kinds of critical values of each supplier and the impacts from the different suppliers on the cost of CPSCN, he can choose the more ideal customized module suppliers by contrasting the delayed differentiation' economy and ask each supplier to take the corresponding postponement degree and the customization degree; thereby CPSCN can pursue the overall optimization by optimally combining these postponement strategies.

Above all, the proposition 2 gives the measurement tools, and lays the judgment foundation for evaluating the economic effect of CPSCN's delayed differentiation.

3.3   Simulation and Verification

We take the delayed differentiation of customization products family consisting of three customized modules as an example to verify the economic effect of the delayed differentiation under the deterministic demand.

Three customized modules have 2, 3, 4 variants respectively, thus the manufacturer can provide the market with 24 customization productions. Set $mc(4) = 5600$, $mc(3) = 2 \times 5600/3$, $mc(2) = 5600/2$, $I = 0.006$, $D = 750$; $fd(3,4) = [0.6, 0.4, 0, 0; 0.28, 0.36, 0.36, 0; 0.24, 0.24, 0.24, 0.28]$, $g(3) = 2 \times 3600/3$, $g(2) = 3600/2$, $q(4) = 6.0e + 6$, $q(3) = 4.0e + 6$, $q(2) = 3.0e + 6$, $u(4) = 3600$, $u(3) = 2 \times 3600/3$, $u(2) = 3600/2$; $S = 4$, $tr = td = 0.001$; $pr = 1.41$, $ra = 0.04$; If not considering the slight differences among the different variants, the customized production conversion cost is: $Ad(4) = 2918$, $Ad(3) = 1914$, $Ad(2) = 1464$; $Mz = 5389$.

$$p(3,4) = [4725, 2250, 0, 0; 12150, 7987.5, 9112.5, 0; 5587.5, 6187.5, 6787.5, 2312.5]$$

Programming in MATLAB and simulating, we obtain the two thresholds of customization production's fixed investment, $z1^* = 6.765e + 6$, $z3^* = 6.495e + 6$. According to expressions of $z1^*$ and $z3^*$, we gain $z1^* = 6.7921e + 6$, $z3^* = 6.4893e + 6$. The two thresholds of the fixed investment, the critical value of the

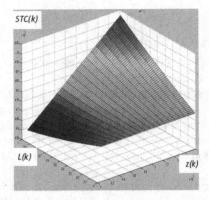

Fig. 2. 3D graphics of supplier' cost, fixed investment, postponement degree

postponement degree, relationship and change trend between $z(k)$, $L(k)$ and $STC(k)$ are also confirmed. Draw three dimensional graphics by the data of $z(k)$, $L(k)$ and $STC(k)$, as shown in Fig. 2.

Draw the 3D curve of the minimal total cost of CPSCN, when the fixed investment $z(k)$ and the postponement degree $L(k)$ change, as shown in Fig. 3. Projecting Fig. 3 to the plane, we get the 2D curve of $z(k)$ and $L(k)$, as shown in Fig. 4. From Figs. 3 and 4, we already know, for a given fixed investment for customization production, there is a postponement degree's threshold, if actual postponement degree is in this threshold, the delayed differentiation is economical. The left of the 2d curve is the ranges of the fixed investment and the postponement degree at which the delayed differentiation is economical; on the right side is the ranges at which the delayed differentiation is not economical.

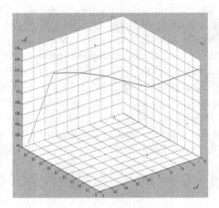

Fig. 3. The curve of the minimum point of $STC(k)$ when $z(k)$, $L(k)$ change

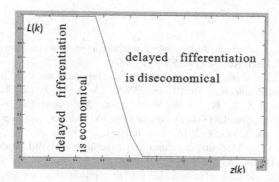

Fig. 4. The delayed differentiation possibility frontier when $z(k)$, $L(k)$ change

For the CPSCN, the situation under the deterministic demand is similar to the module suppliers, here we can omit.

When the demand is stochastic, let $\sigma_D = 0.2D$, and $CSL = 0.90$. By simulation, we have demonstrated the validity of the Propositions 1 and 2.

4 Conclusion

Economic effect of the delayed differentiation in the customized product's supply chain network decides whether postponement should be employed and which postponement strategy should be taken. The main contribution of this paper is that, we have proved the delayed differentiation have three states, economy, economy of scope and diseconomy. Two kinds of identification criteria are provided for the economy analysis and evaluation of the suppliers' delayed differentiation. The fixed investment for the delayed differentiation has both critical values, the economy threshold and the diseconomy threshold;while the delayed differentiation has the economy of scope and the postponement degree has a critical value. At the same time, the impact of different supplier on the total cost is recognized to evaluate the economic effect of CPSCN's delayed differentiation.

The economy analysis of the delayed differentiation can help to enhance the CPSCN's ability to meet the personalized needs, reduce the product cost and raise the competitiveness.

Acknowledgment. This research is sponsored by the Humanities and Social Sciences Planning Foundation of the Ministry of Education, China (Grant No. 12YJAZH151, No. 12YJCZH209), and the Major Project of Innovation Foundation of the Nanjing Institute of Technology, China (Grant No. CKJA201208).

References

1. Shao, X.F., JH, J.: Evaluation of postponement strategies in mass customization with service guarantees. Int. J. Prod. Res. **46**(1), 153–171 (2008)
2. Jian-ming, Y.A.O.: Analysis of supply chain operation mode in mass customization based on cooperators' oriented objects. J. Bus. Econ. **259**(5), 13–21 (2013). (in Chinese)
3. Wang, Z.-L., Yang, Z.-Y., Bai, S.-B., Wang Y.-X.: Joint economic lot sizing model of delayed customization product' supply chain network, solution and supply chain collaboration. Syst. Eng. **34**(7), 78–84 (2016). (in Chinese)
4. Lee, H.L., Tang, C.S.: Modeling the costs and benefits of delayed product differentiation. Manage. Sci. **43**(1), 40–53 (1997)
5. Bin, D.A.N., Kai, R.A.O., Haiyan, L.I.: Cost optimization model of supply chain implementation postponement strategy in mass customization. Comput. Integr. Manuf. Syst. **15**(2), 287–291 (2009). (in Chinese)
6. Clark, A., Almada-Lobo, B., Almeder, C.: Lot sizing and scheduling: industrial extensions and research opportunities. Int. J. Prod. Res. **49**(9), 2457–2461 (2011)
7. Wang, Z., Yang, Z., Wang, Y., et al.: Economic lot scheduling heuristic algorithm based on customized product structure spectrum. J. Nanjing Inst. Technol. **12**(3), 1–7 (2014). (in Chinese)

Concurrency in BIM-Based Project Implementation: An Exploratory Study of Chongqing Jiangbei International Airport's Terminal 3A

Erezi Utiome[1], Sherif Mohamed[1], Kriengsak Panuwatwanich[1], Emerson Lin[2], and Lei Hou[1(✉)]

[1] Griffith University, Gold Coast, Australia
{e.utiome,s.mohamed,k.panuwatwanich,lei.hou}@griffith.edu.au
[2] Chongqing University, Chongqing, China
zhiyang.lin@cqu.edu.cn

Abstract. Many of the shortcomings associated with dated design and construction methods as well as project fast-tracking can be addressed by exploring the concept of concurrency facilitated by Building Information Modelling (BIM). From a BIM perspective, concurrency facilitates the involvement of stakeholders from very early on during the lifecycle of a project. Leveraging the 5 W/H (Who, What, When/Where, Why and How) method of exploratory research, this paper explores how BIM and Concurrent Engineering (CE) at Terminal 3A of the Chongqing Jiangbei International Airport compares with a historical exemplar of BIM deployment in the AEC industry. Based on existing definitions of CE, we compare both projects to determine their conformance to three CE criteria: 1) compressed project duration, 2) enhanced product value, and 3) reduced project costs. We also review their use of collaborative tools and techniques. The paper shows how the success of BIM-based projects can be rationalised by CE.

Keywords: Building information modelling · Concurrent engineering · Fast-track

1 Background

Many of the challenges with traditional design and construction methods, especially in terms of significant problems resulting from fragmentation, have been identified and discussed extensively [1, 2]. In turn, these challenges have served as springboards for exploring various methods of project conceptualisation, modelling, implementation and management. Three of these methods are explored in this paper in exploring concurrency in Building Information Modelling (BIM) based project execution; fast-tracking as well as concurrent engineering and BIM; these last two inform the main content of the research presented in this work.

Unlike fast-tracking, Concurrent Engineering (CE) relies on established theoretical approaches in attaining compressed project duration, enhanced product value, and reduced project costs [3]. Some highlighted benefits of CE include: improved understanding and implementation of client and end-user requirements, improved

© Springer International Publishing AG 2016
Y. Luo (Ed.): CDVE 2016, LNCS 9929, pp. 257–262, 2016.
DOI: 10.1007/978-3-319-46771-9_33

communication and cooperation between project participants, improved team and project effectiveness, reduction in the occurrences of rework (e.g. redesigns, non-conformances etc.) and variations and reductions in project time and cost [4].

A careful consideration of these benefits highlights convergence between CE and the main merits of BIM [5, 6]. The CE-BIM relationship aligns with the idea that through the use of an appropriate parametric database, multidisciplinary teams can access a single design repository with knock on effect on improved project implementation time and effective communication [4]. The use of BIM as such an integrated platform throughout facility lifecycles has been discussed extensively in research and practice [7, 8].

2   Method

Going by the obvious similarities between BIM methods and CE philosophy, this paper explores two case studies, highlighting a strategy for leveraging CE and BIM in facility design and construction delivery. Importantly, aspects of the undertaken project analysis are inspired by the information integration framework (IIF)[1] [9] which is useful for gaining insight in the course of exploratory studies.

This section highlights the use of concurrency and BIM on two projects. The extent to which BIM was used in all stages of project implementation served as the basis for their selection.

Each project is discussed by combining the IIF framework with a matrix derived from the Technology, Organisation, Process/Protocol (TOPP)[2] framework [10] which improves on the IIF by addressing *How* parameters. By comparing two case studies – Eden Medical Centre in the United States and China's Chongqing Jiangbei International Airport – the paper explores points of convergence between BIM and CE in building and infrastructure projects. Consequently, a rationale is presented for teams and organisations to exploit the benefits of BIM in AECO projects.

2.1   Case 1 Overview: Eden Medical Centre Castro Valley

Why: Sutter Health's Eden Medical Centre (EMC) is a USD320 million facility. Following the passing of the Alquist Hospital Facilities' Seismic safety Act (SB1953) in California [11], it was crucial that the EMC building was retrofitted or completely replaced. The Act would ensure that care facilities were earthquake-proof, resilient and provided undisrupted services.

When/Where: BIM was adopted during the conceptual stage and required early commitments by the project team members to collaborate with other stakeholders through the use of BIM methods throughout the project's lifecycle.

---

[1] The IIF framework is useful for gaining a general understanding of information dynamics from a very basic investigative perspective. This approach is widely known as the 5W1H method.

[2] The TOPP framework captures BIM content in three key dimensions depicting unique perspectives for uniformly evaluating BIM-based case-study projects.

Who: The project was the outcome of collaboration between Sutter Health (the Owner), Ghafari Associates (Process and Technology Managers) and the members of an IPD team. The project team was formed by over 240 members spread across the United States.

What – Requirements, Supporting Technologies and Project Management Processes: The Owner envisioned the use of advanced technological tools and processes to undertake the design, construction and re-development of the new medical centre and associated infrastructure, including new car parks [10]. The overarching project goal was to *design and deliver a facility of the highest quality, at least 30 % faster, and for no more than the target cost* [12].

How: The EMC demonstrates that projects delivered through a CE-BIM-IPD approach with strong stakeholder support and backed by appropriate contractual arrangements, will most likely realise early benefits of BIM. Establishing the use of BIM from the inception of the EMC project aided the alignment of all project plans to the overarching BIM implementation strategy.

2.2   Case 2 Overview: The Chongqing Jiangbei International Airport

Why: Against the backdrop of a mandate by Ministry of Housing and Urban-Rural Department of the People's Republic of China (MOHURD) on the use of BIM for publicly procured building and infrastructure projects, tendering for Terminal 3A (T3A) of the Chongqing Jiangbei International Airport (CJIA) was initiated. T3A ranks as Western China's biggest terminal under construction and is projected to cost circa 20 billion Chinese Yuan (4 billion US Dollars) on completion.

When/Where: As a project delivery method, BIM has been integral to CJIA's T3A ongoing design and development. It is expected that BIM and related integrative methods will be used through project execution to operation and maintenance phases. With the appointment of Chongqing University as BIM consultant, a complete model - Architectural, HVAC and MEP - of the entire Terminal (3A), clash detection, 4D simulations during construction, facility management and model up-skilling are some of the services expected to be delivered throughout the facility's lifecycle.

Who: The Client, Chongqing Airport Construction Group Co., Ltd, appointed the China Southwest Architectural Design and Research Institute Corp. Ltd (CSWADI) as the design team, while the construction team consisted of staff from china Construction Eight Engineering Division Corp. Ltd. The project design phase occurred over three stages; Architectural Design Modification, First version of Construction Drawings (Including structural and MEP de signs) and Design Alteration stages. Notably, members of the design teams formed five work divisions, namely: Architecture, Structural Engineering, MEP (Mechanical, Electrical and Plumbing) Engineering, Design Management (Architecture), and Design Vice-Management (Structural/MEP engineering) (see Table 1). Together, these worked to ensure appropriate implementation of CE principles which culminated in substantial cost and schedule savings (Table 2).

Table 1. Distribution of Project Team members across project design stages

Work division	Design phase	
	First stage (Architectural Design Modification)	Last stage (Design Alteration)
Architecture	19	4
Structural engineering	19	3
MEP engineering	29	5
Design management (Architecture)	1	1
Design vice management (Structural/MEP engineering)	2	2
Total number	**70**	**15**

Table 2. Test for BIM-enabled Concurrent Engineering between case studies

CE-BIM criteria	Case studies	
	Eden Medical Centre	Chongqing Jiangbei International Airport
Schedule savings	12 Months	Unknown as project is ongoing
Product value	Achieved	Achieved
Cost target	Achieved	Surpassed (*CNY 57.78 Million saved)
Collaborative tools and techniques	*IPD, BIM, Lean, CE, *Obeya	BIM, CE, MS Project, Navisworks, Inventor, Infraworks and Civil 3D, ARCHIBUS
Project phase(s) affected	Design to *FM	Design to construction (expected for *FM)

What – Requirements, Supporting Technologies and Project Management Processes: To comply with the BIM Mandate across Local Government Projects, T3A included BIM, CE and related methods from the onset of the project by setting out a series of objectives. These drivers include: technical service provision, enabling efficient operation management, improved stakeholder coordination and management, informed onsite problem-resolution, reduction in waste (paper) generation, construction costs and project schedule and effective change management. The project management best practice of continuous improvement [3] was important to the success of the CE processes employed on the project. For instance, through error-checking of the model, error checking revealed that there were 439 identified errors from a first pass which was reduced to 120 after design adjustments.

How: The approach taken in the conceptualisation, design and implementation of CJIA's T3A project shows increased awareness and appreciation for digital construction and the premium placed on process optimisation that accrues from the implementation of

CE. In the application of different suites of software platforms for instance, significant investment in information management and coordination resulted in the effectiveness of interoperability and in leveraging the central digital model.

3   Case Study Comparison

On the premise that each project satisfies the CE-BIM criteria of schedule savings, product value, and cost target, Table 2 compares productivity (the extent to which actual time, cost and quality on the project exceeds the specifications of the project plan) between the case studies.

4   Results and Discussion

As the CJIA project is ongoing, the schedule savings attributable to the systems and processes put in place is unknown. What is sure however, is that there will be circa CNY 57 million (equivalent to USD 9 million) in cost savings due to a refined design underpinned by BIM (Table 3). Overall, this would also bring about a shortened duration, reduced overall cost and enlarged product value, which echo the three CE criteria. For instance, BIM has saved up to 12 months for the completion of the EMC project; BIM has significantly boosted Return-on-Investment (ROI) for the design of the T3A Terminal project considering a ratio of the BIM-aided design cost to the number of design issues identified, etc. Prior to the start of the simultaneous tasks such as mechanical systems installation, cable harnesses layout and pipelines erection, the designers conducted the clash check and optimised the work schedule based on the BIM system, which at a later stage, helped achieve significant schedule and cost savings.

Table 3.   The contributing cost saving items for the CJIA project

Cost saving items	4D simulation	Site planning	Material savings	Design optimisation	Rework reduction
Projected savings (RMB)	5.2 million	3.49 million	30.93 million	5.53 million	12.63 million

5   Conclusions

On the basis of the two projects explored, this paper establishes that the principles of Concurrent Engineering and BIM can be rationalised and explored methodically to deliver on the key project requirements of cost, time and quality. Furthermore, the paper highlights the value of using appropriate collaborative tools and techniques throughout the project lifecycle.

Importantly, the research answers five basic questions – Why, When/Where, Who, What, and How. By answering these questions, we've been able to demonstrate that together, CE and BIM can deliver an integrated platform for achieving project Goals.

The results demonstrate that by focusing on intelligent methods of BIM adoption and implementation as well as making provisions for BIM implementation more measurable project benefits can be realised.

Acknowledgement. The authors wish to thank China Construction Eighth Engineering Division. Corp.Ltd for providing the case study of the CJI Airport Project.

References

1. Latham, M.: Constructing the team: final report of The Government/Industry review of procurement and contractual arrangements in the United Kingdom construction industry. In: The Stationery Office. Department of Environment, London (1994)
2. Egan, J.: Rethinking construction: the report of the construction task force. Department of the Environment, Transport and the Regions, London (1998)
3. Alarcon, L.: Lean Construction. A.A. Balkema, Rotterdam (1997)
4. Love, P.E.D., Gunasekaran, A., Li, H.: Concurrent engineering: a strategy for procuring construction projects. Int. J. Project Manage. **16**(6), 375–383 (1998)
5. Castagna, J.: Benefits of BIM. Environ. Des. Constr. **11**(11), 140–143 (2008)
6. Costin, A., Pradhananga, N., Teizer, J., Marks, E.: Real-time resource location tracking in building information models (BIM). In: Luo, Y. (ed.) CDVE 2012. LNCS, vol. 7467, pp. 41–48. Springer, Heidelberg (2012)
7. Wang, Y., et al.: Engagement of facilities management in design stage through BIM: framework and a case study. Adv. Civ. Eng. (2013)
8. Ren, Y., Skibniewski, M.J., Jiang, S.: Building information modeling integrated with electronic commerce material procurement and supplier performance management system. J. Civ. Eng. Manage. **18**(5), 642–654 (2012)
9. Brandon, P.S., Betts, M.: Integrated Construction Information. Taylor & Francis Group, Boca Raton (1995)
10. Staub-French, S., et al.: Building Information Modeling (BIM) 'Best Practices' Project Report. University of British Colombia, École de Technologie Supérieure (2011)
11. Lichtig, W.: Integrated Form of Agreement (IFoA) (2009) (cited 18 May 2015). http://www.thechangebusiness.co.uk/TCB/ifoa.html
12. Wilson, C. Sutter Medical Center, Castro Valley: IPD Process Innovation with Building Information Modelling (2011) (cited 08 May 2015). http://network.aia.org/HigherLogic/System/DownloadDocumentFile.ashx?DocumentFileKey=69f83720-c575-4029-aea4-418236ec4771

Design of an Architecture for Medical Applications in IoT

Freddy Feria[1(✉)], Octavio J. Salcedo Parra[1,2(✉)], and Brayan S. Reyes Daza[2(✉)]

[1] Universidad Nacional de Colombia, Bogotá D.C., Colombia
{faferiab,ojsalcedop}@unal.edu.co
[2] Internet Inteligente Research Group, Universidad Distrital Francisco José de Caldas,
Bogotá D.C., Colombia
bsreyesd@correo.udistrital.edu.co, osalcedo@udistrital.edu.co

Abstract. This present document presents the design of an architecture of communication oriented to medical and sports applications, in order to bring a series of information collected from a network of portable sensors arranged in the body of the person that will be able to gather vital constants of the user and then transmit them to a web service on the internet, as well as to monitor the State of health and/or the user's physical performance.

Keywords: Internet of things · IoT · WSN · Bluetooth low energy · Web service

1 Introduction

In 1992 they had an estimated, close to a million people with computers, for the year 2003 this number amounted to close to half billion users with portable devices in the world which represent a growth of the 49.900 %, for the year 2012 the number of personnel devices were estimated at close to 8.7 billion units, currently calculations estimate that there are about 14.4 billion devices connected to the Internet every day, and projections estimate that by 2020 they will be 50.1 billion devices connected, 6.6 devices per person on the planet.

This rapid growth of sources of information and interconnection represents great challenges in terms of the volume of data handled by the network and the inherent security that should have that data; however, it presents opportunities in a field that will impact education, communication, business, science, Government and humanity, the Internet of things (IoT). It represents the next evolution of the Internet, and it will bring a huge advance in its capacity to collect, analyze and distribute data, that could be transform in to information, knowledge and, ultimately, in wisdom. The Business solutions for Internet (IBSG) of Cisco group estimated that the term IoT "was born" somewhere between 2008 and 2009, however, since the beginning of the 2000 Kevin Ashton was preparing the way for what would be the IoT in the AutoID laboratory of the MIT. Ashton was one of the pioneers that conceived this notion in the search for ways in which Proctor Gamble could improve their business using RFID tags and Internet.

The concept was simple but powerful: If all the objects of our daily lives were equipped with identifiers and wireless connectivity, these objects could communicate with others and be managed by computers, thus is could follow and tell all, and greatly

© Springer International Publishing AG 2016
Y. Luo (Ed.): CDVE 2016, LNCS 9929, pp. 263–270, 2016.
DOI: 10.1007/978-3-319-46771-9_34

reduce waste, losses and costs. Provide computers to perceive the world and get all the information we need to make decisions. This paradigm of approaching the people, and not just to the Internet devices, needs underlying technologies that facilitate the transition from the real world to the web world and more precisely the use of personal data, that will allow the collection of data from a person, the treatment of the such information and making decisions based on the information collected. At this point technologies such as personal area networks (PAN) or body (BAN), can contribute significantly to the development and conception of an IoT more closer to the user so that allow a user from satisfy a lifestyle, to meet a need or solve a disability.

There have been many advances in this field especially in areas related to health and Medical care, sports and security. The constant Monitoring of the health of a person with any condition is only possible with portable devices that non-invasive and that allow to carry out a comfortable and secure life by alerting and providing information about the development of the State of health to the medical authorities in case of emergency, these data would constitute an integral part in the diagnosis and subsequent treatment. In the sports field, the updated body variable and performance data, are important to track the performance of an activity and to assess and correct the way how the physical activity takes place. These are just a few examples where the use of IoT and portable devices can interact to identify and find the solution to an everyday problem.

2   Related Work

There have been significant advances aiming at defining exactly what IoT is, many of these works propose features that a system must meet to be able to accomplish this paradigm and they assign names to the constituent parts of the system (nodes, gateways, devices, layers, modules, etc.) [3, 11], and based on these definitions propose a number of architectures most of them using Gateways that facilitate the interconnection of a series of sensors and interactions with the web world as well as the design of protocols that allow these devices to comply with specifications of power, speed, reliability, loyalty and security [2, 9]. Besides, the two large existing communication links are explored: one, between portable devices of the user, and two, between these devices and the internet [5, 7]. There is also related research specifically to medical applications and health systems, monitoring of patients both in hospitals [10, 12, 13], as well as in sports activities [1], refining the previously proposed architectures in some cases and generating new architectures in others, depending on the context and strongly oriented to the final application.

3   Description of the Proposed Architecture

The proposed architecture aims to take into account the fundamental aspects of both PAN and IoT technologies and achieve interoperability between them. To bring an object to the Internet it is necessary to meet a series of requirements proposed by the Internet Engineering Task Force (IETF): unique identifiers for each object or service, management of ID for the object (security, authentication, privacy), presence of people and devices, geographical location, modeling of objects for search and discovery, follow-up and support of mobility for moving objects, interoperability and interconnection, global connectivity, scalability, autonomy, restrictions of the object (power, energy), web services and data traffic. Unique identifiers will correspond to the web service that is implemented for the analysis and collection of data, as well as the modeling of objects, global connectivity and web services. The control device will be responsible for the Administration of IDs, geographic location, interconnection, scalability and autonomy, restrictions of the object and data traffic.

As you can see in Fig. 1 the architecture consists of 3 parts, remote portable devices, Portable Control device and the Web service application. The remote portable devices (RPD) are sensors and actuators that interact with the user. Each device is comprised of a sensor or actuator, a microcontroller, a means of communication and a battery. These devices perform the data collection and the shipping of instructions to a Gateway through the Portable Control Device. Such devices must be auto-configurable, autonomous, light and with a very low power consumption.

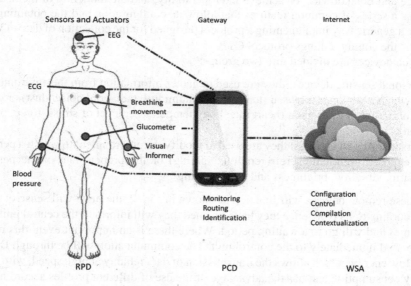

Fig. 1. Proposed network architecture

The Portable Control Device (PCD) is responsible for the administration of devices and data from the system, also manages the connection with the RPDs through Bluetooth low energy technology. On one hand, the device must be capable of performing operations of addiction, reading, updating, and removal of devices on the network, on the other hand, it must carry out the exchange of information between remote devices and web services. It must temporarily save the collected data for later transmission to the internet, as well as having the ability to handle events of importance at local scale. The PCD is the object that will be taken to the Internet and the RPD are the properties and characteristics of that object, which will be consulted and informed according to the user's requirements. The data processing will be at PCD level and RPD reducing traffic to Internet and simplifying the system.

Finally the Web service application (WSA) is responsible for contextualizing the received data, store it and present it in such a way that the user can make decisions based on that information. It has in addition domain rules to filter relevant data and generate events and alerts when necessary.

4   Remote Portable Devices

These devices are deployed in the body or around a person, must not be invasive, must have a low power consumption and tolerate environmental conditions. Each of these devices must have an own identification number and one assigned by the network so it can be addressed and managed, it should distinguish the type of device and the characteristics of the product, and be able to inform the operational status of itself, and report damage and breakdowns. To achieve interoperability, and the modeling of them, they possess a series of common features that allow its configuration and the obtaining of data in a generic way implementing a protocol designed for the collection of data of web objects, the common things protocol CTP.

Such devices are divided into two groups:

- Personal sensing devices: they are used to gather information from the environment to which a person is exposed (temperature, humidity, radiation, noise, dust) or own information of the person (heart rate, body temperature, level of stress, force, position).
- Personal Action Devices: they are used to modify the environment to which a person is exposed (ventilation, refrigeration, lighting) or the proper state of the person (alarm, vibration, brightness and insulin pump).

These remote devices will function as shown in Fig. 2, the units will sense or will act according to its type, once they have finished they will inform to the central unit the outcomes and will go to a waiting period. Where there is an important event this must be reported immediately to the control unit. The communication will be through Bluetooth low energy, which allows the transmission of data reliably at high speed, with low energy consumption and has the advantage of the use of different profiles according to the designed application.

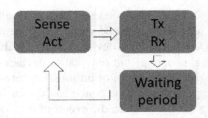

Fig. 2. Operation of the RPD scheme

4.1 Common Things Protocol

This Protocol provides a specification that enables interoperability across different standards of communication and the coexistence of IoT protocols, but giving priority to simplicity, efficiency, and functionality to build specific systems of IoT. CTP takes into account existing standard specifications and the needs of the final applications that are required by the objects. This integrates the strategies, concepts, and terms of some alternatives, such as the concept of TEDs in IEEE1451 to provide information from the devices, working modes in sensors and actuators, and concepts of Zigbee as clusters and endpoints. The definition of CTP is oriented to consider objects, not only as sensors but as electronic devices which develop some kind of function in the IoT application being in contact with the user and the context, and fulfilling the following paradigms:

- Interaction with the context: sensors embedded, actuators, and/or interfaces with the user.
- Computing: having skills of computing and memory that allows them to implement from a simple logic to complicated services or data processing algorithms.
- Communication: have at least one mean of communication, usually wireless, which follows a common standard and is adapted to the requirements of communication.
- Being an electronic object: as any object, electronic or not, everything is unique and "lives" in a specific time and space. In addition like any electronic device, it requires power to operate.

In addition, derived from its capacity to interact with the context, CTP considers that things have three different functionalities: Sensors that collect and process user information which is useful for creating a panorama of what happens in each moment, while it helps the user to understand and evaluate the data objectively to draw conclusions, define guides, or identify patterns. Actuators that provide the ability to act on the user or the environment. IoT applications could act on the environment when the user is not in the ability to do so. Interfaces, human - machine to provide the user relevant information or the notification of events in different ways.

4.2 Bluetooth Low Energy

It is a technology for wireless personal area networks oriented to applications in the field of health, fitness, safety and domestic automation among others. Bluetooth technology offers advantages over other technologies used in the market, with transfer rates of 1 Mb/s, 128-bit AES encryption, 6 ms latency and shipping time of 3 ms, the number of slave devices is dependent on the implementation, the power consumption is 0. 01 W having devices that can run a whole year with a CR2032 battery, also includes profiles of work oriented to applications including medical and fitness applications. In comparison with other technologies it has an improved performance, lower power consumption and higher relationship of power vs transfer rate.

4.3 Portable Control Devices

This is not properly a device, but rather, an application used for the administration of the RPD. This application must add, read, edit, update, and remove peripheral devices on the network. It is deployed using Bluetooth Low Energy technology, where the app will connect from time to time depending on the number of RPDs, in such way the application serves as a gateway between the data collected and the service web, thus simplifying the given architecture by reducing the amount of equipment required and taking advantage of existing technologies.

4.4 Web Service Application

Finally the data are entered in a web service and it becomes information usable by the application. This application must take into account the context in which the data is located, it is not the same, a series of data received by an ECG of a person in medical treatment and a person doing sport, so the context of the information is important when developing applications of this type. Secondly registration and data storage is vital for tracking and traceability procedures. The Interfaces must be clear and should easily expose the information so that it is obvious to a user understand what you want to convey. In some cases the interconnection to other online systems such as databases, social networks, medical records and emergency care systems is required, this means that mechanisms of adaptability and interaction with other systems should be considered, frameworks such as JSON and Restful are recommended by its simplicity in the exchange of information and wide compatibility with current computer systems. From the web service applications the user should be able to configure the RPD and PCD, in a way so that they act as a front-end to the entire system, thus avoiding multiplatform compatibility issues and also avoiding the additional installation of software in some cases.

4.5 Service Oriented Architecture (SOA)

Since we want to implement a web service that manages the data collected, the best design for system architecture corresponds to a service-oriented type. Through this architecture is sought that the system is distributed heterogeneously to achieve greater interoperation with the existing solutions on the market, and low coupling so that you can scale according to the growth of the platform. The Frontend application are the active parties in a SOA given the fact that they initiate and control all activities of the system, for the present design it a web interface is proposed, since it is a multiplatform tool with constant contact by any person, the services are software components of different functionality that encapsulate the business logic, they are composed of contracts that define the functional characteristics of each service as well as its purpose, restriction and applications, such Interfaces expose the functionality of the service to clients connected via the network, and to implementations that correspond to the business logic and data input and output that the service handles.

The Repository of services facilitates the discovery of the services and the acquisition of all the information to use the service, finally the Service Bus connects all the participants of the SOA among themselves (services and applications frontend) (Fig. 3).

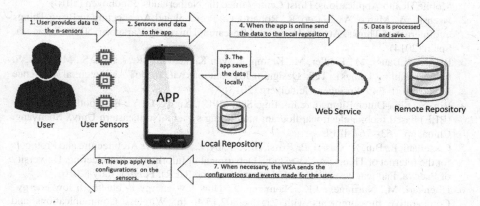

Fig. 3. Flow of information among the architecture.

5 Conclusions

The proposed design is based on different proposed architectures, by extracting the best of each one of them in such a way that it meets the specified objective. The use of Bluetooth in wireless sensing networks is widely documented in the medical field, the technology as well as the proposed architecture have cast out that the system can acquire, transmit, store and display in real time, reliably and accurately, vital signs of a person [4]. In [2, 8] the architecture proposed for different purposes for a system of monitoring of sensors is used with good results in terms of energy consumption and administration of the peripherals and the network. In [6] Bluetooth is compared with its main competitor in the market Zigbee, comparing energy consumption and leaning over Bluetooth.

6 Further Work

Once is the architecture is deployed is necessary to carry out the implementation of it in a way so that it can evaluate performance and make the necessary settings that allow to define factors such as efficiency, quality, QoS, the user experience, etc. There are low cost solutions on the market for the development of the hardware platform, The CC2541 modules of the company Texas Instruments are outlined due to its low size, cost and versatility and the variety of developments that exist in this field. As a platform for the transmission of data, it is important to count with a Smartphone that allows to monitor the data received and sent, in addition it must have Bluetooth technology. For the web service, there are platforms for collection of data with SOA architectures in the market that would be worth exploring.

References

1. Altini, M., Penders, J. Roebbers, H.: An Android-Based Body Area Network Gateway for Mobile Health Applications. Holst Centre/ imec the Netherlands, Eindhoven (2010)
2. Asensio, A., Marco, A., Blasco, R., Roberto, C.: Protocol and Architecture to Bring Things intoInternet of Things. Aragon Institute of Research, University Zaragoza, 50018 Zaragoza, Spain (2014)
3. Bassi, A., Bauer, M., Fiedler, M., Kramp, T., van Kranenburg, R., Lange, S., Meissner, S. (eds.): Enabling Things to Talk, Designing IoT solutions with the IoT Architectural Reference Model, pp. 1–349. Springer, Heidelberg (2013)
4. Bin, Y.; Sina-Dutch Biomed. & Inf. Eng. Sch. (2012). Xu, L., Li, Y.: Bluetooth Low Energy (BLE) based mobile electrocardiogram monitoring system. Northeastern Univ., Shenyang, China, pp. 763– 767. IEEE
5. Castellani, P., Bui, N., Casari, P., Rossi, M., Shelby, Z., Zorzi, M.: Architecture and Protocols for the Internet of Things: A Case Study. Department of Information Engineering, University of Padova, Padova, Italy. Consorzio Ferrara Ricerche (CFR), Ferrara, Italy (2010)
6. Hiienkari, M., Nurminen, J.K., Nieminen, J.: How low energy is bluetooth low energy? Comparative measurements with ZigBee/802.15.4. In: Wireless Communications and Networking Conference Workshops (WCNCW). IEEE (2012)
7. Kumar Singh, K., Sing, M.P., Singh, D.K.: Routing protocols in wireless sensor networks – a survey. IJCSES **1**(2) (2010). http://www.airccse.org/journal/ijcses/papers/1110ijcses06.pdf
8. Lopez Research LLC. An Introduction to the Internet of Things (IoT) (2013). http://www.cisco.com/c/dam/en_us/solutions/trends/iot/introduction_to_IoT_november.pdf
9. Patel, M., Wang, J.: Applications, challenges, and prospective in emerging body area networking technologies. Wireless Commun. **17** (2010). http://csi.dgist.ac.kr/uploads/Seminar/Applications%20challenges%20and%20prospective%20in%20emerging%20body%20area%20networking%20technologies.pdf
10. Poorter, E., Moerman, I., Demeester, P.: Enabling direct connectivity between heterogeneous objects in the internet of things through a network-service-oriented architecture. J. Wireless Commun. Netw. (2011). http://link.springer.com/article/10.1186/1687-1499-2011-61
11. Rashwand, S., Misic, J.: Bridging Between IEEE 802.15.6 and IEEE 802.11e for Wireless Healthcare Networks. University of Manitoba, Department of Computer Science. Ryerson University, Department of Computer Science, pp. 303–337 (2012)
12. WSO: A Reference Architecture for the Internet of Things (2015). www.wso2.com
13. Zhibo P.: Technologies and architectures of the internet-of-things (IoT) for health and well-being. Doctoral Thesis in Electronic and Computer Systems, KTH – Royal Institute of Technology. Stockholm, Sweden (2013)

Vehicle Route Tracking System by Cooperative License Plate Recognition on Multi-peer Monitor Videos

Guofeng Qin, Qiutao Li[⊠], and SichangLi

Department of Computer Science and Technology, Tongji University,
Shanghai 200092, China
gfqing@aliyun.com, liqt91@qq.com

Abstract. With urban transportation problems becoming serious, as an efficient solution, Intelligent Transportation System has been greatly studied and developed. The license plate number can be used as the unique identification of vehicles. In this paper a vehicle route tracking system using automatic vehicle license plate recognition for video images is proposed. The system can extract the driving route of the vehicle in the urban traffic network from multi-peer high-definition monitor video in crossroads.

Keywords: Vehicle license plate recognition · Vibe · Fuzzy matching · Multi-peer cooperation · Vehicle route tracking

1 Introduction

There exist many technologies in vehicle route tracking systems, including GPS (Global Positioning System), RFID (Radio Frequency Identification), wireless communication and sensor network, mobile phone position, video monitor and vehicle license plate recognition. Peter Stopher [1] analyzed the development process of the GPS travel route tracking technology, and pointed out that GPS technology with GIS (Geographic Information System) has many advantages compared to the traditional survey method which depends on non-private traffic data. Bohte, et al. [2] put forward a combination method for GPS, GIS and web service, which was applied to an investigation of large-scale trip in Holland in 2007. Hui Wu [3] proposed an urban traffic information platform on GPS and GIS, and studied the matching technology of GPS positioning data and GIS road model, and analyzed the results of vehicle location and trajectory tracking.

Mobile phone signaling data coverage is wide, and mobile phone positioning technology can directly get the location data from the wireless communication network, so it gradually becomes a new research hotspot in location and trajectory tracking. In 2000,Berkeley used the mobile phone positioning technology to carry out the traffic data collection experiment [4], according to the location result estimate the average travel time and the speed of the vehicle in the road network. Yahsuo Asakura, et al. [5] collected a series of mobile phone continuous positioning points in Kobe City, which are converted to path information, and built the topological characteristics on travel

© Springer International Publishing AG 2016
Y. Luo (Ed.): CDVE 2016, LNCS 9929, pp. 271–282, 2016.
DOI: 10.1007/978-3-319-46771-9_35

behavior with the method of clustering analysis. Calabrese, et al. [6] developed a mobile real-time monitoring system with Italy Telecom, which was located in the mobile network of public transport and taxi, and monitored the urban public traffic flow in real time. Meiling Huang et al. [7] used mobile phone positioning data to study pedestrian travel behavior, to extract the starting and ending points of the travel route, and to obtain their traffic travel information with the area of the polygon algorithm. But the method on GPS or mobile phone positioning belongs to a active tracking method, the followers must carry the related equipment.

Because the pedestrians wish their travel behaviors, data and information should be in private status, vehicle license plate automatic recognition technology on high definition video camera are used to obtain the vehicle information, and protect their travel behaviors. Vehicle license plate automatic recognition technology has applied in high way and park automatic charge, for example, See/CarSystem of Hi.Tech in Israel, and VLPRS system of Optasia in Singapore. The application of license plate recognition and tracking are concentrated in road monitoring, electronic toll collection, how to effectively using the license plate recognition results to obtain vehicle travel path research which is initial. Yasuo et al. [5] establish a traffic data model to carry out traffic planning with the vehicle license plate automatic recognition technique. In order to obtain the complete trajectory of the vehicle in the road network, Feilong Wang et al. [10] proposed a data processing flow for the vehicle travel path analysis with the theory of a reachable network. Ming Zhao [11] proposed a grid division model of the urban road network, through the license plate recognition results recorded inlet and outlet of vehicles in the grid, an approximation Route Tracking map of the target vehicle was setup with data mining technology.

In this paper, a vehicle route tracking system is decomposed into two subsystems: vehicle license plate recognition subsystem and vehicle route tracking subsystem. In vehicle license plate recognition subsystem, there exist two modules: license plate location and character recognition with an improved ViBe algorithm and a multi-classification SVM model on Hadamard error-correcting, which uses Gabor filter to extract character value. In vehicle route tracking system, considering the fact that the accuracy of license plate recognition cannot reach 100 %, a three-level tracking model is proposed. Firstly, it applies accurate matching algorithm to get coarse route. Secondly, for the missing route segments, the model uses branch bounding method based on license plate fuzzy matching algorithm to recover missing segments. If the recovery fails, the A* algorithm is used to get the shortest path as reference solution. At last, the system achieves fundamental functions based on OpenCV and ArcGIS, and has broad application prospects in criminal case detection, vehicle trip survey and traffic analysis.

2 Platform

A fast and efficient algorithm for license plate detection and recognition is studied. Fusion of multi point video license plate detection and intelligent transportation system network video node topology, reconstruction and tracking of vehicle travel path in the urban road network environment. In the road network, the survey points are located at each intersection point by carrying out the high definition video, which could be got the results of the license plate recognition with video analysis. A prototype system for vehicle routing in urban road network on video domain license plate detection was developed.

The prototype system was divided into license plate recognition subsystem and travel route tracking subsystem. The detail of system construction can be seen in Fig. 1. The license plate recognition system is a single point of application among many different location points. License plate recognition data of every point monitoring video is stored in the database. A model of urban topological road network composed of multiple survey sites, and route tracking system is in charge of to remove the path in the network with a multi-peer cooperative applications.

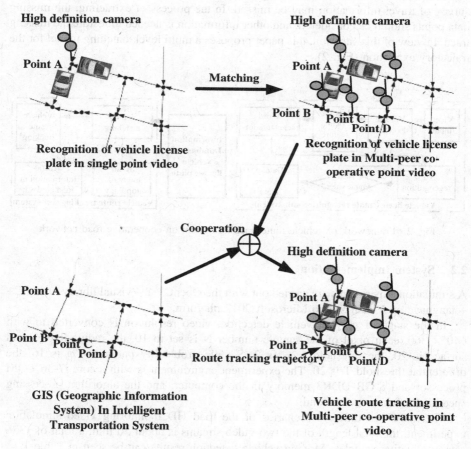

Fig. 1. Platform of multi-peer cooperative points

2.1 Framework of the System

The license plate recognition subsystem mainly consists of three stages: license plate location, character segmentation and character recognition. The tracking subsystem is responsible for the track extraction, which involves a single vehicle trajectory and a large number of vehicle trajectory extraction, as well as the time range or the scope of the search portal, the situation is more diverse. All of these situations can be converted to a single vehicle in a certain period of time of the trajectory extraction, so this paper focuses on the problem of model design. In this paper, we assume that each intersection in the road network is set up the high definition video surveillance survey points. The key is how to get the vehicle line through the survey point sequence, to ensure the correctness and integrity of the sequence. Due to the subsystem to identify the license plate information as the main basis, and the current license plate recognition method can't guarantee 100 % accuracy, possible license plate character recognition errors; and due to equipment failure, climate change and other reasons, vehicle at some point in the survey of travel information may be missed. In the process of extracting, the missing data points should be considered, and other information is needed to restore the missing trace. In view of this situation, this paper proposes a multi level matching model for the trajectory extraction (Fig. 2).

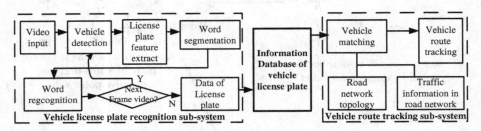

Fig. 2. Framework of vehicle route tracking system on cooperative road network

2.2 System Implementation

A simulation experiments are carried out with the OpenCV 2.4 visual library, using C++ language on Visual Studio Microsoft 2012 platform.

In the stage of moving vehicle detection, video resolution is converted to with 640×360, each pixel of the sample number N is set to 10, the radius R of round surface is 20, the threshold C_{min} is 2. Sample probability parameter φ is 16, the differential threshold T is 20. The experiment environment is with a core i7-3630QM processor and 8 GB DDR3 memory in the computer, and the algorithm processing speed is 25 frames per second.

There are two different scenarios of the road HD monitoring video simulation experiment, the total length of the two video streams is about 50 min, a total of 1376 sets of effective vehicles. Moving vehicle detection results can be seen in Table 1.

Experimental results show that the frame different algorithm is improved to eliminate the interference of the shadow and the ghost region, so the accuracy is higher than that of the original ViBe algorithm. The moving vehicle extraction phase accuracy reached 97.4 %, frame rate reached 25FPS in real-time and high accuracy.

Table 1. Moving vehicle detection ratio

	Right	Missing	Wrong	Accuracy rate
ViBe algorithm	1277	73	26	92.8 %
Improved ViBe algorithm	1340	31	5	97.4 %

Because the vehicle density is too large to make many vehicles' regions integrated into a larger region, some vehicles will be missed with the improved ViBe algorithm. The wrong check is mainly due to the dense pedestrian was mistaken a vehicle area, this kind noise will be filtered in the license plate image extraction phase, the overall accuracy of the license plate will not be affected.

In order to extract the license plate character, the data set is the 1340 vehicle image from the vehicle detection phase. The average size of the vehicle image is 380*420, L_{max} and L_{min} in the edge filtering phase are 70 and 20 respectively, Min_W, Max_W, Min_H and Max_H are 45, 180, 15 and 70 respectively in the screening phase of the connected domain. Vehicle license plate detection results can be seen in Table 2.

Table 2. Vehicle license plate detection results

Right	Missing	Declinational	Wrong	Accuracy rate	Average detection time
1317	9	14	21	98.3 %	27 ms

There are two main reasons of missing check. One is the license plate area is fouled serious, the edge character could not be extracted accurately, the other is the license plate is leaned seriously, in the choice connected domain phase it was treated as a pseudo license plate area removed. The domains of wrong check include Headlight area and Rectangular advertisement area which are similar to license plate. Deviation check include the extraction of the license plate image is too small, too big or not complete, because the edge detection only is in the vertical direction, a portion of the horizontal direction information is lost, the position of the up and low boundary has deviation.

Experimental results show that due to the removal of the complex background, license plate extraction stage achieved higher accuracy rate, the morphological operation method could also be adapted to blurred license plate. In addition the positioning method speed was faster and met the real-time requirements.

3 Grid Arrangement for Multi-peer Cooperative Crossing Point Videos

A cooperative vehicle route tracking system is setup from a single video collection point to many grid multi-peer points at intersections in road network.

3.1 Information and Data of Vehicle License Plate at Single Crossing Point Video

The license plate character image is used after the size of the normalized size of 27×53, using the Gabor filter introduced above to feature extraction, the image of each character will be $27 \times 53 \times 4$, that is, 5724 characteristic values. Feature dimension is too high to make computational complexity of the next recognition process very high, and result in the "Curse of dimensionality". At last, the correct rate of recognition not only will not improve, but will be reduced. In this paper, the PCA method [13] (Component Analysis Principal) was used to get the characteristics of dimensionality reduction processing.

With PCA method, the covariance matrix of the training samples are constructed to extract feature values and vectors, the original high dimensional feature space was projected into a low dimensional space, at the same time as much as possible to retain the original space representation of information and eliminated the redundant data.

The main procedures of the principal component analysis are as follows in sample space X:

(1) Dimension in X is $m \times n_1 \times n_2 \times n_3$, m is number of training samples, $n_1 \times n_2 \times n_3$ is a feature space which was extracted by Gabor filter, for example $27 \times 53 \times 4$. At first, the sample space X was converted into $m \times n$ dimension sample feature set X={x_1, x_2, ..., x_n}, n is equal to $n_1 \times n_2 \times n_3$, namely the feature number of every sample.

(2) The mean value of the sample set is calculated as follow.

$$\mu = \frac{1}{n} \sum_{i=1}^{n} x_i \qquad (1)$$

(3) The covariance matrix of X is calculated as follow.

$$\sum_X \frac{1}{n} \sum_{i=0}^{n} (x_i - \mu)(x_i - \mu)^T \qquad (2)$$

(4) The following equations are solved to calculate the values and vectors of the covariance matrix U.

$$(\lambda I - \sum_X) U = 0 \qquad (3)$$

In Eq. 3, I is a Unit matrix.

(5) The n characteristic values is in descending order, namely, $\lambda_1 \geq \lambda_2 \geq \cdots \geq \lambda_n$. The corresponding feature vectors are sorted to get the feature vector matrix.

$$W_{n \times n} = [U_1 U_2 \cdots U_n] \qquad (4)$$

(6) In the feature vector matrix, the principal component in the front has covered most of the information. The contribution rate threshold is set C, contribution accumulation rate of principal components is added according to characteristic value

of each component. The front m feature values are chosen to satisfy the following equation. The front m columns in $W_{n \times n}$ are chosen to construct a $W_{n \times m}$ matrix.

$$\sum_{i=1}^{m} \lambda_i / \sum_{k=1}^{n} \lambda_k \geq C \tag{5}$$

(7) The principal components of the training samples and testing sample are calculated as Eqs. (6) and (7) respectively.

$$Y_{N \times m} = (X_{N \times n} - \mu)W_{n \times m} \tag{6}$$

$$Y_{1 \times m} = (X_{1 \times n} - \mu)W_{n \times m} \tag{7}$$

In order to recognize the words in vehicle license plate, there are three cooperative classifiers, including a Chinese word classifier, a letter classifier and a letter-number classifier. According to position of the word, letter or number, the correspondent classifier will be chosen. The details of the classifiers can be seen in Fig. 3.

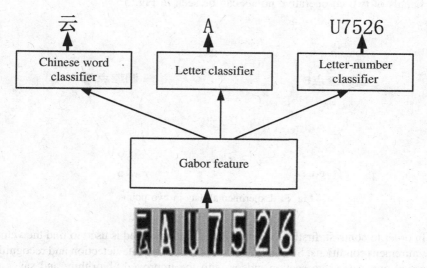

Fig. 3. Three cooperative classifiers of word recognition

3.2 Grid Arrangement for Multi-peer Cooperative Crossing Point Videos in Road Network

In order to construct a cooperative vehicle route tracking system, it is necessary to setup video collection point at intersection in road network, and every video collection point arranges one or many high definition camera. The details of cooperative video collection network can be seen in Fig. 4.

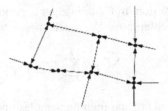

Fig. 4. Multi-peer cooperative video collection points in road network

The route tracking model on vehicle license plate fuzzy matching theory is proposed, trajectory extraction results explain this method have certain fault tolerance rate to restrain recognition errors for the vehicle license plates. In order to illustrate the model is scientific and effective, the experiments and analyses of the fuzzy matching algorithm were carried out by the following example.

The original experimental data is from double adjacent co-operative points of video vehicle monitoring in Shanghai city road network, namely, point A (the cross of Miquan road and Hejing road) and point B(the cross of Moyu road and Hejing road). The details of two co-operative points can be seen in Fig. 5.

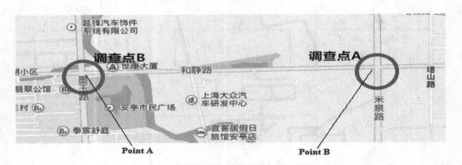

Fig. 5. Experimental data in two points

In order to contrast, firstly, the artificial matching method is used to find the vehicle in requirement conditions. Secondly, the vehicle license plate detection and recognition is carried out in the two section videos with the improved algorithm, and saves the vehicle license plate number and vehicle departure time information. At last, three ways are utilized to match the rows of vehicles through the two points A and B, including exact matching, fuzzy matching point A and fuzzy matching point B. Vehicle license plate fuzzy matching algorithm for point A has similarity weight $w_1=1$, $w_2=1$, $w_3=1$. Vehicle license plate fuzzy matching algorithm for point B has similarity weight $w_1=0.2$, $w_2=0.3$, $w_3=1$.

In order to reasonably select the matching threshold, we analyzed the of similarity value between fuzzy matching point A and fuzzy matching point B in different situations. For one vehicle license plate detection and recognition, the error number of the first word is ER1(ER1∈{0, 1}), the error number of the second word is ER2(ER2∈{0, 1}), the error number from the three to seven words is ER3(ER3∈{0, 1, 2, 3, 4, 5}). When the number of errors of the vehicle license plate recognition is less than 5, the similarity values of the two fuzzy matching weights can be seen in Table 3.

Table 3. Similarity values of the two fuzzy matching weights

ER1	ER2	ER3	Similarity value with fuzzy matching point A (%)	Similarity value with fuzzy matching point B (%)
0	0	1	85.71	81.82
0	1	0	85.71	94.55
1	0	0	85.71	96.36
0	0	2	71.43	63.64
0	1	1	71.43	76.36
1	0	1	71.43	78.18
1	1	0	71.43	90.91
0	0	3	57.14	45.45
0	1	2	57.14	58.18
1	0	2	57.14	60.00
1	1	1	57.14	72.73
0	0	4	42.86	27.27
0	1	3	42.86	40.00
1	1	2	42.86	54.55
1	0	3	42.86	41.82

From Table 3, when the weights are not all 1, the correct rate of the license plate characters in different positions is different to the influence degree of the whole similarity degree. In the experiment, the matching threshold value of fuzzy matching S is chosen as 0.72, the number by manual matching successful license plate is 412, the number by exact matching successful license plate is 324, and the numbers by fuzzy matching point A and B successful license plate are 379 and 401 respectively. The average matching rate among the four matching methods can be seen in Fig. 6.

The result of experiment indicated that the fuzzy matching algorithm of the vehicle license plate with weights can improve matching rate 18.7 % than the exact matching algorithm, and have good fault tolerance for letter recognition, on the other hand, promote its matching velocity evidently. This algorithm can restore the route tracking information of the original vehicle quickly and reasonably.

4 A Vehicle Route Tracking System

A vehicle route tracking system is developed on ArcGIS Engine10.2. Its application interface is shown in Fig. 7, which can practice the map display and operation, layer display and operation, parameter setting, result display and data export. Among them, the map display and operation module can realize MXD map loaded, map zoom, map

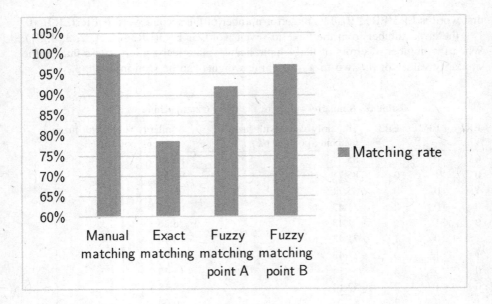

Fig. 6. Average matching rate among the four matching methods

Fig. 7. Application interface of the vehicle route tracking system

translation function. Layer module shows the map layers, each map layer contains several elements or line elements, users can make choice for the different elements.

In the parameter setting blank, a given specific license plate number, time range, the correspondent weights and thresholds are set, then click button "开始检测", a correspondent full track of the vehicle will be obtained.

The full vehicle tracking will be displayed on the interface. The results of different stages are marked by different colors. For examples, the blue line is the exact match, the yellow line is the result of the fuzzy match, and the red line is a shortest route. At the same time, the relevant information of the vehicle trajectory will be listed, including the actual length of the track, the average speed, the number of cooperative points, and the time of each point which vehicle passed through.

5   Conclusion

A route tracking model for multi-peer cooperative domain video license plate detection is proposed in the paper. It can query and reconstruct the vehicle route trajectory in the range of time or route by the license plate recognition of data with GIS of the urban road network. In urban road network, the traffic trajectory analysis is related to big data from multi-peer cooperative point distribution, precision of license plate information extraction and processing is a key factor of the final route trajectory tracking results. The proposed algorithm still has some shortcomings, for example, amount of data storage will increase rapidly with the network size and the number of vehicles increased, real time of the system will decrease. In future, these problems still need to study.

References

1. Stopher, P., FitzGerald, C., Zhang, J.: Search for global positioning system device to measure personal travel. Transp. Res. Part C: Emerg. Technol. 16(3), 350–369 (2008)
2. Bohte, W., Maat, K.: Deriving and validating trip destinations and modes for multi-day GPS based travel surveys: An application in the Netherlands. In: 87th Annual Meeting of the Transportation Research Board, Washington, D. C. (2008)
3. Wu, H.: Research on map matching, vehicle tracking and speed evaluating in urban traffic information system. Jiaotong University, Shanghai (2006)
4. Zhu, L., Sun, Ya., XiaoWen, H.: Dynamic travel time detection based on location of mobile phone. Comput. Eng. Appl. 43(10), 244–248 (2007)
5. Asakura, Y., Iryo, T.: Analysis of tourist behavior based on the tracking data collected using a mobile communication instrument. Transp. Res. 41(1), 684–690 (2007)
6. Calabrese, F., et al.: Real-Time urban monitoring using cell phones: a case study in rome. IEEE Trans. Intell. Transp. Syst. 12(1), 141–151 (2011)
7. Huang, M., Baichuan, L.: Traffic OD data collection technology based on mobile phone location. J. Chongqing Jiaotong Univ. (Nat. Sci.) 29(1), 162–166 (2010)

8. Anagnostopoulos, C.-N.E., Psoroulas, I.D., Loumos, V.: License plate recognition from still images and video sequences: a survey. IEEE Trans. Intell. Transp. Syst. **9**(3), 377–391 (2008)

9. Leelasantitham, A., Kiattisin, S.: A position-varied plate utilized for a Thai license plate recognition. In: SICE Annual Conference 2010, Proceedings of IEEE, pp. 3303–3307 (2010)

10. Wang, F.: Analysis method and practice research of vehicle travel path based on vehicle license plate. Changan University, Changchun (2011)

11. Zhao, M., Wang, H.: Analysis and design of OD survey system based on vehicle license plate recognition technology. J. Highw. Transp. Res. Dev. **48**(12), 188–190 (2008)

12. Jin, C., Chen, T., Ji, L.: License plate recognition based on edge detection algorithm. In: 2013 Ninth International Conference on IEEE Intelligent Information Hiding and Multimedia Signal Processing, pp. 395–398 (2013)

13. Yajing, X., Wang, Y.: An improvement on the application method of principal component analysis. J. Math. Pract. Theor. **36**(6), 68–75 (2006)

SIERA: Visual Analytics for Multi-dimensional Data for Learning Assessment in Educational Organisations

Manuel J. Ibarra[1(✉)], Cristhian Serrano[1], and Angel F. Navarro[2]

[1] School of Informatics and Systems Engineering,
Micaela Bastidas National University of Apurímac, 121 Arenas Av., Abancay, Apurimac, Peru
manuelibarra@gmail.com, cristhiansj@gmail.com
[2] School of System Engineering, Jose Maria Arguedas National University of Apurímac,
380 Juan Francisco Ramos Av., Andahuaylas, Apurimac, Peru
angelnr22@gmail.com

Abstract. Nowadays, data is produced at an incredible rate and the strategy to collect and store is increasing as faster as the strategy to analyse it. The correct analysis of these multidimensional data is very important for decision makers. Some Educational Organisations have a culture of evaluating the student's knowledge, it makes possible to promptly discover weaknesses in the teaching and learning process. This paper describes a proposed strategy to collect multi-dimensional data and visual analytics for assessment that supports the evaluation process of educational organisations. To validate this proposal we used focus group. The proposed strategy was tested with 2677 schools and 160529 students in evaluation process in Apurimac-Peru. The test results show that teachers agree with the proposed strategy.

Keywords: Learning assessment · Multidimensional data · Data visualization · Excel VBA · Visual analytics

1 Introduction

To accomplish with the *first commitment*, one of the *Eight Commitments School Management* given by the government [1], the schools (IE: Institución Educativa in Spanish) organize and propose periodically assessments for students. According to Gonzales et al. [2], an evaluation culture could be defined as the set of values, agreements, traditions, beliefs and thoughts that an educational community attaches to the action of evaluation. Bolseguí and Fuguet [3], point out that the evaluation culture is an evolving concept that refers to the need to evaluate on an ongoing basis; for them, the assessment is a complex and multidimensional process that includes different components: vision, values, behaviours, routines, organisational and social context, past and present experiences and so forth.

Once evaluated, it is necessary to analyze and interpret the results, for his purpose it's important that data has to be properly displayed [4, 5]. An approach is showing relationships between different data groups of a provided statistical selection: in order to compare relative proportions between various indicators [6].

© Springer International Publishing AG 2016
Y. Luo (Ed.): CDVE 2016, LNCS 9929, pp. 283–287, 2016.
DOI: 10.1007/978-3-319-46771-9_36

This article presents a strategy for Visual Analytics to qualify student's test, in primary and secondary level, in *Math* and *Communication* areas in Educational Institutions of Apurimac-Peru, showing the obtained results by statistical charts.

2   Related Works

Visual analytics can be described as *"the science of analytical reasoning facilitated by interactive visual interfaces"* and has evolved in various fields of information and scientific visualization. The transformation of data into meaningful visualization is not trivial task and is not automatically given by computers, rather, is attributed to the creativity of humans being. In this way, according to John Tuckey [7], tools as well as understanding are needed for the interactive and undirected search for structures and trends. Visual analytics is more than only visualization. It can rather be seen as an integral approach combining visualization, human factors and data analysis. In this context, production is defined as the creation of materials that summarize the results of an analytical effort, presentation as the packaging of those materials in a way that helps the audience understand the analytical results [8].

There are techniques for facilitating data selection in the data transformation process [9], techniques for selecting chart type and visual components (e.g., line style, point face, axis range) automatically in the visual mapping process [10]; and techniques for changing visual effects to clarify the user's viewpoint and assertion easily [11] in the view transformation process.

Matsushita et al. [12] made a research titled "Interactive Visualization Method for Exploratory Data Analysis". They propose an interactive visualization method suitable for exploratory data analysis. The method extracts parameters for drawing from a series of user requirements written in a natural language and redraws the drawn chart interactively according to the change in the user's viewpoint.

3   Design, Implementation and Evaluation

To acquire System Requirements of SIERA (in Spanish: Sistema de Evaluación Regional del Aprendizaje) we got information from interviews of the DRE's workers. The goal of these interviews was to define system requirements and test the software functionality; each user used the software and gave us feedback on possible improvements of the tool.

The DRE's server stores the operational data in Mysql Database. This data is related to: number of assessment, student's attributes, answers given by the student, indicators of each question and so forth. It is called the *Data Tier*. In the *Business Tier* a Web server stores *php* pages and procedures to optimize queries. The *Presentation Tier* shows the Excel File that Teacher will use to fill out the student's marked answers. The system makes use of HTML, CSS and JavaScript to decorate and validate webpages of the client side. The system architecture is shown in Fig. 1.

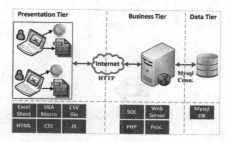

Fig. 1. System architecture

Designing Excel File. An Excel File was designed to fill the answers marked by students, as shown in Fig. 2. Every question can be market with "A", "B", "C", "X" (when students mark two or more answers) or " " (blank, when a student did not mark any answer). Mathematics and Communication have 23 questions, every section has from one to forty five students approximately, and in the *primary* level there are six grades named: "First" "Second" until "Sixth"; and in the *secondary* level there are five grades named: "First" "second" until "Fifth".

	A	B	C	D	E	F		X
1		Answers marked in Mathematics						
2	Name	P1	P2	P3	P4	P5	...	P23
3	Jose	C	B	A	B	A		B
4	Oscar	C	C	B	A	A		B
5	Juvenal	C	B	A	B	A		C
6	Abraham	C	B	A	B	C		B
7	Jonas	B	A	C	B	B		A
8	Anthony	C	A	B	B	A		B

Fig. 2. Sheet to fill answers.

Assigning Reached Level. Each test has 23 questions for each area. To determine the level that student has reached, specialists produce distribution of scores as follows: [0,8] "Initiation"; [9,15] "In process" and [16,23] "Achieved". For example, if a student gets a score of 5, then, the level acquired is "Initiation"; if a student gets a score of 12, then, the level acquired is "In Process"; and if a student gets a score of 20, then, the level acquired is "Achieved".

Example of data visualization. After the teacher fill out the answers, the system rates the assessment using values assigned by Specialists. An example of the Report is shown in Fig. 3.

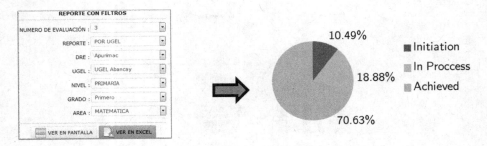

Fig. 3. Report level: primary, grade: first, area: mathematics UGEL: Abancay

Figure 3 shows the multidimensional options for reports (left side) and the results of data visualization (right side). All report filters area automatically built by the system (it is not implemented by hand).

Evaluation of the proposed strategy. The validation of the tool was conducted by five Education Specialists (workers) of the DRE-Apurímac through a focus group. The event took place on: May 15, September 14 and October 15, 2015, in a meeting room of the Pedagogical Management Area of DRE.

Before starting the activity, the developed system was briefly shown to each specialist in evaluation. A simulation of the software functionality was then done. After this simulated process, the Education Specialists provided feedback, suggestions and opinions. When they were asked: *"will the use of the designed software help you to make it easier the data visualization of evaluation assessment results?"*, they all answered that in their opinion that assumption was valid: then they were asked: *"would the decision-making speed and quality of decisions have been better if the Director would have had a support tool that is visual and provides the appropriate suggestions?"*, they all replied that a positive answer would be valid.

4   Conclusions and Future Work

Visual analytics is an emerging field of research, because it makes possible to represent data visually, allowing the users interact directly with the information. This paper describes a way to improve the visualization of the multidimensional data. The tool was tested by teachers in 2677 schools and 160529 students (with three times evaluation process in 2015). According to the Education Specialists opinion, the propose strategy allows them to have visual analytics to know the level (Beginning, In Process, and Achieved) reached by students in every area, level, grade and district; also, Director could have accurate information when making decisions based on the learning achievement indicators. This tool needs to be improved in its flexibility, for this purpose is possible to use drag and drop buttons, this can help users to select dynamically multidimensional data.

References

1. http://www.minedu.gob.pe/campanias/pdf/manual-de-gestion-escolar-2015_10marzo_alta. pd, 5 February 2016
2. González, J.R., Soledad, M., Montoya, R., Rivera, J.A.: Cultura de evaluación en instituciones educativas. Perfiles Educ. **33**(131), 42–63 (2011)
3. Bolseguí, M., Fuguet, A.A.: Cultura de evaluación: una aproximación conceptual. Investigación y Postgrado **21**(1), 77–98 (2006)
4. Guchev, V., Massimo, M., Giuseppe S.: Design guidelines for correlated quantitative data visualizations. In: Proceedings of the International Working Conference on Advanced Visual Interfaces. ACM (2012)
5. Keim, D., Kohlhammer, J., Ellis, G., Mansmann, F.: Mastering the Information Age: Solving Problems with Visual Analytics. Eurographics Association, Goslar (2010)
6. Spence, R.: Information Visualization: Design for Interaction. Pearson Educational (2007)
7. Tuckey, J.W.: Exploratory Data Analysis. Addison-Wesley, Reading (1977)
8. Keim, D.A., Mansmann, F., Schneidewind, J., Thomas, J., Ziegler, H.: Visual analytics: Scope and challenges, pp. 76–90. Springer, Berlin Heidelberg (2008)
9. Ahlberg, C., Shneiderman, B.: Visual information seeking: Tight coupling of dynamic query filters with starfield displays. In: Proceedings of the SIGCHI Conference on Human Factors in Computing Systems. ACM (1994)
10. Fasciano, M., Lapalme, G. : Postgraphe: a system for the generation of statistical graphics and text. In: Proceedings of the Eighth Workshop on Natural Language Generation (1996)
11. Mittal, V.O.: Visual prompts and graphical design: A framework for exploring the design space of 2-D charts and graphs. In: AAAI/IAAI (1997)
12. Matsushita, M., Kato, T.: Interactive visualization method for exploratory data analysis. In: Fifth International Conference on Information Visualisation Proceedings. IEEE (2001)

Visualization of Ranking Authors Based on Social Networks Analysis and Bibliometrics

Xiujuan Xu[1,2], Ruisi Zhang[1,2], Zhenzhen Xu[1,2],
Feng Ding[1,2], and Xiaowei Zhao[1,2(✉)]

[1] School of Software, Dalian University of Technology, Dalian 116620, China
{xjxu,xzz,dingfeng,xiaowei.zhao}@dlut.edu.cn
[2] Key Laboratory for Ubiquitous Network and Service Software of Liaoning Province,
Dalian 116620, China
zruisi@foxmail.com

Abstract. It is interesting to rank scientists in a specific field, which would help researchers to know about the research status of the field and gain valuable insight on future technical trends in the field. Our paper visualizes the results of author ranking with the consideration of authors' contribution. In this paper, every author's contribution to his/her field is calculated according to the co-authorship among papers. By extracting the papers and authors information from a field since they started publication, the co-author network are constructed. We also get the clusters partition of those authors by Girvan-Newman algorithm. For conducting detailed experiments to show the visualized our results, we select the field of Intelligent transportation system (ITS) as an example. Since thousands of papers were published by scientists each year in the ITS field, academic co-authorship in this field expands fast. We design our dataset composed by data from four journals in the ITS field to visualize our algorithm.

Keywords: Visualization · Author ranking · Social network · Intelligent transportation system

1 Introduction

Recent years, scientists cooperation becomes strong and dense. It is a hard challenge for researchers to discover and recognize cooperation of scientists in a specific field. We could rank scientists according to social network analysis. By knowing the scientists' ranking, researchers could follow these scientists to find the new hot topics.

Co-author relationship is one of the important social network relationships. In a co-author network, each node represents an author, and the edges between two nodes stand for co-author relationship between authors. Social network analysis (SNA) is a method for researching and analysing the interpersonal relations or relations between groups and colony morphology in sociology. Since Mark Newman used social network method to analyse the co-author relationship for the

© Springer International Publishing AG 2016
Y. Luo (Ed.): CDVE 2016, LNCS 9929, pp. 288–295, 2016.
DOI: 10.1007/978-3-319-46771-9_37

first time in 2001 [6], social network analysis has been applied to the co-relation investigation frequently. The social network method can effectively reflect the phenomenon of cooperation between researchers. And it can also help us evaluate authors' contribution to their research field.

By studying the co-author relationship network, scientists could easily understand the cooperation status and the development in their research areas. It also provides a new thinking for researchers to understand co-author relationship and to discovery the general features of co-author cooperation in scientific filed.

For many years, the research of American researchers and research institutions are considered to take the lead in the most of scientific fields. However, this viewpoint is an emotional perception rather than scientific conclusions with rigorous experiments and analysis. We could prove the conjecture with more scientific and logical analyses.

The rest of this paper is organized as follows. In Sect. 2, a brief review on related literature is given. In Sect. 3, author rank problem is introduced formally. The visualized experimental results are given in Sect. 4 after introducing the data source from in the ITS field. Remarks are stated under the conclusion in Sect. 5.

2   Related Work

Basically, our work relates to information and literature retrieval category. In this research field, some researchers have done a lot of work. These research work can be generally divided into the following two categories.

2.1   Measurement of Scientific Research

Many researchers work on the measurement of quality of papers and scientific research achievements, which includes the measurement of impact factors of authors, journals, and other scientific ranks of research institutions. Impact factor, as a general international journal evaluation index, is not only an index indicating a journal's usefulness, but also an important index measuring the academic influence of the journals.

Through statistical analysis, researchers can get some useful statistical information, such as the number of published papers in a period of time, the publication time lag, the papers' length, the papers' type and the number of collaborators. With the above information and some criteria, researchers can get comprehensive coefficient of authors, and then, they could measure an author's authority in his/her field. In addition, researchers can also evaluate and rank research institutions and various countries scientific status in the same way.

Journals are the research object in the field of co-author network research. The domestic and foreign scholars have conducted the thorough research. For example, Newman [21] clarified the collaborative patterns of science by analysing the co-author network of different fields. Mane and Borner [20] study on the co-authorship network subject and the most commonly cited topic in the National Academy of Science in 1982 to 2001. Yu and Van de Sompel [27] analyses the citation network among the papers, and analyses the frontier studies. Qinghua and Liang [22] chose the co-authors of 'Journal of Informatics' as dataset, and conducted the empirical research to the co-author network of domestic informatics domain.

As for research methods, previous studies mainly use the social network analysis to do bibliographic statistics. However, in addition to the bibliography analysis methods, the cooperation patterns of research authors also plays important clues to show disciplines hotpot.

2.2   Author Rank Work

The PageRank algorithm is a web page ranking algorithm which was developed by Larry Page and Sergey Brin in 1998 [6]. The main idea is to determine the page rank through hyperlink relationship. We note that this idea is helpful to study the co-relation between the researches. This paper describes a network of co-authorship based on this idea. Recently, Wang and Xie et al. [28] proposed ranking the future popularity of new publications and young researchers by proposing a unified ranking model to combine various available information. Meanwhile, Ding and Yan et al. [9] presented weighted PageRank algorithms in the information retrieval (IR) area from the 1970s to 2008 to form the author co-citation network.

In recent years, many scholars and institutions are studying literature analysis. However, from the scope of research, researchers and the cooperation domain is based on many domains and the scope is very wide. However, data mining deeply in specific direction is much less. And the existing co-author research on intelligent transportation system only use the basic statistical method.

3   Data Analysis Framework

We rank authors based on the PageRank algorithm to identify the co-author relationship, and we visualize each author's academic contribution in a specific field. A co-author relationship between two authors reflects a searching partnership between them. Having co-author relationship between authors represents that several authors published the same paper by cooperation.

When ranking authors, the input set should include: authors, the papers published by those authors, and authors' order in each paper. The output set is every author and his/her ranking values.

3.1   Building Co-author Network and Data Analysis

Our work aimed at deeply analysing the co-author relationship between authors in this field so as to construct a co-author network after processing data. Even in the same paper, the cooperating coefficient of author a to author b differs from that of author b to author a, because every author's weight is different. Thus, the co-author network is a digraph, even though there are always a path from a to b whenever there is a path from b to a.

If two authors (A and B) cooperate a paper, the relationship of A to B and the relationship of B to A have different coefficient. While calculating the cooperating coefficient, we take an author's partners' weight into the calculation of his/her contribution to his/her research field. We could get a series of ranking values associated with authors. These values determine the size of each nodes.

3.2 Visualization

We use Girvan-Newman (GN) algorithm [11] to divide the co-author network into several groups, in that we can get the intimate level of those authors. GN algorithm obtains its results by deleting edges between nodes. By removing the edge with the higher betweenness, the whole network will be divided into several clusters. Members in the same clusters are considered to be more closely connected. Through these results, we can roughly see closeness of the authors.

Comparing to be listed in database tables or described by words, all of the calculating results can be shown more clearly and intuitively in topology graphs. Ucinet is a popular software package to process social networks [4]. It was developed by Borgatti, Everett and Freeman, and incorporates NetDraw, a social network mapping software. We choose to use it for visualization for its strong matrix analysis ability.

In the co-author network topology, each node represents an author. The node's diameter is determined by ranking values. Edges in the network means the two authors connected have been cooperated together. Meanwhile, different colours of the nodes distinguish the clusters we get from GN algorithm.

4 Experiments

In this section, we design a dataset by crawler four journals in the ITS field. We implement our author rank algorithm on our dataset.

4.1 Data Source

Intelligent Transportation System (ITS) is the development direction of transportation system in the future. It integrates advanced information technology, data communications transmission technology, electronic sensor technology, control technology and computer technology into an entire ground traffic management system. It is a real-time and efficient integrated transport management system and can play a role in a wide range. We test our presented method in the ITS field.

Our dataset includes the data from the following journals. IEEE Transactions on ITS (T-ITS) [8], IET ITS (IET-ITS) [16] and Journal of ITS (JITS) [12] are the most famous and authoritative in the ITS field. The data published in T-ITS is from June, 2000 to May, 2016. J-ITS has 40 issues from the spring of 2006 to

March, 2016. ITS journal was the former of J-ITS, so we obtain the data about 19 issues in ITS journal from 1996 to 2004. IET-ITS has 50 volumes from the September, 2007. The statistical results of these journals are listed in Table 1. We gather the above four journals data by crawlers to analyze the co-author relationship in this field.

Table 1. Dataset statistics about every journal

Title	Start time	Volumes	Authors	Papers
T-ITS	June 2000–May 2016	74	4,935	1,701
ITS-J	March 1996–March 2004	19	222	123
J-ITS	March 2006–March 2016	40	606	234
IET-ITS	September 2007–April 2016	50	1,579	502
Summary			6,904	2,562

Our dataset includes all the published paper and the related author's information from the top journals in the ITS field of Table 1. We get these data by crawler and store them in database. However, the data had to be preprocessed for there exists some kind of disunity of data forms. For example, many author's name can be shown as full name or initials. Therefore, we collected authors' full names from the Web of Science as a supplement to our dataset. There are 6,904 authors with 2,562 papers in our dataset. Table 2 shows there are 38,842 relationship between authors in our dataset.

Table 2. Dataset and the number of co-author relations

T-ITS	ITS-J	J-ITS	IET-ITS	Summary
29,145	2,402	7,991	4,399	38,842

4.2 Experimental Results

In the co-author network, higher ranking values mean that authors are of more importance in the ITS field. According to the results, we find these authors are at the core status. Table 3 presents the top 5 authors in four journals. In summary, the five core authors in our dataset: Stiller, Christoph., Trivedi, M.M., Ding Wen, Sotelo, M.A. and van Arem, Bart. They are also at core status in one or several journals.

We use *GN* algorithm during clustering authors, as shown in Fig. 1 since scientists' cooperation forms a big network. However, the dataset has too many nodes to be shown clearly in a single topology. We need to discard some nodes with smaller ranking values and relative edges. We delete the authors who published one paper in our dataset to form Fig. 2. After deleting some unimportant nodes, we get Fig. 3 which shows the final topology of the summary dataset.

Table 3. The five top authors in each journals

Ranking	T-ITS	ITS-J	J-ITS	IET-ITS
Top 1	Wen [13]	Chang [5]	Ran [23]	McDonald [29]
Top 2	Trivedi [25]	Van Aerde [2]	Cheng [23]	van Arem [24]
Top 3	Zhou [10]	Abdulhai [1]	Cetin [18]	Wang [15]
Top 4	Papageorgiou M.	Smith [14]	Khattak [3]	Krems [7]
Top 5	Wang [30]	Lin [17]	Skabardonis [26]	Liu [19]

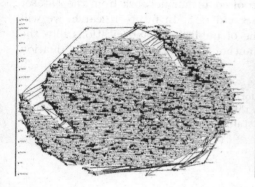

Fig. 1. Co-author network in the dataset   **Fig. 2.** Summary dataset topology

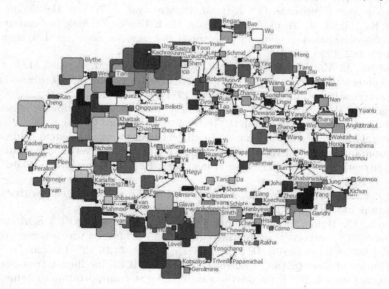

Fig. 3. Co-author network in the dataset

5   Conclusion

Our paper visualizes the ranking of authors that helps to calculate the author's academic contribution in his/her field. The co-author network was divided into clusters by the Girvan-Newman algorithm. The visualized topology graph was produced using the clusters division, the authors' cooperation relationship and their ranking values. We perform the co-author network analysis and present the assessment based on the PageRank algorithm. Our algorithm considers authors' order in papers and the authors' partners' contribution as weight values.

Our paper analyzes the contribution of co-author network from the dataset of several journals: T-ITS, ITS-J, J-ITS and IET. In future research, we will consider other factors, such as the time of publication and citations into the algorithm to get a more optimized co-author network analysis and evaluation method.

Acknowledgments. This work was supported in part by the Natural Science Foundation of China under Grant 615020269, by the Natural Science Foundation of Liaoning under Grant 2015020003, by the Fundamental Research Funds for the Central Universities under Grant DUT15QY40.

References

1. Abdulhai, B., Porwal, H., Recker, W.: Short-term traffic flow prediction using neuro-genetic algorithms. ITS J. Intell. Transp. Syst. J. **7**(1), 3–41 (2002)
2. Ahn, K., Rakha, H., Trani, A., Van Aerde, M.: Estimating vehicle fuel consumption and emissions based on instantaneous speed and acceleration levels. J. Transp. Eng. **128**(2), 182–190 (2002)
3. Bandeira, J., Almeida, T.G., Khattak, A.J., Rouphail, N.M., Coelho, M.C.: Generating emissions information for route selection: experimental monitoring and routes characterization. J. Intell. Transp. Syst. **17**(1), 3–17 (2013)
4. Borgatti, S.P., Everett, M.G., Freeman, L.C.: Ucinet for Windows: Software for Social Network Analysis. Analytic Technologies, Harvard (2002)
5. Chang, G.L., Park, S., Paracha, J.: Intelligent transportation system field demonstration: integration of variable speed limit control and travel time estimation for a recurrently congested highway. Transp. Res. Rec. J. Transp. Res. Board **2243**, 55–66 (2011)
6. Chen, P., Xie, H., Maslov, S., Redner, S.: Finding scientific gems with google's pagerank algorithm. J. Informetrics **1**(1), 8–15 (2007)
7. Cocron, P., Buhler, F., Neumann, I., Franke, T., Krems, J.F., Schwalm, M., Keinath, A.: Methods of evaluating electric vehicles from a user's perspective-the mini e field trial in Berlin. IET Intell. Transp. Syst. **5**(2), 127–133 (2011)
8. Institution of Electrical and Electronics Engineers; IEEE Intelligent Transportation Systems Council: IEEE transactions on intelligent transportation systems. IEEE (2015)
9. Ding, Y., Yan, E., Frazho, A., Caverlee, J.: Pagerank for ranking authors in cocitation networks. J. Am. Soc. Inf. Sci. Technol. **60**(11), 2229–2243 (2009)
10. Fang, Y., Chu, F., Mammar, S., Zhou, M.: Optimal lane reservation in transportation network. IEEE Trans. Intell. Transp. Syst. **13**(2), 482–491 (2012)

11. Girvan, M., Newman, M.E.: Community structure in social and biological networks. Proc. Nat. Acad. Sci. **99**(12), 7821–7826 (2002)
12. Taylor & Francis Group: Journal of Intelligent Transportation Systems. Taylor & Francis Group (2015)
13. Huang, W., Wen, D., Geng, J., Zheng, N.N.: Task-specific performance evaluation of UGVs: case studies at the IVFC. IEEE Trans. Intell. Transp. Syst. **15**(5), 1969–1979 (2014)
14. Kaufman, D.E., Smith, R.L.: Fastest paths in time-dependent networks for intelligent vehicle-highway systems application. J. Intell. Transp. Syst. **1**(1), 1–11 (1993)
15. Li, Z., Wang, W., Chen, R., Liu, P.: Conditional inference tree-based analysis of hazardous traffic conditions for rear-end and sideswipe collisions with implications for control strategies on freeways. IET Intell. Transp. Syst. **8**(6), 509–518 (2014)
16. IET Digital Library: IET Intelligent Transportation Systems (2015)
17. Lin, C.F., Ulsoy, A.G.: Time to lane crossing calculation and characterization of its associated uncertainty. J. Intell. Transp. Syst. **3**(2), 85–98 (1996)
18. List, G.F., Cetin, M.: Modeling traffic signal control using petri nets. IEEE Trans. Intell. Transp. Syst. **5**(3), 177–187 (2004)
19. Liu, P., Lu, J.J., Zhou, H., Sokolow, G.: Operational effects of u-turns as alternatives to direct left-turns. J. Transp. Eng. **133**(5), 327–334 (2007)
20. Mane, K.K., Börner, K.: Mapping topics and topic bursts in PNAS. Proc. Natl. Acad. Sci. **101**(suppl 1), 5287–5290 (2004)
21. Newman, M.E.: The structure of scientific collaboration networks. Proc. Natl. Acad. Sci. **98**(2), 404–409 (2001)
22. Qinghua, Z., Liang, L.: Social network analysis method & its application in information science. Inf. Stud. Theory Appl. **2**, 179–183 (2008)
23. Ran, B., Jin, P.J., Boyce, D., Qiu, T.Z., Cheng, Y.: Perspectives on future transportation research: impact of intelligent transportation system technologies on next-generation transportation modeling. J. Intell. Transp. Syst. **16**(4), 226–242 (2012)
24. Ros, B.G., Knoop, V.L., Van Arem, B., Hoogendoorn, S.P.: Empirical analysis of the causes of stop-and-go waves at sags. IET Intell. Transp. Syst. **8**(5), 499–506 (2014)
25. Sivaraman, S., Trivedi, M.M.: Dynamic probabilistic drivability maps for lane change and merge driver assistance. IEEE Trans. Intell. Transp. Syst. **15**(5), 2063–2073 (2014)
26. Skabardonis, A., Geroliminis, N.: Real-time monitoring and control on signalized arterials. J. Intell. Transp. Syst. **12**(2), 64–74 (2008)
27. de Solla Price, D.J.: Networks of scientific papers. Science **149**(3683), 510–515 (1965)
28. Wang, S., Xie, S., Zhang, X., Li, Z., Philip, S.Y., Shu, X.: Future influence ranking of scientific literature. In: SDM, pp. 749–757. SIAM (2014)
29. Yang, Y., McDonald, M., Zheng, P.: Can drivers' eye movements be used to monitor their performance? A case study. IET Intell. Transp. Syst. **6**(4), 444–452 (2012)
30. Zhang, J., Wang, F.Y., Wang, K., Lin, W.H., Xu, X., Chen, C.: Data-driven intelligent transportation systems: a survey. IEEE Trans. Intell. Transp. Syst. **12**(4), 1624–1639 (2011)

Visual Analytics for Interacting on Cultural Heritage

Thomas Tamisier[1(✉)], Roderick McCall[1], Gabriela Gheorghe[2], and Philippe Pinheiro[1]

[1] Luxembourg Institute of Science and Technology (LIST), 41, rue du Brill,
4422 Belvaux, Luxembourg
thomas.tamisier@list.lu
[2] SnT Centre, University of Luxembourg, 4 rue Weicker, 2721 Luxembourg, Luxembourg

Abstract. We present a framework for location-aware digital storytelling with associated tools and techniques to highlight the connection of different stories. The framework is being implemented in a collaborative editing platform that involves a variety of pilot users, sharing their stories about periods and places selected for their relevance to contemporary history. Complementary studies contribute to knowledge on reducing the intergenerational digital divide (The Locale project is funded by a Core grant from the Fonds National de la Recherche (L).).

Keywords: Visual analytics · Archives mining · Digital heritage

1 Introduction

Cultural heritage initiatives are making an important contribution to industry and economy [1]. This has led to a number of systems dedicated to the exploration of historical content and the addition of semantic information to cultural objects and images [2]. Furthermore, location enabled resources and interactive experiences are becoming increasingly relevant while storytelling and interactions between people and other ambient aspects when telling stories are widely recognised as a powerful mean for explaining complex events [3, 4].

For a story to be even more effective, it should aim to make people feel as far as possible immersed and/or present within the tale. Critical to this task are therefore the underlying models of space and place that allow the preservation and easy sharing of information. At the most basic level space is simply the physical manifestation of the environment e.g. buildings, paths or street furniture. In contrast, sense of place builds on the spatial layout and is fused with aspects such as other people, meaning, sense of self, activities, history and culture (two models are presented in [5, 14]). Early work [13] has shown that people can have a sense of presence and place within location aware stories even when the content provided is relatively simple. We address this issue with the view that sense of presence within storytelling environments is largely derived from co-construction between different elements e.g. physical, narrative and interaction device [6]. We acknowledge differences in the sense of presence and place between virtual reality and digital storytelling environments, in the same way as people can feel immersed within various media types e.g. television, books and films [15]. Furthermore,

Y. Luo (Ed.): CDVE 2016, LNCS 9929, pp. 296–299, 2016.
DOI: 10.1007/978-3-319-46771-9_38

although related to virtual reality, [16] noted that media form and content e.g. methods of display audio and interaction etc., as well as the underlying content, play a part in shaping immersion and hence presence.

We propose an operational framework for location aware and collaborative storytelling that focuses on 3 main challenges identified in this regard. First, encourage people to structure stories in ways that support their perception of place and sense of presence. Second, enable the linking of content and mining of related data to improve how people can navigate within stories and spaces as well as provide people with easier ways to see and interact with the rich content. Last, explore novel interface techniques that are designed to present complex information but avoid information overload.

2   The Locale Authoring Platform

The Locale project aims to allow the authoring and sharing of multi-media historical heritage content about the period 1945-60: from the end of WWII to the dawn of Europe. Targeted users are on the one hand (quasi-)witnesses who keep direct or indirect memories of the period, and on the other hand all people who have historical interest or knowledge about the period. Emphasis will be put on location-based storytelling and sharing experiences that are designed to allow elderly people to share their stories in an intuitive and easy way with younger members of the population. Locale seeks to involve partners for content creation, in particular professional content creators (e.g. local authors etc.), local residents & supporting organization, cultural institutions, local authorities. Technology-enabled passing of stories between generations about the Luxembourg history related to place available to anyone / family. Locale fosters the sharing of personal historical accounts that may not be included in the standard historical literature. The platform is designed to include advanced functionalities to explore multi-dimensional data using various human analyses and data mining strategies, based on metadata, tags, attributes entered by the user, as well as browsing history (e.g. relation between a place and queries about a given historical fact). Interaction between users of the platform will allow following discussions based on data contributed as well as to verify, complete, and put into perspective pieces of historical information.

As users walk around the town or city, they should not have to enter meta-data or filter the vast range of content manually. Instead, we adopt a semi-automatic approach drawn from content-based filtering where implicit and intuitive interaction is used to capture user preferences and behavior [7, 8]. When relevant data are missing, Locale relies on collaborative filtering such as used on popular websites [9], and notably processes ratings and comments by end users. This approach proves successful in linking information between content and users and where appropriate provides a kind of content recommender system. In a next step we will measure the "distance" between content and users within the system. In doing so, the system itself will allow users to see how close other users and content are to their perspective, or to filter out incorrect or irrelevant information or sources.

The ideas highlighted earlier coupled with data mining and extraction approaches can lead to users being overloaded with information, therefore careful consideration must be given to relevant information design approaches. Based on this approach, the underlying rationale is that data must be organized, transformed and presented according to the meaning we want to extract from it. Information design includes both the preparation of the data so as to underline meaning and its visualization according to this meaning [10]. In addition to a tool set for mining data and presenting extracted information, we will draw on the area of data enrichment with two primary objectives: first, refining the presentation and improving the retrieval of the sources [11]; second, providing external references in order to ascertain sources, and build new knowledge through reference linking [12] (Fig. 1).

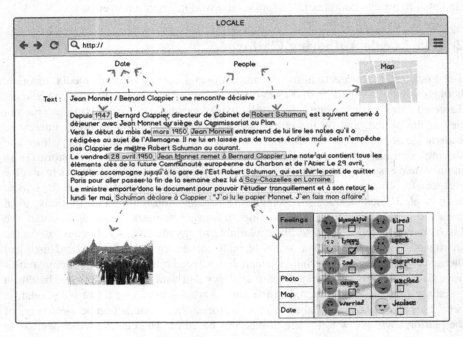

Fig. 1. The Locale Desktop platform for editing stories

3   Locale on the Go

Once the desktop environment for creating stories has been developed, we created an application for mobile devices allowing users to consult stories in the location where they took place, this application have several goals, in particular (1) search stories based on different criteria e.g. by location, keywords, characters stories or timeline, and (2) explore and find stories based on the location of the user. Complementarily, privacy is a key aspect for users, so specific setting includes whether others can browse the stories anonymously or not, whether they can have their location shown. The latter aspect includes the degree of location accuracy and the partial blurring out of content within a pre-set geographical area. The mobile app adds the specific "My stories" area, where the user can see the stories in his geographical area. To this end, we will offer an automatic localization function to the user (with the accuracy that is controllable from the settings panel) and serve content (i.e., a selection of stories) that are related to the location. This feature could be the same as the search of stories by location, just that the location would be in fact the exact location coordinates (with desired accuracy) of the user.

The mobile application allows people to experience the stories on real location. An important feature is to move between different stories as well as gain ambient information about the underlying space during the story period. Building largely on data visualization, we will explore the use of different media forms in order to enhance the sense of immersion within a given story.

4   Conclusion

In a first phase, the Locale project has led to a workable storytelling editing prototype that offers to mine the stories from the perspective of sense of place, and supports interaction between story tellers through tailored visualisations. Extensive testing is being conducted in order to examine the validity of the conceptual model, and explore in what extend there is an increasing convergence between the preservation of cultural heritage and individual or social network based approaches to content creation.

References

1. http://ec.europa.eu/culture/documents/edcci_executive_summary_en.pdf
2. The European competitiveness report (2010). ISBN: 978-92-79-17620-3
3. The Digicult report. European Commission, January 2002
4. Urban Tapestries Project. http://research.urbantapestries.net
5. Gustafson, P.: Meaning of place. J. Environ. Psychol. **21**, 21–39 (2001)
6. Wagner, I.: Consolidated Approach to Presence & Interaction. IPCity Project (2010)
7. Weber, W., Rabaey, J.M., Aarts, E. (eds.): Ambient Intelligence. Springer, Heidelberg (2005)
8. Wan, J., O'Grady, M.J., O'Hare, G.M.P.: Implicit interaction: a modality for ambient exercise monitoring. In: Gross, T., Gulliksen, J., Kotzé, P., Oestreicher, L., Palanque, P., Prates, R.O., Winckler, M. (eds.) INTERACT 2009. LNCS, vol. 5727, pp. 900–903. Springer, Heidelberg (2009)
9. http://www.amazon.com
10. Jacobson, R.: Information Design. MIT Press, Cambridge (2000)
11. http://www.dataflux.com/Products/Data-Management-Studio/Data-Enrichment.aspx
12. Abel, F., et al.: Semantic enrichment, user modeling & mining of usage data on social web. In: Int'l Workshop Usage Analysis and Web of Data, Hyderabad, India (2011)
13. McCall, R., et al.: Mobile phones, subculture & presence. In: Workshop on Mobile Spatial Interaction, ACM Conference on Human Factors in C.S. (CHI), San Jose, Cal. (2007)
14. Relph, E.: Place and Placelessness. Pion Books, London (1976)
15. Lessiter, J., et al.: A cross-media presence questionnaire. Presence **10**(3), 282–297
16. Lombard, M., et al.: The concept of presence. J. CM Com. **3**(2), 149–161 (1997)

socialRadius: Visual Exploration of User Check-in Behavior Based on Social Media Data

Changjiang Wen[1], Zhiyao Teng[1], Jian Chen[2], Yifan Wu[1],
Rui Gong[1], and Jiansu Pu[1(✉)]

[1] CompleX Lab, Web Sciences Center, Big Data Research Center,
University of Electronic Science and Technology of China, Chengdu 611731, China
changjiang.wen@foxmail.com, zhiyao.teng@foxmail.com,
yifan.wu_yfw@foxmail.com, rui.gong_gr@foxmail.com, jiansu.pu@foxmail.com
[2] Graduate School of Information Science and Technology,
University of Tokyo, Tokyo 153-8505, Japan
kenn.chen@hotmail.com
http://www.labcomplex.org

Abstract. The in-depth understanding of the reason why users contribute to the check-in records is of great value in a variety of applications, such as transportation system design, information recommendation, and business intelligence. The widespread application of social media has brought about large-scale and fined-grained data for the exploration of user check-in records from multi-perspectives. However, it is still an arduous task to gain insight into users' check-in behavior due to the complexity and multi-dimensions of the data nature. In this paper, a novel visual analytics system, socialRadius, is proposed to interactively explore spatio-temporal features of check-in behaviors for particular groups and active users extracted from the group. The design in the paper focuses on two major characteristics of check-in data for the specific group: spatio-temporal features and check-in activities. The integration of visualization techniques with new designs has offered us the opportunities to explore and identify the potential patterns based on these two major components. Besides, case studies on real check-in data demonstrate the effectiveness of the system in exploring spatio-temporal features for specific groups.

Keywords: Visual analysis · Spatial and temporal behavior · Social media · Check-in records

1 Introduction

Over the past few years, a great number of user check-in data have been collected through online communication system and location-based services, such as Foursquare, Facebook Places, and Weibo Locations (Chinese Microblog). Such data contain the information about the place the users visit and the activities they have been involved in. The comprehensive check-in data provide us with

© Springer International Publishing AG 2016
Y. Luo (Ed.): CDVE 2016, LNCS 9929, pp. 300–308, 2016.
DOI: 10.1007/978-3-319-46771-9_39

an unprecedented opportunity to explain why users check in at certain places and times with specific activities, which is of great social and business values, such as point of interest (POI) study, transportation system design, and information recommendation. However, it is still a challenging task to achieve an intuitive understanding about the checking-in behaviors of users from spatio-temporal features for specific groups. To best of our knowledges, there are no effective methods which can be employed to cope with the noisy, sparse, and multi-dimensional data for most of current studies.

In this paper, a visual analytics system, called socialRadius, has been developed to capture the behavior features of specific user groups from their check-in data. The system socialRadius, aimed at answering when and where a check-in is occurred, as well as what reason results in it, has been designed to highlight two major features contained in the data: spatio-temporal patterns and check-in activities (*e.g.*, having dinner, working, or exercising). To achieve an intuitive representation, a design enhanced with new features to incorporate the well-established visualization methods, has been proposed to enable the combination of various spatial, temporal, and social attributes display. Meanwhile, it can support the function of exploring the user features from multiple aspects. Thus, socialRadius can facilitate the intuitive comparisons of check-in behaviors at different locations and time scales, of different activities, and from various active users. The output of the system in the paper directly assists the complex analytical tasks such as periodicity pattern exploration, density distribution analysis, and anomaly detection. As for the system mentioned above, it has been deployed in field to demonstrate the usage and effectiveness of our system with real check-in data from millions of users. Interesting findings are obtained and discussed for future research.

To conclude, the major contributions of this work are shown as follows: (1) **System.** The design and implementation of an intuitive and informative visual analytics system, which aims to study the characteristics of social media data, so as to further facilitate the analysis of checking in behavior and uncover people's spatio-temporal patterns from the data. (2) **Visualization.** Several visualization designs enhanced with new features to investigate the user checking in behaviors from the aspects of spatial, temporal, and activity features on specific group, thus exploring so as the reason why users check in. (3) **Evaluation.** Case studies based on real check-in data that demonstrate how our system can guide users to gain insightful recognitions from different aspects of human behavior.

2   Related Work

Visual Analysis of Social Check-in Data. As check-in data from the public have become increasingly available for researchers to analyze, recently, there have been numerous works finding new ways to extract various insights on relations between online and offline interactions ([6,9]), large scale urban dynamics (Noulas et al. [13]; Chang and Sun [3]) and the effects which can be exerted by the location technologies on human behaviors ([4,12]). In [5], researchers utilized millions of check-in users to create a dynamic view of the workings and characters of activities. Based on frequency and a variation heat map of check-in data from the Chinese Jiepang website, Wang et al. [16] proposed a hot spot detection method showing that the check-in data have a high correlation with the urban economy and population. Kim and Xing [11] visualized brand associations from web community photos.

Spatio-temporal Features Exploration. Abstraction and aggregation methods are commonly used in spatio-temporal data analysis and visualization [8]. Crnovrsanin et al. [7] introduced a proximity-based visualization technique to discover the human behavior patterns from movement data. Andrienko et al. [1] systematically summarized possible aggregation methods of movement data. Scheepens et al. [14] presented a density map of vessel movement data, in which process color is used to encode temporal dimensions. An integrative approach was employed in [2] by combining self-organizing map (SOM) with a set of interactive visualization tools. GeoTime [10] displays the 2D path in a 3D space. Tominski et al. [15] proposed a 2D/3D hybrid display stacked trajectories as bands in the third dimension while time is integrated by appropriate ordering of trajectory bands.

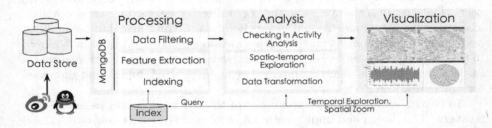

Fig. 1. System overview and data processing pipeline.

3 Visualization Design and System Implementation

The visual analytics system, socialRadius, is designed to aid analysts in understanding what has motived users to contribute check-in records in social media. Thus, capturing how the temporal patterns (*e.g.* frequency, duration), spatial patterns (*e.g.* density, radius of gyration, and traveling distances), and activity patterns (*e.g.* the activities they involved, the interaction around) plays a vital role in revealing the insight of the users' check-in behaviors. As illustrated in Fig. 1 the system starts with the data storage module. All the collected online check-in records are first stored in an offline procedure at this module. Consequently, these data are further processed in the processing module through filtering, feature extraction, and indexing. The analysis module conducts activity analysis and some specific computing tasks. After all these procedures, the results are visualized in the visualization module. The user interface of the social-Radius system consists of multiple components, as illustrated in Fig. 2.

Group Map View (*a*) **and User Map View** (*b*). To support an intuitive spatial exploration, two maps, namely group map (Fig. 2(*a*)) and user map (Fig. 2(*b*)), along with rich interactions are presented to support an in-depth analysis. For both views, the design focuses on the display of users' location from check-in data. Circles are used to indicate the corresponding geographic place. The circle's radius is proportional to the number of check-ins at the place. The style of the circle discriminates whether the check-in has a detailed content. Circles colored in orange encode the check-in records with posted content, while circles colored in blue not. Meanwhile, the check-ins' density distribution is revealed through a heat map layout. Compared with group map view, user map view pays more attention to the certain active users of a specific group. In addition, rich interactions are provided to link the group map with the user map views for further exploration of user spatial features.

Preferences Select Area (*c*). In order to explore the spatio-temporal characteristics of a specific group at an certain time period, the activity type and time span shall be chosen first. The preferences selection area (Fig. 2(*c*)) contains two parameter setting parts and one drawing function selection part. Besides, the paper defines the activity type in *Activities* window and time period in *Time Setting* window. *Activities* window supports multi-selection and hourly data visualization can be set in the *Time Setting* window.

Theme River View (*d*). To provide an overall trend of users' check-in, including that the trend change of the involved activity over time, and the temporal distribution based on different time scales, the paper extends the theme river design, and makes it present within the view. These features facilitate experts to perform an in-depth analysis on check-in behavior from temporal features. Furthermore, coordinate axes have been used to display the activity's trend change over time. The horizontal axis encodes the time line, while the vertical axis represents the number of corresponding check-in. To explore the periodicity of different time granularity, method with various time scales, such as *e.g.* weekly and daily scales, have been adopted in the view. Furthermore, the detailed information can be obtained by zooming in. In addition, trends of multiple activities can be shown and analyzed simultaneously.

Packed Circle View (*e*). In our system, both User Map View and Mircoblog Content View can be used to explore spatio-temporal features of check-in behaviors from different perspectives. However, a further investigation shall be conducted on the diversity of users who have ever checked in the same region, while comparison is made on the their characteristics based on the involved activity types and records left for each activity. As check-in records showing hierarchical structure in both user and activity, so it is proper to adopt circular layout design to visualize the results. Beside, the paper extends the circle packing design algorithm here. In this design (Fig. 3(*e*) and (*f*)), the paper presents four kinds

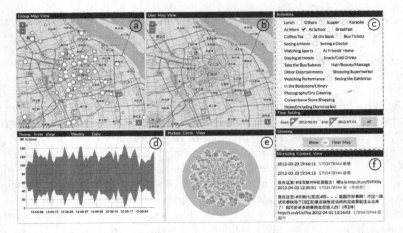

Fig. 2. The user interface of socialRadius system consists of six major views labeled by the letters $a - f$. (Color figure online)

of circular design, including the **Spot Circle**, the **User Circle**, the **Activity Circle**, and the **Check-in Circle**. Spot circle presents all the users who have checked in the corresponding spot in the group map view. User circle means a single user, whose size is determined by the times he/she checked in this spot. In this sense, it is easy to identify those most frequently checking in and the activities they prefer. Moreover, activity circle shows the details of user's activities. Each check-in circle encodes a record of a specific activity for the user. Meanwhile, rich interactions are provided here. When we click on one user circle, all check-in records of the user will be shown in the user map view. At the same time, the activity circle will zoom in and the name of activity will be shown at the center of the circle after clicking the activity circle.

Microblog Content View (f). We can take the advantages of the rich context posted to facilitate the analysis. Content details posted by the users can be found and explored in the Microblog Content View (Fig. 2(f)).

4   Case Study

Data Description and Results Analysis. To evaluate the system's effectiveness and availability, four case studies are conducted based on microblog data from Sina collected from Dec. 1, 2011 to Nov. 30, 2012 in Shanghai, China. Understanding the reason why users check in is of great value, which helps explain many social phenomena and uncover the regularities of human behavior. However, it is difficult to obtain direct solution to this problem for the complex factors affecting human behaviors. It can be observed that each individual has his/her main social role during a certain time period, such as students, commuters, and inhabitants. Based on this common sense, users are classified into different groups based on the activities chosen. Then, the paper explores the specific group from the spatio-temporal features and activities details with post contents. Beside, the paper focuses on the active users extracted from the group and tries to show their characteristics with visualization methods, which provides possible insights for domain experts to verify hypotheses.

Case (1) Exploration of Students' Check-in. First, we chooses the activity type 'At School' from May 1, 2012 to July 1, 2012. As illustrated in the Fig. 3(c), it can be easily found that most of check-ins occurred at sparse area before gathering together at disperse spots. In order to gain deeper insights, we click on some spots, while details of the corresponding posts are displayed in the microblog content view. By analyzing the details mentioned above, almost every spot taken place in or near a campus can thus be found. The characteristics of users' daily behaviors have a very obviously fluctuation and periodicity pattern, with the ups and downs of the curve of the theme river (Fig. 3(a)) and (b)) indicating the fluctuation of check-in behavior over time. In addition, the curve shows a strong periodical pattern over weeks, while some interesting findings can be obtained from other time scales. It is obvious that more check-ins recorded on weekends than weekdays, and the peak point is on Saturday. Students may go out for fun at weekends to leave more chances to be located. The content of posts further verifies the hypothesis.

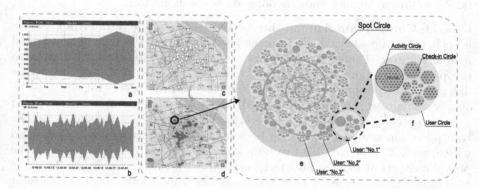

Fig. 3. The process of spatiotemporal exploration of a specific group and individual feature exploration of the most active user.

Case (2) Exploration of the Most Active User. As shown in the Fig. 3(d), an interesting spot (highlighted in a black circle) can be observed. The corresponding packed circle view (Fig. 3(e)) and posts are presented after we selected the spot. The packed circle view extends from inner to outside with the lowest check-in user and end with the most check-in user. It spins along a counterclockwise direction to encode the ascending order of the users based on their number of check-in records. Several outermost circles have been chosen to study with the ranking from first three places in the records since more data can be provided

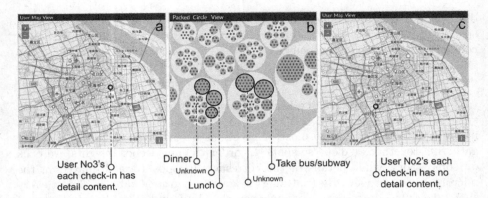

Fig. 4. The comparison between two active users based on Packed Circle and User Map: (a) user No3's User Map View; (b) Packed Circle View of user No2 and No3; (c) user No2's User Map View.

to portray the use's behavior. These outermost users are labeled as 'No1, No2, No3' in the descending order. It is clear that user No1's check-ins distributed (Fig. 5(a)) over a wide area, his/her most frequent visit place is his/her home according to packed circle view (Fig. 3(f)), and his/her other activities such as take bus/subway, dinner and schooling are equal in general.

Case (3) Comparison Among the Active Users in the Same Spot. Active users in the group labeled by location and grouped by activity have demonstrated unique features. Therefore, user pairs are compared with each other through the packed circle and user map view together. For example, user No2 seems like a taciturn person, for all his check-ins are with no posts (Fig. 4(c)), so he simply submitted the places he visited. Moreover, his most frequent recorded activity is taking bus/subway (Fig. 4(b)), which implies his demand for public transportation system by traveling far away from his starting point. Compared with user No2, user No3 likes to be a more active user in social media, as he posted contents at most of his check-ins (Fig. 4(a)), thus revealing the details of his track. Unlike user No2, user No3 looks like a food lover, because his most check-in activities are dinner and lunch (Fig. 4(b)). Besides, it may indicate he is searching for more interaction online and more likely to trust or find communities online.

Case (4) Interesting Findings of the Certain User. Although the activity types 'At School', 'Home', and 'At Work' have shown the similar results, there are also some interesting phenomena. In this case, the 'At Work' activity type is chosen, while the same time range as case study 1 can be used. Then, we choose a user in the packed circle. As can be seen in (Fig. 5(b)), all his check-ins are shown in the user map view. Obviously, this user's major check-ins occurred in the black circle, but it is also found that two check-ins occurred far away from the area. Actually these two interesting check-ins have puzzled us. Why does the user check in at such a faraway place from his routine? The microblog content

Fig. 5. The User Map View of (a) user No1 and (b) the user with interesting check-in features.

view answers the question, and the user goes for a meeting at the place circled by the left bottom dashed circle place. Besides, he was waiting a flight in the right. In summary, the system can effectively detect the abnormal check-in behaviors of specific users and deliver a reasonable explanation from their social content online.

5 Conclusion

In this paper, a novel visual analytics system, socialRadius, has been presented to facilitate the analysis and visualization of user checking in behavior interactively and progressively. It is found that this design is flexible in scale and is compatible to integrate into graphs or tables. As for the sophisticated design with enhanced new features, it can help experts or analysts explore and identify the potential patterns from check-in behaviors for particular groups and selected active users based on these two major components: patio-temporal features and check-in activities. In addition, the system is tested on a real-life SinaWeibo dataset collected from millions of users, with some interesting findings obtained. The experimental results have further confirmed the effectiveness and efficiency of the proposed visual analysis method.

Acknowledgments. This research was supported in part by the National Natural Science Foundation of China, Grant No. 61502083. The authors wish to thank the anonymous reviewers for their valuable comments.

References

1. Andrienko, G., Andrienko, N.: Spatio-temporal aggregation for visual analysis of movements. In: IEEE Symposium on Visual Analytics Science and Technology, VAST 2008, pp. 51–58. IEEE (2008)
2. Andrienko, G., Andrienko, N., Bremm, S., Schreck, T., Von Landesberger, T., Bak, P., Keim, D.: Space-in-time and time-in-space self-organizing maps for exploring spatiotemporal patterns. In: Computer Graphics Forum, vol. 29, pp. 913–922. Wiley Online Library (2010)

3. Chang, J., Sun, E.: Location 3: how users share and respond to location-based data on social networking sites. In: Proceedings of the Fifth International AAAI Conference on Weblogs and Social Media, pp. 74–80 (2011)

4. Cramer, H., Rost, M., Holmquist, L.E.: Performing a check-in: emerging practices, norms and 'conflicts' in location-sharing using foursquare. In: Proceedings of the 13th International Conference on Human Computer Interaction with Mobile Devices and Services, pp. 57–66. ACM (2011)

5. Cranshaw, J., Schwartz, R., Hong, J.I., Sadeh, N.: The livehoods project: utilizing social media to understand the dynamics of a city. In: International AAAI Conference on Weblogs and Social Media, p. 58 (2012)

6. Cranshaw, J., Toch, E., Hong, J., Kittur, A., Sadeh, N.: Bridging the gap between physical location and online social networks. In: Proceedings of the 12th ACM International Conference on Ubiquitous Computing, pp. 119–128. ACM (2010)

7. Crnovrsanin, T., Muelder, C., Correa, C., Ma, K.L.: Proximity-based visualization of movement trace data. In: IEEE Symposium on Visual Analytics Science and Technology, VAST 2009, pp. 11–18. IEEE (2009)

8. Demšar, U., Buchin, K., Cagnacci, F., Safi, K., Speckmann, B., Van de Weghe, N., Weiskopf, D., Weibel, R.: Analysis and visualisation of movement: an interdisciplinary review. Mov. Ecol. **3**(1), 1–24 (2015)

9. Gordon, E., de Souza e Silva, A.: Net Locality: Why Location Matters in a Networked World. Wiley, Malden (2011)

10. Kapler, T., Wright, W.: Geotime information visualization. Inf. Vis. **4**(2), 136–146 (2005)

11. Kim, G., Xing, E.P.: Visualizing brand associations from web community photos. In: Proceedings of the 7th ACM International Conference on Web Search and Data Mining, pp. 623–632. ACM (2014)

12. Lindqvist, J., Cranshaw, J., Wiese, J., Hong, J., Zimmerman, J.: I'm the mayor of my house: examining why people use foursquare-a social-driven location sharing application. In: Proceedings of the SIGCHI Conference on Human Factors in Computing Systems, pp. 2409–2418. ACM (2011)

13. Noulas, A., Scellato, S., Mascolo, C., Pontil, M.: Exploiting semantic annotations for clustering geographic areas and users in location-based social networks. Soc. Mob. Web **11**, 02 (2011)

14. Scheepens, R., Willems, N., van de Wetering, H., Van Wijk, J.J.: Interactive visualization of multivariate trajectory data with density maps. In: 2011 IEEE Pacific Visualization Symposium (PacificVis), pp. 147–154. IEEE (2011)

15. Tominski, C., Schumann, H., Andrienko, G., Andrienko, N.: Stacking-based visualization of trajectory attribute data. IEEE Trans. Vis. Comput. Graph. **18**(12), 2565–2574 (2012)

16. Wang, M., Qin, L., Hu, Q.: Data mining and visualization research of check-in data. In: 2012 20th International Conference on Geoinformatics (GEOINFORMATICS), pp. 1–4. IEEE (2012)

Prediction System for Decision-Making to Improve the Road Environment

Yu-Mi Song[1] and Sung-Ah Kim[1,2(✉)]

[1] Department of Convergence Engineering for Future City, Sungkyunkwan University,
Suwon, Republic of Korea
{hanimyu,sakim}@skku.edu
[2] Department of Architecture, Sungkyunkwan University, Suwon, Republic of Korea

Abstract. The aim of this research was to find the relations among traffic volume, travel speed, and road connectivity in order to predict the traffic congestion. The result showed that when a road has higher connectivity, the travel speed goes lower. Therefore, it was assumed that the congestion on the target area should be affected by high connectivity. The visualization of this prediction would significantly affect the urban planning that is related with the stakeholders of different kind.

Keywords: Traffic congestion · Urban data · Urban information visualization · Space syntax

1 Introduction

The increase in the number of vehicles causes numerous urban problems such as environmental pollution or traffic accident. Traffic congestion is also one of the critical challenges that make urban life inefficient. Predicting congestion or suggesting alternative routes design is a necessity for better urban planning and operation process such as constructing new roads and implementing new transportation system in the cities. The prediction of congestion using numerical statistics, however, is difficult for multi participants to easily understand. In addition, it is hard to compare the prediction of congestion using numerical statistics with the real time data. Predicting and visualizing traffic congestion could help to quickly compare with the current situation and to provide better understanding for the wide range of people. Therefore, prediction and visualization of congestion is essential.

2 Objective

Space syntax refers to the relationship between space and society [1]. The space is an analyzed numerical value. Using these values, space syntax is used as a method that predicts the pedestrian and vehicle flow according to the layout of road in area of urban planning.

© Springer International Publishing AG 2016
Y. Luo (Ed.): CDVE 2016, LNCS 9929, pp. 309–312, 2016.
DOI: 10.1007/978-3-319-46771-9_40

In this paper, the space syntax is used to draw segment map and to calculate the road connectivity. Then the connectivity is compared with the empirical data of traffic volume and travel speed to analyze the relationships. The ultimate objective of this paper is to utilize the empirical data and space syntax method to visualize the road environment of city according to road layout, and to predict the traffic congestion.

3 Traffic Congestion Prediction

3.1 Space Syntax: Segment Map

Space syntax is described as a method that investigates the relationship between space and society from the perspective of structure of space in all its diverse forms: buildings, settlements, cities, or even landscapes [2]. The general idea is that spaces can be broken down into components and then represented as maps that describe the relative connectivity of those spaces using axial line. The connectivity intuitively shows the correlation to pedestrian and vehicle flows [3].

Yet the axial line has some differences with the real road sections. In the real roads, the regulations of roads are changed by the surrounding environment. For example, there is a speed-limit on the roads near by the schools.

The axial line does not consider the possible sections that could have been generated by a single axial line; one axial line may have more than one section on the same road. Therefore, segment map is used in this paper. The segment map breaks axial map into segments and connects it together as a network [4].

The major roads of one city in Republic of Korea were chosen as a target. The map was retrieved from Open Street Map (https://www.openstreetmap.org/) and the DepthmapX program (https://varoudis.github.io/depthmapX/) was applied to calculate the connectivity (Fig. 1).

Fig. 1. Segment map of road's connectivity

3.2 Relation Between Road Traffic and Spatial Connectivity

The three relation graphs were drawn to examine the relations: traffic volume and travel speed, traffic volume and connectivity, travel speed and connectivity (Fig. 2).

The results showed the traffic volume and travel speed did not have a relationship (Fig. 2a). There also was not a causal relationship between connectivity and traffic volume (Fig. 2b). Even if the number of vehicles on the road increased, the travel speed is not affected. Although the road had a high connectivity, the number of vehicles which passed through the road did not increase.

Nevertheless, connectivity and travel speed have a negative relationship (Fig. 2c), meaning that the higher connectivity a road has, the slower travel speed became.

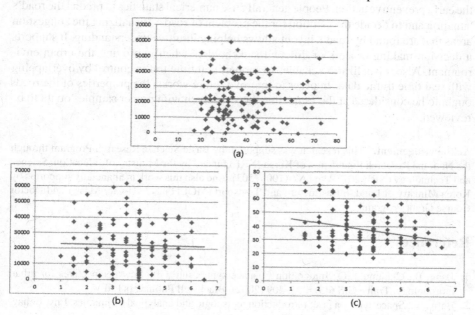

Fig. 2. The relation graphs: (a) traffic volume and travel speed, (b) traffic volume and connectivity, (c) travel speed and connectivity.

3.3 Interpretation of Graph

Generally, the congestion is understood as the situation where there are "too many cars" on the road. But the congestion is the average delay by other vehicles [5]. In fact, there is no relationship between the traffic volume and travel speed. This extraneousness is considered as a result that is inferred from the width and length of road. Also traffic volume has no relationship with connectivity since the reason for passing through a road is influenced by the purpose of passing and surrounding environment.

The connectivity, however, has a relationship with travel speed. When the connectivity of road is increased, the travel speed decreases. Therefore a section with slow travel speed could be predicted by the connectivity of road. The measure of congestion is the difference between the speed at which a vehicle could move without delay caused by other traffic and the actual average traffic speed [5]. In other words, a section with slow travel speed has the higher probability of traffic congestion. The probability of congestion is increased in the road with high connectivity. Conclusively, the congested section of a road would be found by the structure or layout of roads.

4 Conclusion

The travel speed is predicted by the connectivity of roads using segment map analysis. The roads that have slow travel speed could be found before congestion occurs, allowing the early preventive action. People generally use numerical statistics to predict the road's situation and to decide the solution for the problem of roads. Visualizing the congestion areas that are found by road's layout allows helping intuitive understanding. It supports a decision-making process of different stakeholders when improving the urban environment. Also, visualization enables to support real time traffic control by overlapping with real time traffic data. In order to improve future works, the properties of the roads ought to be considered at the same time more research with proper samples ought to be reviewed.

Acknowledgement. This research was supported by Basic Science Research Program through the National Research Foundation of Korea (NRF) funded by the Ministry of Education, Science and Technology (NRF-2013R1A1A2A10057503). And also this work is financially supported by Korea Ministry of Land, Infrastructure and Transport (MOLIT) as 「U-City Master and Doctor Course Grant Program」.

References

1. Jiang, B., Claramunt, C.: Integration of space syntax into GIS: new perspectives for urban morphology. Trans. GIS **6**(3), 295–309 (2002). Blackwell Publishers Ltd
2. Bafna, S.: Space syntax a brief introduction to its logic and analytical techniques. Env. Behav. **35**(1), 17–29 (2003). Sage Publications
3. Jiang, B.: Ranking spaces for predicting human movement in an urban environment. Int. J. Geog. Inf. Sci. **23**(7), 823–837 (2009). Taylor & Francis, Inc., Bristol, PA, USA
4. Turner, A.: Depthmap 4 - A Researcher's Handbook. Bartlett School of Graduate Studies, UCL, London (2004)
5. Verbit, G.P.: The urban transportation problem. Univ. Pennsylvania Law Rev. **124**(2), 368–489 (1975). The University of Pennsylvania Law Review

eduCircle: Visualizing Spatial Temporal Features of Student Performance from Campus Activity and Consumption Data

Yifan Wu, Rui Gong, Yi Cao, Changjiang Wen, Zhiyao Teng,
and Jiansu Pu[✉]

CompleX Lab, Web Sciences Center, Big Data Research Center,
University of Electronic Science and Technology of China, Chengdu 611731, China
yifan.wu_yfw@foxmail.com, rui.gong_gr@foxmail.com, yi.cao_yc@foxmail.com,
changjiang.wen@foxmail.com, zhiyao.teng@foxmail.com,
jiansu.pu@foxmail.com
http://www.labcomplex.org

Abstract. Nowadays, academic performance analysis has become increasingly critical for educational institutes, schools, and universities. Linked with academic achievements the academic performance is widely accepted and used as the assessment indicator for the quality of education. Therefore, it is important for educators and analysts to explore the behavior of enrolled students and investigate the factors affecting their performance. However, due to the existing factors concerning the investigation, such as social interactions, environment influence, and personal reasons related to very limited data collected, the task mentioned above is really challenging. Smart card data used on campus are able to not only provide both activity information and spatial temporal features for enrolled students, but also open a great opportunity for the further understanding about academic performance. In this paper, eduCircle, a visual analytic system, is presented to analyze student behaviors with academic performance based on smart card data. Three sophisticated designs with integrated visualization, mobility map, temporal analysis, and sequence views, have been proposed to analyze spatial temporal features in different time scales. Furthermore, several experiments have been conducted to explore the different student groups in a spatial temporal way. At last, some interesting findings are identified, which have further proved the effectiveness of the system.

Keywords: Visual analysis · Education data · Student performance · Spatial temporal features · Big data

1 Introduction

The measurement of student performance in school plays an important role in education quality assessment. Therefore, recent studies have witnessed considerable attention paid to investigating academic performance. The rapid development of information technologies has resulted in large volume of student data

© Springer International Publishing AG 2016
Y. Luo (Ed.): CDVE 2016, LNCS 9929, pp. 313–321, 2016.
DOI: 10.1007/978-3-319-46771-9_41

collecting and storing in various formats, which has further made the performance factors analysis in a more comprehensive way possible. Moreover, the smart card data analysis has a wide range of applications prospects. It can help tracking student location when used as access control for admittance to restricted buildings, dormitories, libraries, and other facilities. Every day, student card systems, which can generate a vast amount of information about student behavior in various data formats, bring about a great opportunity to explore student behaviors with their academic performances. Analyzing student card data facilitates the understanding of student behaviors, especially the spatial temporal features, as well as gains insights into behavioral differences among various student groups. The datasets can provide valuable analytic resources for student behaviors analysis on one hand, while on the other hand, it can also pose a direct challenge for the useful knowledge extraction from the large-scale spatial temporal data. Therefore, it is significant to seek for an understandable method to further comprehend the data and seek the patterns of different students. Moreover, data visualization provides a great method for the data demonstration and results presentation via an intuitive and understandable way. However, it is an intricate task to design an effective visualization system. There are three problems required to be tackled: (1) Providing a comprehensive and user-friendly system for educators to explore the student card data; (2) Designing appropriate graphs to fully represent the spatial temporal characteristic of the data; (3) Containing different time scale explorations.

To address these problems, we take the advantages of the visual representations and interaction techniques to explore, and analyze student behaviors. In this paper a visual analytic system, the eduCircle, has been presented to interactively explore spatial temporal features of student behaviors based on the smart card data. Moreover, three views, namely mobility map view, temporal view, and sequence view are presented to visualize behaviors on different scales and try to identify certain patterns shared by different groups. Our sophisticated visual analytics system is able to convey a large amount of information in a more efficient way with less cognitive effort. In the experiment section, behavioral data are associated with students academic performance data by choosing 1000 top students and 1000 bottom students from the overall Grade Point Average (GPA). Some interesting findings between the two groups are identified, thus proving the effectiveness of the system.

The major contributions can be summarized as follows: (1) **System.** The design and implementation of a visual analytic system with integrated visualization, eduCircle, to explore the student campus behavioral patterns based on the large-scale student card data. (2) **Visualization.** Several visualization designs have been enhanced with new features, including student mobility map view, temporal view chart, and sequence chart with diversity encoding, to reveal spatial temporal characteristics for smart card data, as well as facilitate multi-perspective pattern discovery and exploration. (3) **Evaluation.** Case studies based on one semester data illustrate several interesting behavior pattern differences between top and bottom student group; meanwhile the studies mentioned above can facilitate the analysis of student behaviors associated with affecting factors.

2   Related Work

Education Data Analysis. The process of learning facilitating or the knowledge acquisition is usually considered as Education [7]. It is important to investigate the factors affecting the quality of education by exploring student performance. Previously, there have been numerous studies exploring the factors which might be related to students academic performance [1,2,4,5,10–12]. Moreover, according to psychologists in 1990, self-regulation [14], self-efficacy, and test anxiety learning have been confirmed as the best predictors for the performance [13]. Furthermore, it is argued that self-discipline even outdoes IQ in terms of predicting the academic performance according to Duckworth [8]. According to Hijazi and Naqvi, students academic performance was highly related to mothers education and students family income [9]. Moreover, Galit [3] conducted a case study to analyze student learning behavior in order to predict the results and risk for students before the final exams. In the past five years, remarkable attention has been paid to the studies of MOOC. Fu et al. [15] utilized the online web clicksteams data to help instructors and educators gain deep insights into the learning behaviors of MOOC student. In addition, forum interactions have been adopted by Dennen [6] to help course instructors improve their teaching.

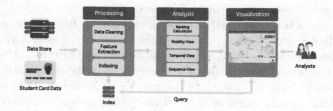

Fig. 1. System overview and data processing pipeline.

3   Visualization Design System Implementation

The design goal of this visual analytics system is to help the educators explore the student behavior data interactively and progressively, in order to further gain insights into factors affecting the academic performance. Figure 1 illustrates the system architecture and the data processing pipeline. The system consists of four modules: (1) the data storage module, (2) the processing module, (3) the analysis module, and (4) the visualization module. The data storage module stores all the raw data of students smart card, while in the processing module, collected

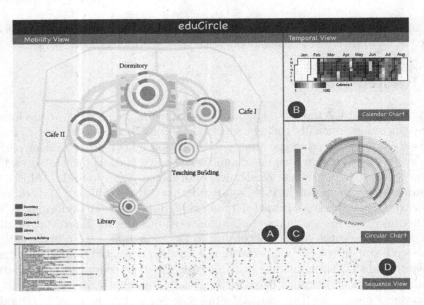

Fig. 2. The user interface of eduCircle system consists of three major views labeled by the characters $A - D$. Section A is the mobility view. Temporal view contains calendar chart (B) and circular chart (C). The sequence view (D) includes two parts: sequence view on the right and condensed one on the left.

data have been subsequently cleaned, indexed, and feature extracted. The analysis module conducts students GPA ranking calculation first to extract top and bottom student groups before presenting the computing tasks, *e.g.* anomalous attendance accumulation, location-based clustering, and filtering. After all these procedures, the results are visualized in three views of the visualization module: Mobility View, Temporal View, and Sequence View. Moreover, the user interface of the eduCircle system consists of multiple components as illustrated in Fig. 2 with labels $A - D$ representing four different charts in three views. Mobility view presents the geographic flow of the selected group of students among recorded locations. Temporal view is integrated with calendar chart and circular chart to demonstrate the temporal features of students from processed data. As for the sequence view, it aims to investigate the trajectory or visited place sequence of specific users in the group.

Circular Chart. In order to fully represent the periodic characteristic of student behavior from smart card data, the circular design is adopted in the temporal view. The chart covers five parts displaying the statistical information of five different locations respectively. Each sector in the graph is designed to encode one period of time. Moreover, color is encoding the popularity of a location in a specific time period, with the darker sector indicating more smart card data generated by students in this location. Furthermore, analysts are also allowed to choose different time scales for different tasks. The part C in Fig. 2 is a circular chart presenting the average student behaviors within 24 h for a semester in different locations on campus.

Calendar Chart. Although circular graph is appropriate to represent behavioral changes within 24 h in a selected semester, the daily variations are still hard to be revealed. Therefore, the calendar chart is introduced to show the statistical changes over the student behavior records of a semester. The chart can illustrate how student behavior varies with the day of the week and how it trends over the semester in different locations. In this chart, a black frame encodes a month and each square in the chart represents a day. The color of the cells encodes the number of the student records collected of a certain location in one day. Besides, the days of the week are labeled with the first letters of Sunday through Saturday at the first column of the left side. Thus, the difference of the temporal pattern between weekday and weekend can be easily identified.

Mobility View. This view is designed to demonstrate the student mobility flows on campus. For each visual item, a circular composition layout is used to show flowing connections between locations and visually organized according to the real campus map in Fig. 3. Color is used to display five different facilities on campus. Grey trajectories connect different locations. Grey will disappear and show the original color with the locations selected. The area of the circle in the item center shows the total amount of student card data over the semester. The outer and inner rings indicate student flow out/in direction. Relative sizes of pieces on rings encode the ratio of students flow out to or into one specific location. Besides, the width of the curves between different locations displays the number of student flow, while the color of the curve also indicates the flow

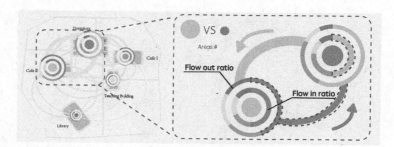

Fig. 3. Mobility view is designed to represent student mobility flows. Five different colors are used to encode five different facilities. The area of the circle shows the amount of student card usage. Grey trajectories connect different locations, and the grey will disappear and show the original color with the locations selected. Two locations are selected and extracted in the dotted box on the right. The curve and destination share the same color. Furthermore, the circle contains outer and inner rings, which represent student flow/out direction. As for different pieces on the ring, they encode the ratio of student flow. Three parts, surrounded by dotted lines, represent student mobility from cafeteria II to dormitory in three different ways. (Color figure online)

direction. In the dotted box, labeled with dotted lines, three parts all share a common message: student mobilities from cafeteria II to dormitory.

Sequence View. The sequence view is designed to provide more details for the exploration of student mobility patterns. The mobility view is an overall analysis for student mobility of different groups considering multiple perspectives. The sequence view presents more details for further explorations. At the right side of the sequence view, each row encodes the behavior sequence of one student; each column encodes one hour in a day of the week. Color of cell encodes corresponding locations, with the white square indicating the lack of records at that time. Moreover, in the left part, we gets rid of white squares and combines all the colored square together to get condense chart, which aims to explore the student mobility patterns. Different days are separated by black squares.

4   Case Study

Data Description. We are authorized to utilize a set of anonymous data from the Institute of Educational Big Data of University of Electronic Science and Technology of China (UESTC). In this study, analysis on the consumption data, library check-in data from smart card data including the time, location, and encrypt student IDs is associated with academic performance records extracted

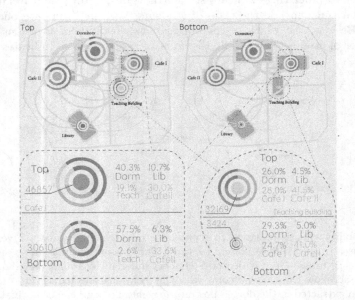

Fig. 4. The comparison between 1000 top and 1000 bottom students flow among locations in one semester. Statistical information is listed, followed by the comparison to identify quite different mobility patterns between two groups. Statistical information of cafeteria I is shown in dotted square box on the left. On the right lies the teaching building information. (Color figure online)

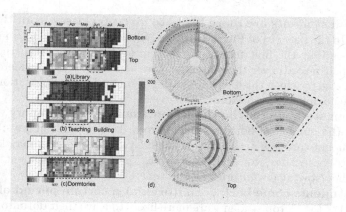

Fig. 5. The comparison between 1000 top and 1000 bottom students with different charts. On the left, (a), (b) and (c) are the calendar charts of different locations between two groups. The major difference is highlighted by dotted boxes. The part (d) is the circular charts between two groups. The dormitory section of top students is extracted for further exploration.

from students final GPA during (2009 − 2012). In this section, 1000 top students and 1000 bottom students are selected to testify the effectiveness of this system.

(1) **Going to the library or not might have limited influence on improving academic performance of bottom students.** In the mobility view of Fig. 4, comparison has been made on the mobility views of top and bottom students, and statistical information of outer rings is shown in the dotted boxes. In the box of cafeteria I, the most obvious difference lies in that the yellow piece in bottom students is much smaller, which means there are rarely students from this group going to the teaching building after their dinner. This difference can be further revealed by the area of yellow circle in round dotted box. The record number of top students is ten times larger than that of bottom students. However, it is unexpected to find that the ratios of library for the both groups are similar. This phenomenon might indicate that going to library modestly improves their poor performance.

(2) **Top students are more cramming for their final exams.** It can be easily observed in Fig. 5 that, students from the bottom group have fewer records in the library, compared with students from the top group. The burst situation in library can be clearly identified for students from top GPA group. This phenomenon can be further demonstrated in the dashed box. In the calendar view, for the top students, they have much more zeal of cramming for final exam than the bottom students. Besides, studying in the library on weekends is an outstanding phenomenon for top student group while the bottom student group seldom goes to the library except during the final periods.

(3) **Bottom students are more likely to give up classes from the beginning.** In the part (b) of Fig. 5, teaching building records for bottom students exists only at the first month of the semester. However, top students can keep their records over three months. Class attendance is considered in final scores, due to which this behavior patterns might be an explanation for their poor academic performance.

(4) **Bottom students maybe the Indoorsmen.** In the dormitory view (c) in Fig. 5, the number of bottom students records is even seven days; while the top students are less active during weekdays. Top students may leave their dormitory weekdays for study. However, for the bottom students, it seems that they stay at dormitories all the time.

(5) **Top students come back dormitories at a certain period of time.** In the (d) of Fig. 5, top students are more likely to leave their dormitory records during the 10 o clock. In contrast, a similar pattern cannot be found for bottom students. This regularity indicates that top students might come back to dormitories later. It can be inferred that top students keep studying late, which can be viewed as their self-discipline. According to Duckworth [8], this self-discipline might explain for their excellent academic performance.

5   Conclusion

In this paper, a visual analytics system, eduCircle, has been presented to facilitate the student academic performance analysis and exploration based on smart card data. In the paper, the sophisticated design is flexible in scale and compatible to integrate into graphs for assisting statistical analysis. Based on the test on the student data over one semester, the experimental results confirm the effectiveness and efficiency of the proposed visual analysis task. Furthermore, according to the analysis of the results, our system is capable of effectively comparing and analyzing complex educational spatial temporal patterns.

Acknowledgment. This research was supported in part by the National Natural Science Foundation of China, Grant No. 61502083. The authors wish to thank the anonymous reviewers for their valuable comments.

References

1. Al-Radaideh, Q.A., Al-Shawakfa, E.M., Al-Najjar, M.I.: Mining student data using decision trees. In: International Arab Conference on Information Technology (ACIT 2006), Yarmouk University, Jordan (2006)
2. Ayesha, S., Mustafa, T., Sattar, A.R., Khan, M.I.: Data mining model for higher education system. Eur. J. Sci. Res. **43**(1), 24–29 (2010)
3. Ben-Zadok, G., Hershkovitz, A., Mintz, E., Nachmias, R.: Examining online learning processes based on log files analysis: a case study. In: 5th International Conference on Multimedia and ICT in Education (m-ICTE 2009) (2009)

4. Bhardwaj, B.K., Pal, S.: Data mining: a prediction for performance improvement using classification. arXiv preprint arXiv:1201.3418 (2012)

5. Bray, M.: The Shadow Education System: Private Tutoring and Its Implications for Planners. Fundamentals of Educational Planning Series, Number 61. ERIC (1999)

6. Dennen, V.P.: Pedagogical lurking: student engagement in non-posting discussion behavior. Comput. Hum. Behav. **24**(4), 1624–1633 (2008). http://www.sciencedirect.com/science/article/pii/S074756320700115X. Including the Special Issue: Integration of Human Factors in Networked Computing

7. Dewey, J.: Democracy and Education. Courier Corporation, New York (2004)

8. Duckworth, A.L., Seligman, M.E.: Self-discipline outdoes iq in predicting academic performance of adolescents. Psychol. Sci. **16**(12), 939–944 (2005)

9. Irfan Mushtaq, S.N.K.: Factors affecting students academic performance. Glob. J. Manage. Bus. Res. **12**(9), 17–22 (2012). http://www.journalofbusiness.org/index.php/GJMBR/article/view/721

10. Khan, Z.N.: Scholastic achievement of higher secondary students in science stream. J. Soc. Sci. **1**(2), 84–87 (2005)

11. Pandey, U.K., Pal, S.: Data mining: a prediction of performer or underperformer using classification. arXiv preprint arXiv:1104.4163 (2011)

12. Pandey, U.K., Pal, S.: A data mining view on class room teaching language. arXiv preprint arXiv:1104.4164 (2011)

13. Pintrich, P.R., De Groot, E.V.: Motivational and self-regulated learning components of classroom academic performance. J. Educ. Psychol. **82**(1), 33 (1990)

14. Tangney, J.P., Baumeister, R.F., Boone, A.L.: High self-control predicts good adjustment, less pathology, better grades, and interpersonal success. J. Pers. **72**(2), 271–324 (2004)

15. Wei, J., Shen, Z., Sundaresan, N., Ma, K.L.: Visual cluster exploration of web clickstream data. In: 2012 IEEE Conference on Visual Analytics Science and Technology (VAST), pp. 3–12, October 2012

Multilevel Psychological Analysis for Cooperative Work Teams

Aurelio Olmedilla[1]([⊠]), Alexandre Garcia-Mas[2], Yuhua Luo[2],
Cristina Llaneras[2], Roberto Ruiz-Barquín[3], and Pilar Fuster-Parra[2]

[1] University of Murcia, Murcia, Spain
olmedilla@um.es
[2] University of the Balearic Islands, Palma, Spain
{alex.garcia,y.luo,pilar.fuster}@uib.es,
cristinallanerasdaniels@gmail.com
[3] Autonomous University of Madrid, Madrid, Spain
roberto.ruiz@uam.es

Abstract. In this study, we try to discover the natural psychological dynamics in a cooperative work team. We have selected a group of individuals that can help us to explore the psychological processes when working in a team. A new tool is used which •has been developed from the most relevant conceptual frameworks existing at the moment, the *Cooperative Workteams Questionnaire*, (CWQ). In this paper, we present the psychometric characteristics and impact encountered by the conceptual framework. We also present an analysis of the results obtained from applying this framework.

Keywords: Cooperation · Cohesion · Coordinative communication · Integration · Identification · Work team

1 Introduction

Nowadays, explanatory attempts for the work team psychological internal dynamics are quite often focused only on partially conflicting theoretical frameworks. This incompleteness of the analysis affects both the theoretical foundations and the applied intervention to maintain or improve the performance of the teams. Based on the traditional and common approach, academics and professionals tried to explain the teamwork through only one model at a time. This simplification leads to some conflict between social and individualistic psychological approaches. In fact, for a long time, there is a need to seek explanation at the group or social level to describe the function of the teams. This leads to excessive use of individualistic approaches to classically describe such dynamics for the groups [1].

Furthermore, one practical issue is the quality of the response to a questionnaire which is greatly affected by the length of the tool [2], as well as other bias stemming from the impact of the questions of the same questionnaires. Therefore, if we want to carry out a comprehensive study, we must use at least five different questionnaires. This affects the reliability of the responses. It generates ecological problems regarding to the

Y. Luo (Ed.): CDVE 2016, LNCS 9929, pp. 322–331, 2016.
DOI: 10.1007/978-3-319-46771-9_42

administration of the stack of questionnaires in performance and the working environments [3].

Our main goal is to try to solve these issues through the generation of a synthetic, comprehensive and global model for the personal relation in a cooperative work team. Firstly, we tried to combine the five major conceptual frameworks related to the cooperative team psychological dynamics: coordination, cohesion, cooperation, integration and identification. And, secondly, we would like to generate a single questionnaire, short, friendly, apt to be applied in an ecological environment.

The paper is organized as follows. First, we present our model based on an overview of the most relevant theories to explain the internal dynamics of work teams psychologically. Secondly we conducted a Delphi analysis to construct a new questionnaire avoiding the shortcomings of existing theories. After, an exploratory psychometric analysis of this questionnaire was conducted. Finally, we discuss both the results of the psychometric endeavour, and the descriptive data obtained in a population working in teams who responded to the questionnaire.

2 The Proposed Model

To overcome the incompleteness in the analysis of the working team psychological internal dynamics, for the first time in the literature, we propose to combine the five theoretical frameworks to be one single pyramid model. At the same time the model retains the conceptual validity and the deep meaning of the five known theoretical frameworks. The organization of the pyramid model is in its increasing complexity. The lowest level is the most basic fundamental one. Going up the pyramid increases the complexity in the working team psychological process. We believe that this can provide a better understanding of the requirements for practical intervention in the work teams.

The five theories are organized in a pyramidal hierarchy in the model(see Fig. 1) in which each level generates greater personal implication, greater workload and more complex psychological process.

2.1 Coordination

Each of these theories occupies one level in the pyramid, starting with the team coordination -the most basic and simple element – the coordination which begins with a fluent and effective communication, based on basic elementary stimuli-motor patterns, and non-verbal communication [4]. As pointed out in [5], a work team is a complex combination of people in which some have to execute a task while others must maintain an emotional positive working environment. For this reason, team coordination also depends on the empathy and communicating skills of the managers. This interaction between the team members can influence the process of decision-making. This can help the team to look for a solution to overcome problems in a more effective and simple way than if the team was not coordinated [5].

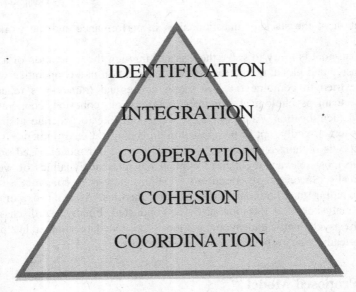

Fig. 1. Proposed model of a pyramidal hierarchy for the psychological dynamics in cooperative teams.

2.2   Cohesion

The next level of complexity is represented by the team cohesion, which was defined by Carron, Brawley and Widmayer as "a dynamic process that can be seen in the inclination of a team not to separate and remains united with the purpose of achieving their goals or satisfying the members' affective needs" [6].

Later, the existence of a double motivation in group cohesion was exposed. This includes the social cohesion by which the members of a team need to remain united and the task cohesion that defines the implication in achieving the team's goals [7]. Furthermore, these two types of cohesion are also influenced by the history of the team and the time since the team were formed and put into motion toward its goals [8].

2.3   Cooperation

The next step in our "climbing the conceptual ladder" of the pyramid, is the team's cooperation [9], a theory rooted in sociological basis [10]. Cooperation includes the communication and trust. By communication, we mean that the team members explain their position regarding to the group cooperation. Trust between the team members is a feeling of responsibility for the company's values and the team identity which is the feeling of being part of a team. The team members have to decide if they want to do their work for their own interests (competition) or they prefer working in cooperation to accomplish the team's goals. If they decide to cooperate, they understand that they will be able to combine individual and the team targets of all the members, in the midterm or long term. There are two different kinds of cooperative workers: the ones who cooperate among themselves, and the others who only show cooperative behaviours in order to obtain their own objectives in a conditioned or casual way [11]. While the team cohesion is a group-affective feature, the team cooperation is an individual characteristic, and acts through the members' interaction to create a collective cooperative or competitive team tendency [12].

2.4 Integration

The last two theories are integration and identification, which are based on social identification theory. They have been shown to help defining the balance between individualism and collectivism in an organization [13]. This theory [14] explains that the feeling of being part of a team is important for the individual self-concept. But at the same time being part of this team can make a person discover similarities and differences with the members of the team and would make him/her change his/her attitude so that he can be accepted and integrated into the group. This process is known as *depersonalisation*, and is greatly influenced by the balance between individualism and collectivism disposition [15].

2.5 Identification

Social identification is also greatly influenced by the team commitment [16]. It represents the motivation of a person to be part of a group, and is based on the concept of personal investment in the relationship with others inside the work team. The social identification is described by a three factors model: the satisfaction level, alternatives and the investment. The satisfaction level is the positive and/or negative feeling obtained from the identification with the team. The alternatives factor is the realization of the existence of other alternative situations to the integration. The third factor is the personal investment which is the effort made to pertain and maintain the team working [17]. Among them, the third factor, the personal investment is the most determining, in relation with the member's integration and/or identification with the team. It is the "resource" of a person investing in this team relationship, but also means everything that the person loses if the relationship with the team and teammates finish. Despite its importance, the other two factors have also relevant weight in helping to maintain or increase the commitment with the team [18].

Considering all the theories outlined before, we discovered the lack of research in this synthesized point of view. The work presented in this paper is try to: (1) unify the theoretical frameworks into one model which may go further from the psychological basic variables to the core psychological dynamics of cooperative team work, and (2) prove that this model can actually elaborate and analyse the psychometric features by a field study using a new questionnaire we created.

3   Method

3.1   Participants

The study uses a real sample set. The sample consisted of 108 male and female workers and managers aged between 23 and 60 years old. The years they have been employed vary from 1 to 34 years, always working in cooperative-type of teams, from different companies, and occupying diverse workplaces. All the subjects completed the questionnaire online voluntarily.

3.2   Instrument

The Cooperative Workteam Questionnaire (CWQ) was generated using a Delphi method in two phases. First, a group of experts in the psychology of performance teams selected 45 items from the five instruments which are more commonly used to evaluate the conceptual frameworks: Non-verbal Sensitivity Questionnaire [4]; Group Environment Questionnaire [6]; Sportive Cooperation Questionnaire [11]; the Sportive Commitment Questionnaire [16], and the Individualism and Collectivism Questionnaire [19]. In the second Delphi phase, authors conducted a three round inter-analysis and review of the selected items. The final CWQ is formed by 12 items with a Likert 5-position answers which covers the five theories and with a .89 index of agreeability among the experts (see Table 1).

Table 1. Cooperative work teams questionnaire (CWQ)

1. The communication among team members is easy and understandable
2. My effort and job level depends on the others' level, and also depends on the situation
3. Our team is solid and united to reach its goals and takes responsibility to face the problems encountered
4. Team workers and staff are integrated into the task and team objectives (How much of "me" has become "us"?)
5. The staff or some key team member spreads their mood to the rest to the team, for good or for bad
6. My working team and its philosophy let me think I belong to something really important
7. Being a member of this work team gives me chances to grow and improve my skills
8. I try my best in cooperate even if the cooperation level of my teammates, or staff is not the same
9. Some of my best friends are also my teammates
10. The staff and the managers recognize the team members' effort to integrate into the team objectives
11. I'm working on my personal objectives, even if they are not the same as the team's objectives
12. The team members choose to have social lives a part from their teammates

3.3   Procedures and Data Analysis

The online tool Google Forms have been used together with the social media, which allowed a fast and efficient distribution of the CWQ to a wide spectrum of individuals who accomplished the inclusion criteria. We believe that this can ensure the heterogeneity of the sample. After the data collection, a psychometric analysis of the questionnaire response was conducted using a software package for statistical analysis in social sciences SSPS 20.1 [20].

4   Results

We have conducted an exploratory factorial analysis of the CWQ response in order to find out what factors would appear in the response, and consequently, what should be the new composition of the cooperative work team conceptual framework. In order to accomplish this goal, we applied a principal component extraction method with the varimax rotation. In order to check whether the data are suitable for conducting an exploratory factor analysis, the Kaiser-Meyer-Olkin (KMO) test and Barlett sphericity test were applied first. These two tests are intended to determine the degree of sample adequacy for the subsequent application of different methods of factor extraction. Results of the Kaiser-Meyer-Olkin test show that the sample responses are satisfactory, with the values Between .500 and 1.00 (KMO = .733, according to Kaiser, mean values: $.80 \geq KMO \geq .70$).

The Bartlett sphericity test result shows a value of $p = .000$ ($p < .001$; *Chi-square* = 285.832), which indicates that the data matrix is appropriate for conducting the analysis of principal components. Considering the criteria for selected factors the

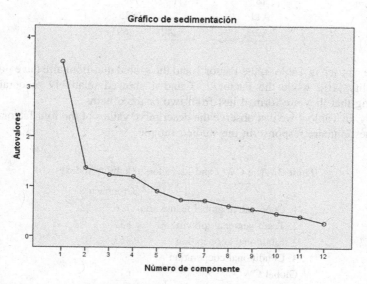

Fig. 2. Sedimentation graphic of the CWQ factors.

selfvalue $\geq$ 1, we included four factors in the analysis. The salfvalue 1 explains the 23.306 % of the total variance, the second one can explains the 15.432 % of the total variance, the third one explains 11.793 % and the fourth one explains the 10.433 %. The total percentage of the variance is explained is t61 %, which is satisfactory if we include just these four factors: *the cooperative global teamwork; the team personal growing; the emotional cooperation* and *the Conditional cooperation*.

The sedimentation curve (see Fig. 2) confirms the suitability to consider just these four factors, according to the degree of the curve between the four factors.

From Table 2 we can see the rotated component matrix obtained after a principal component analysis with a varimax rotation (after six iterations). With a preliminary screening considering the item-factor saturation just over .30, all items showed saturations over .40, sometimes over two factors at the same time.

Table 2.   Rotated component matrix

	Factor			
	1	2	3	4
A3	.838			
A1	.835			
A10	.615			
A4	.613	.458		
A7	.509			
A9		.760		
A12		−.633		
A6	.529	.557		
A5			.794	
A8			−.656	
A11				.835
A2			.428	−.691

As we can see in Table 3, the Factor 1 and the global questionnaire have good level of reliability [20], while the Factor 2, 3 and 4 showed relatively moderate levels considering that they are formed just from two or three items.

Finally, in Table 4 we can observe the descriptive values of the four factors and the global questionnaire response in the studied sample.

Table 3.   The CWQ and its factors reliability indexes

	Cronbach α
1. Cooperative global teamwork	.776
2. Team personal growing	.537
3. Emotional cooperation	.363
4. Conditional cooperation	.378
Global CWQ	.613

Table 4. Descriptive values of the CWQ response in the sample studied

	N	*M*	*SD*	Min	Max
Cooperative global teamwork	108	12.03	2.8	6.00	15.00
Team personal growing	108	6.30	1.54	3.00	9.00
Emotional cooperation	108	3.91	0.96	2.00	6.00
Conditional cooperation	108	4.17	1.07	2.00	6.00
Global CWQ	108	26.40	3.50	17.00	34.00

5 Discussion

According to the results of the psychometric analysis of the CWQ response, we obtained a questionnaire which can integrate the five different and well-known psychological theories of which each only partially explained the dynamics of the work teams. By doing this, we unify the five separated theories into one single integrated model.

The factors obtained in this exploratory analysis and primary attempt have surpassed the basic psychological variables in the original instruments and gone one step further. They built up explanations about how the mind of a team member works. For the first time, we obtained some indications about this "map" for a performance oriented team member. From these factors we recognized the existence of the five theoretical backgrounds to describe the whole team dynamics, from their communicative coordination to the identification to the team. The solid existence of this first factor, factor 1, called cooperative global teamwork factor allows us to think in a new way which can help us to use a more comprehensive approach to apply interventions to cooperative working teams.

Also, considering the second factor is the team personal growing, which shows the importance of the opportunity for the team members to grow personally while pertaining in the team and working cooperatively with other members. The two other factors found are related directly with the conditional cooperation, not derived from the prosocial push to a team member [11]. The 3rd factor, the emotional cooperation indicates that a person may cooperate with his/her teammates moved by the positive emotions derived from the cooperation itself. The factor four, the conditional cooperation, shows a clear and distinct goal to obtain and gain personal interest through belonging to and working in a performance oriented team, perhaps based in a short-term consideration.

Considering that we applied CWQ on this sample set without any generalization, the results already showed a heterogeneous combination of the four factors within this new model. This may allow us to distinguish between individuals and teams with respect to their position in the "pyramid" of the psychological dynamics for a cooperative working team.

This study has some limitations. The first is the need to conduct a confirmatory analysis to the CWQ after this exploratory analysis, using a larger sample. The second is the need to introduce the variable of performance into the descriptive analysis of the results obtained in the follow-up studies.

Acknowledgements. Authors would thank the European Union Grant, "PsyTool: Sport Psychology as a strategic tool for prevention and training on grassroot sports", Code 567199-EPP-1-2015-2-ES-SPO-SCP, to partially fund this study.

References

1. Taylor, D.M., Brown, R.J.: Towards a more social psychology? Br. J. Soc. Clin. Psychol. **18**(2), 173–180 (1979)
2. Galesic, M., Bosjnak, M.: Effects of questionnaire lenght on participation and indicators of response quality in a web survey. Public Opin. Q. **73**(2), 349–360 (2009)
3. Thwaites, D., Murdoch-Eaton, D.: Questionnaire design: the good, the bad and the pitfalls. Arch. Dis. Child Educ. Pract. Ed. **101**(4), 210–212 (2016)
4. Lausic, D., Razon, S., Tenenbaum, G.: Nonverbal sensitivity, verbal communication and team coordination in tennis doubles. Int. J. Sport Exerc. Psychol. **13**(4), 398–414 (2015)
5. López, C.J., Mohamed, K.M., El Yousfi, M.M., Zurita, F., Martínez, A.: Elementos comunicativos en entrenadores de baloncesto en diferentes categorías. Un estudio de caso (Communicative features in basketball coaches from different levels. A Case study). Cultura, Ciencia y Deporte **6**, 199–206 (2011)
6. Carron, A.V., Brawley, R.L., Widmeyer, W.N.: The measurement of cohesiveness in sport groups. In: Duda, J.L. (ed.) Advances in sport and exercise psychology measurement, pp. 214–226. WV, Fitness Information Technology, Morgantown (1998)
7. Carless, S.A., De Paola, C.: The measurement of cohesion in work teams. Small Group Res. **31**, 78–88 (2000)
8. Carron, A.V., Brawley, L.R.: Cohesion. Conceptual and measurement issues. Small Group Res. **31**, 89–106 (2000)
9. Garcia-Mas, A.: Cooperación y competición en equipos deportivos. Un estudio preliminar (Cooperation and Competition in sportive teams. A preliminary study). Análise Psicológica **1**, 115–130 (2001)
10. Rabbie, J.M.: Determinantes de la cooperación instrumental intragrupo (Determinants of the intra-group instrumental cooperation). In: Hinde, E.H., Groebel, J. (eds.) Cooperación y conducta prosocial (Cooperation and prosocial behavior), pp. 97–131. Visor Aprendizaje, Madrid (1995)
11. García-Mas, A., Olmedilla, A., Morilla, M., Rivas, C., García-Quinteiro, E., Ortega, E.: Un nuevo modelo de cooperación deportiva y su evaluación mediante un cuestionario (A new model of sportive cooperation and its evaluatio with a questionnaire). Psicothema **18**(3), 425–432 (2006)
12. Ponseti, F.J., Garcia-Mas, A., Palou, P., Cantallops, J., Fuster-Parra, P.: Self-determined motivation and types of sportive cooperation among players on competitive teams: a bayesian network analysis. Int J. Sport Psychol. (in press)
13. Topa-Cantisano, G., Morales-Domínguez, F.: Burnout e identificación con el grupo: el papel del apoyo social en un modelo de ecuaciones estructurales (Burnout and team identification: role of social support in a model of structural equations). Int. J. Clin. Health Psychol. **7**(2), 337–348 (2006)
14. Scandroglio, B., López Martínez, J.S., San José Sebastián, M.C.: La Teoría de la Identidad Social: una síntesis crítica de sus fundamentos, evidencias y controversias (The Social Identity Theory: A critical synthesis about its foundations and controversies). Psicothema **20**(1), 80–89 (2008)

15. Rivas, C., Ponzanelli, R., De la Llave, A., Pérez-Llantada, M.C., Garcia-Mas, A.: Individualismo y colectivismo en la relación a la eficacia colectiva percibida en jugadores de fútbol (Individualism and collectivism in relationship with perceived collective efficacy in football players). Revista Mexicana de Psicología **32**(1), 68–80 (2015)
16. Sousa, C., Torregrosa, M., Viladrich, C., Villamarín, F., Cruz, J.: The commitment of youg soccer players. Psicothema **19**(2), 256–262 (2007)
17. Rusbult, C.E., Martz, J.M., Agnew, C.R.: The investment model scale: measuring commitment level, satisfaction level, quality of alternatives and investment size. Pers. Relat. **5**, 357–391 (1998)
18. Garcia-Mas, A., Palou, P., et al.: Commitmment, enjoyment and motivation in young soccer competitive players. Span. J. Psychol. **13**(2), 609–616 (2010)
19. Tasa, K., Taggar, S., Saijts, G.H.: The development of collective efficacy in teams: a multilevel and longitudinal perspective. J. Appl. Psychol. **92**(1), 17–27 (2007)
20. Nunnally, J.C.: Psychometric Theory. McGraw-Hill, New York (1978)

An Application of Measuring Aesthetics in Visualization

Badr Al-Harbi[1(✉)], Ali Alturki[1], and Adel Ahmed[2]

[1] Saudi Aramco, Dhahran, Saudi Arabia
badrharbi@gmail.com, ali.turki.2@aramco.com.sa
[2] King Fahd University of Petroleum and Minerals, Dhahran, Saudi Arabia
adelahmed@kfupm.edu.sa

Abstract. It is challenging to efficiently and effectively manage and mine huge-sized scientific and engineering data. The challenge takes another dimension when it comes to visualization and data analytics. Without the use of detail-in-context lenses; it has been found that many important details are missed or misinterpreted. Effectiveness of visual comprehension is one of the main goals of collaborative visualization. Various detail-in-context lenses were developed to increase the visual comprehension of 2D and 3D data types by exaggerating the focused area while maintaining context such as fish-eye lenses. These lenses will enhance the cooperative collaborative visualization environment. In this work, an assessment of the effectiveness of a detail-in-context lens is presented. That is by using a set of aesthetics metrics designed to evaluate the visualizations generated by the fish-eye method to optimize the lens parameters. We have developed a framework to test these metrics on hydrocarbon reservoir simulation grids of different model sizes.

Keywords: Evaluating cooperative visualization environment · Aesthetic · Visualization · Metrics · Measurement

1 Introduction

Scientific visualization is an important part of data analysis. It provides means to illustrate the problem at hand and build relationships that facilitate assessment of data. With the increase in development of new visualization methods, it is logical to provide forms of validation and/or verification of the effectiveness of these methods. In this work, the impact of the detail-in-context variables using shape aesthetics and design principle metrics on scientific data is evaluated.

2 Literature Survey

There are many visualization methods that target volume data types. A set of visualization lenses will be reviewed in addition to perception theory for metric selection.

The most used approaches for the 3D grid is the section view where the user can visualize any number of layers and cross sections using sliced planes in a primitive manner [1]. Figure 1(a) present the full dataset of a hydrocarbon simulation case.

© Springer International Publishing AG 2016
Y. Luo (Ed.): CDVE 2016, LNCS 9929, pp. 332–339, 2016.
DOI: 10.1007/978-3-319-46771-9_43

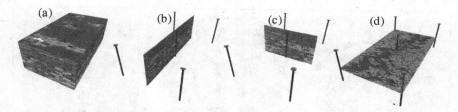

Fig. 1. Present current practice in visualizing volumetric 3-dimentional hydrocarbon reservoir simulation grid

Figure 1(b), (c) and (d) show a column of 2D section of the 3D model, a 2D raw section, a single layer, respectively. From the prospective of collaboration and effectiveness, these visual representations reveal little data to inspect and build decisions on [2].

Deformation is a manipulation lens for exaggerating selected focused area of the data. Visualization techniques such as magic lenses, fish-eye views, or perspective wall are methods developed for 2D data such as maps, graphs or text document to highlight important area or to provide an in-context zoom [3–5].

Several researches have only applied fish-eye views on 3D volume data that combine non-geometric distortion such as transparency and drawing wireframe layers [6, 7]. Luo et al. work has been developed on top of Winch et al. [6, 8]. Which is a fish-eye on 3D data; however, these methods have an issue in which they hide the inner data and only focus on deforming the external layer(s) [8]. Carpendale proposed a novel approach in presenting a detail-in-context view of 3D data [9]. Carpendale's proposed "Visual Access" that reveals the internal information in 3D grids by applying distortion and displacement functions. That is by utilizing line-of-sight that rearrange the gridcells at focus point extending the work done on 2D distortion viewing techniques. Her proposed method is evaluated against basic 3D distortion viewing where issues were identified. The resulted visualization is both understandable and appealing.

3 Detail-in-Context

In this investigation, an implementation of the Visual Access by Carpendale [9] is examined. The used techniques are applied on the different properties that control the visualization. These properties are: displacement function, distorting function area of influence, point-of-view and focus exaggeration. Figure 2 illustrates the Visual Access method adapted by this research work. We have implemented this method in OpenGL/ OpenCL to change the data in real-time.

3.1 Displacement Function

Individual cell displacement provides a mechanism for viewing cells inside a volumetric dataset. This function disperses the cells apart from each other in the three axes. This allows for occluded cells to be revealed as seen in Fig. 3(a). The displacement is a constant value used for the three dimensions; it is considered as a single input parameter

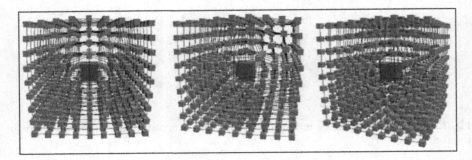

Fig. 2. Visual access

to the method. The default value for displacement is factor of 1 with a range from 0 to 5. Zero displacement translates to the original dataset. Displacements are computed as an incremental on the X and Y-axis in the outward direction from the center point.

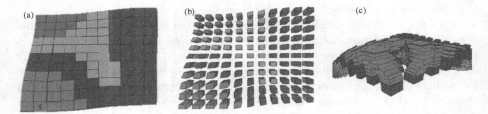

Fig. 3. (a) original data, (b) with displacement (c) with displacement and distortion functions

3.2 Distortion Function

Visual Access has used the normal, bell curve, and distribution shape as the distortion function. Two main variables control the bell curve, the width and the height of the bell curve. The height of the function is the displacement coefficient in the view direction. The width of the function is the displacement coefficient perpendicular to the view direction. Visual Access lens uses the bell curve shape. The default height value of the bell curve is .5 with a range from 0 to 2. Figure 3(c) shows the distortion effect on the data set. The magnitude is proportional to the dataset size.

3.3 Camera Position and Direction

Visual access method uses the camera-position/viewers-eye as a facilitator for the distortion lens. It can change the result of the distortion as it follows the line-of-sight. Some viewpoints reveal more/higher number of cells than others. There are two values governing the position to the data. The X and Y angles are both used, separately, as two input parameters for the camera position that range from 1 to 4 to set the distance.

4   Metrics

Two metrics were designed to evaluate the results of the detail-in-context visualization. The first is based on the perception theory targeting the shape of the result to determine the lie factor [10, 11]. The second metric, ratio of used space, is based on a design guideline that maximizes the use of available space to focus on the data [10].

4.1   Average Relative Change of Mean Curvature (RCMC)

RCMC metric indicates the relative change of the shape represented by the overall averaged mean curvature H (1). The mean curvature is computed from the principle curvature at every vertex. The explanation of the principal curvature is beyond the scope of this paper, however, the details of which are thoroughly discussed in [12]. Figure 4 shows the process of generating RCMC value. Figure 4(b) is the curvature analysis of the base case. Figure 4(d) shows the applied distortion, where Fig. 4(c), (e), and (f) demonstrates the curvature analysis of the new shape. For the computation of the curvature in this work, the authors have implemented the method presented by Griffin et al. [12] which states:

$$RCMC = 1/n \left\{ \sum_{i=0}^{n} |H - H'|/\max(H, H') \right\} \tag{1}$$

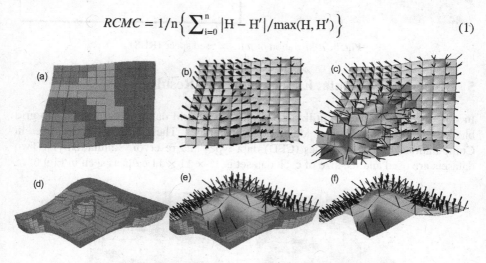

Fig. 4. The process of computing the curvature analysis

Equation (1) is used as the objective function. This metric is used as an objective function that minimize the change to the results of the detail-in-context visualization method to maintain relative relationship to the original shape of the data that translate to better recognition of the "hidden" information.

4.2   Ratio of Used Space (RUS)

The second metric focus on how much space is used after applying the detail-in-context method. This is to maximize the display area and to reduce unutilized view space. As presented in Eq. (2), it is simply computed as the number of used pixels over the total number of pixels in the display area as it shows by Fig. 5.

$$RUS = \text{Used Pixels}/\text{total pixels} \qquad (2)$$

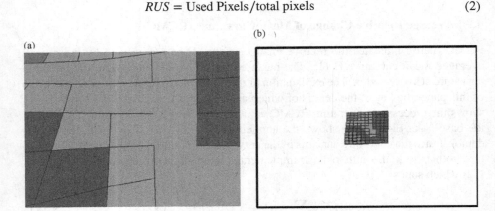

(a)

(b)

Fig. 5.   Illustration of ratio of used space (RUS)

5   Experimental Data, Experiment, and Results

In this experiment, we are utilizing volumetric 3D grid data represented as sub grid blocks. Eight (8) corner points identify each grid block. These grids are mainly used in Computational Fluid Dynamics (CFD) data types and reservoir simulation [1]. Two datasets are used and the size of each dataset is $11 \times 11 \times 11$ cells as seen in Fig. 6.

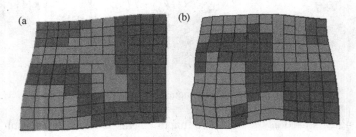

(a

(b)

Fig. 6.   Dataset for the experiment

Five input parameters were carefully selected to be evaluated against the two selected metrics. A total of 60 experiments with different combinations of the input parameters and objective functions were developed and conducted. The experiments were conducted on two 3-dimentional hydrocarbon reservoir model datasets. Each of which is evaluated by five input parameters, two metrics, and three camera setups. The combinations are presented along with the resultant evaluation parameters values. The experiments are grouped by the number of objective functions and then input parameters.

Three sets of camera angles have been used; the first is the top view, which is the same as the one, used in Fig. 6; the second one is set at 45° inclination angle. Finally, the third camera setup is used to optimize the view for the X & Y camera angles. Table 1 summarizes the first set of experiments showing the base case analysis.

Table 1. Base case

Name	Case	Top	45	X &Y
RUS	Case 1	0.3546	.3793	0.4745
	Case 2	.39	.42	.5
	Avg	0.372	0.399	.487
RCMC	Avg	0	0	0

The base case is set as a comparison pivot point against the result generated from the optimization workflow. After conducting the analysis, we have selected the 32 top results from the optimization engine and generated the correlation values. Table 2 presents the highest correlated objective function with the input parameter. Based on the averaged results from both cases (datasets).

Table 2. Highest correlation values between the objective function and input parameters

Objective function	Properties	R2 value	Stnd. Dev
RUS	Camera distance on the 45-degree view	.9	0.0105
RCMC	Bell curve parameter on the 45-degree view	.8	.0165

6 Discussion

From the generated results in this paper, the authors have identified key input parameters that, apparently, have the biggest impact on the results. The discussions of the results are grouping based on their impact on the performance of the objective functions (Table 3).

Table 3. Highest objective function results

Objective function	Properties	Maximum change from base case
RUS	Camera distance on optimized X & Y view	84 %
RCMC	XYZ displacement on optimized X & Y view	500 %

6.1   Ratio of Used Space

From the selected parameters, the camera distance and displacement have the biggest impact. The Gaussian parameter did not show any difference. Camera distance has the biggest impact with when also optimizing for X & Y angles.

6.2   Relative Shape Change

From the conducted experiments, relative shape change metric is not impacted by the size of the cells rather it impacted by the change in the form reflected the change in the curvature of the overall object. It is not affected by XYZ displacement, camera distance or X and Y angle. It is affected by the bell curve parameter and from Table 2 optimizing for the X and Y angle did identify the least shape change for the defaulted value of the bell curve parameter.

7   Conclusion

Aesthetic metrics used in this paper provides insight into the visualization generated from detail-in-context lens. The first metric derived from perception theory shows to the users the degree of which the lens has impacted the accuracy of the data. This is useful in cooperative environment, where users need to know how accurate the representation of the data. The second metric selected from design guideline. This metric provides the designer of a collaboration visualization lens how much of space is unutilized. These metrics were used as objective function in a framework to optimize the view. Based on the correlation analysis conducted, displacement function and camera distance had the major impact on both the used space and the relative shape change. Aesthetic and utility metric analyses are means to identify effectiveness, performance, and compare different lenses for designing visualization lenses. The selected parameters and objective functions used in this work only provides a sense of what can be achieved in the area of heuristic aesthetics evaluation We are looking into expanding on the implemented metrics and evaluate combinations of input parameters and objective functions by incorporating additional utility metrics to evaluate the effectiveness of the visualization method.

Acknowledgment.   We appreciate the support and encouragement of King Fahd University of Petroleum and Minerals, professors, and Saudi Aramco in availing the resources to successfully conduct this research.

References

1. Al-Harbi, B., Al-Darrab, A., Al-Zawawi, A.S., Al-Zamil, K., et al.: Advanced visualization for reservoir simulation. In: SPE Saudi Arabia Section Technical Symposium and Exhibition. Society of Petroleum Engineers (2013). https://www.onepetro.org/download/conference-paper/SPE-168103-MS?id=conference-paper%2FSPE-168103-MS. Accessed 23 Mar 2015

2. Mortelmans, D.: Visualizing emptiness. Vis. Anthropol. **18**, 19–45 (2005)
3. Spence, R., Apperley, M.: Data base navigation: an office environment for the professional. Behav. Inf. Technol. **1**, 43–54 (1982)
4. Sarkar, M., Brown, M.H.: Graphical fisheye views. Commun. ACM **37**, 73–83 (1994)
5. Mackinlay, J.D., Robertson, G.G., Card, S.K.: The perspective wall: detail and context smoothly integrated. In: Proceedings of the SIGCHI Conference on Human Factors in Computing Systems, pp. 173–176. ACM (1991). http://dl.acm.org/citation.cfm?id=108870. Accessed 4 Jun 2015
6. Luo, Y., Iglesias Guitián, J.A., Gobbetti, E., Marton, F.: Context preserving focal probes for exploration of volumetric medical datasets. In: Magnenat-Thalmann, N. (ed.) 3DPH 2009. LNCS, vol. 5903, pp. 187–198. Springer, Heidelberg (2009). http://link.springer.com/chapter/10.1007/978-3-642-10470-1_16. Accessed 5 Jun 2015
7. Cohen, M.: Focus and context for volume visualization. The University of Leeds (2006). http://core.kmi.open.ac.uk/download/pdf/43093.pdf. Accessed 5 Jun 2015
8. Winch, D., Calder, P., Smith, R.: (Focus + context) 3: distortion-oriented displays in three dimensions. In: 2000 First Australasian User Interface Conference (AUIC 2000), pp. 126–33. IEEE (2000). http://ieeexplore.ieee.org/xpls/abs_all.jsp?arnumber=822078. Accessed 23 Mar 2015
9. Carpendale, M.S.T., Cowperthwaite, D.J., Fracchia, F.D.: Extending distortion viewing from 2D to 3D. Comput. Graph. Appl. IEEE **17**, 42–51 (1997)
10. Tufte, E.R., Graves-Morris, P.R.: The Visual Display of Quantitative Informatio. Graphics press Cheshire (1983). http://www.humanities.ufl.edu/pdf/tufte-aesthetics_and_technique.pdf. Accessed 5 Jun 2015
11. Norman, D.A.: The Design of Everyday Things: Revised and Expanded Edition. Basic books, New York (2013). https://books.google.com/books?hl=en&lr=&id=nVQPAAAQBAJA&oi=fnd&pg=PT8&dq=norman+donald+&ots=eSpdL8PTSp&sig=HrJyxmV9UgyqSO6YDpV0_3Is4GU. Accessed 21 Nov 2015
12. Griffin, W., Wang, Y., Berrios, D., Olano, M.: Real-time GPU surface curvature estimation on deforming meshes and volumetric data sets. IEEE Trans. Vis. Comput. Graph. **18**, 1603–1613 (2012)

Generation of 3D Architectural Objects with the Use of an Aesthetic Oriented Multi-agent System

Agnieszka Mars[✉] and Ewa Grabska

Faculty of Physics, Astronomy and Applied Computer Science,
Jagiellonian University, Kraków, Poland
{agnieszka.mars,ewa.grabska}@uj.edu.pl

Abstract. An aesthetic oriented, multi-agent system is proposed for supporting generation of buildings prototypes that fulfill aesthetic criteria. Multi-hierarchical composite graphs are used to represent object's structure, consisting of Biedermann's basic perception elements - geons, grouped into aesthetic measurable components. The approach is illustrated on the example of designing a simple 3d architectural object according to the accepted rules of aesthetics.

Keywords: Aesthetic measure · Computer aided design · Collaborative design · Multi-agent system

1 Introduction

This paper is an attempt to develop a new approach in the area of collaborative design of architecture, where an aesthetic oriented, multi-agent system is proposed for supporting generation buildings prototypes that fulfill aesthetic criteria. The idea to combine Bikhoff's aesthetic measure [1] with Biederman's Recognition-By-Components theory [2] in aesthetic evaluation of architecture has been proposed in [3]. Multi-hierarchical composite graphs are used to represent object's structure, consisting of Biedermann's basic perception elements - geons, grouped into aesthetic measurable components. The proposed system contains several agents, each of them operating on the same graph model and being responsible for developing a project in accordance with a certain aesthetic rule. The result of collaboration between the agents - a building prototype - is expected to be harmonic due to fulfilling aesthetic criteria, but also interesting for a viewer through agents' independence and controlled randomness of added elements.

Geon based aesthetic measure for architecture is based on Bikhoff's formula for assessment of polygonal forms adapted to 3D objects. It assumes division of a building solid into primitive components - Biederman's geons, which are easily identified during the visual perception process and together with a set of spatial relations between them compound an alphabet for an infinite language of images. The most important

© Springer International Publishing AG 2016
Y. Luo (Ed.): CDVE 2016, LNCS 9929, pp. 340–347, 2016.
DOI: 10.1007/978-3-319-46771-9_44

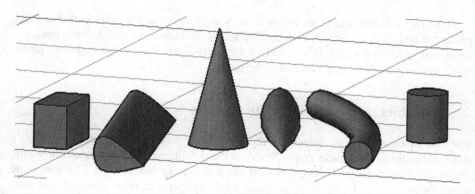

Fig. 1. Examples of geons

feature of geons is that they can be recognized immediately, even when viewed incomplete (e.g. from one side only or partly covered). Figure 1 shows some examples of geons, however a total number is 43, including planar ones.

Judgment of harmony and beauty of a solid can be given due to investigation of aesthetic relations between geons: alignment, vertical symmetry, rotational symmetry, satisfactory form (when an object is not "almost straight" or "almost symmetrical"), equilibrium, fit for a cube- or diamond-shaped network. The more such relations can be found, the more harmonic an object seems to be. However, high cost of perception, i.e., a great number of geons, many different geon types or high complexity of geons can result in decrease of aesthetic value, as well as predictability of components arrangement. In order to achieve optimal results in automatic architectural design, all these parameters should be taken into account, which is a nontrivial problem. However, the proposed method where several agents with different aesthetic motivations which co-operate on the same project seems accurate, because collaboration enables to compromise between many (sometimes contrary) goals. This is why we propose a model of a multi-agent system, which works on graph representation of a building.

There are many approaches to computational design. Genetic algorithms enable to find optimal solutions that fulfill defined criteria or designer's subjective expectations, including aesthetic ones [4]. Shape grammars consist of sets of rules used for derivation of one shape from another. Such rules can by modified dynamically in response to user's interaction with the system, different grammars may also act simultaneously [5]. Despite these possibilities, prototypes generated by shape grammars are restricted by grammar rules, while genetic design may give highly unpredictable results, especially when its fitness function attempts to evaluate aesthetics. Graph grammars, in which rules describe graph transformations, seem to be the most powerful tool in our case. Geons and relations between them can be easily represented by graphs, while graph transformation allows even minor modifications of an object. This makes graph representation appropriate for almost every possible project.

The paper is organized as follows: in Sect. 2 necessary graphs definitions are presented and then, in Sect. 3, their application in the context of architectural design is described. Section 4 contains a model of the multi-agent system for buildings proto-types generation. Section 5 concludes the paper.

2   Multi-hierarchical Composite Graphs

For the purpose of architecture representation we have decided to use a multi-hierarchical composite graph, based on the definitions of an attributed composite graph and a multi-hierarchical graph with its child nesting function [6]. The composite graphs were defined to represent artifacts' structures with their components and relations between them. Artifact components and their fragments are represented by object and bond nodes, respectively. Edges are defined between bond nodes.

Let Σ be an alphabet of labels for object nodes, bond nodes and edges. Let for any sequence $(x_1, \ldots, x_n)$, $SET(x_1, \ldots, x_n)$ be equal to $\{x_1, \ldots, x_m\}$, where $m \leq n$, i.e., to the set of its elements. Let A be a set of attributes for nodes and edges, such that for each a $\in$ A, D_a denotes its domain, i.e., the set of all possible values of this attribute. Let P(A) denote the set of all subsets of A.

Definition 1.   A   composite   multi-edge   graph   over Σ is   a   tuple $g = (V, E, B, bd, s, t, lb, att, val)$, where:

- V, E, B are pairwise disjoint sets whose elements are called object nodes, bond nodes and edges, respectively,
- $bd : V \rightarrow B*$ is a function which specifies a sequence of different bond nodes for each object node, such that $\forall b \in B \exists ! v \in V : b \in SET(bd(v))$, i.e., each bond node is assigned to exactly one object node,
- s, t: $E \rightarrow B$ are mappings assigning to edges source and target bond nodes, respectively, in such a way that $\forall e \in E \exists v_1 \neq v_2$, $s(e) \in SET(bd(v_1)) \wedge t(e) \in SET(bd(v_2))$, i.e., each edge connects bond nodes of exactly two different object nodes,
- lb: $V \cup B \cup E \rightarrow \Sigma$ is a node and edge labeling function,
- att: $V \cup E \rightarrow P(A)$ is a node and edge attributing function, and
- val: $(V \cup E) \times A \in D$ is a partial function assigning values to attributes, where $D = \cup_{a \in A} D_a$ such that $\forall (o, a) \in (V \cup E) \times A$ if $a \in attr(o)$ $val(o, a) \in D_a$.

The above definition differs from the one introduced in [4] in the way of edge assignment - unlike a composition attributed graph, a composite multi-edge graph allows multiple edges assigned to a single bond.

Let G be a labeled graph with U being a finite set of graph atoms (i.e., nodes and edges of a graph). Let $\perp$ be a fixed value, different from all elements of U. If ch is a function $ch : V \rightarrow 2^U \cup \{\perp\}$, then for a node $v \in V$ a set of its descendants of the i-th order is denoted by $ch^i(v)$. Let ch^i, ch^+ and ch^* be defined as follows:

$$ch^0(v) = \begin{cases} \bot \Leftarrow ch(v) = \bot, \\ v \Leftarrow ch(v) \neq \bot \end{cases},$$

$$ch^1(v) = ch(v),$$

$$ch^{i+1}(v) = \begin{cases} \bot \Leftarrow ch^i(v) = \bot, \\ \displaystyle\bigcup_{u \in V \cap ch^i(v)} ch(u) \Leftarrow ch^i(v) \neq \bot, \end{cases}$$

$$ch^+(v) = \bigcup_{i \geq 1} ch^i(v),$$

$$ch^*(v) = \bigcup_{i \geq 0} ch^i(v).$$

Definition 2. A mapping $ch : V \to 2^U \cup \{\bot\}$ is a child nesting function iff:

- $\forall v, w \in V : w \in ch(v) \Rightarrow ch(w) \neq \bot$, i.e., if a node is a child of some other node, then it is a part of the hierarchy and thus must have its own set of children (which may be empty),
- $\forall x \in U \forall v, u \in V : x \in ch(v) \wedge x \in ch(u) \Rightarrow v = u$, i.e., an element cannot have two distinct parents,
- $\forall v \in V : v \notin ch^+(v)$, i.e., no element can be its own child.

Definition 3. A multi-hierarchical composite graph over Σ is a system $G = (V, E, B, bd, s, t, lb, att, val, ch_1, \ldots, ch_n)$, where:

- $(V, E, B, bd, s, t, lb, att, val)$ is a labeled graph, and
- $ch_i : V \to 2^U \cup \{\bot\}$, where $i = 1, \ldots, n$, are child nesting functions.

3 Graph Representation of an Architectural Object

Having introduced multi-hierarchical composite graphs, we can propose an instance of such a structure in order to represent dependencies between architectural object's components. Graph representations of architectural objects need appropriate labels, attributes and numbers of bonds determined as follows:

- child nodes are labeled with geons numbers (1-43), whereas parent nodes refer to aesthetic measure components named - alignment, vertical symmetry and rotational symmetry; geon node bonds are labeled with numbers of geon faces - "1" for a top base, "2" for a bottom base, and next numbers for lateral faces; edges connecting geon nodes are labeled with a type of spatial relation between two geons - "continuation", when their bases are the same and stuck together, or "attachment", when the first geon's side is joined with another one's so as they create concavities;
- edges are only possible between two geon nodes;
- each geon node has at least three bonds, two of them denoting the volume's bases, while other nodes are not equipped with any bonds.
- each attribute set assigned to a geon node may be composed of two subsets of attributes - a subset for "non-accidental" ones, describing properties that are, according to Recognition-ByComponents theory, perceived at once and used in

object recognition process, and a subset for metric properties like exact size or location, which are not perceived immediately, but are important from our point of view due to their power of creating aesthetic relations like alignment or symmetry.

Figure 2 shows an example of a simple building prototype consisting of three geons, two of them aligned to the common plane and two of them arranged in the relation of vertical symmetry, and its graph representation. Numbered bonds denote geon's faces - top base, bottom base and four lateral faces.

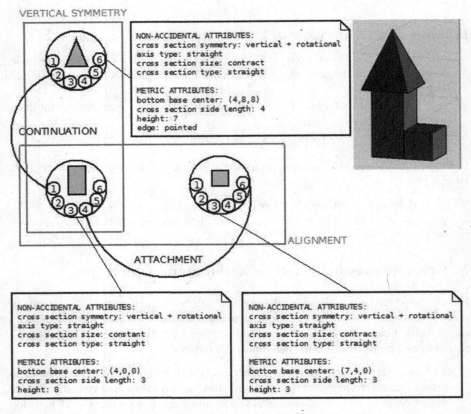

Fig. 2. A building prototype and its graph representation

4 Multi-agent Design System

In this section we consider a multi-agent system that is able to support design process of generating prototypes fulfilling functional requirements and aesthetic criteria. By an agent we understand a computational entity situated in some environment and capable of autonomous actions in the environment in order to satisfy requirements and/or criteria assigned to the agent during design process. Design agents react to changes of the design context by acting upon the environment, exchanging information and interacting with other agents [7]. We propose the system with the following agents:

- **Complexity Agent**, which generates new geon nodes and ensures that the total number of geon types and their complexity are not too high;
- **Equilibrium Agent**, which suggests preferred location of a new geon in case when object's imbalance occurs;
- **Network Agent**, which searches for geon nodes whose attributes' values only need a slight modification to make the component fit to a cube- or diamond-shaped network. The modification is performed only if it does not affect geon's parent relation - e.g. the agent can flatten geon's side in case it is not in a vertical symmetry relation;
- **Alignment Agent**, responsible for generation of new alignment nodes and their child nodes - geons, that fulfill the alignment condition (i.e., one of their side is tangential or inscribed in an alignment plane). The agent also scans the whole graph in order to find new alignment nodes and to find geons that require a slight modification to make them fit for an alignment relation;
- **Vertical Symmetry Agent**, which generates new vertical symmetry nodes and their child geon nodes, scans the graph for unregistered vertical symmetry relations and creates new ones by reflection added to existing geons,
- **Rotational Symmetry Agent**, which acts analogically to Vertical Symmetry Agent.

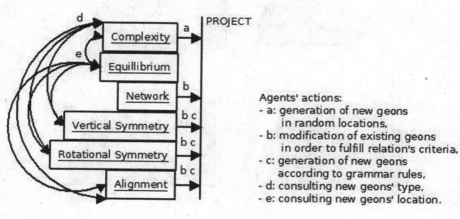

Fig. 3. Design agents and their actions

Alignment and symmetry agents use graph grammars to generate new nodes. A graph grammar consists of a set of graph rules of the form L -> R with L and R being graphs called left-hand side and right-hand side of the rule, respectively. A graph rule is applied to the graph by replacing L by R. Geon nodes are created after consultation with Complexity Agent, which may have some preferences for attributes defining a geon type and complexity. For example, Complexity Agent may decide that geons with straight axis and rounded cross section are most desired, which will have impact on the random function of geon generation. Complexity Agent also uses its own grammar to add new geons, which do not need to be in any aesthetic relation (this ensures the project is not too much ordered and predictable). Each agent communicates with Equilibrium Agent in order to ensure balance of a solid. Figure 3 illustrates agents' actions on the project and interactions with each other.

Let us consider some examples of agents' modifications on a project, illustrated in Fig. 4. Picture (a) shows a production of Symmetry Agent, (b) - generation of a new geon by Complexity Agent, (c) - modification of the project by Alignment Agent, (d) - again, generation of a new geon by Complexity Agent, and (e) - correction of the new geon's location by Alignment Agent.

Besides aesthetic rules to obey, an architectural object should of course comply with multiple functional requirements. At the early stage of prototype generation this task can be performed by graph grammar axioms, i.e., predefined graphs that the agents develop according to their grammar productions. For instance, if a building must have a sloping roof, one can prepare an axiom graph containing a wedge shaped geon on the top of its structure and some non-terminal nodes for further development.

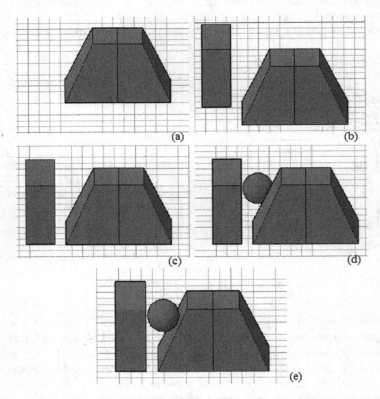

Fig. 4. Examples of agents' modifications on a project

5 Conclusion

Multi-hierarchical composite graph representation of architectural objects combined with a multi-agent approach to design seems to be a powerful tool that allows to gain multiple aesthetic goals while developing buildings prototypes. The proposed model of a multi-agent system can be quite easily enriched with other aesthetic or functional requirements represented by new axioms or by new agents. However, in case of adding agents their behavior should be carefully designed to enable efficient collaboration.

References

1. Birkhoff, G.D.: Aesthetic Measure. Cambridge Massachusetts Harvard University Press, Cambridge (1933)
2. Biederman, I.: Recognition-by-components: a theory of human image understanding. Psychol. Rev. **94**, 115–147 (1987)
3. Mars, A., Grabska, E.: Towards an implementable aesthetic measure for collaborative architecture design. In: Luo, Y. (ed.) CDVE 2015. LNCS, vol. 9320, pp. 72–75. Springer, Heidelberg (2015). doi:10.1007/978-3-319-24132-6_9
4. Case, K., Karim, M.S.A.: Aesthetics considerations in evolutionary computer aided design, applications of digital techniques in industrial design engineering. In: Proceedings of the 6th International Conference on Computer Aided Industrial Design and Conceptual Design (CAID and CD2005). Delft University of Technology, The Netherlands (2005)
5. Knight, T.: Interaction in visual design computing, visual and spatial reasoning in design III. In: Key Centre of Design Computing and Cognition, University of Sydney (2004). (the invited paper)
6. Strug, B., Paszyńska, A., Paszyński, M., Grabska, E.: Using a graph grammar system in the finite element method. Int. J. Appl. Math. Comput. Sci. **23**(4), 839–853 (2013)
7. Saunders, R.: Curious design agents and artificial creativity, Ph.D. thesis, Faculty of Architecture, The University of Sydney (2002)

Synchronized Shared Scene Viewing in Mixed VR Devices in Support of Group Collaboration

Steve Cutchin[✉] and Iker Vazquez

Boise State University, 1910 University Drive, Boise, ID, USA
{stevencutchin,ikervazquezlopez}@boisestate.edu
http://cs.boisestate.edu/~scutchin

Abstract. Virtual Reality devices are available with different resolutions and fields of view. Users can simultaneously interact within environments on head mounted displays, cell phones, tablets, and PowerWalls. Sharing scenes across devices requires solutions that smoothly synchronize shared navigation, minimize jitter and avoid visual confusion. In this paper we present a system that allows a single user to remotely guide many remote users in a virtual environment. A variety of mixed device environments are supported. Techniques are implemented to minimize jitter and synchronize views.

Keywords: VR · Scene sharing · Remote VR

1 Introduction

Classes utilizing virtual reality(VR) devices for directed tours and guided exploration of a virtual environment require guided navigation with a smooth following path of the instructor's view for students in a synchronized and jitter-free manner. Excess jitter can lead to rapid deterioration of the shared views and modest lag can cause nausea for remote students. Because of this it is advisable that shared VR systems utilize view synchronization to minimize these types of extreme events. Additionally, VR devices are available with a variety of different fields of view(FOV). Users can simultaneously interact within VR environments on head mounted displays(HMD), cell phones, tablets, and PowerWalls. Sharing scenes across different types of devices requires solutions that both minimize jitter and deal with different FOVs.

In this paper we present current work on a system that allows a user to guide multiple remote users within a VR environment of stereo panoramas. Specific techniques are implemented to minimize jitter between users and to maintain synchronized views across devices with differing FOV. The implemented system provides a collaborative communal space in mixed device environments of HMD, tablet, and PowerWalls.

Y. Luo (Ed.): CDVE 2016, LNCS 9929, pp. 348–352, 2016.
DOI: 10.1007/978-3-319-46771-9_45

2 Prior Work

Significant research into distributed virtual environments has already been done for a variety of devices. [1] presents a web-based learning environment called Virtual Laboratories (VL). [2] developed a collaborative P2P system which shares a geographic environment to explore complex spatial information and work in a collaborative way. [3] presents Wonderland, an integration of internet accessible physics experiments (iLabs). [4] present a collaborative system to teach students how to use a calligraphy brush with haptic devices. Shared virtual environements, such as [5] and [6], often use specific architectures to synchronize communication between users involving Area of Interest and Dead Level Reckoning techniques. Dealing with differeing FOVs of different devices has been studied in [7] and [8] via experiments involving blinders, software, and augmented virtual systems. The experiments demonstrated the difference in a users experience based on FOV. Prolonged use of virtual enviroments are studied by [9] and [10] examinining cyber-sickness, and task completion in cooperative tele-operation. Reducing jitter and smooth transitions are crucial for shared Virtual Environments. [11] presents a navigation algorithm based on a river flow analogy, following the approximate flow of an anchored river current.

3 Our Approach

Our approach utilizes a basic leader and follower model with one VR system acting as the leader and all other VR systems acting as followers. All VR systems load the same scene (same camera position and looking point) in advance and all system have identical imagery and user interface tools. The actual appearance of the user interface may differ from physical device to physical device but the same functionality is present.

We have implemented two different experimental jitter reduction techniques and one experimental technique for differing FOVs between devices. For jitter reduction we implemented simple Dead Level Reckoning and weighted buffered path smoothing. Dead-Level Reckoning works utilizing the technique as defined in [5]. Buffered path smoothing utilizes a jitter server to buffer and smooth navigation path packets. A weight vector can be used to adjust the smoothing factor based on user preference and testing results. Smoothing the coordinates in the server side provides the same data to all connected users, and thus they will follow the same path. If the smoothing is done in the user side, when some packages are lost over the network, followers will compute different paths differing over the rest of users. Initial testing shows promise for smooth shared navigation. Additionally we implement synchronization of differing FOVs using delayed movement and thresholding.

4 System Architecture

Our testing platform is a stereo panorama viewing application. Multiple users view high-resolution stereoscopic panoramas simultaneously. They connect to

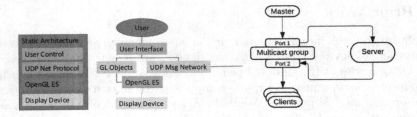

Fig. 1. Static, runtime, and network architecture.

the jitter server which distributes the smoothed packages to lead them on a guided tour. The clients follow the master's view direction and panorama changes. Stereo viewing is supported in GearVR and PowerWall systems, while the WebGL version is limited to monoscopic views. See snapshots in Figs. 1 and 2.

The panorama application presents a partial view of the full panorama with FOV determined by device characteristics. The user may look at any portion of the panorama via device specific controls. The mechanism varies by device: keyboard, mouse, touchpad, or gaze. Once a client slaves itself its view and panoramas are completely controlled by the master. Whenever the master adjusts its view or changes panoramas commands are transmitted to the slaves through the server. Communication is done via multicast UDP with a jitter server used to smooth motion between master and slaves.

iPhone System Display iPad System Display GearVR ScreenShot   Immersion Wall

Fig. 2. Application platforms.

5   Early Results

Early results for buffered smoothing are shown in Fig. 3: the black line represents the master movements while the blue and red lines represent the *non-weighted* and *weighted* smoothed buffers respectively. We have used different buffer sizes to see the differences in the behavior of the smoothing. These results show that the movement of the master can be smoothed to reduce the jitter transitions between frames so the user can be comfortable with the navigation. The next step is to ask real users about which of the approaches and buffer sizes are better for them within different applications.

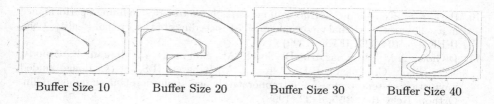

Buffer Size 10   Buffer Size 20   Buffer Size 30   Buffer Size 40

Fig. 3. Buffered results.

6   Conclusion and Future Work

This work in progress requires significant testing to be done in jitter measurement, FOV synchronizing, control curves and movement tracking. Additionally testing of multiple simultaneous users on both homogenous and heterogenous devices in an educational setting is planned to study the use of VR for learning and training.

References

1. Jara, C.A., Candelas, F.A., Torres, F., Dormido, S., Esquembre, F., Reinoso, O.: Real-time collaboration of virtual laboratories through the internet. Comput. Educ. **52**(1), 126–140 (2009)
2. Zhu, J., Gong, J., Liu, W., Song, T., Zhang, J.: A collaborative virtual geographic environment based on p2p and grid technologies. Inf. Sci. **177**(21), 4621–4633 (2007)
3. Scheucher, B., Bailey, P.H., Gütl, C., Harward, J.V.: Collaborative virtual 3d environment for internet-accessible physics experiments. iJOE **5**(S1), 65–71 (2009)
4. Ishibashi, Y., Asano, T.: Media synchronization control with prediction in a remote haptic calligraphy system. In: Proceedings of the International Conference on Advances in Computer Entertainment Technology, ACE 2007, pp. 79–86. ACM, New York, NY, USA (2007)
5. Macedonia, M.R., Zyda, M.J., Pratt, D.R., Barham, P.T., Zeswitz, S.: Npsnet: a network software architecture for largescale virtual environments. Presence Teleoperators Virtual Environ. **3**(4), 265–287 (1994)
6. Gossweiler, R., Laferriere, R.J., Keller, M.L., Pausch, R.: An introductory tutorial for developing multiuser virtual environments. Presence: Teleoperators Virtual Environ. **3**(4), 255–264 (1994)
7. Jeo, S., Kim, G.J.: Providing a wide field of view for effective interaction in desktop tangible augmented reality. In: Virtual Reality Conference, VR 2008, IEEE, pp. 3–10. IEEE (2008)
8. Bowman, D.A., Stinson, C., Ragan, E.D., Scerbo, S., Höllerer, T., Lee, C., McMahan, R.P., Kopper, R.: Evaluating effectiveness in virtual environments with mr simulation. In: Interservice/Industry Training, Simulation, and Education Conference (2012)
9. LaViola Jr., J.J.: discussion of cybersickness in virtual environments. ACM SIGCHI Bull. **32**(1), 47–56 (2000)

10. Park, K.S., Kenyon, R.V.: Effects of network characteristics on human performance in a collaborative virtual environment. In: Proceedings of the Virtual Reality, 1999. IEEE, pp. 104–111. IEEE (1999)
11. DiGioia, A.M., Jaramaz, B., Blackwell, M., Simon, D.A., Morgan, F., Moody, J.E., Nikou, C., Colgan, B.D., Aston, C.A., Labarca, R.S., et al.: Image guided navigation system to measure intraoperatively acetabular implant alignment. Clin. Orthop. Rela. Res. **355**, 8–22 (1998)

Larchiveum as an Augmented Historical Place: Blended Space Approach

Sun-Young Jang and Sung-Ah Kim[✉]

Department of Architecture, Sungkyunkwan University, Suwon, Republic of Korea
{abyme1204,sakim}@skku.edu

Abstract. This study proposed a composition logic of blended space in which the evolution of experience is possible constantly in terms of the augmented space experience of a historical site. On the basis of the blended space theory proposed as a methodology for organizing the user space experience between the physical space and digital space regarding a problem called the reproduction of experience, an augmented space experience method for overcoming it was composed. It composes an active learning environment, including the meaning and connective logic by linking the story composition and delivery method of digital storytelling to the space experience framework of the blended space. In particular, the application to digital tourism was represented through *Hwasung Castle* case. The prototype of the system is implemented using Unreal Engine. Implications deduced from building the prototype for simulation are used in composing an experiment environment targeting users.

Keywords: Blended space · Larchiveum · Augmented place · Multimedia · Urban regeneration

1 Introduction

Recently, the importance of the cultural strategy to develop the cultural environment has been emphasized in urban regeneration [1]. In particular, in successful cases of urban generation, such as Barcelona in Spain, Bologna in Italy, and Seattle Pioneer Square Historic District in the U.S., they innovated their space by utilizing historical resources and helped the community to overcome economic recession. There are an increasing number of cases involving introducing cultural complexes as a part of urban regeneration through cultural fusion. The British DCMS report 'Evidence-based case studies of culture's contribution to regeneration' explains this trend well [2].

Among various types of cultural complexes, experts are paying attention to the larchiveum. The larchiveum, a complex of a library, archive, and museum, is a concept Megan Winget introduced while proposing the necessity of a multidisciplinary collecting institution of massively multiplayer online (MMO) game material [3]. According to the International Federation of Library Associations and Institutions, libraries, archives, and museums will be practical partners within communities, since they all support and enhance the opportunity for lifelong education, preserve local cultural heritage, and protect and provide relevant information [4]. There are several

© Springer International Publishing AG 2016
Y. Luo (Ed.): CDVE 2016, LNCS 9929, pp. 353–361, 2016.
DOI: 10.1007/978-3-319-46771-9_46

factors in the background to consider the cooperation and integration of the three facilities: the digitization of materials to preserve and use them efficiently, the generalization of electronic publishing, increased web resources, and the increasing need for an integrated service that can be provided regardless of user type. Modern technologies, including Augmented Reality (AR)/Virtual Reality (VR), telecommunication devices, various detecting sensors of human motion, identity, and state change, network environments, or miniaturized computers, can be used to visualize the materials in a larchiveum and help users obtain relevant knowledge. Considering technology is in the process of advancement and the devices are generalized, it will be possible to provide an augmented experience readily to users in real time [11–13]. The existing digital larchiveum concept cases should enable the integrative facilitation of huge data derived from the cooperation of various institutes. Trove, established by the National Library of Australia, provides a digital image library service integrating libraries, archives, museums, colleges, historical academies, and other cultural facilities in cooperation with related organizations [14]. Europeana in Europe connects 2.3 million digital items, including documents, museum materials, artworks, music, images, and videos, and has implemented a user service through which users can sort the items by categories of interest [15]. Others, including services accessed by QR code providing the origin and information of the object or providing a navigation function and historical information according to the specific location of a historical place (Location-Based Service, LBS) by extracting the historical or geographical data of three institutions – a library, archive, and museum – are operated in *Hwasung Castle* historical places, the Cleveland Museum of Art, the National History Museum in Vienna, etc.

While the information from digital media offered by the larchiveum enables people to gain information about exhibits conveniently, it has caused a negative aspect called the reproduction of experience. LBS-based humanities GISs or relevant services guiding users in the larchiveum still do not generally consider the users' characteristics, knowledge level, and concerns, but reproduce automated experiences that provide certain information repeatedly in a specific position. The automated experiences provide the same experience to every user and can generate stereotyping errors by providing fixed ideas regarding the object of experience. While the original works in historical places or the larchiveum have an "aura," according to Benjamin, they can lose their value as a historical cultural resource due to changes to accommodate the attitudes of users and repetitive and typical content. Therefore, the providing way of digital information on historical cultural resources should consider changing to accommodate the attitudes of people and the generation method of experience that a lot of affects accommodation attitude.

2   Research Objectives

The methods of composing an experiential environment have problems receiving content at a specific place through humanities GIS or creating similar experiential content from web resources. The purpose of the research is to compose a blended space for the evolution of experience and solving the problem of the reproduction of experience, which provides the same experience to users. For this, the augmented space is composed based on the blended space theory to create a meaningful experiential environment for users. The connection and composition methods of related data are grafted onto the digital storytelling mechanism to create general content for composing the blended space. Digital tourism represents a method of applying elements of the blended space theory to a historical place appropriately. The proposed augmented space of the historical place presents the main elements and composition method for composing the augmented space based on the user experience method of digital tourism. This composition method is defined as a blended space unit. Sequences of units constitute the augmented space. The effect of the system will be verified through a simulation with a prototype before a full-scale introduction to a real space. The prototype of the system is implemented using Unreal Engine. Implications are deduced from the simulation process to build an experiential environment targeting users.

3 Concept of Larchiveum as Blended Space Integrating Historical Place and Media Enhanced Space

3.1 Blended Space Theory and Digital Tourism

Benyon's blended space theory is proposed as a methodology for organizing the user space's experiential manner through the combination of physical space and digital space. This theory can be a suitable background theory for developing experience content because the theory considers user activity in a space and focuses on the whole design of the experience at the human scale. Blended space is a theory that was presented on the basis of the conceptual blending theory [5]. It is used to formulate a mixed-reality experience focusing on the response between the digital space and physical space [6]. This theory has four key characteristics for describing the information space, spanning between the digital space and physical space: ontology, topology, volatility, and agency. Benyon described digital tourism as the utilization of blended space. Digital tourism involves the design of a user experience (UX) through the blended space framework in the context of historical content combined with personal interests. The four core features used in digital tourism are as follows [7].

- Ontology concerns the object of the target space. The core point of ontology for a tourist attraction is high-level points of interests (POIs). They are natural objects, buildings of historic sites, squares, and utilities. Ontology can relate to other POIs with a story or a temporal method for considering the property and function information of the object.
- Topology explains how different POIs are associated with each other in a given position. The relation of POIs derives from a restriction of various levels of the physical environment, tour, educational program, individual preference, and interest.
- Volatility is a concept related to the time of a place. The objects and people move through the space, and the topology changes according to the time flow. The space regularly changes depending on the day, time, and certain events.

– Agency is a core feature that affects the usefulness and enjoyment of the blended space in the digital space. It describes the possible ways of interacting with visitors in the space. Tourists typically rely on street signs or hire a guide. However, in a blended space, they can use the digital agency properly and pivotally. The digital agency can guide the tour with certain POIs.

Benyon tries to create an improved user experience by applying these four features of blended space. The key point is to use these four features in blended space UX and to find corresponding features between physical space and digital space.

3.2   System Design of Larchiveum Based on Blended Space Concept: *Hwasung Castle* Heritage Case

While tour services using smart devices have been used for *Hwasung Castle* by necessity, it does not provide a user experience at the level of augmented space. This study proposes a configuration method of augmented space through the blended space approach. *Hwasung Castle* was declared a UNESCO World Heritage Site in 1997. More than 2 million people visit this historical place every year. Thus, *Hwasung Castle* requires various tour services for visitors. The surrounding university and city have taken the lead to try to develop smart tour services. Some of the services are in the pilot stage or are being operated now.

The "Suwon *Hwasung Castle* mobile guiding service for smartphones" provides guidance for visitors regarding the main facilities located in *Hwasung Castle* through NFC or QR codes. This service provides the location of visitors and historical information on the facilities depending on users' current positions. Thus, it prevents visitors from experiencing confusion in the large area. "*Hwasung Castle* Histour" began a pilot service in 2010 through a game-based tour service using LBS. This service provides mission performances, simple games, and the delivery of event information related to specific locations. The "U-seum" of Suwon *Hwasung Castle* Museum was developed and demonstrated in 2011 to provide an event pop-up service using LBS in Suwon *Hwasung Castle* Museum. This pop-up service offers interesting game-based elements, such as quizzes, puzzles, and a listening service for descriptions.

The applications among the mentioned services are in the trial testing or discontinued state at present. While these services arouse visitor's interest by adding games and events with historical information, they have limitations for attracting attention from visitors because the information about the remains or facilities is fragmentary and lacks user context. The limitations exist because the services are not designed considering the context of user. Therefore, the service composition method of augmented space is proposed for the blended space approach focused on user experience.

- **Augmented Larchiveum of *Hwasung Castle* Heritage**
  The utilization scenario that applies the blended space framework is as follows (Fig. 1). The user can start the augmented space experience by selecting a physical object related to *Hwasung Castle*. The user tries to investigate a related subject to "the construction of *Hwasung Castle*." At the beginning of the story, they can choose a typical apparatus used in the construction of *Hwasung Castle* called "Geojunggi."

The Geojunggi is connected to other physical objects, such as ramparts, bricks, and design drawings, based on the relationship of functions or applications (ontology). The choice of the physical object is connected to the digital media device's existing surroundings. It can connect the digital agency related to the subject through digital devices. The representative digital agency related Geojunggi is Jung Yak-Yong, a designer of *Hwasung Castle*. The user listens to an explanation about working or receives directions to other places (POIs) related to the story in the design process through the digital agency. The completion degree of construction is exhibited differently according to the visiting season of the user (volatility). If the user visits in October, they can participate in the completion ceremony.

Fig. 1.   (a) Blended space framework [6] (b) Larchiveum as an augmented space: *Hwasung Castle* heritage

4   Evolution of Experience in Blended Space

4.1   Blended Space Structure

Although the "reproduction of experience" and "evolution of experience" have the same content resources, the structure of experience is made differently according to what the user chooses first and involves context. The origin of this structure can be found from the structure of the digital storytelling featuring the interactivity. Intelligent Video Editor, the most similar system to the "evolution of experience," has a structure that automatically classifies and extracts the existing fragmentary information by the rules defined by the user by means of multimedia and combines it with more advanced subjects to restructure it into a useful information resource [8]. Manovich said it was hard to see the users making their own route by choosing the records of the database in a certain order to make their distinctive narrative structure, and they had to adjust the meaning of elements and the logic of the connection to satisfy the narrative standards [9].

The structure creating the "evolution of experience" suggested from this context does not mean a simple connection of resources existing in the database. The evolution of experience lets the content experience be reproduced with various stories and meanings in response to the method of digital storytelling and the framework of the blended space, forming the meaning of the space experience. The structure of the evolution of experience creates a different experience structure every time through various combinations as a kind of unit or set containing essential components. This unit defines the Blended Space Unit (BSU). Blended Space is made by the sequence of units. The BSU is generated by associating Benyon's blended space framework and the digital storytelling mechanism (Fig. 2). The digital storytelling mechanism is made by combining a content database of various images, texts, video clips etc. and the user context, which is the user's profile (age, gender, job, areas of interest, recent visiting information, etc.), the purpose of the visit, or the task. The generated BSU has three components: the Physical Object, Media Object, and Content. The detailed classification of each element is shown in Table 1.

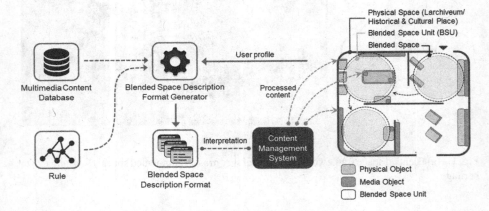

Fig. 2. System diagram for composing the blended space

Table 1. Classification details of the Blended Space Unit (BSU)

Elements of BSU	Classification Details
Physical Object	Natural object with historical stories in the physical space, artifact (ex. old tree, Korean traditional totem pole, rampart, building, door attached to the building, book, artwork etc.)
Media Object	The type of digital media is classified as installed, projected, embedded, personal. The media object works as single or complex object by selecting an appropriate type according to content.
Content	Types of text, graphics, audio and visual as multimedia-containing mediums related to the historical place

Figure 2 represents the system configuration of the composite blended space. The blended space description format (BSDF) generator creates the BSDF, which processes the content of the multimedia content database through rules referring to the user profile transmitted from the physical space. The rules select a media representation method suitable for the content type and configure the result according to specific conditions related to the user or story. The generated BSDF is interpreted by a content management system (CMS). The processed content creates the BSU by transmitting the media of the physical space.

4.2   Prototyping and Simulation of the BSU

The prototype aims to simulate whether the proposed augmented space functioning as an active learning environment is possible for the intuitive and active learning about the cultural heritage. Figure 3 shows a prototype of the BSU implemented by Unreal Engine to compose the interactive virtual reality. It represents combinations of physical objects, media objects, and content and changing states according to the user context and choices. As a result of composing the environment through the prototype, the computer program environment is more simplified than a real experiment and describes the utilization of various media simultaneously within one program environment. Therefore, it has an advantage of composing an environment rather than constructing a whole system by connecting each digital media device in a real environment. On the other hand, the presence of physical objects is insufficient because the physical objects exist in a virtual environment.

Fig. 3. Simulation environment of Blended Space Unit (BSU) using game engine

The augmented space works by mixing with physical objects and media objects simultaneously. Therefore, the precise effects of the augmented space will be tested by applying physical objects in the real space to add to the reality of the experiment space. The communication function with other people can be considered an extension of the function provided by the system. Exchanging opinions with other people and gaining feedback on ideas can work for the improvement of the understanding of the historical place and the formation of the thoughts of the user. The implementation of the prototype helps for developing the direction of development on functions for more positive effects in an experiment for an active learning environment in the future. The experiment targeting actual users reflects the mentioned points and refers to the principles of active learning [10] to develop measures as a standard for user evaluation.

5   Conclusion

This study proposed a composition logic of blended space in which the evolution of experience is possible constantly in terms of the augmented space experience of a historical site. On the basis of the blended space theory proposed as a methodology regarding a problem called the reproduction of experience, an augmented space experience method for overcoming it was composed. It composes an active learning environment, including the meaning and connective logic by linking the digital storytelling to the space experience framework of the blended space. In particular, the application to digital tourism was represented through the *Hwasung Castle* case. Through this, it will be possible to overcome the disadvantage of a fixed experience, which is a common limitation of the smart tour services in *Hwasung Castle*. This study proposed the content-composing principle and has a limit that the actual use and evaluation are inadequate. Implications deduced from building the prototype for simulation are used in composing an experiment environment targeting users.

A future study based on the results of this study could involve a learning environment formation with the test and evaluation. This smart learning environment will be a way of heightening the accessibility to knowledge compared with the existing larchiveum or historical site tourism and is differentiated from the previous augmented space through the formation of a dynamic experience, real-time sharing from various contexts, and contributing to the reproduction of knowledge by inducing civil participation. While the existing smart services provided technology that was anticipated to be useful for the introduction stage, in the present, the advanced technology of AR/VR makes it possible to embody experiences improved by widespread equipment, and the demand for services beyond information delivery is increasing.

Acknowledgment. This research was supported by Basic Science Research Program through the National Research Foundation of Korea (NRF) funded by the Ministry of Education, Science and Technology (NRF-2013R1A1A2A10057503).

References

1. Miles, S., Paddison, R.: Introduction: the rise and rise of culture-led urban regeneration. Urban stud. **42**(5–6), 833–839 (2005)
2. Evans, G., Shaw, P.: The Contribution of Culture to Regeneration in the UK: A Review of Evidence, vol. 4. DCMS, London (2004)
3. Kuzyk, R.: LJ talks to Megan Winget, who studies preservation of online games. Libr. J., July, 2008 http://www.libraryjournal.com/article/CA6582968.html
4. Yarrow, A., Clubb, B., Draper, J.L.: Public Libraries, Archives and Museums: Trends in Collaboration and Cooperation. International Federation of Library Associations and Institutions, The Hague (2008)
5. Fauconnier, G., Turner, M.: The Way We Think: Conceptual Blending and the Mind's Hidden Complexities. Basic Books (2008)
6. Benyon, D.: Presence in blended spaces. Interact. Comput. **24**(4), 219–226 (2012)
7. Benyon, D.: Spaces of interaction, places for experience. In: Synthesis Lectures on Human-Centered Information, vol. 7, no. 2, pp. 1–129 (2014)

8. Kim, S.-A.: Development of the intelligent video editor for the research and education of architectural history. J. Architectural Inst. Korea **13**, 67–74 (1997). (in Korea)
9. Manovich, L.: The Language of New Media. MIT press, Cambridge (2001)
10. Barnes, D.R.: Active Learning. Leeds University TVEI Support Project, p. 19 (1989)
11. www.ted.com/talks/blaise_aguera. 20 May 2016
12. www.ted.com/talks/marco_tempest_a_magical_tale_with_augmented_reality. 20 May 2016
13. www.youtube.com/watch?v=aThCr0PsyuA&feature=player_embedded. 20 May 2016
14. http://trove.nla.gov.au/. 20 May 2016
15. http://www.europeana.eu/portal/. 20 May 2016

Understanding the Impact of Mobile Augmented Reality on Co-design Cognition and Co-modelling

Leman Figen Gül[1(⊠)], Müge Halıcı[2], Can Uzun[2], and Mustafa Esengün[3]

[1] Faculty of Architecture, Istanbul Technical University (ITU), Istanbul, Turkey
fgul@itu.edu.tr
[2] Architectural Design Computing Program, ITU, Istanbul, Turkey
{halici,uzunc}@itu.edu.tr
[3] Faculty of Computer Engineering, ITU, Istanbul, Turkey
esengun@itu.edu.tr

Abstract. With the development of the computer technology, new ways of model making become an alternative for the representation of the design ideas. In this paper, we present a new design platform based on the mobile augmented reality technology for a co-design situation. A marker-based mobile augmented reality platform for the early phase of the co-design process is presented. A pilot study is conducted and the data is analyzed with the protocol analysis method. In the paper we provide some insights of the impact of the employment of the mobile augmented reality technology in the co-design situation.

Keywords: Collaborative design · Mobile augmented reality · Protocol analysis

1 Introduction

Over the last decade, with the proliferation of the mobile communication technologies, there has an increase in the development of the applications and devices of augmented reality. In general, Augmented Reality (AR) technology includes a combination of the real and the virtual by providing 3D real time interactivity [1]. The early version of the AR technology is mainly considered as a representation tool for the evaluation of the design proposal [2, 3]. The recent mobile AR technology has the potential to offer new opportunities to designers as a new design platform that the visual and the physical models are superimposed for the real time designing and visual analysis of the idea. Thus, the AR technology can provide the shared virtual model for co-designers to discuss and interact with.

The aim of this study is to understand the changes of co-designer's design reasoning and communication activities while they are working on the virtual model using a mobile AR technology. In order to understand the changes of their reasoning, we compare the dialogues and actions of designers: 1. When they are co-designing with the physical models, and 2. When they are co-designing with the augmented digital model,

© Springer International Publishing AG 2016
Y. Luo (Ed.): CDVE 2016, LNCS 9929, pp. 362–370, 2016.
DOI: 10.1007/978-3-319-46771-9_47

employing the Protocol Analysis method (see [4]) which is widely used in collaborative design settings [5–7]. In this paper, the proposed AR platform is presented and the result of a pilot study is discussed.

2 Studying Marker-Based AR in Collaborative Design

In general, design process has complex components as well as static and dynamic relationships between those components. Researchers attempt to offer new design tools and technologies to overcome those complexities facilitating alternative visualization and representation techniques. In the co-design situation, the shared representation of the design idea plays a key role as the communicative resource of the interaction between the designers. In particular, the model making is one of these shared representations. Making the model represents the concretization of ideas, by getting as close as possible to the actual construction of the design proposal. In addition, models can help with the creative process of visualizing 3D space directly by functioning to help with the inspection of the complex visual relationships, so the models outperform drawings [8]. Kvan and Thilakaratne [9] pointed out that models offer benefits of approachability, tangibility, manipulability and collaborative engagement.

The augmented digital models can be considered as the new design representations that could have a consistency and long life span which may not require continues reconstruction, in contrast to analogue tools such as sketches and physical models, which 'involve considerable redrawing, tracing and scale model making' [10]. There are many studies to employ the AR technology in the design field, for example; developing an augmented sketching tool for the early phase of the design process [11, 12]; developing a tool for urban design [13]; and for civil engineering [14]. Although the employment of the physical model making and sketching in the design process have been extensively studied in the individual cases [15, 16], and also in the group processes [17, 18], there is a limited number of studies of employing mobile augmented reality technology in the collaborative model making. This research is concerned with designers' cognition and communication activities while they are carrying out collaborative design tasks using a marker-based mobile AR environment.

Collaborative Marker-based AR Platform. A marker-based mobile AR environment is developed for the study using the Unity3D (www.unity.com) game engine with the Vuforia AR plugin. In the Vuforia AR, a library of markers is adapted to match several target objects that are sets of basic primitives (cubes, spheres and cylinders). In order to augment the objects on the scene, the Vuforia AR plugin requires the definition of image targets for each of the target objects. The image targets are the unique predefined 2D shapes, similar to the QR codes, which are recognized by the mobile device's camera. In the developed application, nine image targets are defined and assigned to the basic primitive objects. The application has the interface components to manage and manipulate the augmented objects, as shown in Fig. 1. The users are able to operate dragging, rotating, scaling and changing the color of the objects. In addition, the Vuforia AR enables extended tracking, that is, once the image target is detected, it

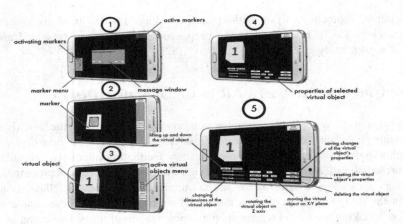

Fig. 1. The mobile AR interface. The smart phones and Android-IOS tablets can be used.

keeps the objects on the screen, even the image target is moved out of the vision of the mobile device's camera.

3 Methodology: Protocol Analysis of Co-design with Mobile AR

In order to analyze and document the collaborative behavior of designers in two different design settings, a pilot study is conducted at the Department of Architecture in the Istanbul Technical University: 1. Co-designing with the physical modelling environment (PM), and 2. Co-design with enhanced marker-based mobile AR environment (AR). A pair of architects collaborating on two different design tasks with the similar complexity are examined. The assumption of the study is that a comparison of the same architects in two different environments would provide better indication of the impact of the environments than using different designers and the same design task. With these ideas in mind, the pilot study with two design settings is developed. In order to have a collaborative working environment, one tablet view is shared and a glass-top table that has the shared view of the tablet's display projected onto is provided. A physical model and the plan of the site in 1:500 scale are also provided to help the visualization of the given design context. The designers are able to inspect the site in both physically and virtually in the 2D and 3D environments, as shown in Fig. 2.

The first phase, co-design with the physical modelling tools (PM), the site model and the plan are given in 1:500 scale. The cardboard plates and small boxes in different sizes, pen, paper, knives, and some other modelling materials are also provided. The second phase, co-design with the enhanced mobile AR platform (AR): Android and IOS tablets, the markers, the physical site model and plan in 1:500 scale and the glass-top table with the shared view of the AR interface are provided to the designers. The designers had a training session followed by the experiments. During the

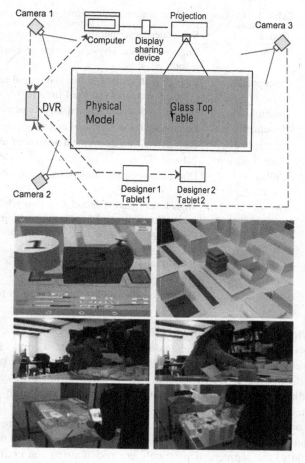

Fig. 2. The experiment setup: the AR display is projected onto the glass-top table and the sessions are recorded onto the DVR (top). The experiments screen shots are at the bottom: the final models are on the top from the AR and PM sessions.

experiments, three cameras are used to capture the designers' actions and verbalizations, as shown in Fig. 2.

In addition, in the second phase (AR) the screen view of the shared tablet is also captured. All the video and audio data are fed into a DVR (Digital Video Recording) system.

3.1 Protocol Analysis

First adopted by Eastman [19] to study design cognition, protocol analysis was used as the research technique. Early design studies used the method to study individual's design cognition. In the late1980 s, a prompt shift observed in the protocol studies by

Table 1. Co-design and communication coding scheme

Category	Codes	Sub-codes/Description
Co-design cognition	Physical	Engage with the physical aspects of elements (size, form etc.)
	Perceptual	Engage with visual features and spatial relationships of design elements (adopted from [6])
	Functional	Engage with the functional aspects of elements
	Structural	Engage with the structural aspects of elements
	Conceptual	Engage with the conceptual aspects of elements
Communication	Representation	2D and 3D
	Collab. content	Discussions on making/discussions on designing
	Design exchanges	High level (making broad decisions which affect significant aspects)/Low level (making more focused decisions for individual elements) (adopted from [23])
	Collab. mode	Individual/Team
	Shared content	On Given Model/on Proposal
	Agent actions	Gesture/on Element/on Tools (adopted from [6])

extending individual's design activity to the team's design activity [20, 21]. A team's design protocols resembles the 'think aloud' method, since a joint task seemed to provide data indicative of the cognitive abilities that were being undertaken by the team members [22]. Consequently, we examine the communication protocols by using a customized coding scheme that has two main categories: co-design cognition and communication, as shown in Table 1.

The data is analyzed using the protocol analysis method that requires transcription, segmentation and coding the data. We have done the transcription and then, the data is segmented. Finally, the segmented protocols are coded using the coding scheme, as shown in the Table 1.

4 Results and Discussion

The data is analyzed with the behavioral analysis software (INTERACT 15) that enables multiple tasks, such as managing codes, accessing multimedia stream, and seeing the coding scheme as well as the management of the data, to be undertaken in one interface, as shown in Fig. 3.

The results show that the designers are able to adapt the mobile augmented reality system showing similar behavioral patterns in the PM and AR environments with some exceptions. Table 2 shows the counts, the durations and the duration percentages of the categories in both sessions (PM and AR): In general, there is an increase in the duration percentages of the co-design cognition codes (conceptual, functional, physical) in the AR phase (23,7 %, 9.8 % and 24,8 %) with a drop of the percentages in the brief inspection code, the perceptual and the structural codes, as shown in Table 2. This

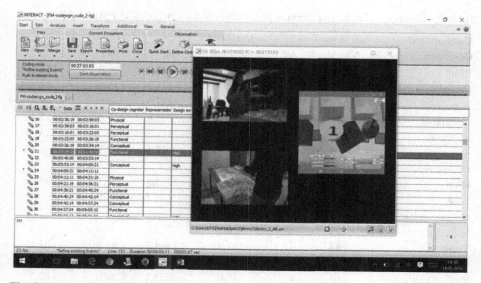

Fig. 3. The interface of INTERACT software, showing the scene, segments, codes and video.

means that the AR environment supports the discussions on the conceptual, functional and physical aspects of the design idea. The reason of having low structure related discussions might be the 3D mass target objects (cube, cylinder, sphere) provided by the AR system that may not initiating discussions on the structural issues. The sharpest decrease is observed in the design exchanges categories: The duration percentage of low-level design exchanges is null (0.4 %), and the duration percentage of the high level design exchanges (99,6 %) increases in the AR phase. This shows that the designers talk about overall design concepts and ideas, and they did not talk much on the individual design elements in the AR environment.

The analysis shows that the AR environment supports the team work; there is an increase in the duration percentages of the team codes (83 %). In addition, the designers focused on the making of the virtual model (57,5 %), and spend more time on the given interface in order to make the model (65,8 % about_making and 49.5 % onTools actions) in the AR environment, as shown in Table 2. This result shows that having a shared display and shared design tools encourage designers to work together on the development of the design proposal. In addition, a drop in the duration percentages of the gesture codes is observed in the AR phase.

The drop of the gesture and the increase of the making actions might suggest that the designer's focus shifts on the production of the design idea in the AR phase. We may argue that as the visual stimulation is supported by the AR, spatial imagery is not necessary and thus, gestures is reduced. This result may suggest that the AR environment reduces the cognitive load of the designers by providing direct visual stimulation of the design artefact. This result needs to be examined in more detail in the future studies.

Table 2. Durations, counts, and duration percentages of the categories in PM and AR sessions

Category/code	Count		Duration		Duration in Class	
Co-design Cognition	PM	AR	[sec] PM	AR	[%] PM	AR
Brief	19	18	353,6	282,0	28,3	22,5
Conceptual	20	20	198,0	297,1	15,8	23,7
Functional	5	7	57,3	123,0	4,6	9,8
Perceptual	18	7	212,4	192,8	17,0	15,4
Physical	16	21	266,5	311,3	21,3	24,8
Structural	10	3	163,9	48,1	13,1	3,8
Design Ex-change						
High	52	63	721,3	1075,5	56,1	99,6
Low	28	1	563,6	4,7	43,9	0,4
Collaboration mode						
Individual	28	16	624,8	293,1	34,4	16,4
Team	88	91	1192,9	1494,2	65,6	83,6
Collaboration Content						
about_Design	65	41	885,0	633,1	54,0	42,5
about_Making	34	45	754,3	857,8	46,0	57,5
Sharing Content						
On_Given_Model	44	41	798,1	551,3	42,5	34,2
On_Proposal	72	58	1079,0	1060,7	57,5	65,8
Agent Actions						
Gesture	45	21	539,6	287,2	31,3	17,4
onTools	27	48	493,6	815,6	40,1	49,4
OnElements	35	27	691,2	547,9	28,6	33

5   Conclusions

In this paper, we present the results of the pilot study to examine the collaborative design activity of the mobile AR technology users. The results of the analyses show that the physical and the mobile AR modelling sessions produce parallel processes in terms of the designers' co-design activities, with some exceptions: The content of the discussion is broad conceptual and high-level and the intensity of the collaborative design actions is different in the AR session. During both sessions, we observed that the participants inspect the relationship of the prisms by orienting and changing the locations of the objects. This means that the mobile AR technology encourages the designers to co-examine the alternative solutions and configurations of the blocks through visual inspections. We also noted that in the mobile AR session, they have spent more time on the bodily engagement by standing up, looking around and bending their body around the table. This might happen because they are trying to keep the markers on the field of vision to establish smooth object registration that is always considered as a difficult task in AR systems.

A further study will be conducted to evaluate more on the use of AR based collaborative design environments providing more and varied design objects (geometric primitives and library of customized building elements) to understand the effects of the affordances of the objects on design cognition and behavior. We consider this knowledge would be informative for the development of the innovative collaborative design environments and be guidance for the further developments.

Acknowledgements. The research is funded by the Scientific and Technological Research Council of Turkey (TUBITAK), PN:115K515.

References

1. Azuma, R.T.: A Survey of Augmented Reality. Presence Tele-operators Virtual Environ. **6**(4), 355–385 (1997)
2. Kim, M., Maher, M.L.: Comparison of designers using a tangible user interface & graphical user interface and impact on spatial cognition. In: Proceeding Human Behavior in Design, vol. 5, p. 14 (2005)
3. Ko, C.H., Chang, T.C.: Evaluation and student perception of augmented reality based design collaboration. Management **6**(6), 6 (2011)
4. Ericsson, K.A., Simon, H.A.: Protocol analysis. MIT Press, Cambridge (1993)
5. Gabriel, G.C.: Computer Mediated Collaborative Design in Architecture: The Effects of Communication Channels on Collaborative Design Communication (Doctoral Dissertation, University of Sydney) (2000)
6. Gül, L.F.: Understanding Collaborative Design in Different Environments: Comparing Face to Face Sketching to Remote Sketching and 3D Virtual Worlds. Key Centre for Design Computing and Cognition. (Doctoral Dissertation, University of Sydney) (2007)
7. Gül, L.F., Maher, M.L.: Co-creating external design representations: comparing face to face sketching to designing in virtual environments. Co-design Int. J. Co-creation Design Arts **2**, 117–138 (2009). ISSN: 1571-0882
8. Porter, T., Neale, J.: Architectural Supermodels. Architectural Press, Oxford (2000)
9. Kvan, T., Thilakaratne, R.: Models in the design conversation: architectural vs engineering. In: Proceedings of AASA Conference. Association of Architecture Schools of Australia, Melbourne (2003)
10. Achten, H., Joosen, G.: The digital design process -reflections on a single design case. In: Digital Design, 21st eCAADe Conference Proceedings, Graz, Austria, pp. 269–274 (2003)
11. Seichter, H.: Sketchand + A collaborative augmented reality sketching application. In: Proceedings of the 8th International Conference on Computer Aided Architectural Design Research in Asia. Bangkok Thailand, 18–20, October 2003
12. Yee, B., Ning, Y., Lipson, H.: Augmented Reality In-Situ 3D Sketching of Physical Objects. In: CHI (2009)
13. Seichter, H.: Benchworks augmented reality urban design. In: Proceedings of the 9th International Conference on Computer Aided Architectural Design Research in Asia Seoul, Korea (2004)
14. Riera, S.A., Redondo, E., Fonseca, D.: Geo-located teaching using handheld augmented reality: good practices to improve the motivation and qualifications of architecture. Univ. Access Inf. Soc. **14**(3), 363–374 (2014)
15. Janke, R.: Architectural Models. Academic Editions, London (1978)

16. Goldschmidt, G.: Interpretation: its role in architectural design. Design Stud. **9**(4), 235–245 (1988)
17. Schön, D.A.: The Design Studio: An Exploration of its Traditions and Potentials, pp 30–32. RIBA, London (1985)
18. Ward, T.: Design archetypes from group processes. Design Stud. **8**(3), 157–169 (1987)
19. Eastman, C.M.: Explorations of the Cognitive Processes in Design, in Department of Computer Science Report. Carnegie Mellon University, Pittsburgh (1968)
20. Cross, N.: Design cognition: results from protocol and other empirical studies of design activity. In: Newstetter, W. (ed.) Design Knowing and Learning: Cognition in Design Education. Elsevier, Amsterdam (2001)
21. Schön, D.A.: Problems, frames and perspectives on designing. Design Stud. **5**(3), 132–136 (1984)
22. Cross, A.C., Cross, N.: Observations of teamwork and social processes in design. In: Cross, N., Christiaans, H., Dorst, K. (eds.) Analyzing Design Activity, pp. 291–317. Wiley, West Sussex (1996)
23. Vera, A.H., Kvan, T., West, R.L., Lai, S.: Expertise, collaboration and bandwidth. In: SIGCHI, CHI 1998, pp. 502–510. ACM, Los Angeles (1998)

Cooperative and Immersive Coaching to Facilitate Skill Development in Construction Tasks

Lei Hou[1(✉)], Hung-Lin Chi[2], Erezi Utiome[1], and Xiangyu Wang[2]

[1] Griffith University, Gold Coast, Australia
{lei.hou,e.utiome}@griffith.edu.au
[2] Curtin University, Perth, Australia
{hung-lin.chi,Xiangyu.wang}@curtin.edu.au

Abstract. At present, construction operations training offered by qualified organisations and associations for the Australian oil and gas, mineral and chemical industries have been provided at only limited levels. Moreover, the relevant training facilities and centres being established or considered in the construction agenda are insufficient to meet the growing standard of operators and industry expansion. These facts illustrate the need for developing effective cooperative coaching and learning systems for expediting the acquisition of fundamental construction skills. Accordingly, the aim of this ongoing study is to establish scientific principles for developing appropriate Virtual Reality (VR) and Augmented Reality (AR) supported cooperative and immersive training prototypes and curriculum to meet the above mentioned purposes. Through the application of pertinent learning theories, system prototyping and experimentation techniques, this study is envisioned to significantly supplement interactive and immersive site experiences from immersive training environment, and produce cost-effective and efficient ways to manage the skill shortage challenges in mega construction projects.

Keywords: Immersive training · Skills acquisition · Virtual Reality (VR) and Augmented Reality (AR) · Cognitive theories · Concurrent Engineering (CE)

1 Background

To gain hands-on skills and work experience in a recognised qualification in construction sectors, traineeships should usually be workplace-based or encompassing both off and on-the-job training options. Within the traditional construction industry, the usual source of human resource supply of site workers and technicians is from vocational education or work-based, second-class education [1]. However, a significant impact on the present day transfer of professional knowledge and skills is noticeable; on the one hand, joining the construction profession is becoming much less attractive to the younger generation, on the other hand, there is a dearth in training tools and current approaches aligned with contemporary complex construction projects and activities [2]. These issues materialise in the form of well-known construction bottlenecks such as: low labour productivity, frequent schedule delays and increased occurrences of workplace accidents [3–5].

© Springer International Publishing AG 2016
Y. Luo (Ed.): CDVE 2016, LNCS 9929, pp. 371–377, 2016.
DOI: 10.1007/978-3-319-46771-9_48

Regrettably, a lack of work-based learning curricula and training opportunities has, to some extent, impeded the acquisition of necessary competences and proficiencies for construction practitioners [6–8].

2 Literature Review

An overview of the present literature illustrates that there is still a dearth of effective training approaches for improving workforce performance in the field of construction [9, 10]. As a mighty remedy for the issue, visualisation technologies-based training such as Virtual Reality (VR) and Augmented Reality (AR) can afford new opportunities for effectively training novices with lower cost and fewer hazards [11]. Using visualisation as the training platform could significantly improve people perception about the geometrical features and spatial locations of components in operation task and considerably lower the difficulty in cognition and information retrieval. Rezazadeh et al. [9] indicated that visualisation could facilitate coaching and learning progress along a steep learning curve and enable effective rehearsal of future operations in actual construction sites. The promise of such effectiveness is also evidenced from mental health research fields which reveal that a virtual experience can evoke the same reactions and emotions as a real experience [12].

3 Objectives and Methodology

Based on an ongoing study, this paper accordingly aims at establishing scientific principles for developing appropriate VR and AR prototypes and curricula that will promisingly expedite the process of mastering the fundamental skills in mega project construction. The two particular objectives are (1) to create a usable VR plus AR framework that supports comprehensive and practical experience of operating heavy equipment as well as conducting other complex activities of construction, and (2) to scientifically verify the merits of applying a set of VR plus AR paradigms to acquire cognitive and sensorimotor skills that are essential in the real practice.

4 Research Implementation

4.1 Establishment of Critical Performance (Proficiency) Metrics with Quantitative Indicators

There are numerous critical indicators identified for evaluating training performance. Through consulting with a large number of practitioners from Liquefied Natural Gas construction projects, the researchers will formulate a break-down structure incorporating performance measurement metrics by taking into account the measurable variables related to work stages, environmental variables and ergonomics evaluation to create a comprehensive analysis.

4.2   Process of Implementing Training Curricula

Once the guiding inquiry metrics have been formulated, the implementation plans for exploring these metrics must be established for curricula development, in which trainers can make explicit statements about learning effects. Therefore, the curricula should be inclusive of a series of activities from which knowledge or skills can possibly be constructed and acknowledged based on learners' performance indices.

4.3   Modelling, Design and Development of Proficiency-Based Training Systems

Game engines such as Unity and Ngrain will be used to develop virtual training and coaching systems given the features of simple operation, cross-platform compatibility, powerful maintainability and expansibility. Another consideration is that gaming techniques can also support scenario customisation via user scripting in various languages such as JavaScript, C# or Boo (users are allowed to retrieve different scripts that are open-sourced and formulate their own scripts). An AR system will be prototyped under Objective C, an iOS programming language, and integrates various software development kits (SDK) such as mobile AR SDK, sensing/tracking SDK and real-time communication SDK.

4.4   Design and Implementation of Experimentation to Validate Training Effects

All experimental scenarios will be simulated at the Curtin Immersive Hub and the hypotheses of the experiment include: (1) the developed training curricula can enhance the learning performance of participants in terms of a number of skill capacities defined in the proposed proficiency metrics; (2) comparative results show similar trends for the proficiency level growth between the proposed trainings and the counterparts operated in actual facilities.

4.5   Data Evaluation and Conclusion

Performance criteria for the skill transferability assessment in the training scenarios will be established as they are important to recognise that a key element of the proposed proficiency-based training approach is the use of criteria for assessment. Rather than passing written tests to prove declarative knowledge, the trainee will have to demonstrate knowledge by solving problems that encapsulate the knowledge.

4.6   System Development

Currently, a series of mixed reality training scenarios by integrating AR and VR environments derived from real construction field environment have been tentatively developed and perfected. These applicable training programs include scenarios of earth work for operating a track backhoe excavator, lifting work for tower crane operation and assembly work for construction fitters. The current settings are based on desktop VR

Fig. 1. Development of backhoe excavator scenario

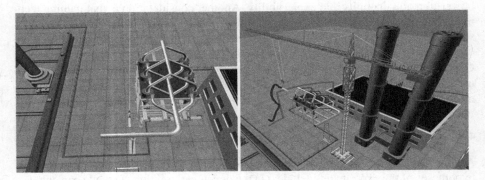

Fig. 2. Path guidance (Red Line) and actual operation trajectory (Blue Line). (Color figure online)

and AR, where the users can use a desktop monitor and mouse to interact with mixed reality context (Figs. 1 and 2).

4.7 Rationalising VR and AR Assembly Scenarios Through Concurrent Engineering (CE)

In the field of construction and maintenance, AR has been tentatively deployed as a very practical and promising assistive tool/technique for improving task comprehension, component location recognition and task execution accuracy [13–16]. The current training platform supplements a trainee's natural visual aptitude with assistive cues such as texts, arrows and animated construction guidance in relation to parts assembly and/or location (Fig. 3). Furthermore, the study also adopts a VR ergonomic analysis tool to evaluate the design of workflow and workplace activities (Fig. 4). To deliver a better and effective workplace-driven learning curriculum in constructing an LNG facility, DELMIA – regarded as a helpful and handy solution – was adopted to support a comprehensive array of activity simulations by trainees. This can be set forth and reviewed after VR-based construction has been implemented. This solution is envisaged to facilitate the trainees to understand and re-plan their own activities accordingly.

Fig. 3. AR-supported construction scaffolds assembly

Fig. 4. VR-supported LNG pipeline assembly using ngrain engine

Therefore, this paper argues that far reaching implications in the delivering of immersive instructional training for Mega construction projects through the use of VR and AR tools can be rationalised by CE. This rationale can be best understood by first determining what training applications are best suited to AR or VR and by understanding the principles of CE.

While the basic distinction between AR and VR lies in the greater extent of user-immersion involved in the later over the former, CE is concerned with how trainees can take advantage of these platforms to attain efficiencies by way of compressed project duration, enhanced product value, and reduced project costs. Knowledge of CE will thus empower trainees to leverage AR and VR technologies to simulate crucial scenarios during various stages throughout the lifecycle of megaprojects, thereby reducing, if not completely eliminating, the significant levels of uncertainty that belie traditional training approaches.

Thus, by establishing and preserving the integration of CE and AR/VR, trainings organised on mega construction projects stand to derive significant benefits such as: improved understanding and implementation of stakeholders' requirements, improved communication and cooperation between trainees, improved understanding of team work and project effectiveness, reduced probability that rework (e.g. redesigns, non-conformances etc.) will occur, and significant reduction in project time and budget.

5   Summary and Future Study

In conclusion, immersive VR plus AR have become the promising technologies for coaching and learning purpose particularly in a wide range of architecture, engineering and construction disciplines. It allows a training paradigm with features of both context and location awareness so that information acquisition and interpretation are reasonably handy and rapid. Apart from repetitive activities, e.g. civil work, lifting work and construction work, most jobsite environments also encompass unpredictable variables, for instance, potential hazards, inconsistency of as-planed and as-build scheme, and intricate workflow. The flexibility of customizing the ad hoc scenarios is deemed as vital for developing pertinent apprenticeship programs in a VR and AR session. Notwithstanding the learning curve may not necessarily grow as fast as that under the jobsite based training, constructing such a system is less costly and for any of the trials made therein it is risk free. Imminent work will give special attention to system deployment and integration, and data interpretation based on the as designed quantifiable indicators for rating skill and proficiency.

References

1. Construction Training Council. Construction Industry Workforce Development Plan 2014. Retrieved 4 Nov. 2014. bcitf.org/upload/documents/research_reports/CTCWDPforCTF website2014v20141003e.pdf
2. Abdel-Wahab, M.: Rethinking apprenticeship training in the British construction industry. J. Vocat. Educ. Training **64**(2), 145–154 (2012)
3. Hu, K., Rahmandad, H., Smith-Jackson, T., Winchester, W.: Factors influencing the risk of falls in the construction industry: a review of the evidence. Constr. Manage. Econ. **29**(4), 397–416 (2011)
4. Zhou, W., Whyte, J., Sacks, R.: Construction safety and digital design: a review. Autom. Constr. **22**, 102–111 (2012)
5. Sacks, R., Perlman, A., Barak, R.: Construction safety training using immersive virtual reality. Constr. Manage. Econ. **31**(9), 1005–1017 (2013)
6. Goulding, J., Nadim, W., Petridis, P., Alshawi, M.: Construction industry offsite production: a virtual reality interactive training environment prototype. Adv. Eng. Inf. **26**, 103–116 (2012)
7. Chappelow, C.: Managing the Australian LNG Skill Shortage. *Interpro.com.au*. Retrieved 16 Sep. 2015. http://www.interpro.com.au/managing-australian-lng-skill-shortage
8. Harrier Human Capital. (2012). LNG Talent Strategies: Time for a Re-think? *Harrierhumancapital.com*. Retrieved 16 Sep. 2014. www.harrierhumancapital.com/wp-content/uploads/2014/01/LNG-Recruitment-Time-for-A-Rethink_0.pdf
9. Rezazadeh, I.M., Wang, X., Firoozabadi, M., Hashemi Golpayegani, M.R.: Using affective human–machine interface to increase the operation performance in virtual construction crane training system: A novel approach. Autom. Constr. **20**(3), 289–298 (2011)
10. Hou, L., Wang, X.: A study on the benefits of augmented reality in retaining working memory in assembly tasks: a focus on differences in gender. Autom. Constr. **32**, 38–45 (2013)

11. Wang, X., Truijens, M., Hou, L., Wang, Y.: Application of collaborative mobile system in ar-based visualization. In: Yuhua, Y. (ed.) EuroGP 2009. LNCS, vol. 8091, pp. 221–226. Springer, Heidelberg (2013)

12. Schuemie, M.J., Van Der Straaten, P., Krijn, M., Van Der Mast, C.A.: Research on presence in virtual reality: A survey. CyberPsychology Behav. **4**(2), 183–201 (2001)

13. Wang, X., Dunston, P.S.: A user-centered taxonomy for specifying mixed reality systems for aec industry: ITcon (2011)

14. Hou, L., Wang, Y., Wang, X., Maynard, N., Cameron, I.T., Zhang, S., Maynard, N.: Combining photogrammetry and augmented reality towards an integrated facility management system for the oil industry. Proc. IEEE **102**(2), 204–220 (2014)

15. Behzadan, A.H., Kamat, V.R.: Visualization of construction graphics in outdoor augmented reality. In: Paper Presented at the Proceedings of the 37th Conference on Winter Simulation (2005)

16. Golparvar-Fard, M., Peña-Mora, F., Savarese, S.: D4AR–a 4-dimensional augmented reality model for automating construction progress monitoring data collection, processing and communication. J. Inf. Technol. Constr. **14**(13), 129–153 (2009)

Visualizing Electricity Consumption in Qatar

Engy Soliman[(⊠)], Al-Hanouf Al-Mohannadi[(⊠)], and Noora Fetais

College of Engineering, Department of Computer Science & Engineering,
Qatar University, Doha, Qatar
{es1204833,aa1202270}@student.qu.edu.qa, n.almarri@qu.edu.qa

Abstract. Data related to electricity consumption is a global problem, particularly here in Qatar. Thus, a customized tool to analyze this data is made. The aim of this research is to present a new software, which would help the Qatar General Electricity & Water Corporation (KAHRAMAA) to identify trends, patterns and relationships of the consumptions and waste of electricity. Analyzing the electricity consumption would help in finding any abnormal trends. This tool will help in overcoming the challenges of analyzing such data and in gaining a deeper insight into its large and complex data sets. This software will ultimately help managers understand the processes that generated the data, which can be used to improve decision making in their target domain.

Keywords: Information visualization · Consumption · Electricity · Interactive tools · Maps

1 Introduction

Data visualization is an effective analytical tool for effective research communications as the amount of data is increasing rapidly which would challenge both our ability to both use such data for making decisions and avoid the danger of getting lost in that data. This could not only waste time and money, but also could lead to the loss of industrial and scientific opportunities.

The aim of this project is to present a software tool, which visualizes trends, patterns and relationships based on the consumption data [1–5]. However, this tool will be expected to provide a deeper understanding of abnormal trends if they exist, as well as insights into the details such data provides. This would help in gaining a deeper insight into large and complex data sets in order to enhance the understanding of the generated data and support the decision-making and problem solving in the target domain.

The proposed tool has an interactive map of Qatar, where the clients can view instant or historical data and they can zoom into the data to view the consumption at magnified levels of Qatar's consumption as a whole to the smallest household's consumption. This data is presented by different visual representations that will show the general statistics.

2 Methodology

For the development of this tool, the first step was to collect the requirements and meeting with the managers at KAHRAMAA to identify their normal, expected and

© Springer International Publishing AG 2016
Y. Luo (Ed.): CDVE 2016, LNCS 9929, pp. 378–381, 2016.
DOI: 10.1007/978-3-319-46771-9_49

exciting requirements. The next step was to evaluate the meeting results, and to set decisions on how the overall tool should perform and how the software will add value to the clients. Another step was setting the boundaries of consumptions for each area in Qatar so the clients see which areas are exceeding a certain consumption level and then they can take the necessary actions towards guiding consumers to save electricity or setting a penalty amount.

Figure 1 shows an overview of the tool's functionality. After a successful login to the system, the clients can view both the map of Qatar generated using Google Virtual Maps and the charts. There are colored light bulbs that present the consumption level (high, medium, low). The color is based on the consumption of the area relatively compared to the average consumption of all areas in Qatar. They can move around the map and zoom in/out. If the initial statistics are not enough, the clients can filter the data depending on the year using the line graph. The clients, who want to query the data, have the ability to choose the axis of the graph to compare different data sets, which will allow different perspectives of results. Moreover, functionalities such as emailing, printing and downloading any chart for report making is added to the system. In the background, there would be authentication services, Google API, extraction of data from database, updated calculation of statistics, and authorization service for database uploading.

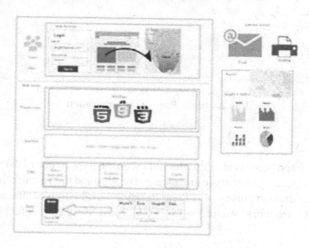

Fig. 1. High-level architecture of the proposed system

Figure 1 also represents the high-level architecture such that; the Interface layer (presentation) which allows users to login to the Electricity Visualization system by submitting their emails and passwords. The logical layer (web server) which is responsible for all of the processing done by the system. The application layer (coding of the web pages) which has the HTML (Hyper Text Markup Language Protocol), JavaScript, CSS, AJAX and Google Maps API [6]. The data layer is responsible for the system database; on this layer data is transferred from the excel file to a database. SQL commands will be used to test the database before using it to figure out the most significant combinations of queries to be generated for the clients.

Figure 2 shows the home-screen of the software. After a successful login, for each click on the map, the client can view 6 different types of charts; pie, scatter, column, combo, line and table. The map has three zoom levels; the first level focuses on Qatar as a country, the next level focuses on the seven zones of Qatar, the area level till the individual consumer level. For each area, the consumption is divided into three categories to represent the different sectors; governmental, residential and industrial. The client can change the charts through the 'graph type' button. The charts are combined with options like saving, printing or emailing. Furthermore, the pie, scatter, line and column can be viewed as data tables which would give the clients a good chance to compare whether the visual solution in the form of chart is better or having big numbers in tables is better.

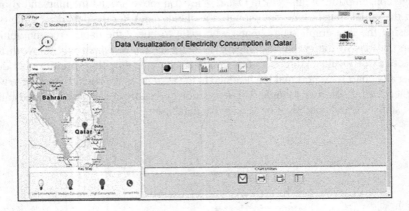

Fig. 2. Home Page of the application

3   Results

A maintainable interface was created which showed the importance of using information Visualization at Qatar University to enhance and understand the visualization techniques and tools. A satisfaction survey was done to see the evaluation of the application and enhance it for future work. According to Fig. 3, most users gave a feedback that they

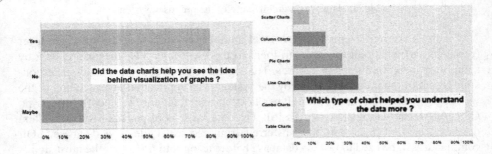

Fig. 3. Survey results

can understand the represented charts better than the data tables and that they prefer the line charts more than the other visualization charts.

4 Conclusion

The system is created in accordance with Qatar vision 2030 for saving time and electricity. The system aims to make the data understandable using different visual representations using interactive visualization tools such as maps and charts. The interaction between the maps and the charts is achieved by the merging of the Google Maps markers clicks to the Google charts loading and rendering the chart image, the purpose the chart utilities such as print, save and email. Making the zones highlighted was a problem because they have to be static images, since we are using a live map we cannot add colors to the zones or areas.

The research aim is to provide better solutions for the future by giving an insight of the data. As top level managers understand how each zone and area consumes, they will be able to take immediate decisions on how this zone, area in Qatar should start saving electricity. They can make a decision whether the consumption in the area is mostly affected by the governmental, residential or industrial consumption. They can customize the required campaigns for each zone. Basically, more customized advertising campaigns would be targeting the required areas and sectors.

References

1. Costanza, E., Ramchurn, S.D., Jennings, N.R.: Understanding domestic energy consumption through interactive visualisation: a field study. In: Proceedings of the 2012 ACM Conference on Ubiquitous Computing, pp. 216–225 (2012)
2. Dove, G., Jones, S.: Using information visualization to support creativity in service design workshops. In: Paper presented at the ServDes. 2014, 09-04-2014 - 11-04-2014, Lancaster, UK (2014)
3. Fischer, C.: Feedback on household electricity consumption: a tool for saving energy? Energy Effi. **1**, 79–104 (2008)
4. Fitzpatrick, G., Smith, G.: Technology-enabled feedback on domestic energy consumption: Articulating a set of design concerns. IEEE Pervasive Comput. **8**, 37–44 (2009)
5. Yi, J.S., Kang, Y.A., Stasko, J., Jacko, J.: Toward a deeper understanding of the role of interaction in information visualization. ieee trans. visual. comput. graphics. IEEE Trans. Visual. Comput. Graph. **13**(6), 1224–1231 (2007). doi:10.1109/tvcg.2007.70515
6. Ruthkoski, T.L.: Google Visualization API Essentials. Olton, Birmingham, GBR: Packt Publishing Ltd (2013). http://www.ebrary.com

A Space Optimized Scatter Plot Matrix Visualization

Wen Bo Wang[1](✉), Mao Lin Huang[1], and Quang Vinh Nguyen[2]

[1] School of Software, University of Technology, Sydney, Australia
wbwang09@hotmail.com, Mao.Huang@uts.edu.au
[2] School of Computing Engineering and Mathematics,
University of Western Sydney, Sydney, Australia
q.nguyen@westernsydney.edu.au

Abstract. This paper proposed a Space-Optimized Scatter Plot Matrix that used for the presentation of multi-dimensional dataset. This technique achieves the display space utilization in a 2D geometrical space. Our strategy is to maximize the utilization of computer space by optimizing the distribution of the plots in a geometrical plane of a display screen; We also apply interact mechanism, user query and visual cues, to support users' communication with variables and the discovery of deeper contents.

Keywords: Multi-dimensional data visualization · Space optimization · Scatter plot matrix · Visual cue · User query

1 Introduction

Scatter Plot Matrix (SPM) [1, 2] is one of the most frequently applied multi-dimensional visualization methods, it roughly displays the linear correlation between multiple variables; and it is helpful in pinpointing specific variables that might have similar correlations to the dataset.

During the past years, several variations on the representation of scatter plots have been proposed. Brushing [3] is a dynamic graphical method to interact with each scatter plot in real time by a screen input device, when the mouse is brushing over a certain scatterplot, the related data appears simultaneously on all the other scatterplots; The generalized scatter plots [4] is proposed to solve the problem of overlap, which allows an overlap-free representation of large data sets to fit entirely into the display; The third variation is dimension reordering method [5], which was mainly dealing with the crowded and disordered visual entities that obscure the structure in visual displays.

Although many optimisation methods have been proposed in the past to improve the visual data processing, little research work has been done in the field of display space optimisation. Specifically, in a matrix, the plots above the diagonal have the same contents with the plots which are below the diagonal, and the plots on the diagonal don't contain too much meaning in the visualization point of view; these two matters would greatly affect the clarity of data presentation especially when the number of variables is increased, and the working efficiency of the tools would be influenced consequently.

Y. Luo (Ed.): CDVE 2016, LNCS 9929, pp. 382–385, 2016.
DOI: 10.1007/978-3-319-46771-9_50

Therefore, this paper presents a space optimised [6] SPM with a clear explanation of pairwise variable relationships.

2   Technical Specification

The basic concept of the scatterplot matrix is simple. Give a set of n variables, SPM contains all the pairwise scatter plots of the variables on a single panel in a matrix format. That is $\{X_1, X_2, \ldots, X_{n-1}X_n\}$, if there are n variables, the scatterplot matrix will have n rows and n columns and the ith row and the jth column of this matrix is a plot of $X_i * X_j$.

2.1   Geometrical Layout

The proposed method is based on the balance of a suitable view with clear variable correlation with the SPM paradigm. Particularly, it inherits the principals of drawing rectangles from processing approach to ensure the maximum utilization of geometrical space for displaying plots, while they can also discover the relationships with each other by highlighting with different colors. The series of procedures for constructing such visualization can be divided into three steps:

Number Calculation (Row & Column) - This procedure calculates the number of plots per row and per column. Suppose the dataset contains n variables, the number of plots is $N = n * (n - 1)/2$; the number of plots per row is $NR = Roundup\sqrt{N}$; the number of plots per column $NC = ceiling(NR/N)$.

Space Partitioning - In a constraint space (the maximum is the size of the display screen, the minimum is size 0), procedure 2 needs to repartition the entire display space into a set of rectangle called plots when the size of the screen is resettled. The position of a plot is defined as four vertex value pairs, associated with the location of a plot. Specifically, we describe a point as $P(x_i, y_i)$ and a line as, $line(x_i, y_i, x_j, y_j)$ where (x_i, y_i) is the start point of the line, (x_j, y_j) is the end point.

Repeat Drawing - until all plots are drew.

2.2   Data Exploration and Interaction

As one of the main concerns for changing the plots' location in "matrix" visualization is whether the neighbor variables' relationships can be displayed clearly. So we use a data highlight method to discover the pairwise relationships among all variables. See Fig. 1 (right), an example of data highlighting on X-axis.

In addition, to make this tool more user friendly, we employed an interaction scheme, dynamic queries [7], see Fig. 1 (left): the users can choose specific variables according to their requirements; Furthermore, we apply two visual cues [8], Color and Shape, to support the query results, see Fig. 2, which is better for viewer to gain more information from different perspectives dynamically and clearly.

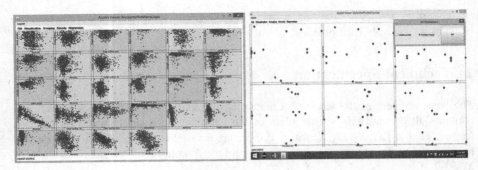

Fig. 1. Examples of data exploration and interaction by space-optimized SPM; (Left) data highlighting on X-axis; (Right) user query

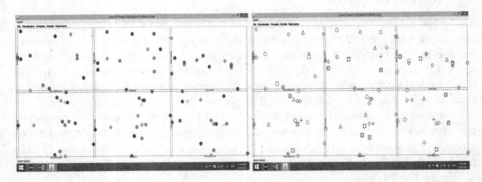

Fig. 2. Display with visual cues (Left) using color metaphor (Right) using shape metaphor (Color figure online)

3   Evaluation

We conducted a usability study with users who most of them are unfamiliar with SPM. The goal was to test whether the approach toward the design improved the user satisfaction on the challenges of visualization techniques: Space Utilization, Visual Clarity, and Information Navigation.

We involved 10 participants, who are students from different majors. Four questions are designed for the evaluation, and all the participants need to do a comparison between our space-optimized SPM with the original SPM, and the participants also need to give their overall preference on using the space-optimized SPM and the original SPM.

From the evaluation process, our result is shown in Fig. 3: Space-optimized SPM is more preferable than the original SPM in respect to the above three perspectives and the subjects showed high preference to using the space-optimized SPM on their own dataset.

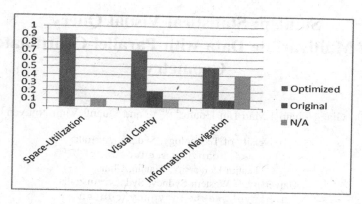

Fig. 3. Usability study test result

4 Conclusion and Future Work

This proposed Space-Optimized SPM can fully utilize the display space without missing the clarity of the visualization for multi data relationships, and this also allows viewers to explore the data patterns with the assistant of visual cues and user query technique.

We are currently investigating on new algorithms to improve the visual exploration function of this tool, such as: viewing the density distribution. Another improvement over the interactive mechanism is also being implemented, such as zooming in and out, which could make the tool to be more user-friendly. In addition, we are working on formal usability test to demonstrate the benefits of our technique.

References

1. Engineering Statistics HandBook. Scatterplot matrix (1995)
2. Niklas, E., Pierre, D., Daniel, F.J.: Rolling the dice: multidimensional visual exploration using scatter plot matrix navigation. IEEE Trans. Vis. **14**, 1141–1148 (2008)
3. Friendly, M., Denis, D.J.: Milestones in the history of thematic cartography, statistical graphics and data visualization (2009)
4. Keim, D.A., Chao, M., Dayal, U.: Generalized scatter plots. Inf. Vis. **9**(4), 301–311 (2010)
5. Ferdosi, B.J., Roerdink, J.B.T.M.: Visualizing high-dimensional structures by dimension ordering and filtering using subspace analysis. Comput. Graph. Forum **30**(3), 1121–1130 (2011)
6. Huang, M.: A space efficient clustered visualization of large graphs. In: Image and Graphics (2007)
7. Stockinger, K., Shalf, J., Wu, K., Bethel, E.W.: Query-driven visualization of large data sets. In: IEEE Visualization (2005)
8. Peter, M., Keller, M.: Visual Cues Practical Data Visualization. IEEE Computer Society, Los Alamitos (1993)

SumUp: Statistical Visual Query of Multivariate Data with Parallel-Coordinate Geometry

Phi Giang Pham[1], Mao Lin Huang[1,2(✉)], and Quang Vinh Nguyen[3]

[1] University of Technology, Sydney, Australia
mao.huang@uts.edu.au
[2] Tianjin University, Tianjin, China
[3] University of Western Sydney, Sydney, Australia
q.nguyen@westernsydney.edu.au

Abstract. One of the most noticeable issues of parallel coordinate visualization is how to quantitatively analyze density caused by polyline growth in a limited space on axes. The existing visualization tools only support the comparison among single dimensions and single ranges of polylines, which could face limitation in cases of complicated analytics. This paper proposes a new visual-query technique, named SumUp, for statistical analysis of multiple attributes of dimensions and multiple ranges of polylines. The methodology of SumUp is primarily based on developing dynamic queries using brushing operations to deliver summary stacked bars adaptive with parallel coordinates. Users can easily observe quantitative information from data patterns and compare multiple attributes over the density of polylines in the parallel coordinate visualization. Early experiments show that our proposed technique could potentially enhance the manipulation on parallel coordinates, showing by a typical case study.

Keywords: Visual query · Multivariate data visualization · Parallel coordinates

1 Introduction

Parallel coordinates, a well-known approach in multivariate-data visualization, represents data instances by intersection points between polylines and parallel axes. The intersection points encode dimension attributes, and the axes represent data dimensions. However, it might make the challenges of understanding and interpreting the pattern meaning to users [12]. Applying appropriate interaction on parallel-coordinate browsers is able to improve the effectiveness of visual data mining and analysis; a number of interaction techniques thus have been being proposed. Most popular manipulations are about brushing, ordering and scaling [7]. Brushing enables users to select and highlight considered instances by drawing and dragging selected zones on polylines and ranges of axes [4, 6, 10]. This method allows the parallel-coordinate browsers to be more adaptable with focus+conext views for better navigation. While brushing targets to data instances filtering, ordering and scaling help reduce overlapping and adjust density opacity [1, 8]. In parallel coordinates, correlative comparison of

© Springer International Publishing AG 2016
Y. Luo (Ed.): CDVE 2016, LNCS 9929, pp. 386–393, 2016.
DOI: 10.1007/978-3-319-46771-9_51

dimensions is much considered; however, one axis is not always placed next to the others, which causes an increase of users' efforts to trace patterns and match details together. Therefore, ordering purpose is to reorder axes automatically or manually for more flexible views of analytics. Another challenge in the area is about the increase of the number of traversing polylines through axes. A large number of intersection points displayed in a limited range can make difficulties for statistical analysis. Dimension zooming is a simple way for polyline counting support, but not suitable in case of overlapped polylines [3]. Hierarchical clustering of dimensions and instances can enhance scalability by similarity-based computation of axes and their attributes [2, 3]. Although the methods accomplish handling a large volume of data, they do not concentrate on quantitative comparison. Models applying box plots and bar charts are the existing approaches for quantitative mining of density measurement [5, 11]. However, the techniques are designed for analysis based on a single dimension attributes and single ranges of polylines, which might not fulfill complex analytics requiring multiple-attribute and flexible-range comparison.

This paper introduces SumUp: a statistical visual-query technique associated with parallel-coordinate visualization for multivariate data analytics. SumUp enables users to perform statistical queries by direct and flexible manipulation. Our approach is to building interactive stacked bars embedded in parallel axes to encode and represent statistical results of multiple attributes and to featuring dynamic queries based on conventional brushing operations. By using this method, users are able to arbitrarily analyse summaries of polylines in multiple ranges of attributes on multiple dimensions. We demonstrate SumUp abilities via a case study of high-dimensional data analysis. The main contributions of this paper include:

- A visual-query technique named SumUp and its prototype applying interactive stacked bars and multiple-attribute-based queries for enhancing statistical direct manipulation on parallel coordinates,
- A case study for demonstration of SumUp utility.

2 Statistical Visualization Technique

2.1 Basic Design and Interaction

The primary design of SumUp includes two overlaid layers of the parallel coordinates and stacked bars where the parallel axes are the baselines of stacked bars and the component for the attribute and range selection (Fig. 1). While parallel coordinates plays the role of a basic browser, horizontal stacked bars encode statistical results associated with the ranges on each axis. The purpose of this method is to utilize the vertical space between the axes, and to allow tracing the statistical results directly in the same view of data browsing.

The length of a total bar represents the total number of polylines based on all the target attributes, and that of each stacked bar encodes the number of polylines given by a corresponding attribute. The height of stacked bars encodes the range size of traversing polylines through an axis and selected as inputs of queries. The size of a bar is proportionally represented in statistical values. As a consequence, the stacked bars

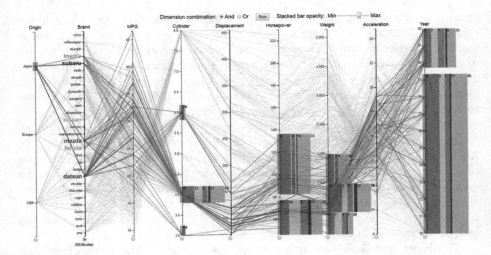

Fig. 1. SumUp interface visualizing a query on Car data set with nine dimensions and 398 instances [9]

can show statistical results towards multiple attributes of dimensions, which enriches amount of information encoded in the display space of parallel coordinates.

SumUp query components are designed to be embedded in parallel-coordinate axes for data discovery manipulation. A query is created primarily by conventional brushing operations. The brushing operations are adaptive with multiple brushes for selecting ranges of traversing polylines or intersection points to be involved in the query. The function of query is to compute the number of traversing polylines through all axes grouped by a set of attributes.

The formal definition of SumUp query function is described as follows.

- R_k is the axis of target attributes, $D' \subset D$ and $D' \not\supseteq R_k$, where D and D' are the sets of all dimensions and activated ones.
- $A = \{a_i | i = 1, 2, \ldots n\}$ is a set of attributes selected from axis k, and a_i is either a single value (one intersection point) or a range of values (a set of intersection points).
- $R_q = \{r_{qj} | j = 1, 2 \ldots m\}$: a set of traversing-polyline ranges on axis q ($R_q \in D'$) and r_{qj} is either a single value or a range of values.

Functions S_q (A, R_q) and S'_q (A, D') are to compute the statistical results by operators Or and And. Computation by operator Or considers the polylines of ranges in R_q satisfying A while that by operator And takes A and D' into account as a satisfactory condition for R_q.

2.2 Statistical Visual Comparison

Figure 2 shows a query example, that compares car models of three representatives from Europe, Japan and USA, including Volkswagen, Toyota and Ford based on

25-and-lower MPG (Miles per gallon) and all cylinder numbers. To perform the query, we select all the origins as target attributes, select the three brands, then select associated ranges of traversing polylines as requirements on axes MPG and Cylinder. The resulting pattern indicates that the majority of models were owned by Ford, with 39 ones whereas the minority of that belonged to Toyota and Volkswagen, with 9 and 3 ones. While all of the brands employed 4-cylinder engines, only Ford employed 8-cylinder engines, and only Volkswagen did not install 6-cylinder engines for their cars with the fuel economy for MPG 25 and lower.

As common employment of stacked bars, the size, colour and data label representing attribute value summary are visual comparison principles. The height of the stacked bars is equivalent to the height of associated traversing-polyline range. The length of the total bar at range r_{qj} is computed by

$$l(r_{qj}) = \sum_{i=1}^{n} S(ai, rqj) \text{ and } l'(r_{qj}) = \sum_{i=1}^{n} S'(ai, D')$$

Where l and l' are the lengths resulted with operators Or and And.

The colour variety assigned to stacked bars depends upon the number of attributes involved in the query, with a defaulted range of twenty categorical colours. For graphic legend, coloured labels and coloured brushes are corresponding to single attribute values and ranges of ones.

2.3   Visual Enhancement

That the layout of SumUp browser is stacked bars overlaid on parallel coordinates might cause loss of visual patterns of polylines due to their overlapped position. For dealing with this, the transparency of the stacked-bar layer can be freely customized, which keeps both layers clearly visible and switchable in the same display space without loss of visual pattern. Besides, in case of lengths of stacked bars in very small values, their labels would be shown when the space is sufficient, or mouse-over interaction is applied.

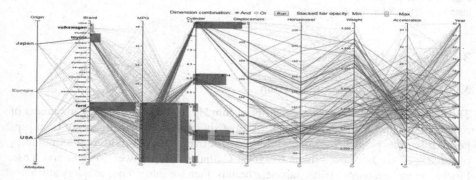

Fig. 2. SumUp query example using Car data set (Color figure online)

A common visual challenge of parallel coordinates is representing a large number of polylines in a 2D space. This might cause high density and affect to navigation tasks. We develop an adaptive filtering feature using stacked-bar interaction to handle the challenge. Users can highlight and trace polylines by selecting clustered colours on associated stacked bars. Thus the polyline clusters can be kept visible by groups of colours according to user needs, and navigation tasks can be performed easily, which could make density decreased and appropriate for comparison and analysis (Fig. 3).

Although current parallel-coordinate browsers support statistical functions, they would focus on numerical data rather than categorical one. Motivated by this reason, SumUp delivers a statistical query feature that can work with both of the data types. Categorical data can be mapped as either inputs for creating target attributes or ranges of selected traversing polylines.

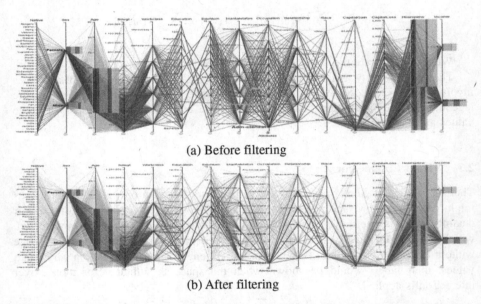

(a) Before filtering

(b) After filtering

Fig. 3. Filtering feature applied to a set of Census income data with fifteen dimensions and 9998 instances [9]. (Color figure online)

3   Case Study

3.1   Multiple-Attribute Comparison

This use case demonstrates the capability of SumUp in statistical visual comparison of multiple attributes with flexible ranges of traversing polylines, which has not been supported by current parallel-coordinate browsers. The overall purpose is to compare numbers of models of six Japanese brands based on Cylinder, Horsepower, Weight and Year. Firstly, we make a brush to filter Japanese brands, then we select those as query attributes including Toyota, Subaru, Nissan, Mazda, Honda and Datsun. From the highlighted details of the browser, we configure query ranges as follows. For Cylinder attribute, we select three filtered Cylinder numbers 3, 4 and 6. We divide Weight by three ranges including the weights (in kilogram) from 2500 to 3000, from 2000 to 2500, and below 2000. For Horsepower (hp), we take two ranges from 80 to 140 hp, and below 80 hp. We consider two periods of model production up to 1980 and later years.

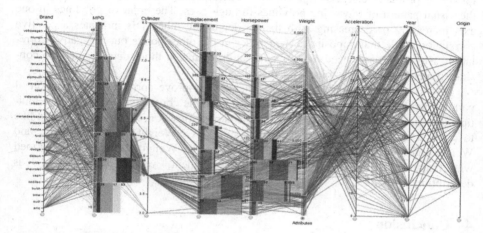

Fig. 4. Correlative analysis. For MPG summary towards Weight, the number of low-weight models (the red, orange and green stacked bars) occupied in most of the ranges of high MPG (25 and over), and conversely the number of high-weight ones (the blue, violet and yellow stacked bars) appeared in most of the ranges of low MPG (lower 25), which indicates their relationship was reaching a negative correlation with high probability. For Displacement, the number of low-weight models filled with the majority of the ranges of low Displacement (lower 200), and the number of height-weight ones appeared in the majority of the ranges of high Displacement (200 and over), which points out their relationship was reaching a positive correlation with high probability. Similarly, the relationship between Weight and Horsepower was a positive correlation as well. (Color figure online)

Once the query is performed, the browser shows a meaningful pattern (Fig. 1). Generally, the model numbers of Toyota, Mazda, Honda and Datsun were more than that of Subaru and Nissan. There were significant differences in the numbers of models of axis Cylinder and at 4-cylinder level; while all of the brands used 4-cylinder engines, with 68 in total, only Mazda featured 3-cylinder engines, with 4, and just Toyota and Datsun featured 6-cylinder engines, with 6 in total and 3 for each. The greatest number of level of 4-cylinder engines was for Toyota, with 23 models compared to just 1 model of Nissan. The number of models for Horsepower under 80, with 45, was slightly more than that from 80 to 140, with 33. For weight criterion, the highest figure was at the range from 2000 to under 2500, with 38, and around double of the remaining ranges, with 18 and 22 of 2500–3000 weights and under-2000 ones. Although before 1980 Toyota and Datsun were produced, with over 14 models of each, more than others, with under 7 of each, from 1980 to 1982 the model delivery of those, Mazda and Honda became more balanced, with about 8 of each. While Subaru delivered 2 in each period of the time, Nissan only introduced 1 model in the latter one.

3.2 Correlative Analysis

Parallel coordinates can show the correlative relationship between two dimensions by the visual pattern of traversing polylines through axes. The order of polylines in one axis increasing or decreasing with their order in the other axis indicates a positive correlation while that opposite to their order in the other points out a negative correlation. However, users need much mental effort to match those details since the considered axis is not always placed next to the others.

This use case explores how SumUp helps to improve correlative comparison of parallel coordinates. SumUp enables users to examine correlative coefficients of multiple dimensions without effects from their axis positions. It is supposed we would like to make a correlative analysis of Weight and MPG, Weight and Horsepower, and Weight and Displacement. Once the query focused on Weight attributes is performed with ranges of MPG, Horsepower and Displacement, we analyse the results as description of Fig. 4.

4 Conclusion

This paper has presented a new visual-query technique for improving statistical functions of parallel coordinates. The methodology is mainly based on integration of stacked bars and parallel axes with multiple-attribute queries on flexible ranges of traversing polylines. This technique enables users to perform statistical tasks with more useful information and rich interaction for visual comparison and navigation. A case study with two typical use-cases has been introduced for the prototype demonstration, which indicates SumUp is probably useful for the addressed problems.

In the future, we will enhance operators for SumUp queries, improve the animation and optimize data mapping modules. Further, data performance tests and usability study will be conducted for SumUp in-depth evaluation. We plan for extended investigation of this work to deal with hierarchical clustering of dimensions and instances on parallel coordinates in cases of high polyline density.

References

1. Andrienko, G., Andrienko, N.: Constructing parallel coordinates plot for problem solving. In: 1st International Symposium on Smart Graphics, pp. 9–14 (2001)
2. Andrews, K., Osmić, M., Schagerl, G.: Aggregated parallel coordinates: integrating hierarchical dimensions into parallel coordinates visualisations. In: Proceedings of the 15th International Conference on Knowledge Technologies and Data-Driven Business, i-KNOW 2015, pp. 37:1–37:4 (2015)

3. Fua, Y., Ward, M., Rundensteiner, E.: Hierarchical parallel coordinates for exploration of large datasets. In: Proceedings of the Conference on Visualization 1999: Celebrating Ten Years, VIS 1999, pp. 43–50 (1999)

4. Fua, Y.-H., Ward, M.O., Rundensteiner, E.A.: Structure-based brushes: a mechanism for navigating hierarchically organized data and information spaces. IEEE Trans. Vis. Comput. Graph. 6(2), 150–159 (2000)

5. Ho, Q., Lundblad, P., Åström, T., Jern, M.: A web enabled visualization toolkit for geo visual analytics. In: International Society for Optics and Photonics on IS&T/SPIE Electronic Imaging, p. 78680R (2011)

6. Hauser, H., Ledermann, F., Doleisch, H.: Angular brushing of extended parallel coordinates. In: IEEE Symposium on Information Visualization, INFOVIS 2002, pp. 127–130. IEEE (2002)

7. Heinrich, J., Weiskopf, D.: State of the art of parallel coordinates. In: STAR Proceedings of Eurographics 2013, pp. 95–116 (2013)

8. Lu, L.F., Huang, M.L., Huang, T.-H.: A new axes reordering method in parallel coordinates visualization. In: 2012 11th International Conference on Machine Learning and Applications (ICMLA), vol. 2, pp. 252–257. IEEE (2012)

9. Lichman, M.: UCI machine learning repository (2013). http://archive.ics.uci.edu/ml

10. Martin, A.R., Ward, M.O.: High dimensional brushing for interactive exploration of multivariate data. In: Proceedings of the 6th Conference on Visualization 1995, p. 271. IEEE Computer Society (1995)

11. Siirtola, H.: Direct manipulation of parallel coordinates. In: Proceedings of IEEE International Conference on Information Visualization, pp. 373–378. IEEE (2000)

12. Siirtola, H., Raiha, K.-J.: Interacting with parallel coordinates, pp. 1278–1309. doi:10.1016/j.intcom.2006.03.006

Author Index

Printed in the United States
By Bookmasters